The Primordial Violence

Why do parents hit those they love? What effect does it have on children? What can be done to end this pattern? These are some of the questions explored in *The Primordial Violence.* Featuring data from over 7,000 U.S. families as well as results from a 32-nation study, the book presents the latest research on the extent to which spanking is used in different cultures and the subsequent effects of its use on children and on society. It presents longitudinal data showing that spanking is associated with *subsequent slowing* of cognitive development and *increase* in antisocial and criminal behavior. Both cross-sectional and longitudinal studies are explored in an accessible fashion. An abundance of high quality research has produced findings that are highly consistent from study to study, which show that spanking is a risk factor for aggressive behavior and other social and psychological problems. Because of these findings, the authors argue for policy changes and recommend never spanking. Policy and practical implications are explored in most chapters.

The Primordial Violence highlights:

- The benefits of avoiding spanking such as the development of better interpersonal skills and higher academic achievement;
- The link between spanking and behavioral problems and crime;
- The extent to which spanking is declining and why, despite the unusually high level of agreement between numerous studies that found harmful effects from spanking, most parents continue to spank.

This book is clearly written. Technical material is in an appendix. It is readable by a general audience and suitable for undergraduate and graduate courses in child development, parenting, child abuse, family violence, juvenile delinquency, criminal behavior, social development, sociology of the family, family relations, human development, family studies, education, social work, and social policy.

Murray A. Straus is Professor of Sociology and founder and Co-Director of the Family Research Laboratory at the University of New Hampshire.

Emily M. Douglas is an Associate Professor of Social Work at Bridgewater State University.

Rose Anne Medeiros is Quantitative Methodologist in the Department of Sociology at Rice University.

The Primordial Violence

Spanking Children, Psychological Development, Violence, and Crime

Murray A. Straus
University of New Hampshire

Emily M. Douglas
Bridgewater State University

Rose Anne Medeiros
Rice University

 Routledge
Taylor & Francis Group

NEW YORK AND LONDON

First published 2014
by Routledge
711 Third Avenue, New York, NY 10017

Simultaneously published in the UK
by Routledge
27 Church Road, Hove, East Sussex BN3 2FA

Routledge is an imprint of the Taylor & Francis Group,an informa business

Library of Congress Cataloging in Publication Data

Straus, Murray A. (Murray Arnold), 1926–
  The primordial violence : spanking children, psychological development, violence, and crime / Murray A. Straus, Emily M. Douglas, Rose Anne Medeiros. — First Edition.
     pages cm
  Includes bibliographical references and index.
  1. Violence—Psychological aspects.   2. Corporal punishment of children.   3. Child rearing.   4. Child abuse.   I. Title.
  BF575.A3S77 2013
  362.7′874—dc23
  2013007416

ISBN: 978-1-84872-952-0 (hbk)
ISBN: 978-1-84872-953-7 (pbk)
ISBN: 978-0-203-80885-6 (ebk)

Typeset in Times New Roman
by Apex CoVantage, LLC

To Dorothy who, years before we met, brought up her wonderful children without spanking.

—Murray A. Straus

For L. L. Perkins, who taught me to look past barriers and to only see possibilities

—Emily M. Douglas

For my dear friend Catherine

—Rose Anne Medeiros

Contents

Charts

Tables

Tables in Appendix

Preface

Being spanked for misbehavior is part of growing up for almost all children, in all but a few nations of the world. What explains parents hitting those they love, what effects does it have on children, what can be done to end this millennia-long pattern of violent child rearing? Those are the questions addressed by *The Primordial Violence*. Part I documents the worldwide use of spanking and presents research showing that misbehavior by the child is only one of many reasons parents spank. The chapters in the next three parts give the findings from our research on the effects of having been spanked: child behavior problems in Part II, mental ability and academic achievement in Part III, and crime as an adult in Part IV. The chapters in the concluding section, Part V, examine trends in spanking, with the emphasis on the social factors that have triggered the movement away from spanking and also the social factors that have obstructed the trend. The concluding chapter argues that changing just this one aspect of parenting is likely to have profound benefits, not only for the children and families specifically involved, but for the society as a whole. A nation without spanking is likely to have less crime and violence and, as the saying goes, be "healthier, wealthier, and wiser."

What Stands in the Way?

If bringing up children without spanking has benefits for children, for their parents, and for society as a whole, what stands in the way? Some of the many obstacles are discussed in Chapter 20 and in a few other places such as Chapter 18. In that chapter we describe what seem to be contradictory opinions about whether to spank. Although there are no clear survey results, we believe that, in the United States, most parents and most professionals who provide information and services for parents have come to believe spanking should be avoided if possible. However, for the reasons explained in that chapter, they also believe that spanking is *sometimes necessary*. These are not contradictions because toddlers are notorious recidivists. After several instances of "No" and other corrections, a parent is likely to conclude that this is an instance when it is not possible to avoid spanking, and a parent who "doesn't believe in spanking," spanks. Our solution to this dilemma is presented in Chapter 18.

Another obstacle is touched on in Chapter 2. Textbooks in courses on child development, criminology, pediatrics, social work, etc. present almost nothing on spanking and the results of the large body of research showing that the less spanking the better off the child. We hope that *The Primordial Violence* contributes to changing that by providing the results of 15 years of empirical research conducted at the Family Research Laboratory of the University of New Hampshire on spanking.

It is even possible that the evidence presented will help lead to public policy to ban spanking children. We dare to entertain this hope because the information in *The Primordial Violence* is both comprehensive and scientifically sound. Of course, not everything that needs to be known is covered, but the following seems to be a good start.

- ***Why parents spank.*** It is much more than whether the child misbehaves. It is also determined, for example, by the cultural norms and beliefs of the society and the social and psychological characteristics of the parents. Evidence from national and international surveys is presented showing the relation of these social and psychological characteristics to whether parents spank and how much they do it.
- ***The link between spanking, and child and adult problems, and crime.*** Three of the five parts of the book provide evidence on this crucial issue. As mentioned previously, we present empirical evidence showing the relation of spanking to 15 problem behaviors on the part of children and adults.
- ***Longitudinal evidence.*** Over 90% of the studies that investigated the effects of spanking have found that children who were spanked have more problems, both as children and as adults. This is an unusually high degree of agreement between studies. However, most of the studies used a cross-sectional design, and that type of study cannot determine if the problem behavior was caused by the child being hit, or whether the problem behavior caused the parents to hit, or whether it works both ways. Most of the studies in *The Primordial Violence* are cross-sectional and, therefore, subject to that important limitation. However, the chapters on the relation of spanking to antisocial behavior (Chapter 6), to IQ (Chapter 10), and to crime as a young adult (Chapter 15) are longitudinal. The chapter on child antisocial behavior, for example, shows that spanking is associated with a *subsequent increase,* not a decrease, in antisocial behavior. In addition to those three longitudinal studies, Chapter 19 summarizes results of 16 additional studies by others. Twelve longitudinal studies found that spanking is associated with a *subsequent increase* rather than decrease in the probability of antisocial and aggressive behavior. Four longitudinal studies of adult crime are summarized, and all four found that the more spanking, the greater the probability of the child later in life perpetrating a crime.
- ***International in scope.*** Most research on spanking has been done in the United States. How broadly applicable are the results? On the issues of

the high percent of parents who spank, the relation of spanking to physically assaulting a romantic partner later in life and forcing sex on a partner (Chapters 3, 13, and 16) found remarkable similarity in 32 nations.

- *Controls for 32 confounding variables.* The results of correlational studies, including longitudinal studies, can be "spurious" if there are variables that result in both spanking and problematic behavior. For example, parents with low-education and living in poverty have repeatedly been found to do more spanking, and their children have repeatedly been shown to have higher crime rates. It might be dire life circumstances, not the spanking *per se,* which produces the relation of spanking to crime. Fortunately, modern statistics let us take that into account. This was done in one chapter or another for 32 such sources of a spurious correlation, yet the link of spanking to problematic behavior remained.

- *Trends in spanking and what stands in the way of further decline. The Primordial Violence* pays particular attention to the paradox that, in the United States, more and more parents and professionals think spanking should be avoided, but the decrease in the percent who spank has been extremely small for preschool-age children—the age when spanking is most likely to occur.

- *Policy and practice implications.* This is part of most chapters, and the main focus of two chapters.

- *Understandable.* Although complex statistical methods were used in the research, we tried to present the results in a way we hope is understandable by any college educated person. One of the devices to achieve this was to put the necessary technical documentation of statistical procedures and results in the appendix.

Influence of Social Science on Public Policy

Will the evidence on the harmful effects of spanking lead to change in public policy and what parents do? Some understanding of whether this is likely can be gleaned by putting the issue in historical context and comparing the history of legislation and policy statements about spanking with that on corporal punishment by teachers.

Medical research has frequently led to new public policies. Research from psychology, sociology, anthropology, and social work (the disciplines most concerned with spanking by parents), however, has seldom been the basis for new public policy. These disciplines have nevertheless made important contributions to public policy. Weiss and Bucuvalas's historical analysis showed that the contribution of social science has mainly been to justify, revise, and sometimes correct policies that had been previously initiated in response to changes in social circumstances, including changes in cultural norms and values.

A specific example is the effort by feminists starting in the mid 1970s to change police treatment of domestic violence. The change was happening, but slowly. However, the pace quickened dramatically after publication of the results of an experiment comparing three modes of police action: separating and calming down the parties, referral to services, and arrest of the offender. The study found that those arrested were less likely to reoffend. This experiment is unlikely to have been done, and the results are unlikely to have been the subject of an information brief sent to *all* police departments in the United States, were it not for changes in public tolerance for what came to be called domestic violence, brought about by the women's movement.

Policies to end corporal punishment in the armed services and in schools occurred because of a change in values and beliefs, not because of research evidence. Similarly, the Swedish no-spanking law of 1979 was enacted primarily on the basis of moral principles. In the United States, about half the states and almost all large school districts prohibit spanking by teachers. This change began long before there was empirical research, and even now, the quality of research showing harmful effects of spanking *in schools* is minimal.

The sequence of events for policy on spanking *by parents* in the United States has been almost the opposite. There has been a large amount of research, much of it of high quality. It has produced findings that are highly consistent from study to study showing that spanking is a risk factor for aggressive behavior and many social and psychological problems. Despite that, this research has largely been ignored. We suggest that this will continue until there is what Gusfield (1963, 1981) calls a "moral passage" that brings about policy changes and with it receptivity to the empirical evidence to justify and improve the policy. Such a moral passage is starting to occur in respect to spanking, but in the United States it is minimal and has extremely strong opposition. But perhaps, if the research on spanking continues to grow in quantity and scientific quality, and if it continues to consistently find harmful side effects, together with the increasing demand for evidence-based interventions and policies, spanking will be one of the few examples of research resulting in a new social policy.

Intended Audience

This book is intended for a general audience of readers who are interested in child development and parenting, and for courses in child abuse, family violence, juvenile delinquency, criminal behavior, social development, sociology of the family, or parenting and family relations taught in psychology, human development, family studies, criminology, education, social work, sociology, and social policy.

Acknowledgments

Coauthors

Fifteen of the 21 chapters were coauthored. It is obvious that this book would not exist without their contributions, for which we are extremely grateful.

Nancy L. Asdigian (Chapter 4)

John P. Colby (Chapter 15)

Emily M. Douglas (Chapter 13)

Manuel Gámez-Guadix (Chapter 16)

Jean Giles-Sims (Chapter 6)

Scott Hershberger (Chapter 16)

Kimberly A. Hill (Chapter 8)

Sean Lauer (Chapter 14)

Anita K. Mathur (Chapter 11)

Rose A. Medeiros (Chapters 9 and 15)

Vera E. Mouradian (Chapter 7)

Mallie J. Paschall (Chapter 10)

Julie H. Stewart (Chapters 2 and 5)

David B. Sugarman (Chapter 6)

Carrie L. Yodanis (Chapter 12)

Members of the Family Research Laboratory Seminar

This unique seminar consisted of the faculty, post-doctoral fellows, and graduate students of the University of New Hampshire Family Research Laboratory. The seminar reviewed drafts of most of the chapters in this book and made extremely valuable suggestions.

The Reviewers

We are very grateful for the hard work and insights of the six scholars who reviewed the draft of the book for Routledge/Taylor & Francis: Penelope Leach (University of London), Patricia K. Kerig (University of Utah), Chan Yuk-chung (The Hong Kong Polytechnic University), Brigitte Vittrup (Texas Woman's University), Elizabeth T. Gershoff (the University of Texas at Austin), George Holden (Southern Methodist University), and four anonymous reviewers. Their reviews enabled us to avoid errors, and their many important suggestions greatly improved the book. Peer review is a sometimes painful but wonderful part of science, and this book benefitted from that process.

Doreen Cole

It is a pleasure to thank Doreen Cole for her many contributions, not only to this book, but to the operation of the Family Research Laboratory. Over the many years of research for this book, she trained and supervised student office assistants who worked on the research. She managed the publication process for the papers that are the basis of almost one-half of this book and managed the long and involved task of producing the final manuscript of the book. This included tracking down hundreds of references and maintaining the EndNote library of references. Anyone who has created a reference list for a book knows what a daunting task that is, even with the help of a reference manager program. She found and enabled us to correct numerous inconsistencies and omissions in the text, tables, charts, and references. For example, she pointed out a table with the footnote $* p < .0$, $** p < .01$, but the table did not have any statistics marked with $*$ or $**$.

Financial Support

The work was supported by National Institute of Mental Health grant T32MH15161 and the University of New Hampshire. We are grateful for this crucial support.

Permissions

Nine of the 21 chapters are extensively updated revisions of published articles and are printed with the permission of the original publisher, as listed below.

Straus, M. A., & Stewart, J. H. (1999). Corporal punishment by American parents: National data on prevalence, chronicity, severity, and duration, in relation to child, and family characteristics. *Clinical Child and Family Psychology Review, 2,* 55–70.

Straus, M. A., Sugarman, D. B., & Giles-Sims, J. (1997). Spanking by parents and subsequent antisocial behavior of children. *Archives of Pediatric and Adolescent Medicine, 151,* 761–767.

Straus, M. A., & Mouradian, V. E. (1998). Impulsive corporal punishment by mothers and antisocial behavior and impulsiveness of children. *Behavioral Sciences & the Law, 16,* 353–374.

Straus, M. A., & Paschall, M. J. (2009). Corporal punishment by mothers and development of children's cognitive ability: A longitudinal study of two nationally representative age cohorts. *Journal of Aggression, Maltreatment, and Trauma.*

Straus, M. A., & Yodanis, C. L. (1996). Corporal punishment in adolescence and physical assaults on spouses later in life: What accounts for the link? *Journal of Marriage and the Family, 58,* 825–841.

Douglas, E. M., & Straus, M. A. (2006). Assault and injury of dating partners by university students in 19 countries and its relation to corporal punishment experienced as a child. *European Journal of Criminology, 3,* 293–318.

Gamez-Guadix, M., Straus, M. A., & Hershberger, S. (2011). Childhood and adolescent victimization and perpetration of sexual coercion by male and female university students. *Deviant Behavior, 32:* 712–742.

Straus, M. A., & Mathur, A. K. (1996). Social change and trends in approval of corporal punishment by parents from 1968 to 1994. In D. Frehsee, W. Horn, & K. D. Bussmann (Ed.), *Family violence against children: A challenge for society* (pp. 91–105). New York, NY: Walter deGruyter.

Straus, M. A. (2005). Children should never, ever, be spanked no matter what the circumstances. In D. R. Loseke, R. J. Gelles, & M. M. Cavanaugh (Eds.), *Current controversies about family violence* (pp. 137–157). Thousand Oak, CA: Sage.

About the Authors

Murray A. Straus is professor emeritus of sociology and founder and codirector of the Family Research Laboratory at the University of New Hampshire. He has been president of the National Council on Family Relations, the Society For the Study of Social Problems, and the Eastern Sociological Society. He is the author or coauthor of over 200 articles on the family, research methods, and South Asia and 17 books, including *Corporal Punishment by Parents in Theoretical Perspective* (Yale, 2006), *Beating the Devil Out of Them: Corporal Punishment in American Families* (Transaction, 2001), *Physical Violence in American Families: Risk Factors and Adaptations to Violence in 8,145 Families* (Transaction, 1990), *Four Theories of Rape in American Society* (Yale, 1989), and *Stress, Culture, and Aggression* (Yale, 1995). He is widely recognized for his research on partner violence and on spanking and other legal forms of corporal punishment and for efforts to reduce corporal punishment as part of primary prevention of child physical abuse and partner violence.

Emily M. Douglas is an associate professor of social work at Bridgewater State University. Her research focuses on child and family well-being with strong implications for programmatic and policy interventions. Her areas of expertise include corporal punishment, fatal child maltreatment, male victims of partner violence, and divorced families. She is the author of 30 articles and two books: *Mending Broken Families: Social Policies for Divorced Families* (Rowman & Littlefield, 2006) and *Innovations in Family Policy* (Lexington Books, 2010). Her degrees are in psychology and public policy, and she is the founder and director of the National Research Conference on Child & Family Programs & Policy.

Rose Anne Medeiros received her PhD in 2010 in sociology from the University of New Hampshire. Dr. Medeiros is interested in a variety of statistical topics, including latent variable modeling (including SEM) and handling of missing data. Dr. Medeiros' substantive work has included research on partner assault, corporal punishment of children, and the parent-child relationships of LGBT young adults. Her research on partner assault focused on the role of gender in partner assault, with a special interest in partner assault in same-sex couples.

Part I

Prevalence and Social Causes of Spanking

1   The Social and Scientific Context of Research on Spanking

Spanking and other forms of legal corporal punishment by parents is the primordial violence in two senses. First, as shown in the next chapter, over 90% of U.S. parents spank or slap toddlers. Of this 90%, at least one third of parents start hitting their children when they are less than a year old. Thus, for almost everyone in the United States and most other nations, the first experience of being the victim of a deliberate physical attack is in the form of being slapped or spanked by parents who wish to correct what they perceive as misbehavior.

The second way in which spanking is the primordial violence became evident when this book was being considered for publication. Some reviewers objected to the title *The Primordial Violence* because, as one put it, *primordial* has connotations of the beginnings of the earth and the primordial soup. But, for better or worse, that is exactly the connotation we intended. We believe that spanking is the primordial violence, not only because it is usually a child's first experience with violence, but even more because research shows that it is one of the bases out of which almost all other violence grows. Ironically, this is because parents spank for the morally correct and socially important purpose of correcting misbehavior and preparing a child to be a law-abiding citizen. Thus, spanking teaches the morality of violence. Chapter 5, for example, shows that approval and use of spanking is correlated with approval of other types of violence, even including torture. All five chapters in Part IV and the longitudinal studies summarized in Chapter 19 show that the more a child was spanked, the greater the probability that he or she will approve of or engage in violence and other crime later in life.

What Is Spanking?

We define corporal punishment as the use of physical force with the intention of causing a child to experience pain, but not injury, for the purpose of correction or control of the child's behavior. This definition is discussed in more detail in Straus (2001a).

What to Call It?

In the United States and Canada *spank* and *spanking* are sometimes used to refer to slapping a child on the buttocks and also to slapping a child on other parts of the body. In Great Britain and other English-language nations, the equivalent terms are *smack* and *smacking*. Although these are the most common terms, there are many others such as thrash, beat, belt, paddle, warm his butt, whipping, and whupping. Even U.S. President Barack Obama, who is on record as not spanking, used one of those terms in a speech at the centennial convention of the National Association for the Advancement of Colored People on July 17, 2009. He said, "And by the way, we need to be there for our neighbor's sons and daughters. We need to go back to the time, back to the day when we parents saw somebody, saw some kid fooling around and—it wasn't your child, but they'll whup you anyway."

When Obama and others use terms like *whup him* or *beat him,* they usually mean hitting on the buttocks or slapping a child, not the severe attacks that they would signify for relationships between adults. They refer to forms of spanking that are legal in every state in the United States and in most other nations. In the United States, legal spanking includes hitting with traditionally accepted objects such as a hairbrush or belt, provided that no serious injury results. Chapter 2, which is on the prevalence of spanking in the United States, shows that 28% of parents of children age 5 to 12 had hit their child with one of these traditionally approved objects in the previous 12 months.

Hit is a synonym for spank that we use from time to time. Those who believe spanking is appropriate and necessary may object to hit because, as Rosemond (1994b) says in his widely read book *To Spank or Not To Spank,* "calling spanking *hitting* is nothing more than misleading propaganda. Even people who are not on one side or the other of the spanking debate may object on the basis of biased terminology because hit has a negative connotation." Our view is that hit is no more biased than spank. The difference is in the direction of the bias. Spank and smack describes hitting a child, but with the connotation of a socially and legally approved act. When an adult physically punishes another adult for some misbehavior such as flirting with his wife, it is called *assault.* However, the assault laws of all U.S. states and most other nations contain a specific exemption for hitting a child to correct misbehavior. It is only in the case of children that we search for neutral words or euphemisms. We do not think there is a neutral word in everyday English that describes using spanking against a child. In this book, we use spank most of the time because that word is in the questions asked parents or children to obtain the data analyzed. In addition, as previously noted, parents use spank and smack to mean hitting in general (as defined above) not just hitting on the buttocks.

Outside the academic world, almost no parent uses *corporal punishment* to describe what they do to correct misbehavior. We have found that when we talk about corporal punishment, some parents don't realize we are talking about spanking or slapping a child's buttocks or hand. This was illustrated when one of us was interviewing the mother of a four-year-old. The child repeatedly interrupted the mother despite the mother's pleas. Finally, she slapped the child on the shoulder. Then, somewhat embarrassed, she explained "There are times when nothing except *spanking* will get a child to mind" (emphasis added). It is also illustrated by a book for parents that says that at about 18 to 24 months, "spanking means a brief swat on the fingers or leg at the instant of infraction" (Guarendi & Eich, 1990).

Spanking, Violence, and Child Abuse

Is Spanking Violence?

Some parents we have talked to say they don't hit their kids, even though they have just told us about spanking the child when necessary. Few Americans think of an occasional slap on the hand or butt to correct a child's misbehavior as a physical attack or violence, although they would think of an occasional slap of another adult as a physical attack or violence. This is because violence refers to *culturally disapproved* uses of physical force. People who favor the death penalty do not think of executions as violence, but people who are opposed to the death penalty do. Similarly, the three quarters of Americans shown in Chapter 18 who believe that a good hard spanking is sometimes necessary, dismiss the idea that spanking is a form of violence. Before the largely feminist-based effort to end violence against women, if a husband occasionally slapped his wife, it was considered a family fight, not family violence. Before the 20th century, slapping a wife was often legally identified as *physically chastising.* Until the 1870s in the United States, husbands had the legal right to physically chastise their wives (Calvert, 1974); that is, they were permitted to use corporal punishment, just as parents still have this right with children. For most of the 20th century, police, in some jurisdictions, followed an informal "stitch rule." This directed them to avoid making an arrest in family disturbance cases unless there was an injury that required stitches or other immediate medical attention (Straus, 1976). In economically developed nations today, very few still believe that an occasional slap by a husband to correct misbehavior by his wife is harmless, but many believe that an occasional slap by a parent to correct misbehavior by a child is morally correct and harmless.

To understand the reasoning behind identifying spanking as a form of violence, it is necessary to start with the definition of violence:

> Violence is "an act carried out with the intention of, or perceived as having the intention of physically hurting another person." (Gelles & Straus, 1979, p. 553)

The *physical hurt* can range from slight pain, as in a slap, to murder. The basis for *intent to hurt* may range from a concern with a child's safety (as when a child is spanked for going into the street) to hostility so intense that the death of the other is desired (Gelles & Straus, 1979, p. 554). Now compare the definition of violence with the definition of spanking given in the previous section: "The use of physical force with the intention of causing a child to experience pain, but not injury, for the purpose of correction or control of the child's behavior."

The difference between the two definitions is that the definition of spanking is restricted to attacks that are not intended to cause injury and to attacks that are for purposes of correction and control. This makes spanking an example of *instrumental violence* (Gelles & Straus, 1979), that is, violence perpetrated to achieve some end other than pain or injury as an end in itself, such as hitting a wife or husband just because of anger and fury. The latter is called *expressive violence.* When parents are angry at the child for repeated misbehavior, it is often also an act of expressive violence. Another example of violence that is both instrumental and expressive is someone hitting a neighbor who dumps trash on their property. However, unlike hitting a child who misbehaves, which is legal and socially legitimate in most of the world, hitting the repeatedly misbehaving neighbor is an example of illegal violence. Empirical data on the theory that spanking is part of a pattern of violence in other spheres life are presented in the chapter on spanking and the approval of violence (Chapter 5).

The Line between Spanking and Physical Abuse

It is important to keep in mind that this book is about socially acceptable and legal corporal punishment, not *physical abuse* of children as that term is used in law, social work, and social science. Legal definitions of physical abuse vary, and there is tremendous ambiguity concerning the line between physical punishment and physical abuse, discussed in Gelles and Straus (1988) and Straus (1990b). However, in practice the *de facto* definition is almost always an attack on a child that *results in an injury.* According to the law in most U.S. states, parents can be charged with physical abuse if it exceeds the frequency and severity of violence allowed by cultural norms for disciplining children. In fact, that rarely happens, because child protective services seldom have the resources to attend to such cases. This largely happens because the norms are not clear and because numerous court decisions in many states have not accepted as *abuse* cases where the child is not injured or does not show bruises (Associated Press, 1995; Olson, 2008). In addition, the laws exempting parents from prosecution for assault do not provide a clear guideline because they permit parents to use *reasonable force* but fail to specify what acts are and are not reasonable. At one extreme, the attorney general of Texas told a reporter that corporal punishment becomes abusive "only if observable and material impairment occurs as a result" (Work, 2011).

Why Focus on Just One Narrow Aspect of Discipline?

Spanking is just one of many methods of discipline. The *Dimensions of Discipline Inventory* (Straus & Fauchier, 2011), for example, measures four punitive and five non-punitive methods of correction. Only one of these nine is spanking. However, as shown in Chapter 2, over 90% of U.S. parents spank toddlers. Any parental behavior that is that close to being universal needs to be examined and understood, it is part of the socialization experience of nearly all children in the United States and in most of the world's societies. A second reason for focusing on spanking is the extensive body of research that found harmful side effects, many of which are presented in this book. The combination of something that is nearly universal and engenders a risk of harm to children and to society needs to be understood to provide a basis for protecting children and lowering the level of violence in society.

Harsh Discipline

Many child researchers prefer to study the more general concept of *harsh discipline*. They usually believe that spanking is just one aspect of harsh discipline and that a better understanding of the effects of discipline on children can be obtained by investigating the broader concept of harsh discipline, for example by also studying verbal attacks on the child. We believe that both harsh discipline in general and the spanking component of harsh discipline need to be understood. They overlap, but are not the same. Many parents who spank do not use other modes of harsh parenting. Moreover, using a composite harsh parenting index seems to assume that spanking is best viewed as one manifestation or symptom of inadequate parenting. This is not likely to be true. Consider the fact that more than 90% of U.S. parents spank. No one knows the percent of parents that are inadequate, but over 90% is not plausible. So there must be a sizable number of good parents who spank. Another reason for not treating spanking only as part of a more general pattern of harsh parenting is that it ignores an extremely important question: Does spanking by good parents, who do not use other methods of harsh discipline, have harmful side effects? A large part of this book is devoted to that question.

Public Attitudes and Beliefs about Spanking

Whether to spank or not has always been a question that interests parents and professionals concerned with children and families. The interest dates to biblical times, and no doubt long before. In the last decade both public interest and research on spanking has substantially increased.

The high level of interest by parents and Americans in general was shown dramatically by the reaction to a *Time* magazine article in April 2010, *The Long Term Effects of Spanking*. It described the results of a large-scale study using a gold-standard longitudinal design. The study found that spanking had the long-term effect of *increasing* the probability of aggressive and antisocial behavior. The day after publication, over 1,000 comments were posted in response to a copy of the article on *Yahoo! News*. Six days after publication, there were over 10,000. One of us read the first 30 and then a few in each of the next few days. At least 95% of the individuals who commented doubted the validity of the study or condemned the study.

This is just one bit of evidence showing that spanking is a controversial issue. It is very likely that this book will be controversial, and that the results will be denied, condemned, or ignored. This has been the fate of much of the other research on spanking, as shown by the response to the study described in *Time* and as shown by the virtual absence of spanking in child development and child psychiatry textbooks described below.

A major obstacle to accepting research showing that spanking has harmful side effects occurs because the research contradicts deeply embedded cultural beliefs in many societies. The 2006 General Social Survey found that three quarters of the U.S. population believe that spanking is sometimes necessary. Many parents are very strongly committed to spanking as necessary for the well-being of their children, and their right to do so is protected in many state statutes, as we show in Chapter 17. Several have put it to us as necessary to keep their children from being delinquent and jailed as an adult. During a 20/20 segment on spanking in which one of us discussed spanking with parents, two parents said, that they needed to use spanking to make sure their children do not end up in the electric chair. This book is testimony to the irony of those beliefs. Spanking does usually work in the immediate situation, but as shown by the studies in Part II (Spanking and Child Behavior Problems), Part IV (Spanking and Crime), and in Chapter 19 (on spanking and crime), spanking increases the *probability* of antisocial behavior, delinquency, and crime later in life. Probability is emphasized in the previous sentence to indicate that the link between spanking and antisocial behavior is not in the form of a one-to-one relationship. Rather, as explained later in this chapter, it is in the form of a risk-factor relationship.

Part of the relationship between spanking and crime probably occurs because spanking is part of a culture of violence. For example, in Chapter 5, which addresses spanking and crime, Chart 5.6 shows that the U.S. states with a population that has the strongest commitment to spanking are also the states with the highest homicide rate. Spanking does not directly cause murder, but it provides the behavioral model that characterizes almost three quarters of murders in the United States—use of physical attacks to correct or punish the person attacked. The chapters in Part IV give the results of studies that have found direct links between corporal punishment and adult violence and other crime, including a longitudinal study that followed up children to find whether spanking resulted in less or more crime years later when they were young adults.

The national surveys we analyze in Chapter 17 show that the percent of the U.S. population who believe that spanking is sometimes necessary has dropped from 94% in 1968 to about 70% in 2010. Seventy percent is still a lot. But, the culture is changing. Most Americans now probably also think spanking is something to be avoided when possible. Fewer are spanking older children and teenagers. The 70% who think it is sometimes necessary are probably thinking about toddlers, which is why the next chapter shows over 90% of parents continue to spank toddlers, even though somewhat less often than previously.

The research in this book and the other research found that even in the short run spanking does not work better than nonviolent modes of correction, and in the long run spanking makes the child's behavior worse more often than it makes it better. We believe that this research is one of the causes of the decrease in spanking described in Part V. However, the concluding chapter suggests that the main driving forces for the decrease in spanking are, and will continue to be, changes in the organization of society and changes in values that are not directly about corporal punishment. This includes the century's long expansion of the scope of human rights to include not only people of all races and ethnicities, social classes, and women, but also children. The Convention on the Rights of the Child (UNICEF, 1997), which has been ratified by all United Nations members except Somalia and the United States, is one manifestation of that change. Our concluding chapter discusses the change in human rights explanations of the decrease in spanking, and it is analyzed in more detail by Smith and Durrant (2011) and Newell (2011).

We believe that even though the shift away from corporal punishment is mainly the result of social evolution, research has made an important contribution. The results presented in this book from the past 15 years of research by members of the Family Research Laboratory at the University of New Hampshire concerning spanking provide part of the needed scientific evidence. This research, along with research by others, found that, on average, children whose parents correct their behavior without spanking are better behaved, have better relations with their parents, and are smarter and less likely to be delinquent. As adults, they are less likely to suffer from mental health and family problems and are less likely to commit crime.

The Scientific Climate

The opinions of professionals concerned with child development such as pediatricians, developmental psychologists, family life/parenting educators, and social workers generally parallel the views of the general public, even though some professional organizations such as the American Academy of Pediatrics and the National Association of Social Workers have taken a stand against spanking. There is both a growing belief that spanking has harmful side effects and should be avoided and, at the same time, a continuing belief that spanking is sometimes necessary. We suggest these contradictory beliefs coexist because the United States and many other nations are in a period of cultural change in respect to spanking. This paradoxical contradiction is part of the explanation offered in Chapter 18 on why nearly everyone resorts to spanking and for the continued high rate of hitting toddlers as compared with the large decreases in the percent of parents who hit school-age children and teenagers.

The commitment to the folk beliefs that spanking is sometimes necessary and is harmless if done in moderation shows up in surveys of child development by child abuse professionals and in the content of child development and child psychiatry textbooks. A study of 237 clinical child psychologists (Schenck, Lyman, & Bodin, 2000) found that, although they were generally opposed to corporal punishment, two thirds considered it ethical to advise using corporal punishment under some circumstances. A study of 380 lawyers and physicians, who were members of a national professional listserv concerned with child abuse, found that 90% of the lawyers and 70% of the physicians believed there are occasions when it is OK to spank a 6- to 10-year-old child (Burgess, Block, & Runyan, 2010). A study by Knox and Brouwer (2008) of 98 medical professionals, residents, mental health professionals, child development specialists, and early childhood service coordinators may seem to contradict the Schenck and Burgess studies. Knox and Brouwer found that approximately one third had recommended spanking at least once in the past year to parents of children age 5 years or younger. This is far from the two thirds and 70% found by the Schenck et al. (2000) and the Burgess et al. (2010) studies. However, it does not necessarily contradict the studies showing much higher rates of approval of spanking by human service professionals because those who had not advised spanking in the past year may not have encountered a situation for which they felt the misbehavior was persistent enough to advise spanking. In addition, they were not asked if they believed that spanking was sometimes necessary. If they had been asked that, we believe that most of those who had not advised spanking would have agreed it is sometimes necessary. Moreover, that one third of child care professionals had actually advised spanking is itself important.

Another indication that U.S. professionals concerned with children continue to believe that spanking is sometimes necessary and harmless when done by loving parents is the minimal, and sometimes zero, coverage of spanking in child development textbooks. At the 2009 conference of the Society for Research in Child Development, one of us examined the child development textbooks with a 2009 or 2010 copyright at the first five publisher's booths. There were 10 such books. The number of pages on spanking in these 10 books ranged from 0 to 2.5, with a mean of 1.5 pages. This is remarkably little coverage for something which, as shown in Chapter 2 is experienced by over 90% of children in the United States and many other nations. In addition, *none* even mentioned the meta-analysis by Gershoff (2002) that analyzed 88 studies of the effects of spanking and found 93% agreement with spanking showing harmful side effects. None advised readers to never spank. Nevertheless, even the tiny average of 1.5 pages on spanking is more than triple the mean number of pages in child development textbooks published in previous decades (Straus & Stewart, 1999).

The risks associated with spanking are also given little attention or ignored in child psychiatry textbooks (Douglas and Straus, 2007) and in discussions of of steps to prevent physical abuse of children. Special-topic issues of the two leading journals on child abuse do not mention the research showing that at least two thirds of cases of physical abuse confirmed by child protective services began as spanking and then escalated into physical abuse (Straus, 2000; Straus, 2008a). The two-volume compendium on *Violence against Women and Children* edited by White, Koss, and Kazdin (2011) has nothing on spanking as a risk factor for child abuse or anything else.

An important indicator of the continuing belief that spanking is sometimes necessary comes from a careful reading of the policy statement of the American Academy of Pediatrics published in 1998 and reaffirmed in 2004 (American

Academy of Pediatrics, 1998). The policy statement defines spanking as "strik-ing a child with an open hand on the buttocks or extremities." It reviews the evidence on the effects of spanking and concludes that "Corporal punishment is of limited effectiveness and has potentially deleterious side effects. The American Academy of Pediatrics recommends that parents be encouraged and assisted in the development of methods other than spanking for managing un-desired behavior." However, it then says that "other forms of physical punish-ment than spanking . . . are unacceptable . . . and . . . should never be used." This is, in effect a denial of the previous statement because the only thing that should never be used is other forms of corporal punishment. Thus, it permits "striking a child with an open hand on the buttocks or extremities" in the very document that says it is of limited effectiveness and has potentially deleterious side effects.

That policy statement was more than a decade ago. Have things changed? We believe they have changed but not enough to put never-spanking very high on the agenda of pediatricians. This is illustrated by the American Acad-emy of Pediatrics, Committee on Early Childhood, Adoption, and Depen-dent Care, and Section on Developmental and Behavioral Pediatrics. Neither the policy statement on "Early Childhood Adversity, Toxic Stress, and the Role of the Pediatrician: Translating Developmental Science into Lifelong Health" (Garner et al., 2012) nor the technical report on which it was based (Shonkoff et al., 2012) mention spanking, despite the research showing that spanking adversely affects brain development and IQ (see Chapter 10) and increases the probability of antisocial behavior and many other child behav-ior problems, as shown by the studies in this book and the meta-analysis by Gershoff (2002).

Despite the continuing belief among parents and professionals in the United States concerned with children in the necessity of sometimes spanking, as noted previously, there is also a growing concern with the harmful side effects of spanking and a growing amount of research on spanking. Chart 1.1, which we created on the basis of a search of studies in the Social Science Citation Index, shows that the annual number of journal articles on corporal punishment is growing rapidly. We tabulated articles on spanking, corporal punishment, etc. in the Social Science Citation Index from 1900 to 2010. Chart 1.1 shows that almost nothing was published in the period 1900 to 1929, slightly more in the period 1930 to 1969, and an exponential growth since 1970. Just over 100 articles were published in 2010.

Another indication of the growing recognition of the harmful side effects of spanking is the *Report on Physical Punishment in the United States: What Research Tells Us about Its Effects on Children* (Gershoff, 2008). It docu-ments the harmful side effects of spanking and it has been endorsed by over 70 organizations, including the American Academy of Pediatrics, the Ameri-can Medical Association, and the American Academy of Child and Adoles-cent Psychiatry. Nevertheless, the American Psychological Association has not endorsed the statement. On the other hand, a similar Canadian report

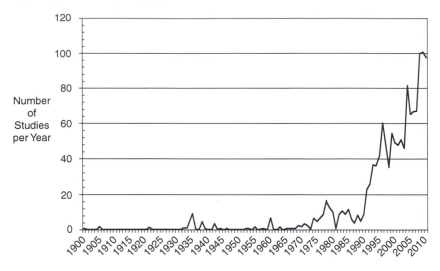

Chart 1.1   Exponential Growth in Articles on Spanking

(Durrant, Ensom, & Coalition on Physical Punishment of Children and Youth, 2004) has been adopted by the Canadian Psychological Association and adopted the conclusions of the Canadian Joint Statement as its official position statement, and more than 400 Canadian organizations have endorsed the statement.

The above discussion, and Chapter 17 on trends in approval of spanking, indicate that, although there is a growing belief that spanking is not appropriate, the majority of parents and professionals continue to believe spanking is sometimes necessary. Chapters 18 and 20 in this book and "Ten Myths that Perpetuate Corporal Punishment" in Chapter 10 of Straus (2001a) discuss some of the many reasons, both common sense and technical, used to justify continuing to spank when necessary.

Our Research on Corporal Punishment

This book provides the results of empirical research on the extent to which spanking is used by different groups of parents, the causes of spanking, the effects on children, and by inference, the effects on society in the form of the rates of mental health problems and crime. These same issues were addressed in the previous book *Beating the Devil Out of Them: Corporal Punishment in American Families and Its Effects on Children* (Straus, 2001a). Key parts of the current book represent a major advance. The previous book was based entirely on cross-sectional studies. In the current book, three key chapters (Chapters 6, 10, and 15) report results of *prospective* studies. Moreover, unlike 15 years ago, in Chapter 19 we are also able to cite many prospective studies by other researchers. This is crucial because only prospective studies and experiments can determine the extent to which corporal punishment, although usually effective in the immediate situation, tends to make things worse in the long run.

One of the most unique contributions of our research are the studies that found that spanking by parents interferes with the development of mental ability among young children. It increases the probability of poor academic performance and reduces the chances of earning a college degree. Some other important characteristics of this book include:

- Several chapters report data for representative samples of U.S. children. There are also four chapters that report results from a 32-nation study. Some other chapters discuss developments in other nations, but the bulk of our analyses, discussions, and references are to spanking in the United States.
- Our approach is a multidisciplinary analysis that does not assume knowledge of any of these disciplines on the part of the reader. Our goal was a book that is understandable by any college-educated person. To accomplish this, the chapters provide the results using graphs, not tables, and the technical methodological information such as tests of significance and regression coefficients are in an appendix.

The concluding chapters take a historical, theoretical, and social policy perspective. They show that corporal punishment is decreasing and explain the reasons for the decrease in spanking. For example, they suggest an explanation for why, despite a large decrease in corporal punishment of older children, over 90% of U.S. parents continue to spank toddlers. They discuss the implications of the findings for efforts to prevent and treat mental health problems and make projections regarding the effect on society as a whole of a continued reduction in spanking. The final chapter concludes that the continued reduction in spanking is likely to result in a population with better parent-child relationships, a higher average IQ, less delinquency, fewer adult mental health and family problems, and less crime.

Except for concluding that parents should never spank, *The Primordial Violence* is not an advice book. But it does have important practical implications for parents. It provides scientific evidence showing the benefits of not spanking, such as less antisocial behavior and higher IQ. Parents need this information because the harmful side effects of spanking do not show up for months or even years. As a consequence, parents can't perceive these side effects. Because parents can't perceive the harmful effects, professionals need to provide that information and advise parents to never spank. As we showed earlier, very few do that. We hope that *The Primordial Violence* will enable child psychologists, educators, parent educators, pediatricians, sociologists, and social workers to alert parents to the risks to which spanking exposes their children and the benefits of never spanking.

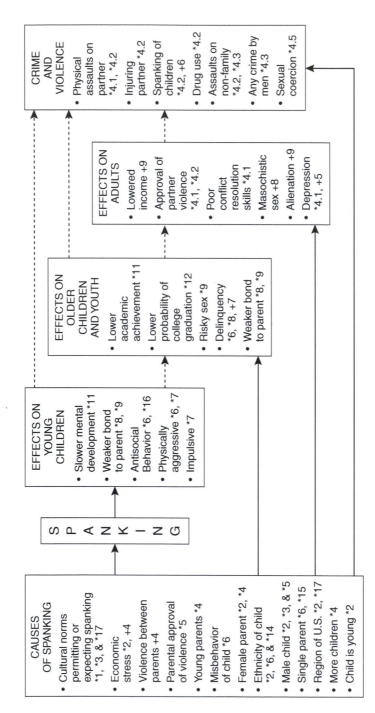

CAUSES OF SPANKING
- Cultural norms permitting or expecting spanking *1, *3, & *17
- Economic stress *2, +4
- Violence between parents +4
- Parental approval of violence *5
- Young parents *4
- Misbehavior of child *6
- Female parent *2, *4
- Ethnicity of child *2, *6, & *14
- Male child *2, *3, & *5
- Single parent *6, *15
- Region of U.S. *2, *17
- More children *4
- Child is young *2

S P A N K I N G

EFFECTS ON YOUNG CHILDREN
- Slower mental development *11
- Weaker bond to parent *8, *9
- Antisocial Behavior *6, *16
- Physically aggressive *6, *7
- Impulsive *7

EFFECTS ON OLDER CHILDREN AND YOUTH
- Lower academic achievement *11
- Lower probability of college graduation *12
- Risky sex *9
- Delinquency *6, *8, +7
- Weaker bond to parent *8, *9

EFFECTS ON ADULTS
- Lowered income +9
- Approval of partner violence *4.1, *4.2
- Poor conflict resolution skills *4.1
- Masochistic sex +8
- Alienation +9
- Depression *4.1, +5

CRIME AND VIOLENCE
- Physical assaults on partner *4.1, *4.2
- Injuring partner *4.2
- Spanking of children *4.2, +6
- Drug use *4.2
- Assaults on non-family *4.2, *4.3
- Any crime by men *4.3
- Sexual coercion *4.5

Chart 1.2 Partial Theoretical Model of the Processes Linking Spanking, Child Development, and Crime

*Indicates chapter numbers in this book.

+Indicates chapter numbers in *Beating the Devil Out of Them*.

The Theoretical Framework

As previously noted, this book is the product of the past 15 years of research on corporal punishment at the Family Research Laboratory of the University of New Hampshire. The results from the 15 years before that were presented in *Beating the Devil Out of Them: Corporal Punishment in American Families and Its Effects on Children* (Straus, 2001a). Chart 1.2 summarizes the evidence from this 30-year effort. The variables in bold type identify results in this book. The chart provides an overview of the theoretical framework that guided our research.

The central theoretical ideas in Chart 1.2 are first, that spanking has many causes, only one of which is misbehavior by the child, and second, that there are multiple direct and indirect links between spanking and antisocial behavior. These include effects on personality and cognitions, such as beliefs and attitudes about violence and mental ability. Third, there are separate blocks to indicate that these effects of spanking manifest themselves in different ways among young children, older children, and adults. The solid lines in Chart 1.2 indicate our empirical results. The dashed lines indicate the mechanisms (i.e., mediating processes), which could explain why spanking results in violence and crime. Although some of these mediating processes have been confirmed by empirical research (see, for example, Chapters 8, 9, 12, and 16), dashed lines are used because most of the mechanisms in Chart 1.2 that could explain why spanking causes violence and other crimes have not yet been confirmed by empirical research.

Some Things to Keep in Mind about Research Results

The low effect size for a single variable. It is important to keep in mind that the results summarized in Chart 1.2 identify only a few of the differences between children and adults in characteristics and experiences that could explain differences in beliefs about violence, and in violent and criminal behavior. To fully understand why some children and adults are smarter or more violent than others, and to fully understand why some commit crimes and others do not, requires information on a vast array of characteristics and experiences. This includes innate differences as well as social experiences such as spanking (Farrington, 2011; Fergusson, Boden, Horwood, Miller, & Kennedy, 2011). Because almost all human behavior has multiple causes, no single cause, such as spanking or poverty, will explain more than a small part of the difference between people in a specific behavior. Examined separately, each of those causes will, therefore, be found to have a small *effect size*. (Effect size is a measure of the strength of the relationship between spanking and any adverse outcome.) The small effect size also applies to other single characteristics or experiences. Yet, as will be shown in Chapters 20, even a small effect size can make a large difference. In fact, small effect sizes, smaller than those for spanking, have been the basis for important public health and social programs such as protecting children from exposure to lead.

Tests of statistical significance. As explained previously, the details of such tests, such as the specific test used, degrees of freedom, F tests, and *p* values are in sections of the Appendix or the references cited in the chapter. In the chapters themselves, we use the term *dependable* to refer to results that have been found to be statistically significant. We have used this wording because years of experience with many students has shown that, despite having had a course in statistics, most continue to think that *significant* means *important* in the sense of a large difference or large effect, when it actually refers to the probability that the result could occur by chance. Just because a research result is statistically dependable, in the sense of being unlikely to have occurred by chance, it does not necessarily mean it is significant in that sense.

Context. It is also true that we can fully understand the effects of spanking only by taking into account many other aspects of the parent-child relationship and other aspects of the child's life circumstances. However, that perspective can be pushed too far. For example, Ross Parke, one of America's leading developmental psychologists, argues that "attempts to treat punishment as a separate variable are bound to failure. Instead, the inherent packaged nature of parental discipline renders the attempt to answer the question about the effects of corporal punishment on children a misguided one" (Parke, 2002). This is a classic false dichotomy. It is like saying it is futile to try to separate out the effects of Vitamin C because the effects depend on the whole nutritional context or futile to study the effect of reading to children because the effect depends on the inherent package nature of the parenting context. In fact, both specific parenting practices, and the broader parenting context and the social circumstances in which a family lives, need to be considered. In this book, we do focus primarily on one part of the package—spanking—but whenever the data are available, we have also controlled for how other aspects of "the parenting package" influence the effects of spanking. This includes:

Social Characteristics of the Parents and Family

- Educational level of parents
- Income, including very low income
- Racial/ethnic group
- Socioeconomic status (SES)
- Child's age
- Mother's age
- Single-parent versus two-parent families
- Number of children in the family
- Sex of the parent
- Age of the parent

Parenting Behavior

- Adequacy of parent's supervision of children
- Parental warmth and emotional support

- Whether parents established clear rules and expectations
- Use of other disciplinary strategies such as time-out
- Parental consistency in discipline
- Parental use of reasoning
- Parental involvement and cognitive stimulation provided by the parent
- Father presence or absence

Psychosocial Problems of Parents

- Conflict between the parents
- Violence between the parents
- Violence in the families in which the parents grew up
- Parental alcohol abuse
- Parent attitudes approving violence
- Whether the parent also engaged in more severe violence ("physical abuse")
- Depression of parents

Child Characteristics

- Sex of the child
- Age of the child
- Child's weight at birth (a proxy for possible physical or mental limitations)
- Child's misbehavior at Time 1
- Child's cognitive ability at Time 1
- Child-to-parent bond

When the variables just listed are controlled, it means that the results on the relation of spanking to child behavior problems are *in addition* to the effects of the variables controlled. Or another way of putting this is that the results show that spanking makes a unique contribution, to whatever side effect was studied, that is over and above the contribution of the variables controlled.

Risk Factors: The Real Meaning of Social Science Results

"I was spanked as a child and I turned out fine, so what's the big deal?" We have heard this hundreds of times. In this section, we explain how it can be a big deal even though they turned out fine. To understand this, readers need to be familiar with the concept of a *risk factor*. The term risk factor has been used in several different ways (Murray, Farrington, & Eisner, 2009). We use it to indicate the relation of an event, behavior, or characteristic to an increased *probability* of experiencing being spanked rather than a one-to-one relationship. We refer to spanking as a risk factor for antisocial behavior and later crime to indicate that spanking is associated with an *increase in the chances* of crime, not to indicate that every child who has been spanked will commit crimes as an adult. If that were the case, because almost all children in the United States and most other nations have been spanked, we should all be criminals. The next section uses the example of the relation of heavy smoking to dying of a smoking-related disease to illustrate that, even though heavy smoking is proven to cause early death, it is also a risk factor in the sense that most people who experience the cause, do *not* experience the harmful effect.

Smoking and the Fallacy of Personal Experience

A well-known example of a risk-factor relationship rather than a one-to-one relationship is the research on the relationship of heavy smoking to dying of a smoking-related disease. The research leaves no doubt that smoking causes lung cancer and other diseases. It shows that about one third of heavy smokers die from a smoking-related disease (Matteson, Pollack, & Cullen, 1987). That is a big enough risk for governments to take steps to reduce smoking and for many people to stop smoking—both of which have happened across the United States and throughout many parts of the world. The same statistic, however, also means that two thirds of heavy smokers do *not* die of a smoking-related disease. As a consequence, the majority of heavy smokers may doubt the research because they can say that they have smoked all their lives and are in good health. If they are in good health, that is a correct statement. But when people say that, it is intended to imply that smoking does not cause lung cancer and other diseases, which is not correct. The correct interpretation is that the person still in good health is one of the lucky two thirds. This is because smoking is only one of the large number of things that increase or decrease the probability of developing or dying from a smoking-related disease.

The relation of smoking to disease is in the form of a *dose-response:* the more smoking, the greater the probability of illness. Large amounts of smoking are associated with a large increase in the probability of illness, but even small amounts are associated with a significant but smaller increase in the chances of illness. For example, even relatively small amounts of *passive* exposure to smoking is associated with an increased chance of chronic obstructive pulmonary disease (Jordan, Cheng, Miller, & Adab, 2011). As a consequence, many jurisdictions and some nations have policies to protect people from *any* exposure to smoking, just as we think it should be national policy to protect children from exposure to *any* amount of spanking.

Other Examples of Risk-Factor Relationships

* Research on binge drinking and wife beating shows that in a given year about 20% of binge drinkers assault their partners (Kaufman Kantor & Straus, 1987). That is 3 times the percent of abstainers. But this finding also means that 80% of binge drinkers did *not* attack their partner during the year covered by the study (see also Hines & Straus, 2007; Testa, Hoffman, & Leonard, 2011).

- Research on male dominance and partner violence shows that, in a given year, men in male-dominant relationships are almost 7 times more likely than men in egalitarian relationships to assault a partner (Straus, Gelles, & Steinmetz, 2006, p.194). The rate increases from 3% to 20%. Therefore, despite the seven-fold increase, the results of that study also show that 80% of the men in male-dominant relationships did *not* assault their partners.
- Protective factors are also in the form of a lessened probability of harm. Aspirin does prevent heart attacks, but in the form of a decreased *probability* of a heart attack. Many people who take aspirin have heart attacks, but fewer of them than those who should take aspirin and do not.

Examples of Risk-Factor Relationships in This Book

All the results in this book on the presumed causes or consequences of spanking are in the form of risk-factor relationships. Here are some examples:

- In the next chapter, Chart 2.3 shows that low socioeconomic status is associated with an increased *probability* of spanking. Those results do not mean that *all* low socioeconomic status parents spank more than high socioeconomic status parents. Some low socioeconomic status parents spank less than high socioeconomic status parents, and some high socioeconomic status parents spank more than low socioeconomic status parents. The results in that chapter, like all the results in this book, are what happen *on average*. There are always people who are above or below the average for their group, but that does not mean the average gives incorrect information.
- Chapter 4 on family size and spanking found that having more than two children is associated with an increased *probability* of spanking and an average increase in the frequency of spanking. Those results do not mean that *all* parents with three or four children spank more than those with one or two children. Those results, like all of the results presented in this book and like the results of almost all social science and most medical research, are in the form of what is true on average or what is true generally. Fortunately or unfortunately, depending on whether the study investigates a potential source of harm or a potential benefit, there are always exceptions to the general trend of things. Moreover, the exceptions are usually the majority of people who experience the risk factor, as is the case with smoking. Not everyone is harmed by a risk factor and not everyone gains from a beneficial factor. The studies showing that more children in a family is associated with more spanking of each child are likely to be doubted by parents who point out that, "I have four children, and I don't spank a lot." For many parents that is correct, but the implication that the number of children makes no difference in spanking is just as incorrect as a smoker who is healthy believing that smoking makes no difference in health.

- Chapter 6 shows that spanking is associated with a subsequent increased probability of antisocial behavior—the very thing it was designed to correct. This does not mean that all, or even most, children who are spanked will be antisocial, just as the results on smoking do not mean that all, or even most, heavy smokers will die of a smoking-related disease.

Risk and Causation

As we noted earlier, the results of almost all social science and medical research are in the form of risk-factor relationships, that is an increased probability of a harmful (or beneficial) outcome, not a one-to-one relationship. This applies even when there is a proven causal relationship, as in the examples of smoking. Another example of a causal relationship in the form of an increased probability, rather than a one-to-one relationship, is that only a minority of children born to mothers with HIV, have HIV.

The converse is also important: There may be clear evidence that a certain event or behavior is associated with an increased probability of a harm or benefit, but that does not necessarily mean that the risk factor is the cause. Research showing that spanking is a risk factor for an adverse outcome, like everything else in science, needs to be carefully evaluated. In this case, the crucial question is whether the evidence showing that spanking is *associated with* an increased probability of a negative side effect also indicates that the risk factor *causes* the negative side effect. This question has been the subject of much discussion, which is well summarized by Murray et al. (2009). Many things are involved, but a core element in determining whether a risk factor is also a causal factor is whether the study was experimental, longitudinal, or cross-sectional.

Experiments.   Experiments are the gold standard for research answering causal questions on issues such as whether spanking causes or prevents crime. An experiment on this question would involve randomly assigning half the parents to a spanking group and the other half of the parents would be assigned to a no-spanking group who would agree to never spank and instead correct misbehavior in other ways. There are no experimental studies in this book, partly because we believe it would be unethical to randomly assign parents to spank. However, those who think that spanking is sometimes necessary might also think an experimental study would be unethical, but for almost the opposite reason: because they would not want to deprive the child of what they think is sometimes necessary for the child's well-being. Nevertheless, one research group has conducted experiments (Day & Roberts, 1983; Roberts, 1988; Roberts & Powers, 1990). They randomly assigned one group of parents to spank when a child left time-out and another group to use nonviolent alternatives such as simply putting the child back in the time-out place.

They found that it took an average of about eight repetitions of putting the child back in time-out before the child would stay. What happened with the children who were spanked? It took an average of eight spankings. Thus, as we explain in more detail in Chapter 18 on why most parents resort to spanking, spanking does work but on average no better than nonviolent modes of correction, and spanking has harmful side effects that nonviolent methods of correction do not have. In this study, the side effects were that the spanked children engaged in more disruptive behavior (such as yelling and whining) before achieving compliance.

Regardless of the reason, the absence of experiments is a weakness in the evidence on the harmful effects of spanking, but it does not provide a basis for disregarding all the other evidence indicating that spanking causes harmful side effects, especially the evidence from longitudinal studies (also called prospective studies).

Longitudinal studies. In this type of research, children are followed over a period of time such as one, two, or four years. Prospective studies can provide data on *change* in the behavior of the spanked children compared with those not spanked. Examples are Chapter 6 on the relation of spanking to antisocial behavior by the child, Chapter 10 on the relation of spanking to the child's mental ability, and Chapter 15 on the relation of spanking to crime as an adult. We also describe prospective studies by others, especially in Chapter 19 on the link between spanking and violent societies. If other variables that are linked to spanking, and which could be the real underlying cause, are controlled, longitudinal studies provide strong, although not conclusive, evidence of a cause-and-effect relationship.

Cross-sectional studies. A cross-sectional study (also called a correlational study) simply establishes whether or not differences in a presumed cause (such as spanking) are linked to differences in the probability of a presumed effect, such as delinquency. Most of the chapters in this book describe the results of cross-sectional research. They can show that the more spanking, the greater the probability of some harmful side effect, but they cannot prove that spanking causes the increased probability of the side effect. Cross-sectional research could, however, *dis*prove the theory that spanking has harmful side effects. This would be the case if the cross-sectional studies failed to show the hypothesized correlation between spanking and the side effect investigated. The opposite has happened. There have been more than 100 cross-sectional studies testing the theory that spanking has harmful side effects. Gershoff's meta-analysis (Gershoff, 2002) of the results of 88 studies found that 97% were consistent with the theory. That is, almost none failed to find that spanking is linked to a harmful side effect. That is also true of the studies that have been published since then. This is especially important because the studies since Gershoff's review include many longitudinal studies, such as MacKenzie, Nicklas, Waldfogel, and Brooks-Gunn, 2011. Longitudinal studies provide evidence of a causal relationship that is second only to random assignment experiments. It is also important to keep in mind that when we conclude, for example, that spanking *causes* antisocial behavior, we do not mean it is the only cause. Almost everything in human behavior has multiple causes.

Summary and Conclusions

Despite the absence of experimental data, we believe the evidence is sufficient to conclude that spanking does cause child behavior problems and crime. We base this on the longitudinal studies in this book, the longitudinal studies by others identified in Chapter 19 on the relation of spanking to antisocial behavior and crime and the fact that almost none of the very large number of cross-sectional studies conducted over decades has failed to find the theoretically predicted link between spanking and a harmful side effect.

The idea of a risk-factor relationship is extremely important for understanding these results and for the practical implications of most social science and medical research. It explains the seeming contradiction between research and personal experience; for example, the discrepancy between research on the relation of spanking to assaulting a marital or dating partner and the fact that most people do not hit their partners. The research has consistently found that the more spanking, the greater the probability of assaulting a partner (see Chapter 12). But the personal experience of most people who were spanked is that they have not physically assaulted their marital or dating partners. Both statements are correct. One does not contradict the other, just as a chaotic or abusive family does not doom children to failure and a wonderfully warm and supportive family does not guarantee success. The worst parenting only increases the *probability* of bad outcomes, and the best parenting only increases the *probability* of good outcomes for the child. Risk-factor relationships are what is presented in this book. We hope that this explanation up front provides a foundation for understanding the results in the following chapters and for understanding why we argue that spanking is, indeed, the primordial violence.

2 Corporal Punishment in the United States

As we pointed out in Chapter 1, whether parents should spank children is the subject of a huge debate among both parents and professionals concerned with children. But regardless of whether one favors or rejects spanking as a method of correcting misbehavior, parents and the professionals who advise parents need to know the extent to which spanking and other legal methods of corporal punishment are actually used. They also need to know how effective spanking is and whether there are unintended side effects. This book provides information on all those issues. This chapter addresses the following questions:

- What percent of parents use corporal punishment such as spanking, and how often do those who spank do it?
- To what extent does use of corporal punishment differ depending on:
  - The child's age?
  - Whether the child is a boy or a girl?
  - Whether the parent correcting the misbehavior is the mother or the father?
  - Whether the parent has little education or is a college graduate?
- If, for example, low-education parents do more spanking, does that mean that all children of low-education parents are spanked a lot? Obviously not. Underneath that obvious answer is a general principle that is extremely important for properly interpreting *all* the research results in this book, not just this chapter. That principle is explained in Chapter 1, in the section on "Risk Factors: The Real Meaning of Social Science Results."

This chapter provides information on the questions just listed for a nationally representative sample of American children in 1995. It also provides an update on current use of corporal punishment from a national survey of American children in 2006. The next chapter and Straus (2010b) provide some of that information for other nations.

Julie H. Stewart is the coauthor of this chapter.

To understand what children experience when parents use corporal punishment, more needs to be known than just the percentage of different ages who are hit by parents. As a consequence, the chapter also provides information on:

- Six specific acts of corporal punishment that vary in severity
- The chronicity of corporal punishment, that is among those who used corporal punishment, and how often did they do it
- The duration of corporal punishment (the number of years until corporal punishment ceases)
- The extent to which corporal punishment differs by seven characteristics of the children (such as boys versus girls) and of the families (such as low-and high-education parents)

Information on the extent to which corporal punishment differs according to these characteristics of children and families can suggest some of the social causes of corporal punishment. This can have practical value because there is a growing professional interest in helping parents shift from spanking to non-violent forms of discipline. Such programs need to be guided by data on the extent to which spanking occurs at different ages and in different sectors of the population. For example, if poor Black parents and parents of other races or ethnic groups with low educational attainment are more likely to approve of and use spanking (Alvy, 1987; Deater-Deckard, Bates, Dodge, & Pettit, 1996; Giles-Sims, Straus, & Sugarman, 1995; Ispa & Halgunseth, 2004; Polite, 1996), parent education intended to reduce spanking may need to take into account the culture of these groups. If, in recent years, fathers have taken on additional child care responsibilities, the additional effort needed to include fathers in parent education programs may be even more important than it was previously.

The Survey

Most of the information in this chapter was obtained from a survey of a nationally representative sample of 986 parents (333 fathers and 653 mothers) that was conducted for us by the Gallup Organization in 1995. Each parent was interviewed about one child under age 18. When there was more than one child at home, the child to be the focus of the interview was randomly selected. Additional information on the method of sampling and the characteristics of the sample is in Straus and Stewart (1999).

Some of the many methods of measuring corporal punishment are discussed in Holden and Zambarano (1992) and Straus (1998) and others have been developed since then. The instrument used for this study is the parent-child version of the Conflict Tactics Scales (Straus, Hamby, Finkelhor, Moore, & Runyan, 1998). The questions ask how often the parent did each of the following in the previous 12 months:

- Spanked on the bottom with your bare hand
- Slapped on the hand, arm, or leg

- Pinched
- Shook (for children age 3 and over only)
- Hit on the bottom with something like a belt, hairbrush, a stick, or some other hard object
- Slapped on the face, head, or ears

All six of these acts are legal forms of corporal punishment in every state in the United States, provided that they do not result in an injury that leaves a lasting mark and that they are not done so frequently and severely that the child is at high risk of injury. However, three acts were judged to carry a higher risk of injury and be less widely accepted, and will be referred to as *severe corporal punishment*. They are slapping a child's face or head, hitting with a belt or hard object, and pinching. Two of the six (spanked on the buttocks and slapped on the hand or leg) will be referred to as ordinary corporal punishment. Shaking

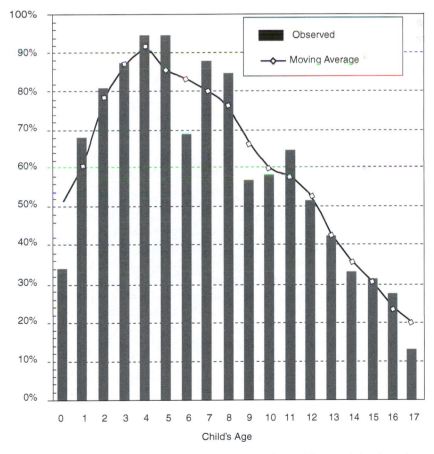

Chart 2.1 Spanking Begins with Infants, Is Highest for Toddlers, and Continues into the Teen Years for Many Children

a child was considered separately because of the extreme danger if done to infants. Additional information on how the Conflict Tactics Scales was used to measure corporal punishment is in Straus (1998).

In addition to the rates for the sample as a whole, we examined whether there are differences in corporal punishment for the following seven variables: fathers compared with mothers, boys compared with girls, the age of the child, the ethnic group of the child, single parents, and region. The tests of statistical significance for the differences between groups are in Straus (1999).

How Corporal Punishment Changes as Children Grow Older

A child's age is uniquely important for understanding the place of spanking because young children are spanked or hit much more often than older children. It is also important because the age at which spanking is appropriate is something that parents worry about and professionals debate. The professional debate about the age for spanking took up much of the time at a conference on spanking sponsored by the American Academy of Pediatrics that one of us attended (Friedman & Schonberg, 1996b) and had two noteworthy features. The first is that the debate was carried out within the context of what ages to recommend and what ages to avoid, rather than whether it is ever appropriate. Second, the debate took place in the absence of scientific evidence on how the age of the child influences the effects of spanking. The so-called consensus statement said that spanking should not be used with children under 2 or over 6 years of age. However, not a single member of this distinguished group presented even one study showing less harm at the ages they approved. They could not provide evidence on that issue because that research has never been done. However, the chapters on child behavior problems (Chapter 6) and mental ability (Chapter 10) contain a bit of the needed evidence on the age when corporal punishment has the greatest adverse effect. Ironically, they show that corporal punishment is just as harmful or more harmful for toddlers (the permitted age) than it is for older children (the prohibited ages). This is precisely the opposite of what the conference recommended and the opposite of what we think most parents, like professionals believe.

Returning to the issue of the prevalence of corporal punishment, Chart 2.1 gives the percentage of parents who used corporal punishment at each age, starting on the left side with infants (children under 1 year of age). The percent who spanked or slapped an infant is one of the most important results because it shows that just over one third of American parents did this. Typically this was a slap on the hand for touching something forbidden or dangerous or for repeatedly pushing food off a high chair tray, etc. One out of three is probably a minimum estimate because parents may be reluctant to tell an interviewer that they spanked or slapped an infant. Not many studies have looked into hitting infants, but the studies that have found rates that are this high or higher (Bugental, Martorell, & Barraza, 2003; Korsch, Christian, Gozzi, & Carlson, 1965; Newson & Newson, 1963; Socolar & Stein, 1995).

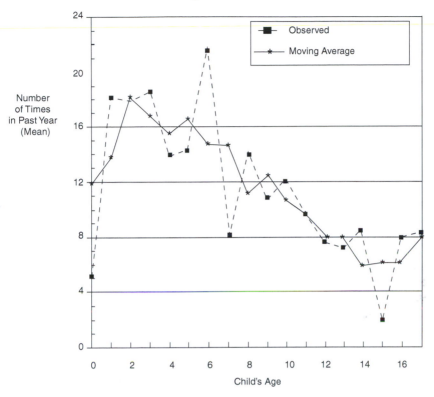

Chart 2.2 Parents Who Use Spanking Do It Often

After infancy, the percent of children who were spanked rises to a peak at ages 4 and 5, when 94% of parents said that they had used one or more of the six types of corporal punishment, during the previous 12 months. From there on, the rate declines steadily to age 17. However, it is important to note that as late as age 13, over 40% of parents used corporal punishment as a disciplinary technique. These rates are consistent with previous studies that have found that corporal punishment increases from infancy to age 2, stays at or above 90% for ages 3 through 5, and decreases steadily from age 6 through 17 (Bachman, 1967; Straus, 1991, 2001a; Wauchope & Straus, 1990).

Chronicity and Severity

Chronicity. Although Chart 2.1, shows the percent of children who were hit at each age, it does not indicate how often parents hit the children in this study. This is in Chart 2.2. It refers to the subsample of parents who used corporal punishment at least once during the previous year, and it gives the average number of times they used corporal punishment. The term *chronicity* is used to distinguish this data from data on the average frequency for *all* parents of children of a given age. The average frequency for all parents would be misleading because almost one half of the children age 9 to 11 and more than one half of older children would have a score of zero (no corporal punishment that year). Therefore the average frequency would turn out to be less than once a year. This is very different than the chronicity data in Chart 2.2, which shows that the chronicity, among those who do use corporal punishment, is in the 4 to 8 times a year range.

Chart 2.2 shows that spanking was most chronic by parents of 2-year-old children—the "terrible two's." They spanked an average of 18 times during the previous year. Except for what are probably random fluctuations around the trend line, the chronicity of spanking declined from there on, to an average of 6 times per year by parents of 14-, 15-, and 16-year-old children. However, these chronicity figures are almost certainly large underestimates, especially for toddlers. Other studies show averages of about 3 times a week for toddlers (see Chapter 10 and Giles-Sims et al., 1995; Holden, Coleman, & Schmidt, 1995; Stattin, Janson, Klackenberg-Larsson, Magnusson, & McCord, 1995). Three times a week multiplies out to about 150 times a year. The difference between the 18 times a year in Chart 2.2 and 150 or more times a year found by these other studies occurs because our study asked parents how often they did it *in the past year.* The problem with asking parents about the last year is that spanking children is such a routine, taken-for-granted, and unremarkable event that few parents realize how often they have done it over the course of a year. This and other problematic aspects of measuring corporal punishment, and alternative procedures, are discussed in Straus (1998). Fortunately, response categories are now available for the CTS and other instruments which avoid this large underestimate (Fauchier & Straus, 2011; Moore, Straus & Winstok, 2013).

Severity. It is important to distinguish between ordinary spanking and severe spanking such as hitting a child with a belt or paddle. As we pointed out earlier, the legality of using a belt or paddle has been confirmed by high court rulings in many states (Olson 2008). The rates of ordinary and severe corporal punishment follow a developmental pattern. The milder forms of corporal punishment, spanking and slapping, were used most often with toddlers (ages 2 to 4). The more severe and less culturally approved forms of corporal punishment were most prevalent in middle childhood. Twenty-eight percent of children ages 5 to 12 were hit with a belt, paddle, or hairbrush during the year covered by this study. Teenagers had the lowest prevalence rates, but 16% being hit with an object is still a remarkably high rate.

We believe that hitting a child on the bottom with objects such as a belt, hairbrush, or stick was extremely common as recently as the 1940s and 1950s. It is still legal in every state in the United States, providing it leaves no lasting mark on the child. Even as recently as the 1970s, two thirds of a random sample of the population of Texas believed that hitting a child with such objects is acceptable (Teske & Parker, 1983). The actual use of belts and paddles has also not disappeared by the time of this survey in 1995. Table A2.2 in the section of the Appendix for this chapter gives the percent of parents who used each of the modes of corporal punishment, including hitting a child with an object such as a belt or hairbrush for children in each of five child age categories.

We also asked about threats to spank or slap. Strictly speaking this is a form of verbal aggression, not an act of corporal punishment as previously defined. Therefore, it was not one of the items in the corporal punishment scale used to obtain the rates in Chart 2.1 and Chart 2.2. However, we consider it a part of violent children rearing, just as threats to hit a wife or husband would be considered part of a violent relationship. The rate of such threats is greatest for children 5–8 (71%) and then decreases, but even during the teen years, 39% of the parents reported threatening to hit (see Appendix Table A2.2).

Other Characteristics of Children and Parents Associated with Spanking

Age of Parent

Studies of three nationally representative samples of parents found that the younger the parent, the more likely they were to spank (Day, Peterson, & McCracken, 1998; Giles-Sims et al., 1995; Straus, 2001a). This relationship parallels what has been found for psychical abuse (Connelly & Straus, 1992). For this study, although there was a tendency for younger parents to be more likely to spank, the differences were not significant. However, we did find that the younger the parents, the more often they spanked. Parents age 18 to 29 used corporal punishment an average of 17.1 times during the previous 12 months. Parents age 30 to 39 did it an average of 12.6 times, and parents age 40 and over who used corporal punishment did it an average of 9.1 times during the year of the study. This difference is not the result of younger parents having younger children (who, on average, are hit more frequently) because the analysis adjusted for the age of the child.

Socioeconomic Status

Although most studies have found that the higher the socioeconomic status, the less use of spanking (Giles-Sims et al., 1995; Straus, 2001a) some have found no important difference (Erlanger, 1974). In this study, Chart 2.3 shows that, after controlling for the other seven independent variables (age and gender of the parent and the child, the ethnicity of the child, single parent and region), higher socioeconomic status parents tended to spank less.

We also found that the relation of socioeconomic status to spanking depended on the age of the parent. The finding that the higher the socioeconomic status, the lower the percentage using corporal punishment, applies

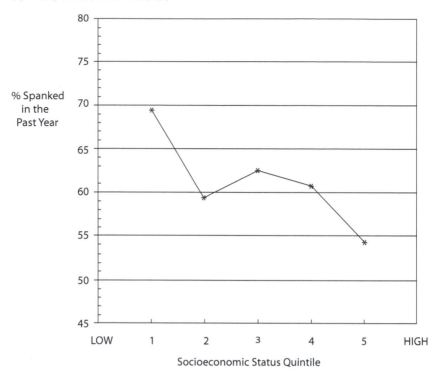

Chart 2.3   The Higher the Socioeconomic Status, the Lower the Percent Who Used Spanking

*Adjusted for age and sex of parent and child, race of the child, single parent, and region.

only to the two older age groups (ages 30 to 39 and ages 40 and over). Among younger parents, the percentage who spanked was high regardless of socio-economic status. This could be due to the combination of younger parents tending to have children in the toddler ages and the fact that almost everyone (over 90%) hits toddlers. However, having younger children is not likely to be the explanation for the greater use of spanking by young parents in this study because we controlled for age of the child. Perhaps the higher propensity to violence of all types by young people overrides the violence-reducing effect of high socioeconomic status.

There are important theoretical reasons for expecting spanking to be more prevalent among the lowest socioeconomic sectors of society. For example, low socioeconomic status parents are under greater stress and have more children, both of which are related to spanking (see Chapter 4 and Turner & Finkel-hor, 1996). In addition, low socioeconomic status families tend to reside in areas of high violence. As a consequence, despite the inconsistency of previous research, we expected to find, and did find, that the lower the socioeconomic status, the higher the percentage of parents who spanked.

Ethnic Group

Previous research on ethnic differences in spanking is also contradictory. For example, Straus (2001a) found no important difference between Blacks and Whites. Day et al. (1998) found more spanking by Black parents, but only for children age 5 to 11 years, and among younger children, only by unmarried mothers. On the other hand, many other studies such as Barkin (2007), Deater-Deckard et al. (1996), Giles-Sims et al. (1995), Ispa and Halgunseth (2004), Lee (2011), and Taylor (2010) found more spanking by Black parents.

For the parents in this sample, corporal punishment was used by 77% of Black parents during the previous 12 months compared with 59% of Whites. This large difference was mostly due to differences in socioeconomic status and six other sociodemographic characteristics (age of child, age of parent, single parent, gender of parent and child, and region). When these variables were controlled, the difference dropped greatly but remained statistically dependable (70% of Black parents compared with 62% of other minority parents and 60% of White parents).

It is important to keep in mind that statistical controls do not change the fact that Black parents used 30% more corporal punishment than White parents. The contribution of the statistical control is to help explain why the group difference exists. In this case, it shows that a large part of the difference is due to such characteristics as lower socioeconomic status, having younger children, and single parenthood. The analysis suggests that if Black parents did not differ from White parents on these characteristics, there would be a much smaller difference in the prevalence and chronicity of spanking. Because use of these controls reduced, but did not eliminate the difference, these results also suggest that there may be cultural explanations. There is debate over whether the approval and use of corporal punishment by Blacks is a legacy of their culture prior to enslavement, a legacy of the physical brutality to which Blacks were subjected during slavery (Alvy, 1987; Grier & Cobbs, 1968; Polite, 1996), a reflection of the violence and the "code of the streets" found in inner-city Black neighborhoods (Anderson, 1999; Brown, 1965), or some combination of these. There is also a debate about whether the harmful side effects of spanking documented in this book apply to Black children. That issue is addressed in Chapter 14.

Although these results are consistent with the evidence that more Blacks than Whites think spanking is necessary, (see Chapter 17), some of the results are not that clear and caution is needed in evaluating race and ethnic group differences. This is because, despite the higher percentage of Blacks who approved spanking and who actually spanked, in this study, Whites who spanked did so just as often as Black parents who spanked.

Boys and Girls

Previous research indicates that boys are spanked more than girls at all ages (Day et al., 1998; Giles-Sims et al., 1995; Graziano & Namaste, 1990; Straus, 2001a). In view of the movement toward treating boys and girls more similarly, previous findings might not apply to this sample. However, we found the same tendency for parents in this nationally representative sample to hit boys more than girls (65% of boys compared with 58% of girls). There was also a difference in how often boys and girls were hit. For boys, it occurred an average of 14.3 times, compared with an average of 12.9 times for girls. However, for children age 2 to 4 there was no difference at all in the chronicity of hitting boys and girls. Perhaps this is a ceiling effect because at those ages, over 90% of the parents spank. Finding that boys were hit more than girls is consistent with previous studies cited, and even with a study of homicides of infants (Straus, 1987). Despite a trend toward equality in methods of bringing up boys and girls, boys are still subjected to more violent child rearing.

An ironic aspect of this gender difference in socialization is that spanking is intended to produce a better behaved child, but numerous studies show that boys tend to have higher rates of misbehavior than girls. Perhaps there is an innate tendency of boys to be less compliant and this leads to more spanking of boys. Whatever the role of genetic difference between boys and girls, socialization differences are also likely to be important. For example, the studies of antisocial behavior as a child and crime later in life (Chapters 6 and 19) found that spanking tended to be counterproductive in the long run, and that the counterproductive effect was stronger for boys than for girls. Because spanking starts in infancy, it is even possible that the greater misbehavior rate of boys may reflect their higher rate of having been exposed to this form of violent socialization more than girls, starting when they were infants. Even lethal violence is directed at more infant boys than girls (Straus, 1987).

Mothers and Fathers

Mothers have been shown to spank more than fathers (Straus, 2001a). Of the mothers interviewed for this study, 64% spanked in the previous 12 months, compared with 58% of the fathers. However, parents of children age 9 to 12 were an exception. For this group, the percent who spanked was almost identical for mothers and fathers (57% of mothers and 58% of fathers).

Although in this study, as in many others, more mothers than fathers spanked, mothers who spanked did not do it more often than fathers. Perhaps in some families, the father is the disciplinarian and this may explain why their rates are close to those of mothers despite spending less time with children. It also needs to be noted that the difference between mothers and fathers is only six percentage points (64% for mothers and 58% for fathers). If, for example, mothers spend twice the amount of time with children as fathers, the rate for fathers would need to be doubled to equalize the time at risk. That would raise the rate for fathers to over 100%! Although we do not have any reasonable way of statistically adjusting for time at risk, the much greater time for mothers, the small difference between mothers and fathers probably indicates a lower propensity to hit children by mothers than fathers. That interpretation is consistent with the chapter that shows that fewer mothers than fathers believe that spanking is necessary (Chapter 17). It is also consistent with research on teachers. Male and female teachers spend about the same amount of time with students, but Checks (1979) found a higher rate of corporal punishment by male teachers. It is important to keep in mind, however, that even if this interpretation is correct, it does not necessarily mean that mothers actually hit less. It may only mean that the greater time spent with children is one of the reasons the mothers hit children more than fathers.

Single Parents

Although we found no research that directly demonstrates a relationship between single parenthood and spanking, research on physical abuse (i.e., severe physical assaults on children) shows higher rates for single parents (Bolton & MacEachron, 1987; Gelles, 1989; Giles-Sims & Finkelhor, 1984). These findings can plausibly be extended to spanking because the risk factors for spanking parallel those for physical abuse (Straus, 1990b). On average, single parents are under greater stress and therefore may also be more likely to spank. Although this is plausible, we did not find a statistically significant difference between parents who were living with a partner as compared with single parents, and among those who spanked, there was no significant difference in the chronicity of spanking. If stress is a determinant of spanking, perhaps the stress of bringing up children without the financial and supervisory contributions of a partner are counterbalanced by being freed from a stressful marriage.

Region

Research on regional differences in attitudes and norms concerning spanking has consistently shown more widespread endorsement of spanking in the South than in other regions (see Chapter 17 and Ellison & Sherkat, 1993; Flynn, 1994). These studies also found that spanking was least favored in the Northeast. In addition, Giles-Sims et al. (1995) found the same regional pattern for actual spanking. We also found the highest prevalence of spanking in the South (69%) and the lowest in the Northeast (53%). The age of the child made a difference: For the youngest and oldest children (ages 1 to 2 and 13 to 17), the lowest rates of spanking were in the West.

Although the regions differed significantly in the percentage of parents who used corporal punishment, there was not a significant difference between regions in the chronicity of spanking. So, although more Southern parents spank, those who do, do not hit more often than parents in other regions.

Five Recent Studies

There has not been a comprehensive national survey since the 1995 study described in this chapter. However, there are five more recent, although less complete, studies. Although they are more limited in scope and used different methods, they are not studies of high-risk or other special populations and can help bring the overall picture up-to-date.

The Harris Youth Report survey in 2006 asked a national sample of children age 8 and over whether they had been hit by parents that year. Thus, there is no data on toddlers, the age group when spanking is most prevalent. Nevertheless, the results are important because they show that the percentage who were hit by a parent in the previous 12 months remain as high as was found for children age 8 and over a decade earlier:

- 44% of children age 8 to 10
- 33% of children age 11 to 13
- 22% of children age 14 to 15
- 15% of children age 16 to 18

Although the 2006 survey did not include toddlers and therefore could not determine if the percentage in 2006 remained at over 90%, the rates for children age 8 and over are as high as the 1995 rates. This suggests that, had the study included toddlers, the results would have been about the same as in 1995, as has been the case since the 1950s when Sears, Maccoby, and Levin (1957) found that 99% of the kindergarten children they studied were spanked at least occasionally. Similarly, Bryan and Freed (1982) found that 95% of a sample of community college students had been spanked. Numerous other studies, (e.g., Giles-Sims et al., 1995; Goodenough, 1975; Holden et al., 1995; Straus, 2001a; Wauchope & Straus, 1990) also show extremely high rates of spanking toddlers.

A study by Regalado, Sareen, Inkelas, Wissow, and Halfon (2004) of a nationally representative sample focused on infants and toddlers age 4 to 35 months. They asked the mothers whether they spanked often, sometimes, rarely, or never and found that 6% reported spanking infants between the ages of 4 and 9 months, with the rate increasing to 29% of parents with children between 10 and 18 months and 64% of parents of 19- to 35-month-old children. These percentages are also comparable with those reported earlier in this chapter.

The third more recent study is a national survey of parents in Great Britain conducted for a television documentary, *I Smack and I'm Proud* (Bennett, 2006). It found that 70% of parents smacked their children and would strongly resist any move to ban corporal punishment in the home. The same survey included nonparents who, along with the parents, were asked about approval or disapproval of spanking. This uncovered even greater support for spanking. Eighty percent said that they believed in smacking, while 73% said that they believed a ban would lead to a sharp deterioration in children's behavior.

A fourth recent study (Zolotor, Theodore, Runyan, Chang, & Laskey, 2011) surveyed a probability sample of 1,435 parents of children age 3 to 11 in North and South Carolina. They found that 82% of the parents of children age 3 to 5 had spanked or slapped the child with an open hand that year, 81% had spanked children age 6 to 8, and 64% had spanked children age 9 to 11. Moreover, they also found that 40% of parents of children age 3 to 5 had hit the child with a traditionally accepted object such as a hairbrush or belt. If some of those 40% were added to the percent who spanked or slapped, the rates would probably be about the same as we found in 1995. Zolotor et al. point out that, when they compared their results with those of the Gallup Survey described in this chapter and our 1975 and 1985 national surveys, they found an overall decline in the spanking and slapping of children, but that "for the youngest children, there was little change in corporal punishment" (Zolotor, 2011, p. 60). These statistics cry out for explanation. In decades when the use of spanking has been declining for older children, why do just about all American parents hit toddlers? Chapter 18 suggests a likely explanation.

Finally, a study by Erath, El-Sheikh, Hinnant, and Cummings (2011) of 251 families obtained data on spanking from both the parents and the child. The sample was from three school districts surrounding a small town in the southeastern United States. The children were in second or third grade (mean age was 8.2 years), from two-parent families, and did not have diagnoses of physical illness, attention-deficit or hyperactivity disorder, learning disability, or intellectual disability. Spanking was reported by 95% of the parents and 89% of the children. These rates are even higher than those from our 1995 national survey, perhaps because the sample is from a small city in the south.

Summary and Conclusions

Prevalence, Duration, Chronicity, and Severity of Corporal Punishment

Prevalence and duration. We found that almost all toddlers (over 90%) were hit by parents, and that for more than a third (35%) of children, spanking starts as an infant. This is a lower rate of hitting infants than found by Korsch et al. (1965), which is to be expected because the Korsch study was for a time period when spanking was more prevalent and the parents in her sample were predominantly low in education and income.

Our informal observation suggests that spanking infants is typically a slap on the hand for something such as pushing food off a tray or touching something forbidden. Although this is not a severe form of corporal punishment, the fact that over one third of a nationally representative sample of parents hit infants in any way is a startling and sad characteristic of American patterns of child rearing. Moreover, the 35% should be regarded as a minimum estimate because there is less public approval of spanking infants compared with wide approval of spanking toddlers and, therefore, a greater likelihood of nondisclosure. Even if the folk belief that the risk of *psychological* harm to an infant from being hit by a parent is less than the risk of psychological harm when older children are hit (which we doubt), spanking of infants poses a greater risk of *physical* injury for infants.

At age 12, just over half of the parents in this study were using corporal punishment. This can be interpreted as indicating that corporal punishment typically continues for 12 years. It means that, although about one half of parents stop hitting their child by age 12, corporal punishment continues beyond that age for the other half. Further, about one out of five parents of children age 16 and 17 hit them during the year of this study.

Chronicity of corporal punishment. As the chapters in Parts II, III, and IV and Chapter 19 show, at every age, the more often parents use corporal punishment, the greater the probability of subsequent behavior problems such as aggression, antisocial behavior, lower academic achievement, and crime. Because chronicity affects the risk of harmful side effects, it is fortunate that even though spanking toddlers is nearly universal in the United States and many other nations, there are large differences in how often the parents who spank do it. The chronicity estimates for toddlers in this study (for example, 18 times in the past year for 2-year-olds) are, as we noted earlier, almost certainly vast underestimates because the study used a 1-year reporting period. Studies using a 1-week reporting period, such as the chapter on spanking and college graduation rates (Chapter 11) and Giles-Sims et al. (1995), Holden et al. (1995), and Straus and Paschall (2009), find averages of 2 to 3 times a week. If two or three times a week is multiplied by 52, it suggests a seven times higher level of chronicity. We think the underestimate occurs because spanking is such a taken-for-granted and unremarkable event that many parents do not realize how often they do it.

The same underestimate is much less likely for hitting older children because corporal punishment is not an everyday event at older ages, and when it happens, it is often more dramatic. Among teenagers in this sample, the chronicity ranged from just once that year to 35 times. On average, parents who hit teenagers did so 6.7 times (median = 4). This indicates that when parents hit a teenager, it is not usually, as some might think, an isolated event triggered by some extreme circumstance, but rather a recurring pattern of violence in the relationship of these parents with their child.

Severity. Although most corporal punishment is in the form of slapping hands or buttocks, use of traditionally approved implements such as a hairbrush, paddle, stick, or belt has by no means died out. Among the parents of children, age 5 to 12 in this study, 28% had hit their child with one of these traditionally approved objects in the previous 12 months. As noted earlier, using such implements is still legal in every state, provided there is no injury or, in some states, no mark that lasts more than about a day. At the same time, there is a growing belief that using a belt or paddle on a child's bottom is physical abuse. If use of these implements were illegal, the results of this study would lead one to conclude that, among parents of children in middle childhood, more than one quarter engaged in a criminal assault on their child during the year of this study. In addition, 10% of parents of a 1-year-old child reported shaking the child, which is an act that carries a high risk of brain injury for children that young.

Accuracy of estimates. The prevalence rates from this study are extremely high and comparable with other studies. However, the chronicity of spanking is much lower than is shown by studies that asked about spanking in the *last week*. This is because we ask our parents about the number of times in the *past year* that they hit toddlers, and parents can't keep track of how many times they spank in a year. On the other hand, for teenage children, our rates may be fairly accurate because those are less frequent and more dramatic events. When something dramatic happens 6 or 7 times in a year (the average for our teenagers), it is more easily remembered. But there may also be pressure to not disclose corporal punishment of older children and toddlers. The cultural norms that allow for, and in many neighborhoods require, parents to use corporal punishment (Carson, 1986; Straus, 2001a; Straus & Mathur, 1996; Walsh, 2002) have changed. In 21st-century America, although legal, the use of corporal punishment against teenagers is no longer widely regarded as sometimes necessary, as is still the case with young children (see Chapter 17). Slapping and spanking infants is also not favored. So for infants and teenage children, there are cultural norms that parents may not want to admit violating by disclosing they hit children of those ages, and this may make our numbers lower bound estimates.

Putting it another way, the 1-year recall period used for this study, although it probably provides the best estimate of *prevalence*, it also results in a large underestimate of how often parents do it (chronicity), especially for toddlers. As suggested previously, at this age, corporal punishment tends to be such an everyday occurrence (almost literally as well as figuratively) that many parents would have to use a calculator to provide a reasonable annual estimate. The fact that many parents do not realize how often they spank was demonstrated in a pioneer study of corporal punishment that found that the frequency of spanking, as recalled during an interview, was only one sixth of the frequency as recorded in a parenting diary (Goodenough, 1975 [1931]). On the other hand, because many toddlers and most older children are not hit every week, the best estimate of prevalence probably requires data for both a 1-week and a 1-year reporting period. However, there is no need to choose the lesser of two undesirable modes of asking about corporal punishment. In designing a new instrument—the *Dimensions of Discipline Inventory* (Straus & Fauchier, 2011)—we developed new response categories that are sensitive to both events: those that happen only rarely and those that happen frequently.

The budget limitations of the study restricted the interviews to only one parent in each family. If the other parent had been interviewed, the prevalence rate would be higher because there are families where one parent spanks and the other does not. For the more typical situation, where both parents spank, chronicity would have been higher.

Chronicity is less variable. We examined the relation of eight child and family characteristics to spanking. Six out of the eight were found to be significantly related to the prevalence of spanking, but only three of the eight were related to the chronicity of spanking. For example, although more low-socioeconomic parents used spanked, high-socioeconomic parents who hit their children did it just as often as low-socioeconomic parents who spanked. Moreover, among the three variables that were significantly related to the chronicity of spanking, there seemed to be less difference between categories of those variables than there was for prevalence. Research on why chronicity is relatively constant may lead to important insights about the processes underlying parental use of corporal punishment.

Implications for Parents and Professionals

Although we found differences between different groups of parents, and big differences according to the age of the child, the differences are really about the degree to which spanking is prevalent, not about whether spanking occurs or does not occur. For example, 69% of parents in the South hit their child during the previous 12 months, compared with 53% in the Northeast. It is equally or more important to read this finding as showing that over one half of parents in the low region (the Northeast) hit their child in the previous 12 months. Moreover, that is the average for children of all ages. For toddlers, the rate is 90% in the South and 74% in the Northeast. Thus, almost all children in the South experience violent child rearing, but so do three out of four children in the least violent region of the United States.

The results of the research in this chapter show that spanking is a nearly universal aspect of the way young American children are brought up. The frequency and severity of spanking does decline rapidly with age, and it differs greatly from child-to-child in the severity and duration of their experiences. Despite this, almost all American children have been spanked. Unfortunately, few Americans, including few pediatricians and child psychologists, realize this because the information is not in the textbooks they have read. Even fewer explicitly recommend *never* spanking, that is, never hitting a child. Perhaps the lack of knowledge about the near-universal nature of hitting children by parents partly explains why so few have been alarmed by the strong evidence that, even when done by loving and supportive parents, it is associated with an increased risk of serious problems later—described in this book—such as increased aggression and crime and lower IQ. However, another part of the explanation for not being concerned about the near universality of spanking in the United States and most other nations may be the widespread belief (documented in Chapter 17) that spanking is sometimes necessary and the belief that if it is done in moderation by loving parents, it is not harmful (see Chapter 17 and Straus, 2001e).

End or reduce spanking. On the basis of the research in this book, and about 100 other studies (Gershoff, 2002; Straus, 2001a) that have found that spanking is associated with many serious and lifelong problems, we believe that parents should *never* spank (i.e., never hit children as a method of correcting misbehavior). Although a number of studies used a longitudinal design from which one can infer that spanking is a cause of these problems, even the best of these have limitations. For example, no longitudinal study to date has provided data on children who were *never* spanked. As a consequence, the empirical evidence indicates only a need to reduce the frequency and severity of spanking. Our belief that children should never be hit represents a plausible extrapolation from the results showing that the more spanking, the greater the probability of behavior problems later in childhood and as an adult. It also reflects our antiviolence values, just as the view that it is sometimes necessary to spank represents the scientifically unproven values and beliefs of those who hold that view.

Fortunately, the issue of reduction versus total elimination of spanking does not need to be resolved for the results in this book to have important implications for parents and clinical practice. This is because the results indicate such a high prevalence and chronicity of spanking. As a consequence, even those who believe that spanking is sometimes necessary are likely to agree on the need for remedial steps. For example, the pro-spanking members of the American Academy of Pediatrics conference on discipline believe that spanking should be confined to children age 2 to 6 and that only the open hand should be used, and even this should be done only rarely (Friedman & Schonberg, 1996b). By contrast, this chapter revealed high prevalence rates for children outside the permissible ages: 35% for infants, 60% for both 1- and 10-year-olds, 44% for 13-year-olds, and 20% for 16- and 17-year-olds. In addition, for 28% of children age 5 to 12, spanking included spanking with a hairbrush, paddle, or belt. Ironically, even though those recommendations accept spanking, achieving them would be a net gain for children and for the society they will grow into.

Make information on spanking available. The extremely high frequency and frequent severity of spanking by parents applies, on average, to both mothers and fathers, to parents of all ages, to both boys and girls, to all ethnic and socioeconomic groups, and to all regions. This needs to be part of the information base of parents, researchers, and clinicians. One obvious way to accomplish this would be an increase in the space devoted to spanking in child development and child psychology textbooks from the present average of less than a page. If that were to occur, we believe the information would be perceived as so inconsistent with the standard of only rarely and only with children age 2 to 6 (Friedman & Schonberg, 1996a), that it will lead many parents to reconsider the extent to which they spank and lead many clinicians to include information about spanking in their assessment and work with clients. Perhaps in the next generation, we will get to never at any age.

The evidence that spanking is an almost universal aspect of American parental behavior (although to widely varying degrees), together with the increasingly conclusive evidence that spanking has harmful side effects, suggests that pediatricians, psychologists, social workers, and others who advise parents should address spanking in their research, clinical work, and books for parents. We recommend determining the extent to which a client uses spanking as a routine procedure and discussing the pros, cons, and alternatives with parents. There are brief and easily used tests that can make routine screening for spanking and other modes of discipline practical, for example, the short form of the *Parent-Child Conflict Tactics Scales* (Straus & Mattingly, 2007) and the *Dimensions of Discipline Inventory* (Straus & Fauchier, 2011). Along with the screening, there needs to be unambiguous advice recommending never using a child rearing practice which, when stripped of euphemisms such as "a good spanking" and "a quick swat on the behind" can be seen as a culturally approved system of physical attacks on children.

3   Spanking in World Perspective

The previous chapter showed that in the United States almost all young children experience at least some physical attacks by their parents in the name of discipline. However, the severity, frequency, and duration of this form of violence by parents vary from family to family and depends on the age of the child. This chapter shows that it also depends on the cultural context. It provides information on three questions:

*   To what extent does the percent who spank young children differ in 32 nations located in all major world regions?
*   To what extent are teenagers in these 32 nations hit to correct misbehavior?
*   To what extent are national differences in attitudes approving spanking linked to actual spanking?

Cross-National Differences in Spanking

We know that parents in almost all parts of the world bring up children violently by spanking (Levinson, 1989; Segall, Ember, & Ember, 1997). Just as there are large differences between parents in how often and how severely they hit their children, there are likely to be large differences between nations in how often and how severely children are typically hit. There is little evidence that has documented where the United States stands in comparison with other nations. This is because different methods have been used to obtain the information on corporal punishment in different nations. Often the information is in the form of case studies and other qualitative data that does not permit direct comparison. Although qualitative studies provide a rich understanding of the phenomenon, they do not provide information that permits comparing nations on the percentage of children who were spanked.

There is quantitative data for a few nations, but it is usually not comparable from one nation to another (Straus, 2010b). In some nations, the figures refer to acts that are considered legally and socially acceptable corporal punishment in the nation in which the data was collected, but would be considered physical abuse in other nations. In other instances, the data lump corporal punishment together with more severe violence by parents. Moreover, the wording of the questions also influences the rates, so what appear to be cross-national differences could actually be due to differences in question wording. However, a growing body of research has dealt with this issue by using a standard set of questions about corporal punishment in several nations. For example, the United Nations Children's Fund (UNICEF) conducted studies of child well-being in low economic development nations. In some of those nations, questions on corporal punishment from the *Parent-Child Conflict Tactics Scales* (Straus et al., 1998) were included, and some of the results are in the next chapter. Bussmann (2011) obtained detailed information on trends in corporal punishment from surveys of parents in five nations in Europe, and those results are described in Chapter 17 on the decline in the use of spanking. A study by Runyan and colleagues also used the *Parent-Child Conflict Tactics Scales,* in six nations: Brazil, Chile, Egypt, India, Philippines, and the United States (Runyan et al., 2010). They examined parental discipline strategies used by community samples in each nation, for a total of over 14,000 mothers. They found that corporal punishment is usually used more frequently than in the United States. In fact, according to this study, the United States has among the lowest rates of corporal punishment compared with other nations. However, there were individual research sites within each nation that ranked below the averages for their own nation and the United States.

Sample and Measures

The data on spanking in this chapter are for university students in the 32 nations in the International Dating Violence Study. Nations in all major world regions are included in the sample: two nations in sub-Saharan Africa, seven in Asia, thirteen in Europe, four in Latin America, two in the Middle East, two in North America, and two in Oceania. Over 17,000 students participated in the study. A table listing the characteristics of the sample in each nation is in Chan, Straus, Brownridge, Tiwari, and Leung (2008). This table, a detailed description to the study methods, including the questionnaire, and the data itself canbe downloaded from the Inter-university Consortium for Political and Social Research (dx.doi.org/10.3886/ICPSR29583).

One limitation of the study is that it is based on convenience samples of university students. However, there is evidence that the behavior and beliefs of these students reflects the national context in which the students lived. Analyses of the degree of correspondence between seven concepts as measured by the International Dating Violence Study and as measured by studies using representative samples found correlations that ranged from .43 to −.69 (Straus, 2009b).

Another limitation of the study is that it included only two questions on spanking. Moreover, the validity of these questions can be questioned because it depends on the degree to which university students can report about what happened when they were children or teenagers. Despite these limitations, the results in Chapter 13, on the relation of spanking to later in life assaulting or injuring a dating partner, provides evidence suggesting that the measure has *construct validity.* The analysis in Chapter 13 using these questions found that spanking is associated with an increased probability of physically assaulting a dating or marital partner later in life, even after controlling for a number of other characteristics. This result is consistent with the theory and research evidence that spanking is associated with an increased probability of antisocial and aggressive behavior, shown by:

- A huge volume of research summarized in the meta-analysis by Gershoff (2002, p. 3008)
- The many studies summarized in Chapter 19 on the relation of spanking to crime
- The results in other chapters of this book, such as the longitudinal study, which found that data from mothers about spanking in the last week was associated with a subsequent increase in the child's antisocial behavior (Chapter 6)

How Corporal Punishment Was Measured

Students in the study were asked whether they strongly disagreed, disagreed, agreed, or strongly agreed with the following statements:

- When I was less than 12 years old, I was spanked or hit a lot by my mother or father.
- When I was a teenager, I was hit a lot by my mother or father.

Instead of measuring the percent of students in each nation by the percent who answered agree or strongly agree, we used the percent of students in each nation, who did *not* strongly disagree. The logic behind this decision was that students who did not strongly disagree had probably experienced at least some spanking. To determine if this was appropriate, we computed the correlation of spanking measured in these two ways with 16 other variables to determine which method of scoring resulted in a stronger correlation. If the *not strongly disagree* method is wrong, it should have resulted in lower correlations. Instead, for every one of the 16 comparisons, the correlation was larger using the not strongly disagree method of determining the percent of students in each nation who had been spanked or slapped.

How Cultural Norms about Spanking were Measured

The International Dating Violence Study also obtained information on differences in the strength of cultural norms supporting corporal punishment in each of the nations in the study using the following two statements:

- It is sometimes necessary to discipline a child with a good, hard spanking.
- It is sometimes necessary for parents to slap a teen who talks back or is getting into trouble.

These two questions asked the students about their individual attitudes and beliefs, but the results in this chapter are for nations rather than for individual persons. The percentage for each nation is the percent of students who did *not* strongly disagree with the statement—the higher the percentage who did not strongly disagree, the greater the strength of cultural norms and cultural beliefs about spanking in each national setting.

It is also important to keep in mind that the percentages refer to the experiences and opinions of university students rather than the population in general. This is a limitation, but if it biases the results, it probably biases them toward indicating less support for spanking than for the rest of the population because, as shown in Chapter 2 on the prevalence of spanking in the United States and other studies in the United States, and Chapter 18 on trends in approval of spanking, more educated people tend to be less approving of spanking and are less likely to actually spank. Another limitation is that the questions on experiencing corporal punishment refer to being spanked or hit *a lot* by parents. This probably leads to an underestimate of the prevalence of spanking because it omits those who were spanked or hit by parents, but not a lot, and it omits those who were hit a lot as toddlers (the peak age for spanking in the United States) but is not remembered. It also introduces ambiguity in the data because we do not know what the students had in mind by "a lot."

Spanking Worldwide

Spanking as a Child

The first row in the column headed Total in Table 3.1 gives the median percent for all 32 national settings. After that, listed in rank order is the percent of students in each nation who were spanked or hit a lot before they were 12 years old. The highest percent was in Taiwan, where three out of four students reported that they were spanked or hit a lot before age 12. At the bottom of the list is the Netherlands, where 15% reported being hit a lot before age 12. Halfway down the list, the bold 53.4 indicates that at the middle ranking (median) nation, over half of the students indicated that they had been spanked or hit a lot as a child. Thus, corporal punishment varied tremendously among the nations in this study.

The next two columns in Table 3.1 show the percent of boys and girls who reported being hit a lot, and the final column shows the ratio of girls to boys in being hit a lot. This final column shows that in 30 of the 32 nations in the study, a somewhat smaller percent of girls than boys were hit as a child. Taking the median of the 32 nations, the percent of girls hit a lot was 95% of the percent for boys—that is, girls were hit a lot as a child almost as much as boys. This is consistent with the results for the nationally representative sample of American children in the previous chapter and with many other studies of corporal punishment (Giles-Sims et al., 1995) that also found that more boys than girls are hit by parents, but only by a small difference.

Table 3.1 Percent Who Agree* That "When I Was Less Than 12 Years Old, I Was Spanked or Hit a Lot by My Mother or Father"

Nation	Total	Boys	Girls	% Girls to Boys
All Nations	**52.3**	**54.3**	**51.7**	**95.2%**
Taiwan	74.7	80.6	72.0	89.3%
Tanzania	74.1	76.1	71.7	94.3%
South Africa	70.3	71.8	69.9	97.2%
Mexico	66.4	72.2	65.1	90.1%
Singapore	65.9	68.5	64.6	94.4%
Hong Kong-China	61.4	66.2	59.5	89.8%
United States	61.4	70.0	56.8	81.2%
Germany	60.4	63.7	58.8	92.3%
China	59.8	66.7	56.0	84.0%
India	59.7	63.2	57.6	91.1%
South Korea	59.3	63.3	56.7	89.7%
Russia	58.8	65.1	54.3	83.4%
Iran	58.2	65.4	55.6	85.1%
New Zealand	56.8	53.5	57.2	107.0%
Great Britain	54.7	61.4	53.2	86.5%
Australia	**53.4**	**60.7**	51.6	**84.9%**
Greece	52.6	69.7	43.8	62.8%
Canada	52.5	56.4	50.7	89.9%
Hungary	51.0	47.7	**52.5**	110.0%
Lithuania	49.1	57.1	44.9	78.6%
Switzerland	47.6	54.3	43.9	80.9%
Romania	41.8	54.5	40.5	74.2%
Malta	39.2	53.8	33.3	61.9%
Japan	36.0	47.5	25.0	52.7%
Guatemala	35.8	42.6	26.3	61.7%
Sweden	30.1	42.8	24.3	56.8%
Venezuela	29.8	42.6	21.7	50.8%
Israel	24.3	25.3	24.1	95.2%
Belgium	23.8	30.0	21.8	72.7%
Brazil	21.3	27.7	17.8	64.5%
Portugal	21.1	27.1	17.8	65.7%
Netherlands	14.8	35.8	11.6	32.4%

*As explained, this is the percent of students who did *not* strongly disagree.

Spanking as a Teenager

The first row of Table 3.2 shows that taking all 32 nations into consideration, about a third of these students were hit a lot when they were teenagers. Of course, there were important differences between nations. The Netherlands was again lowest (10%). Tanzania was highest (71%).

Table 3.2   Percent Who Agree* That "When I Was a Teenager, I Was Hit a Lot by My Mother or Father"

Nation	Total	Boys	Girls	% Girls to Boys
All Nations	**33.4**	**39.1**	**28.3**	**72.3%**
Tanzania	70.6	73.5	67.0	91.2%
Taiwan	64.9	67.3	63.8	94.7%
South Africa	57.2	62.0	55.9	90.3%
South Korea	51.5	53.9	49.8	92.3%
China	49.5	58.6	44.4	75.8%
India	49.0	56.9	44.1	77.4%
Hong Kong-China	49.0	55.3	46.3	83.8%
Singapore	45.5	51.1	42.9	84.0%
Lithuania	43.4	49.4	40.2	81.3%
Russia	41.2	**43.7**	39.4	90.3%
Portugal	41.0	50.3	35.9	71.4%
Brazil	40.6	49.1	36.0	73.4%
Iran	39.7	50.0	35.9	71.8%
Greece	38.5	51.5	31.8	61.7%
Venezuela	37.3	50.4	29.1	57.7%
Germany	**33.9**	40.4	30.7	75.9%
Japan	33.5	41.5	25.8	62.1%
Guatemala	31.9	36.4	25.5	70.2%
Romania	31.5	45.5	**29.9**	65.9%
Mexico	30.4	40.7	28.1	68.9%
United States	27.8	33.9	24.5	72.2%
Malta	27.6	32.7	25.6	78.2%
Australia	27.2	39.3	24.2	61.6%
Canada	25.5	30.2	23.3	77.2%
Sweden	22.1	32.3	17.3	53.5%
Switzerland	21.9	24.1	20.2	84.0%
Hungary	21.4	21.5	21.3	98.8%
Great Britain	21.3	26.5	19.9	**75.1%**
Israel	20.0	25.3	18.7	74.1%
New Zealand	18.4	25.6	15.9	62.0%
Belgium	13.7	19.1	12.0	62.9%
Netherlands	10.1	19.4	8.6	44.6%

*As explained, this is the percent of students who did *not* strongly disagree.

The columns in Table 3.2 for boys and girls show that parents hit a larger percentage of boys than girls when they were teenagers. The median of the 32 nations in the first row shows that the percent of girls hit a lot as teenagers was 75% of the percent for boys hit a lot as teenagers. This is a larger difference between boys and girls than was found for hitting children under 12 a lot. Thus, the more violent child rearing experienced by boys is greatest in the teenage years.

Support for Spanking Worldwide

What could account for the fact that so many parents in so many different societies spank? One of the reasons is that there are cultural norms that define spanking as something that is correct or necessary to bring up children properly. This section examines the extent to which such norms exist in the diverse cultural settings included in the International Dating Violence Study. The section that follows tests the hypothesis that the stronger the belief in the necessity of spanking among university students, the more students who have been spanked or slapped.

Table 3.3 shows the 32 nations in rank order for believing that spanking is necessary, starting with the national setting with the most students who believed that corporal punishment is necessary. The three top nations, South Korea, Singapore, and India, are all Asian, and in all three nations, at least 90% of the students we surveyed believed that spanking is sometimes necessary. The average for students in these 32 nations was 71%, i.e., nearly three quarters of the students thought that spanking was necessary.

The worldwide belief in the necessity of spanking is shown by the fact that, in 29 of the 32 nations, more than one half of the students thought that spanking a child under 12 was sometimes necessary. Even in the national setting with the lowest percent who believed that spanking is necessary, the rate was 31%.

The far right column of Table 3.3 shows that in most of the nations, more male than female students believed that spanking is necessary. However, in most nations, the differences are not large. Thus, in general, there was strong support for spanking by women as well as men.

Table 3.4 ranks the national settings according to the percentage who approved of parents hitting a teenager. The results are not quite what was expected. Because Table 3.2 in this chapter and the results in Chapter 2 on the use of spanking in the United States show that a much smaller percent of teenagers are hit than younger children, we expected the percentage of students in each national setting who approved of hitting a teenager to be lower than the percent who approved of hitting a younger child. But Table 3.4 shows the percentage of students who approve of hitting a teenager is as high or higher. Even in the national setting that is least approving, nearly one half (43%) of the students thought it was sometimes necessary to hit a teenager who talked back or was in trouble.

A possible explanation is that the question about teenagers refers to a teenager "who talks back or is getting into trouble." This may provide a socially acceptable justification that could have led more students to think it is necessary. As was true of the approval of hitting younger children, despite the percentages being lower for women, very high percentages of female students approved of hitting a teenager.

Table 3.3 Percent Who Agree* that "It Is Sometimes Necessary to Discipline a Child with a Good, Hard Spanking"

Nation	Total	Men	Women	Women/Men%
All Nations	**71.0**	**76.3**	**68.5**	**88.6%**
South Korea	94.8	91.4	96.7	106.0%
Singapore	94.1	94.6	93.9	99.3%
India	89.5	86.1	91.4	106.0%
Taiwan	88.9	93.9	86.7	92.4%
Tanzania	88.0	89.9	85.5	95.2%
Portugal	86.4	90.6	84.0	92.8%
Russia	86.0	87.7	84.9	96.8%
Hong Kong-China	83.1	88.4	80.9	**91.6%**
Japan	83.1	85.6	80.6	94.2%
South Africa	81.6	**77.5**	82.6	107.0%
United States	79.3	86.9	75.2	86.5%
Brazil	78.3	84.3	75.1	89.1%
Lithuania	77.8	82.4	75.4	91.5%
China	77.5	80.7	75.8	94.0%
Mexico	76.5	75.9	76.6	101.0%
New Zealand	**73.2**	76.7	**71.7**	93.5%
Iran	72.2	67.3	73.9	110.0%
Switzerland	70.8	75.9	68.2	89.8%
Great Britain	68.2	80.7	65.6	81.2%
Hungary	68.0	78.5	63.1	80.4%
Australia	67.0	76.8	64.6	84.1%
Malta	63.5	69.2	61.2	88.5%
Romania	61.7	60.6	61.8	102.0%
Canada	61.6	69.8	58.1	83.2%
Germany	60.8	70.5	56.0	79.5%
Guatemala	57.8	63.6	49.6	78.1%
Belgium	57.5	65.9	54.8	83.1%
Israel	57.2	56.0	57.5	103.0%
Venezuela	50.6	60.5	44.3	73.3%
Greece	44.4	62.9	34.9	55.5%
Netherlands	41.1	59.7	38.3	64.1%
Sweden	30.6	49.8	21.9	44.0%

*This is the percent of students who did *not* strongly disagree.

Table 3.4   Percent Who Agree* that "It Is Sometimes Necessary for Parents to Slap a Teenager Who Talks Back or Is Getting into Trouble"

Nation	Total	Men	Women	Women/Men%
All Nations	**74.8**	**79.3**	**70.7**	**89.2%**
Portugal	91.5	93.9	90.2	96.0%
Lithuania	89.0	89.4	88.8	99.3%
India	88.2	90.3	86.9	96.3%
South Korea	86.6	90.6	84.2	92.9%
Russia	86.4	87.3	85.7	98.2%
Japan	86.0	89.0	83.1	93.3%
Tanzania	85.6	87.3	83.3	95.4%
Iran	84.0	84.6	83.8	99.0%
Singapore	83.4	89.1	80.8	90.7%
Brazil	80.7	84.3	78.8	93.5%
China	78.0	83.1	75.1	90.4%
Switzerland	77.1	82.7	74.3	89.8%
Great Britain	75.4	85.5	73.3	85.7%
South Africa	75.1	71.8	75.7	105.0%
Hong Kong-China	75.0	81.2	**72.5**	89.2%
Malta	**74.6**	**80.8**	72.1	89.3%
Mexico	74.0	75.9	73.6	97.0%
Taiwan	73.7	90.8	66.1	72.7%
Guatemala	73.2	79.5	64.2	80.8%
Hungary	72.8	75.4	71.6	95.0%
United States	72.2	79.2	68.4	86.3%
Belgium	68.4	76.8	65.7	85.6%
Greece	67.9	78.8	62.4	79.2%
Australia	67.4	80.4	64.1	79.8%
Romania	66.5	72.7	65.8	**90.5%**
Venezuela	66.3	74.4	61.1	82.1%
Canada	64.2	72.9	60.4	82.8%
Israel	62.8	65.9	62.0	94.1%
Germany	61.8	68.9	58.3	84.6%
New Zealand	59.5	62.8	57.9	92.3%
Sweden	46.1	63.6	38.3	60.2%
Netherlands	42.7	64.2	39.4	61.4%

*This is the percent of students who did *not* strongly disagree.

The Experience of Spanking and Approval of Spanking

Children dislike being hit and dislike their parents for doing it (see Chapters 7 and 8 and Straus, 2001a, p. 154; Willow & Hyder, 1998). This might lead one to think that children who were hit a lot by their parents are likely to grow up being opposed to spanking because they know firsthand that it is something they resented or even hated. Most, but not all of the research, however, shows the opposite. It shows that the more spanking a child experiences, the more likely a child is to endorse spanking and actually spank (Deater-Deckard, Lansford, Dodge, Pettit, & Bates, 2003; Graziano, Lindquist, Kunce, & Munjal, 1992). The International Dating Violence Study provided a way of investigating whether this link between experiencing spanking and favoring spanking is present in social contexts other than North America. The International Dating Violence Study allows this issue to be examined at both the individual level using the students in the study as the cases and also at the societal level using the 32 nations as the cases. The individual level data will tell us about the relationship between experiencing spanking as a child and later approval, whereas the societal-level analysis will tell us about the link between cultural norms that define spanking as necessary and the actual use of spanking.

Individual Experience with Spanking and Attitudes toward Spanking

Chart 3.1 shows that having been spanked as a child is associated with believing that spanking is necessary. That is, the more a student reports being spanked or hit a lot as a child, the more they agree that it is sometimes necessary to spank. This relationship exists even after controlling for the student's gender and age, and the tendency to avoid disclosing undesirable behavior as measured by the Limited Disclosure Scale of the Personal and Relationships Profile (Chan & Straus, 2008; Straus, Hamby, Boney-McCoy, & Sugarman, 2010; Straus & Mouradian, 1999).

The relationship applies to both male and female students but is stronger for the male students in this study. However, the students who experienced the most spanking (e.g., strongly agree) were slightly less approving of spanking than students who experienced one lower degree of spanking. Thus, at least for this sample, once spanking becomes very frequent or very harsh, that approval rates start to decline.

We also examined the relationship between being hit a lot as a teenager and agreeing that it was sometimes necessary to slap a teenager, and found a similar relationship. These results are consistent with the theory that being hit by parents, rather than turning children against spanking, predisposes them to approving this behavior. The modeling effect seems to override the pain of the experience. In other words, individuals, who as children experience violence at the hands of their caregivers, are likely to believe such violence is necessary to raise children and, hence, probably more likely to use violence as a child rearing tactic. However, very few people think of spanking by parents as

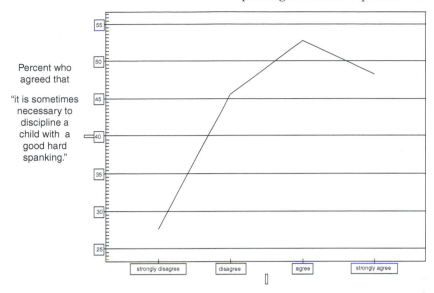

Percent who
agreed that

"it is sometimes
necessary to
discipline a
child with a
good hard
spanking."

| strongly disagree | disagree | agree | strongly agree |

Chart 3.1   The More Spanking as a Child, the More Approval of Spanking as an Adult

violence and would, therefore, not agree that these results show that spanking teaches violence. From that perspective, the real question is whether people who favor spanking are also more favorable to less socially legitimate forms of violence as a husband slapping his wife. Does approval of spanking go hand-in-hand with thinking that there are occasions when it is acceptable to slap a partner and actually hitting a partner? These are issues that are addressed in the chapters on the approval of violence and spanking (Chapter 5); the link between spanking and partner violence (Chapters 12 and 13); spanking, crime, and ethnicity (Chapter 14); and the implications of spanking, crime, and violence (Chapter 19).

Cultural Norms Approving Spanking and the Use of Spanking

The questions about approval of spanking and slapping children and teenagers provide information on the attitudes of individual students. By computing the percentage of students in each national setting who approve of spanking, these questions also provide information about cultural norms concerning spanking in each nation. This let us investigate the extent to which cultural norms about spanking are related to the actual spanking. Chart 3.2 was computed for this purpose. It shows that the larger the percentage of students in a nation who were spanked, the more students who approved of corporal punishment. A similar relationship was found between being hit a lot as a teenager and agreeing that it is sometimes necessary for parents to slap a teenager.

Percent who agreed that: "when I was less than 12 years old, I was spanked or hit a lot by my mother or father."

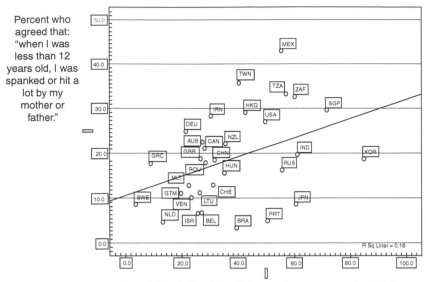

Percent Who Believed That "It is sometimes necessary to discipline a child with a good hard spanking"

Chart 3.2   The Stronger the Belief in a Nation that Spanking Is Necessary, the Larger the Percent of Students Who Were Spanked

AUS Australia; BEL Belgium; BRA Brazil; CAN Canada; CHE Switzerland; CHN China; DEU Germany; GBR Great Britain; GRC Greece; GTM Guatemala; HKG Hong Kong; HUN Hungary; IND India; IRN Iran; ISR Israel; JPN Japan; KOR South Korea; LTU Lithuania; MEX Mexico; MLT Malta; NLD Netherlands; NZL New Zealand; PRT Portugal; ROU Romania; RUS Russia; SGP Singapore; SWE Sweden; TWN Taiwan; TZA Tanzania; USA United States; VEN Venezuela; ZAF South Africa

Summary and Conclusions

There are large differences in national settings and within nations in the extent to which parents hit children and to which there are cultural norms that approve of parents hitting children. However, in 27 of the 32 national settings studied, more than 20% of the students surveyed were spanked or hit a lot before they were 12 years old, and in 31 of the 32 nations, more than 10% were hit a lot as teenagers. In the middle ranking national setting, more than one half of the students were hit a lot as a child and more than one quarter were hit a lot as teenagers. It is important to keep in mind that these statistics do not refer to occasionally being hit, but to being hit a lot by parents. Moreover, because most people cannot remember much about what happened when they were toddlers, we could not ask about preschool-age children, which is when children are most likely to be hit by parents (see Chapter 2). But even without that data, it is clear that university students around the world were brought up violently.

In respect to attitudes and cultural norms, the fact that, in the middle ranking nation, nearly three out of four students believed that it is sometimes necessary to discipline a child with a good, hard spanking and that it is sometimes necessary for parents to slap a teen who talks back or is getting into trouble, indicates the presence of cultural norms that permit, and in many circumstances require, parents to hit children. The violent child rearing actually experienced by these students is consistent with the cultural norms of the societies in this study.

Chart 3.2 clearly shows that there is a link between cultural norms that assert the necessity of sometimes hitting children and actually hitting children and teenagers a lot. However, that chart does not provide evidence on which, if either, is cause and which is effect. There are at least three possible explanations. A cultural explanation argues that the norms are part of the reason so many children are hit a lot. A social-organizational explanation argues that a society where parents hit children a lot will develop social norms specifying that hitting a child who misbehaves is necessary. A social-context explanation argues that a society with a high level of violence between adults will be a society in which the violence spills over to the definition of appropriate parental and actual parent behavior to include hitting children. It is likely that all three of these processes take place.

Anthropologists who have studied violent and nonviolent societies agree that the presence of cultural beliefs and norms that support or require violence is part of the explanation for society-to-society differences in all forms of violence, including spanking (Montague, 1978; Segall, Ember, & Ember, 1997). The experience of the students in the International Dating Violence Study graphed in Chart 3.2 is consistent with that conclusion. It shows that nations where there is a high level of approval of spanking are also nations in which children are hit a lot. Runyan and colleagues (2010) found a similar relationship for six nations. Thus, as will be explained in the chapter on why almost all parents resort to spanking (Chapter 18), one of the steps needed to reduce the level of societal violence is to change those norms.

Changing cultural norms is not as difficult as might, at first, be imagined. In fact, cultural norms are constantly changing, especially in modern societies. Often they change in response to shifts in the organization of society. There are also many examples of successful efforts to change norms. The feminist movement, for example, has been able to change the legal system and the informal cultural norms that tolerated men hitting their wives. It is no longer a behavior that is regarded as just a family problem. It is now regarded as outrageous and intolerable, and as a crime calling for arrest and prosecution (Smithey & Straus, 2004). That change in norms, in turn, is part of the explanation for the decrease in violence against women in the United States (Smithey & Straus, 2004; Straus, 1995b; Straus & Gelles, 1986). The same thing is happening in respect to parents hitting children. Sweden, the first nation to prohibit corporal punishment by parents, has gone from a nation in which, like the United States, just about all parents hit children (Stattin et al., 1995) to one in which spanking is rare. Consistent with that, the Swedish students in this study have the lowest percentage of students who believe that spanking is sometimes necessary. In the United States, Chapter 17 shows that cultural support for the idea that spanking is necessary has dropped substantially in about a generation. Consistent with the change in norms, Chapter 17 also shows that fewer American parents are hitting children for purposes of correction and control, although the change is minimal for toddlers.

4   There Was an Old Woman Who Lived in a Shoe

Like other aspects of parent behavior, spanking has multiple determinants. The cultural determinants were shown by the results in the previous chapter that suggest that one determinant of whether parents spank is the degree to which the society has cultural beliefs and norms that accept or require spanking children who misbehave. The next chapter shows that those who approve of violence in other spheres of life are more likely to approve of spanking and to spank. There are many other causes. From a psychological perspective, other determinants are such characteristics as depression (Silverstein, Augustyn, Young, & Zuckerman, 2009) and the degree to which the parent's worldview is characterized by anger and resentment (Tsang, 1995). Kim, Pears, Fisher, Connelly, and Landsverk (2010) found that maternal alcohol abuse and maternal age were related to their measure of harsh parenting, which included spanking.

There are also social organizational differences related to spanking, such as social class, race or ethnicity, neighborhood, and kinship networks. Some of these were shown in Chapter 2 on the prevalence of spanking in the United States, and they will come up in other chapters. Moreover, cultural norms expecting parents to spank a misbehaving child are more likely to be followed if the parent is part of a social network that believes that a good hard spanking is sometimes necessary (see Chapter 17 and Walsh, 2002).

The class structure of society is an important aspect of social organization that can influence whether and how often a parent will spank. But important as knowing about class difference is, that is not sufficient. It is also necessary to understand why low socioeconomic status parents spank more. Is it a difference in cultural norms or is it the stress of dealing with children in crowded households with minimal other resources, or both? This chapter addresses one aspect of that question and the following specific questions:

- Are parents with more children more likely to spank?
- If parents with more children spank more, is this because those with more children tend be lower in socioeconomic status?

Nancy L. Asdigian is the coauthor of this chapter.

- Can the inconsistency between previous studies of the number of children and spanking be resolved by taking into account methodological differences between the studies?

Family and Child Characteristics Associated with Spanking

Although spanking is a pervasive child rearing technique, as we reported in Chapter 2 on the use of corporal punishment in the United States, the frequency and duration differ a great deal from family to family. These differences are partially explained by certain parental and child characteristics, such as whether the parent is dealing with a difficult child. Analyses of large representative samples (see Chapter 2 and Giles-Sims et al., 1995; Molnar, Buka, Brennan, Holton, & Earls, 2003; Straus, 2001b) reveal that spanking is more likely to occur under a number of social circumstances and social roles, including lower social classes, mothers more than fathers, younger parents, and parents who were corporally punished as adolescents. As pointed out in the previous chapter, parents who are violent to each other are more likely to spank. In a previous study, we found that this is probably a bidirectional relationship. Parents who hit each other are more likely to hit their children and hitting children provides role practice in using violence to correct misbehavior that can spillover to correcting the misbehavior of the other parent (Straus, 2001a, p. 105). Moreover, boys are somewhat more likely than girls to be corporally punished. Additional examples show that spanking reflects much more than the level of misbehavior by a child.

For example, a Swedish study found higher rates of spanking by single parents (Annerbäck, Wingren, Svedin, & Gustafsson, 2010), as did the Project on Human Development in Chicago Neighborhoods (Molnar et al., 2003), especially among low-education mothers (Heckman, 2008). The higher rate of spanking by single parents was also found for the single parents in the national sample described in the chapter on spanking in the United States (Chapter 2) and in the International Parenting Study. One can think of this as indicating the effect of the ratio of the amount of parental resources (number of parents) to the amount of parenting (number of children). If one less parent can mean more spanking, so can one or two additional children with the same number of parents. As a consequence, it is not implausible to expect that there is some truth to the nursery rhyme that identifies the number of children as one of the social organizational factors associated with more spanking.

This chapter considers a simple but fundamental aspect of family social organization: the number of children in the family. The relatively small attention to the effect of the number of children on spanking is somewhat surprising given its recognition in the Mother Goose nursery rhyme, "There was an old woman who lived in a shoe. She had so many children she didn't know what to do. She gave them some broth without any bread and whipped them all soundly and put them to bed."

Number of Children and Spanking

There are several reasons to expect spanking to be more common in larger families. As the number of children in a family increases, parents have less time and energy to monitor, explain, and reason with each child and may therefore use spanking as a quick form of behavioral control. In addition, larger families place more emotional and economic burdens on parents. Parents have to devote more time to child care and may also have to spend more time working outside the home to meet the economic needs of more children. These commitments detract from the time that parents have to spend in pleasurable, stress-relieving activities with children. More children take more time and, therefore, may diminish the size and quality of personal support networks and also the quality of the marital relationship itself. Increased stress, combined with reduced social support from the marital relationship, might give rise to anger and resentment, which may in turn manifest itself in the form of punitive discipline strategies such as corporal punishment. Thus, we hypothesize that the larger the number of children, the greater the use of corporal punishment.

Previous Studies

Number of Children and Spanking

One early investigation, Elder and Bowerman (1963) found that girls from lower class families, with four or more siblings, were twice as likely as their counterparts, with only one or two siblings, to report being corporally punished by mothers or fathers. However, for girls from middle class backgrounds or for boys of any social class, the number of children was not related to corporal punishment. Using data from a large community survey, Nye, Carlson, and Gerrett (1970) found that the more children, the more spanking was used by both mothers and fathers. They also found that the more children, the less parents used discussion and explanation as a discipline strategy. Kidwell (1981) found that the number of children was related to adolescents' ratings of parental punitiveness (which included questions about actual spanking), even after controlling for the effects of family socioeconomic status, race, parental structure, and sibling spacing. A 10-year longitudinal study by Dubowitz et al. (2011) found that, among a sample of high-risk families, each additional child was associated with a 26% increase in the odds of the child being maltreated. The results of three other studies are also consistent with the Mother Goose rhyme (De Zoysa, 2005; Eamon, 2001; Xu, Tung, & Dunaway, 2000). However, there is also contradictory evidence. However, as mentioned previously, Elder and Bowerman (1963) found no relationship for middle class girls. Straus and colleagues' (2006) analysis of a large nationally representative sample of American children found somewhat more spanking among two-child than among one-child families, but no increase in spanking with additional children. Thus, the evidence on this seemingly plausible hypothesis is not entirely consistent. Because the issue of the extent to which the use of spanking grows out of factors other than the level of misbehavior of a child is so important, both for theories about why spanking occurs and for prevention efforts, there is a need for additional evidence.

Number of Children and Other Parent Behaviors

Despite the not entirely consistent evidence from studies just reviewed, the case for expecting the number of children in a family to be linked to more corporal punishment is strengthened by the results of two bodies of research on parent behavior that is consistent with the hypothesis that having more children is associated with more hitting of children.

Parent-child relationship quality. With only a few exceptions (Philliber & Graham, 1981; Richardson, Abramowitz, Asp, & Petersen, 1986), studies that examined the relationship between the number of children and the quality of parent-child relationships indicate that parents with more children engage in more authoritarian and controlling behavior. Zussman (1978), for example, found that the larger the family, the greater the tendency for parents to use power assertion techniques (physical or material sanctions, including spanking) to deal with typical childhood transgressions of boys. Peterson and Kunz (1975) also found that ratings of parental control were two to three times as high among middle class adolescents with six or more siblings compared with those from single-child families. In addition, Scheck and Emerick (1976) found that a larger number of children was significantly associated with less parental support, stricter disciplinary practices, and more conflicted parent-child relations, even after controlling for differences in socioeconomic status.

Number of children and maltreatment. Support for the hypothesis that the more children, the greater the likelihood of corporal punishment is also suggested by research on physical abuse. Studies by Zuravin (1988a, 1988b, 1991; Zuravin & Greif, 1989) and Connelly (1992) found that the more children in a family, the greater the probability of physical abuse.

Confounding with Age and Birth Order

One reason for the inconsistent findings on the number of children and corporal punishment may be that the studies did not control for the inherent confounding of the number of children with the child's age and birth order. The confounding occurs because, (except for multiple births) as the number of children increases, their average age must also increase. The average age is important because, as shown in Chapter 2 on spanking in the United States, the use of corporal punishment decreases rapidly as children grow older. With experience, parents may also be less inclined to strike their later-born children relative to earlier-born children. Without statistically controlling for age and birth order, children from larger families may appear to be at a lower risk for corporal punishment because they are more likely to be older or later born. Thus, the failure to control for age and birth order could obscure the association between the number of children and corporal punishment. Our analyses therefore controlled for both age and birth order.

Sample and Measures

Sample

The data for this chapter were obtained from the 1985 National Family Violence Survey (Gelles & Straus, 1988; Straus, 2001a; Straus & Gelles, 1986). Because the focus of the chapter is spanking, the analyses included only the 3,360 respondents who had one or more minor children living at home at the time of the survey. Information on one child was gathered from each household with children. If there was more than one child, a procedure was used to randomly select the child about which to gather information.

The Minor Violence scale of the original *Conflict Tactics Scales* (Straus, 1979) was used to obtain the information about spanking by the parent during the 12 months prior to the interview.

Number of Children and Spanking

Our first look at whether parents with more children were more likely to use corporal punishment found that parents with two children were more likely to hit them than parents with just one child. Of those who did use corporal punishment, the parents with two children also hit more often than parents with just one child. However, contrary to the hypothesis, neither the percentage who hit nor the frequency with which they did it went up with additional children beyond two. This is the same pattern we found years before (Straus et al., 2006). This time however, as explained above, we realized that children in larger families were more likely than those in smaller families to be later born and older and therefore less likely to have experienced corporal punishment during the year of the survey. In addition, *the parents* with more children were on average, older and lower in socioeconomic status. Because corporal punishment tends to be more common among young, lower socioeconomic parents, the effects of the number of children per se can only emerge after disentangling the overlap with the age of the child, birth order, and the age and socioeconomic of the parents. We did this using analysis of covariance (see the section of the Appendix for Chapter 4)

Prevalence of corporal punishment.   There are two plot lines in Chart 4.1. The dashed line shows that, as previously mentioned, when no controls are used, having more than two children is not associated with more corporal punishment. However, the solid line in Chart 4.1 shows that, after taking into account the age of the child and other family characteristics, the more children, the greater the percent of parents who used corporal punishment.

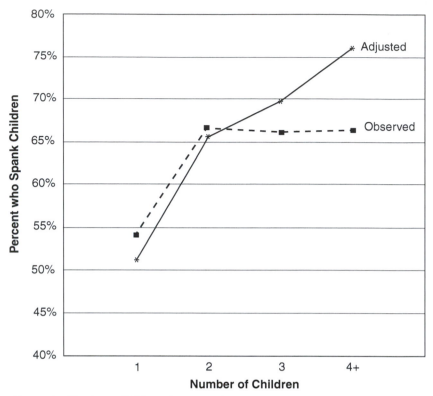

Chart 4.1   The More Children, the More That Parents Spank

* Adjusted for parent and child age, birth order, and socioeconomic status.

Chronicity of corporal punishment. The results for chronicity of corporal punishment (the number of times the parents who use corporal punishment do so) are similar to those for prevalence. The dashed line in Chart 4.2 shows an increase in the chronicity of corporal punishment as the number of children in the family increased from one to three, followed by a decrease from three to four or more children. However, the solid line in Chart 4.2 shows that when the effects of other variables were controlled, scores on the chronicity scale increased up to three children and then leveled off in families with four or more children.

Summary and Conclusions

The results of this study of a nationally representative sample of U.S. parents found that as the number of children in the family increased from one to four or more, the percentage of parents using corporal punishment increased. Among the parents who used corporal punishment, those with more children also hit more frequently. Both the percentage hitting and the number of times the parents in this sample did it, support the hypothesis that the more children

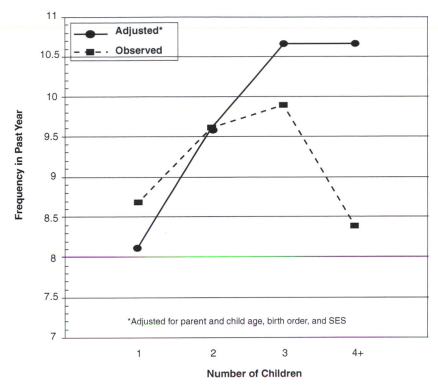

Chart 4.2　The More Children, the More Often They Are Hit

in a family, the more likely parents are to use corporal punishment. This pattern was discernible, however, only after using statistical controls to take into account the fact that children in larger families have to be older, later born, and have older parents. All three of these are characteristics associated with *less* use of corporal punishment and thus obscure the tendency for more children in a family to mean more corporal punishment.

These results suggest that the decrease in the number of children per family was probably one of the factors that contributed to the decline in the use of corporal punishment shown in Chapter 17. Also, the tendency for more children to be linked to more corporal punishment illustrates the way changes in family structure can reduce or increase the level of violence used to bring up children. Our concluding chapter suggests that the trend away from violent child rearing is likely to continue and even accelerate and identifies many processes that are driving this change, including fewer children per family.

The link between the number of children and corporal punishment is also theoretically important because it suggests that more corporal punishment may be one of the processes that explain why only-children tend to have a higher IQ after controlling for the socioeconomic status of the parents, and average IQ declines with the increasing number of siblings (Blake, 2011). The chapters in this book provide evidence that the adverse side effects of spanking, including lower mental ability (Chapter 10) delinquency, and adult crime (the chapters in Parts II and IV and Chapter 19). That is, a large number of children can lead to more use of corporal punishment, slower cognitive development, and more delinquency and crime. The concluding section of Chapter 1 on Risk Factors: The Real Meaning of Social Science Results explains how this can be true, whereas at the same time, millions of people can say that "I was spanked a lot and I graduated from college and never committed a crime."

In view of the evidence in this book and elsewhere showing that corporal punishment is linked to a wide variety of undesirable outcomes for children, the finding that more children is associated with an increased probability of the children being spanked indicates that larger families increase the risk to children, and that this is something few people perceive. Parents need to know that additional children are associated with an increased likelihood of engaging in a mode of child rearing that, in principle, is opposed by more and more parents and professionals (see Chapters 17 and 20). Moreover, this information may be especially important because we found that parents who believe that corporal punishment is not an appropriate method of discipline are less likely to use corporal punishment. For toddlers, however, for the reasons explained in the chapter on why parents tends to resort to spanking (Chapter 18), not believing in corporal punishment made little difference in spanking (Straus, 2001a, Chart 4–1). But perhaps if the increased risk of harmful effects were known to parents of toddlers, they would spank less.

Another theoretical contribution of this chapter is that it provides additional evidence that the causes of corporal punishment include the social organization and position of the family in society, not just the level of misbehavior of the child and the personality and child rearing skills of the parents. These social causes include the age of the parent, single- versus two-parent households, the level of violence in the neighborhood (Winstok & Straus, 2011b), and cultural norms that permit or require parents to use corporal punishment as shown in the chapters on the approval of violence and spanking (Chapter 5), spanking and partner violence throughout the world (Chapter 13), and why parents resort to spanking (Chapter18 and in Taylor, Hamvas, & Paris, 2011).

Coping with a first child is often seen as the most stressful part of parenthood, and parent educators and pediatricians have traditionally tended to emphasize helping parents deal with their *first* child, as exemplified by the *What to Expect* series and the "just-in-time" newsletters that provide month-by-month information about infant and child development. Although helping parents deal with a first child is very important, the results of this study indicate that the need to help parents avoid corporal punishment may be even greater with subsequent children.

5   Approval of Violence and Spanking

As we pointed out in Chapter 2 on the prevalence of spanking in the United States, for spanking to be legally permissible, it must be for purposes of correction and control. That is, the right of parents to hit children applies only when it is for purposes of correcting misbehavior. Consistent with this, very few parents just spank a child out of the blue and for no good reason. But what is a good reason for hitting a child? The answer depends on the cultural setting and the historical era. A good reason that was common earlier in American history was to "drive out the devil" because he was believed to possess children at birth (Miller & Swanson, 1958). The religious basis for beating the devil out of them has almost ceased to exist except among some fundamentalist Protestants; however, it persists in the idea of a willful child.

Although there is abundant evidence that parents' decision to spank depends on the type and severity of children's misbehavior (Dix & Grusec, 1985; Dix, Ruble, & Zambarano, 1989; Grusec, Dix, & Mills, 1982; MacKinnon-Lewis et al., 1994; Nix et al., 1999), the same misbehavior in one family will lead to a spanking, but not in another. Some parents spank frequently, some rarely, and a few not at all. There are many reasons for the difference as shown in the two previous chapters. For example, young parents and parents with more children are more likely to hit. The many other causes of spanking, other than misbehavior by the child, is one of the reasons the correlation between misbehavior and spanking are typically between about .20 and .35. Correlations that size are more than enough to be confident that one of the reasons parents spank is to correct misbehavior, but not large enough to allow researchers and educators to ignore other causes. A correlation of .30, for example, when squared to obtain the *coefficient of determination,* shows that only 9% of the differences between parents in the use of spanking is attributable to differences in the misbehavior of their children. If spanking were the only cause or the main cause, the correlation between misbehavior and spanking would have to be much higher. A study of a nationally representative sample of mothers in Israel (Winstok & Straus, 2011b) found that the

Julie H. Stewart is the coauthor of this chapter.

mothers' approval of spanking explained 2.5 times more of the differences between mothers in the use of spanking than was explained by misbehavior of the child.

Although it may be obvious that more than the child's misbehavior determines who spanks, professionals advising parents and researchers have not paid sufficient attention to this obvious fact. Efforts to end spanking are primarily focused on alternatives to spanking. Providing parents with alternatives is very important, but it is not sufficient. This is because many things other than misbehavior by the child lead to spanking. We do not know enough about why some parents spank when others do not. A few social scientists have gone beyond the belief that spanking is only a response to children's misbehavior and investigated the other social and psychological causes of spanking, mostly in the form of examining the effects of demographic variables such as age, gender, race, and education of the parents.

Because spanking is so prevalent and, as shown in this book, has so many harmful side effects, it is important to investigate other potential influences, in addition to demographic factors, to further understand why parents spank and how often they do it. There are many possibilities. This chapter is a step in that direction. It examines the relation of attitudes approving violence and the cultural norms underlying those attitudes. This book is based on the assumption that spanking is a form of violence. This chapter provides empirical data on that issue. It presents the results of our analysis of a nationally representative sample of U.S. parents on the following questions:

- To what extent is approval of violence and actual violence in other aspects of life associated with more approval of spanking?
- To what extent is more approval of violence and actual violence in other aspects of life associated with an increased probability of parents spanking?

In addition, we present data from three other studies to determine if the following are related to an increased probability of approving of or using spanking:

- Approval of torture of suspected terrorists
- Living in a state with a high rate of homicide
- Living in a nation where a high percent of women think it is appropriate for a husband to hit his wife under certain circumstances

Is Approving Violence One of the Reasons Parents Spank?

Many people we talk to about spanking are repelled, and even angered, by the idea that approving violence has anything to do with whether parents spank their children. They may indignantly proclaim "I spank my kids once in a while when nothing else works, but I don't believe in violence and I'm not in favor of violence and I'm not violent." Americans believe they are a peaceful and nonviolent nation. As a consequence, the United States has supported a great deal of research through government and private foundation funds to understand and ultimately prevent violence. However, because of the culturally established acceptance of the necessity and acceptability of sometimes spanking, spanking is rarely considered an act of violence, and research that could end spanking is not seen as research that could help end violence.

The idea that spanking is one of the roots of adult violence is not new. In 1941 the distinguished anthropologist Ashley Montague wrote an essay "Spanking the baby may be the psychological seed of war" (Montague, 1941). Investigating that issue is only now starting to seem credible. As just noted, few Americans perceive spanking as violence. This may be one of the reasons why, despite much research on violence, there has been little on understanding the links between spanking and other forms of violence, and why some scholars reject the evidence that does exist (Baumrind, Larzelere, & Cowan, 2002; Larzelere, Cox, & Smith, 2010; Parke, 2002). Even those who do not reject the evidence are doubtful. This may be one of the reasons why, as shown in Chapter 1, child development textbooks devote little or no space to the results of research showing that spanking is associated with an increased probability of the child being physically aggressive and, later in life, having social and psychological problems such as depression and crime.

The main focus of this chapter is whether one of the root causes of spanking is approval of violence and a propensity toward violence on the part of parents. At least one study found that among college students, the greater an individual's approval of war, of violence to control prison inmates, and of violence between dating and marital partners—the greater their approval of spanking tends to be (Anderson, Benjamin, Wood, & Bonacci, 2006). This study is particularly interesting because the types of violence included in the study, and the wording of the specific questions used, often involve the perception that one party has misbehaved. Thus, it provides examples of using violence to correct misbehavior, regardless of whether that misbehavior is a child throwing food, a spouse who flirts with someone, or a country that does not respect international borders.

There is reason to believe that both approval of violence and a propensity toward violence increases the approval of spanking and may be one of the root causes of parents hitting children. The research described in this chapter, therefore, tested the following two hypotheses:

1. *Parents who approve violence by children are more likely to also approve spanking by parents.*
2. *Parents who approve violence by children are more likely to actually spank.*

If the results confirm the hypotheses, that parents who approve of other types of violence (in this case violence by children in the form of fistfights) are more likely to approve of spanking and more likely to actually spank than other parents, it suggests that the approval of hitting children is partly a manifestation of a more general approval of violence for socially desirable ends. It also suggests another reason why helping parents avoid hitting children requires more than teaching nonviolent modes of correcting misbehavior.

Sample and Measures

The data for the main part of this chapter were obtained by interviews with a nationally representative sample of 986 parents that was conducted for us in 1995 by the Gallup Organization. Information on the method of sampling and the characteristics of the sample is in Chapter 2. We were able to supplement the results with analyses of data from four other studies. These are described in the sections on the results from those studies.

The following variables were analyzed for the main part of this chapter.

Approval of violence. Approval of violence was measured by a question first used by the National Commission on the Causes and Prevention of Violence (Baker & Ball, 1969; Owens & Straus, 1975). We asked the parents about the extent to which they agreed or disagreed with the statement that "When a boy is growing up, it is important for him to have a few fistfights."

Attitudes approving spanking. Attitudes approving spanking were assessed by asking the parents the extent to which they agreed with three questions: (1) "It is sometimes necessary to discipline a child with a good, hard spanking," (2) "It is OK for parents to slap their teenage children who talk back to them," and (3) "Parents who spare the rod, spoil the child."

Spanking. Spanking in the previous 12 months was measured by the Parent-Child Conflict Tactics Scales (Straus et al., 1998) and also used for Chapter 2.

The analysis of the relationship between violent attitudes and spanking took into account five other variables that are known to be associated with spanking: the age of the parent and child, gender of the parent, the racial and ethnic group of the child, and region of the country.

Relation of Approval of Violence to Approval of Spanking

Percent Who Approve Violence and Spanking

To identify parents who approved of violence, we asked the parents whether they agreed or disagreed that "It is important for boys to have a few fistfights." Seventeen percent of the parents strongly disagreed, 62% disagreed, 20% agreed, and 1% strongly agreed. Because only 1% strongly agreed, we combined them with those who chose the agree response and, from here on, used three categories: strongly disagreed, disagreed, and agreed.

The questions on the approval of spanking showed that 50% agreed that "A good hard spanking is sometimes necessary," 19% agreed that "It is okay to slap a teenager who talks back," and 40% agreed that "sparing the rod means spoiling the child" (see Appendix Table A4.1 for details).

Charts 5.1, 5.2, and 5.3 show that the more the parents in this sample approved of boys fist fighting, the more likely they were to approve of spanking. The specific results in each chart are:

- Chart 5.1 shows that only a small percent of parents who disagreed that boys need to get in fistfights believed that a good, hard spanking was sometimes necessary; but among parents who agreed that when a boy is growing up, it is important for him to have a few fistfights, 80% believed that a good, hard spanking is sometimes necessary.
- Chart 5.2 shows that the more a parent approves of boys getting into fistfights, the more likely they are to believe it is OK to slap a teenager who talks back.
- Chart 5.3 shows that parents, who believe that when a boy is growing up, it is important for him to have a few fistfights, are 2 times more likely than other parents to agree that sparing the rod spoils the child.

The results in these three charts show that parents who approve of violence have much higher rates of approving of spanking than other parents, but that does not answer the question of whether parents who believe that fistfights are good for boys actually hit their children more.

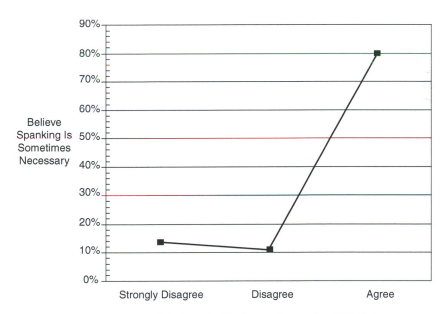

"It is important for boys to have a few fistfights"

Chart 5.1   Parents Who Believe Fighting Is Good for Boys Are More Likely to Believe Spanking Is Sometimes Necessary

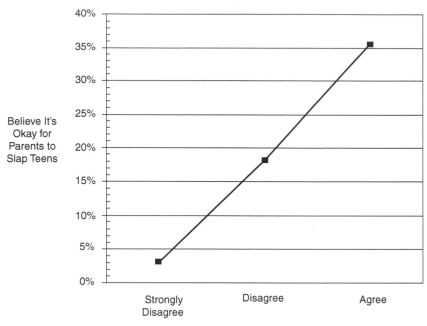

Chart 5.2 Parents Who Believe Fist Fighting Is Good for Boys Are More Likely to Believe It's OK for Parents to Slap Teenagers

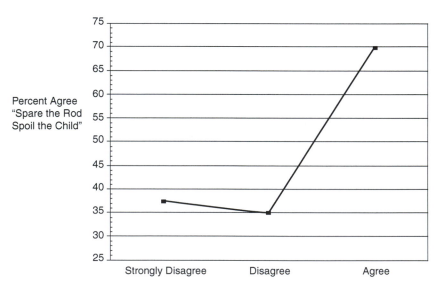

Chart 5.3 Parents Who Believe Fist Fighting Is Good for Boys Are More Likely to Agree with "Spare the Rod, Spoil the Child"

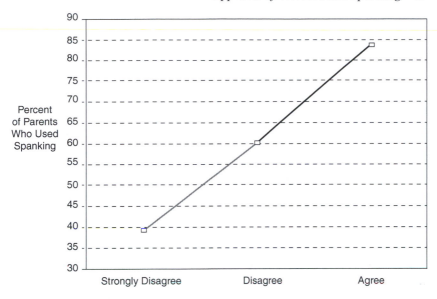

Chart 5.4   Parents Who Believe Fist Fighting Is Good for Boys Are More Likely to Spank

Chart 5.4 provides that information. It shows that the more a parent approves of violence (as measured by believing that it is good for boys to get into a few fistfights), the more likely the parent is to use spanking. Eighty percent of the parents, who agree that it is important for boys to fight, spanked, compared with only about one half that percentage of parents who disapprove of boys fighting.

Other Child and Family Characteristics Related to the Approval of Spanking

The idea that parents who approve of violence are more likely to spank is part of a general theoretical perspective that holds that the degree of misbehavior of children is only part of the explanation for differences in the use of spanking, and perhaps only a minor part of the explanation. The data for these parents permitted us to investigate five of the multitude of other factors that affect whether parents approve of hitting children (see Straus, 2010b, and Chapters 1, 2, 3, 4, and 18 for additional discussion of the causes of spanking).

Age of child. Twenty-nine percent of parents of infants (children up to age 1) agreed that it is sometimes necessary to spank compared with 62% of parents of teenagers (age 13 to 17). This is consistent with the percent who actually spanked shown in Chapter 2 on spanking in the United States.

Fathers and mothers. More fathers approved of spanking than mothers. This reflects the fact that men condone and use violence more than women as evidenced by the much higher violent crime rate for men. Men in the United States commit murder at a rate that is around 9 times higher than the rate for women (Bureau of Justice Statistics, 2001).

Race or ethnic group. Whites approved of parents slapping a teenager who talks back less often than other groups.

Age of parent. Younger parents are more accepting of spanking: 55% of younger parents (age 18 to 29), compared with 42% of parents over age 40, agree that it is sometimes necessary to spank. This is not surprising as they are more likely to have younger children or toddlers, the group most commonly spanked for misbehavior.

Region. Consistent with previous research (Ellison & Sherkat, 1993; Flynn, 1994) and the study in Chapter 17 on the decline in the approval of corporal punishment, the South stands out as the region where the most people approve of spanking. Seventy percent of Southern parents agreed that a good, hard spanking is sometimes necessary, compared with 32% parents from the Northeast. There was also a large difference between the South (58%) and the Northeast (26%) in the percent who believed that parents who spare the rod, will spoil the child. This is consistent with research by Cohen and Nisbett. They analyzed data from three surveys and found that Southern White males endorse violence when it is used for self-protection, to defend one's honor, and to socialize children. In one study, they gave respondents two different scenarios: one in which their son was being bullied and another in which their son was being beaten up in front of a crowd. In both situations, Southern respondents were more likely to say that their son "should take a stand and fight the other boy" than individuals from other regions of the country.

Three Other Studies

As we were working on this chapter, four other studies that could throw additional light on the issue of the links between violence in other spheres of life and spanking came to our attention.

Torture and Spanking

The results of a national by the Scripps Survey Center at Ohio University became available (Stempel, 2006). This is a study of a nationally representative sample of 1,031 adults selected by random digit dialing. The completion rate was 70%.

The survey was, in part, prompted by the national anguish over the invasion of Iraq and the steps taken to combat terrorism. It included the following question: "Do you think the United States is sometimes justified in using torture to get information from a suspected terrorist, or is torture never justified?" Overall, 37.8% of the participants in the survey believed torture is sometimes justified, 51% that it is never justified, and 10% said they did not know or gave some other answer.

The survey also happened to include the following question on spanking children: "Do you think spanking is sometimes necessary to maintain discipline with children or do you think spanking is not necessary?" Overall, 73% of the participants agreed that spanking is sometimes necessary. At this point, the crucial question is not the overall rate of approval of spanking because it is clear that Americans approve of spanking. Instead, the point of interest is an additional test of the theory that social norms concerning violence, and other violent tendencies, are factors that help explain why some people approve of spanking and others do not, and why some do it to correct misbehavior that other parents correct nonviolently.

Chart 5.5 shows strong support for this theory. To be more specific, participants in the Scripps survey study who said that torture was sometimes justified were about one third more likely to believe that spanking was necessary than those who said torture was never justified. The underlying factor seems to

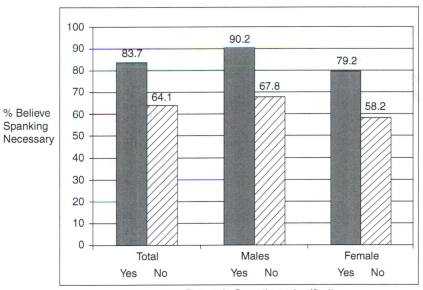

* P <.001 For All Differences between Yes & No Groups

Chart 5.5   Americans Who Believe that Torture Is Sometimes Necessary Are More Likely to Believe Spanking Is Necessary

be willingness to inflict physical pain to achieve socially desirable ends. We believe that most such people would probably insist that they do not approve of violence (Blumenthal, Kahn, Andrew, & Head, 1972). Why don't they see a contradiction between disapproving of violence and believing that torture is sometimes justified and that spanking is sometimes necessary? We suggest that it is because, for such individuals, violence is restricted to physical attacks that are not morally and socially justified. Therefore, in their view, torture for national security and hitting children for bad behavior do not constitute violence because these are morally and socially desirable ends. This probably also explains the view of a leading political scientist and human rights advocate who said, "we need to be careful that the concept of rights is not overstretched. When the prohibition against torture in the European Convention on Human Rights is extended to include spanking, the idea of 'human rights' has been transformed and trivialized. No matter what one's view is of child rearing norms, domestic discipline and torture are not meaningfully categorized together" (Pinto-Duschinsky, 2011). The evidence just presented suggests that they do go together.

Homicide and Spanking

Molnar and colleagues (2003) analyzed the Project on Human Development in Chicago Neighborhoods data on 8,782 study participants in 343 neighborhoods. Controlling for other neighborhood characteristics, such as, concentrated poverty and the age and sex of the child, they found that the higher the neighborhood homicide rate, the more physically aggressive the parenting.

We tested the same theory using the 50 U.S. states as the societal units. The level of violence in each state was measured by the 2006 Uniform Crime reports data on homicides per 100,000 population (Federal Bureau of Investigation, 2007). The data on spanking are from a 2005 national survey (SurveyUSA, 2005). Attitudes toward spanking were measured by a survey that asked a representative sample in each state, "Do you think it is OK to spank a child?" For the United States as a whole, 72% said they thought it was OK. The percent varied from state to state with Alabama at the top (87%) and Vermont at the bottom (62%). Chart 5.6 shows that the higher the level of violence in a state (as indicated by homicides), the higher the percent of a state's population who believed that spanking is OK.

Violence between Parents and Spanking

UNICEF (The United Nations Children's Fund) is conducting ongoing studies of child well-being in many nations (www.childinfo.org/mics.html). Large and representative samples of mothers, of children age 2 to 14, were interviewed in each nation. Eighteen of the nations participating in this effort asked the mothers about the use of spanking and also about whether they would approve of a husband hitting his wife under five circumstances such

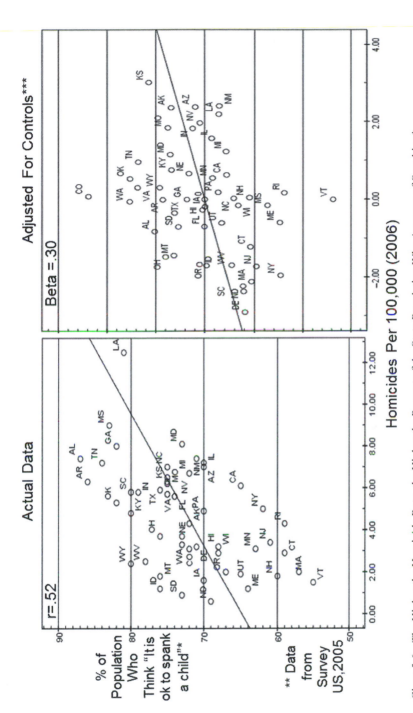

Chart 5.6 The Higher the Homicide Rate, the Higher the Percent of the State Population Who Approve of Spanking*

*Analysis controlled for Below poverty, Black, College-educated, and Metro resident. X and Y axes are for centered variables.

as neglecting the children or burning his food (Fluke, Casillas, Capa, Chen, & Wulczyn, 2010). The percent who approved a husband hitting his wife in one or more of the five circumstances ranged from 7% in Bosnia and Herzegovina to 76% in Ghana (the average was 35%). The percent who had used spanking in the last month ranged from 45% in Bosnia and Herzegovina to 88% in Jamaica (the average was 66%). These data enabled us to compute the correlation between approving a husband hitting his wife and hitting a child in the past month. We found that the higher the percent in a nation who believed husbands were justified in hitting a wife, in one or more of the five circumstances, the higher the percent who had hit their child in the past month. (The correlation is .30 if the raw data is used and .46 if the percentages are first converted into low, low middle, high middle, and high quarters to smooth out irregularities in the data.)

Thus, our analyses using data from four very different studies (the Gallup survey of U.S. parents, a Scripps Survey Center, homicide rates and Survey-USA data on the 50 U.S. states, and the UNICEF study of 18 economically developing nations) all show that the more other types of violence, the more approval of spanking and use of spanking. The data from the Gallup survey from 1995 may seem dated, but the studies described in Chapters 2 and 17 on the use of spanking show that almost all parents continue to hit toddlers and almost three quarters of the population continue to believe that spanking is sometimes necessary. Thus, the findings in this chapter are relevant and timely today.

Summary and Conclusions

We found clear evidence, from several independent sources of data, that suggests that one of the factors that influences whether parents approve of and use spanking is whether they approve of other forms of violence. The greater the approval of violence, the more approval of spanking and the more likely parents were to actually spank. Because these results are based on cross-sectional data, it is equally plausible to interpret the results as showing that when parents hit children, it makes them more favorable to other kinds of violence such as boys punching other boys. Probably there are causal influences in both directions. Regardless of which causes which, the results in this chapter are consistent with the *cultural spillover* theory of violence (Archer & Gartner, 1984; Baron & Straus, 1988, 1989). This theory argues that the use of violence in one sphere of life tends to increase the probability of violence in other spheres of life. Moreover, the spillover from one sphere of life to another applies to the effect of using violence for socially legitimate purposes and for criminal purposes.

Socially legitimate violence, such as executing criminals and waging war on an enemy nation, tends to legitimize other kinds of violence including criminal violence such as assault, rape, and murder (Bailey, 1998) The link between spanking and approval of violence is also shown by data from the General

Social Survey (McClure, 2002). McClure found that people who approved of executing criminals and those who owned a gun were more likely than others to approve of spanking by parents.

The spillover from the socially legitimate use of violence to discipline children to the criminal violence of hitting a spouse or dating partners is illustrated in Chapters 12 and 13. Chapter 12 shows this relationship for individual persons, and Chapter 13 shows that nations where spanking is prevalent tend to be nations with higher rates of violence toward dating partners. Thus, at both the individual and the societal level, experiencing spanking as a child, which is legitimate violence, is associated with an increased probability later in life of hitting a marital or dating partner, which is criminal violence.

Criminal Violence and Spanking

The link between belief in the death penalty or gun ownership and spanking partly reflects the fact that both are culturally defined as legitimate. However, the level of *criminal* violence in a society is also related to spanking, as shown in the sections of this chapter showing that the higher the homicide rate of a state, the higher the percent who approve of spanking.

Another study that found a link between criminal violence and spanking was conducted by Zhang and Anderson (2010) using a sample of low-income single mothers. Community violence was measured by whether the mothers had witnessed or been a victim of violence. They found that mothers who experienced moderate and high levels of community violence were 2.1 times and 2.4 times more likely to use spanking than mothers with no exposure to violence.

Winstok and Straus (2011b) studied a large and nationally representative sample of mothers in Israel and found that, after controlling for socioeconomic status and other variables, the more violent the study participants perceived their neighborhood, the more frequent was their use of spanking.

Another type of criminal violence that is associated with spanking is physical assaults between the parents (Annerbäck et al., 2010; Fergusson & Horwood, 1998; Silverstein et al., 2009; Straus, 2001a). Chart 5.7 graphs the link between interparental violence and spanking. Not surprisingly, parents who hit each other are more likely to hit their children. Straus (2001a) has suggested that it also works the other way—that each time a parent hits a child, it is role practice in violence. This not as big a leap as it might seem. Contrary to the patriarchal-dominance theory about the causes of violence between married couples, in most of the world, including nations with male-dominant cultures, about the same percent of women as men hit their partner (see Chapter 13 and Straus, 2008b). What is most relevant in this context is that the predominant cause of hitting a partner, by both men and women, is to correct what is perceived as a persistent, unacceptable behavior by the partner. The misbehavior ranges from not taking out the trash to infidelity (Ansara & Hindin, 2009; Bookwala, Frieze, Smith, & Ryan, 1992; Capaldi, Kim, & Shortt, 2007;

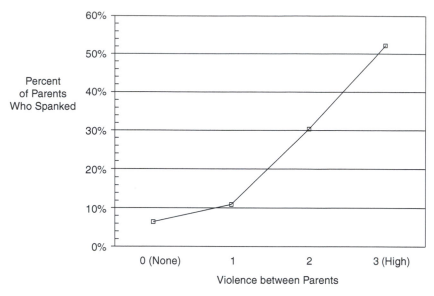

Chart 5.7   The More Violence between Parents, the Larger the Percent Who Spanked*
*Data from Fergusson and Horwood (1998, Table 4).

Carrado, George, Loxam, Jones, & Templar, 1996; Cascardi & Vivian, 1995; Fiebert & Gonzalez, 1997; Foshee, Linder, MacDougall, & Bangdiwala, 2001; Harned, 2001; Hettrich & O'Leary, 2007). Just as parents hit children to correct a persistent misbehavior, so do marital and dating partners hit to correct misbehavior. Or put another way, spanking by parents is part of a larger pattern of violence in society.

The same conclusion can be drawn from the study of university students in 32 countries who participated in the International Dating Violence Study. At universities where a large percent of the students believed that spanking was necessary, a large percent also approved of a husband slapping his wife (Chapter 13). A similar, but even stronger, relationship was found between cultural norms permitting a husband to "make her do it" when a wife does not want to have sex and spanking. Nations where a high percentage believed that spanking was necessary tended to be nations where a large percentage of students believed it was acceptable for husbands to "make her do it" ($r = .70$).

Conclusion

Somewhat ironically, the results showing that spanking is partly an expression of a more general pattern of violence in society leads us to conclude that this link is a basis for optimism about ending violent parenting. This is because there has been a long-term and historical decrease in interpersonal violence (Eisner, 2001; Elias, 1978; Straus, 2001a, Chapters 11 and 21), including physical abuse of children and wife beating (Straus & Gelles, 1986). The question on approval of boys getting into fistfights is an example of that trend. When this question was answered by another nationally representative sample in 1968, 70% agreed. By 1995 when the parents for this chapter were interviewed, only 21% favored boys getting into fistfights. Part of the difference may be because the 1968 sample included all adults, whereas this sample included only adults who were parents. Nevertheless, a substantial part of the decrease from 70% to 21% probably represents a change in cultural norms about acceptable violence. Because this centuries-long trend is likely to continue, that alone suggests there will be a further decline in the still widespread pattern of parents hitting children.

Finally, the results in this chapter suggest that efforts to help parents avoid hitting children will be aided by capitalizing on the historical trend toward less approval of, and less actual, interpersonal violence. This can be done by unequivocally declaring that spanking is violence and is not an acceptable method of discipline by parents. Sweden did that in 1979. By 2011, a total of 29 nations had banned spanking by parents, and both the United Nations (Pinheiro, 2006) and the European Union (Council of Europe, 2005) have called on all member nations to prohibit all spanking by parents.

Part II
Spanking and Child Behavior Problems

6   The Boomerang Effect of Spanking

Public approval of spanking has declined drastically in the past generation. Actual use of corporal punishment (spanking) on *older* children has dropped by about half since 1975 (see Chapter 17). Despite this, spanking remains an almost universal experience of children in the United States because, as was shown in Chapter 2 on spanking in the United States, at least 94% of parents spank and slap toddlers. Because every child was a toddler, this means that being hit by parents at least occasionally is an almost universal part of growing up in an American family. The 94% rate also suggests that parents are either not aware of, or choose to ignore, the possible harmful side effects of slapping and spanking. Surveys of pediatricians, psychologists, and sociologists have found that they also seem to give little attention to the possible harmful side effects of spanking. A clear indication is the virtual omission of spanking in child development textbooks shown in Chapter 1 and the surveys of pediatricians and psychologists (Anderson & Anderson, 1976; Schenck et al., 2000; White, 1993). Ignoring the harmful side effects of spanking flies in the face of a large and highly consistent body of research indicating that spanking is associated with an increased probability of physical aggression and other antisocial behaviors. Gershoff's meta-analysis documents the results of 27 studies of the relationship of corporal punishment to aggression by children (Gershoff, 2002). All 27 found that corporal punishment was associated with an increased probability of aggression. Since then, all studies conducted on this relationship have found that spanking is associated with an increased probability of aggression and antisocial behavior.

There are many reasons this evidence has been ignored. One of the most important is the belief that spanking is more effective than nonviolent discipline and is, therefore, sometimes necessary, despite the risk of harmful side effects. The *sometimes* refers to occasions when a child engages in repeated misbehavior, dangerous behavior such running out into the street, or morally offensive behavior such as hitting other children. These situations occur in the lives of almost all children and that is why, as will be explained more fully in the chapter on why parents are driven to spank (Chapter 18), the belief that spanking is sometimes necessary means that almost all children will be hit by parents.

David B. Sugarman and Jean Giles-Sims are coauthors of this chapter.

As we pointed out in Chapter 3 on spanking throughout the world and in Chapter 4 on the relationship between family size and spanking, the child's behavior is only part of the explanation for spanking. As we previously suggested the evidence on harmful side effects has probably also been ignored because of the belief that spanking is more effective than other modes of correction. Spanking is widely believed to teach a lesson that children will not forget. The results of the study described in this chapter confirm that belief, but in a way that parents do not envision. In fact, they show that the lesson is often the opposite of what parents have in mind when they say, "I don't like to spank, but I had to teach him a lesson."

The specific questions to be addressed in this chapter are:

- What type of study could provide evidence that spanking causes antisocial behavior? This is an important question because, although many studies have found a correlation, a correlation does not provide evidence that there is a causal relationship.
- Does the relation of spanking to antisocial behavior apply to toddlers as well as older children? This is an important question because some argue that it has no harmful effects at early ages (Friedman & Schonberg, 1996a).
- Does the context in which spanking occurs make a difference? This is an important question because it is widely believed that if parents spank in the context of a warm and supportive relationship or that if spanking occurs within a culture where it is the prescriptive or statistical norm, it will not have adverse side effects.
- If parents spank only rarely, will it still cause harm? This question is important because many argue that the rare and judicious use of spanking could have beneficial outcomes.

Spanking and Behavior Problems

There are theoretical reasons to think that the link between spanking and an increased probability of physical aggression by the child is strengthened because parents use spanking for the socially approved and moral purpose of correcting behavior—and because spanking itself is socially approved and viewed as morally correct. Therefore, we could predict that when parents, albeit unintentionally, teach that it is morally appropriate to hit to correct misbehavior, their children will learn to hit others to correct their behavior. Children are continuously faced with situations in which other children are doing something they consider seriously wrong and who persist in that behavior, such as "he squirted water at me and wouldn't stop," "she took all the dolls and won't give me even one," or, later in life, "he made a pass at my girl." If children have learned that it is socially and morally appropriate for parents to hit others to change their behavior, they are more likely to hit others themselves. This is one of the reasons why study after study has found that the more spanking a child experiences, the more likely that child is to hit another child. In addition, other processes, such as those investigated in Chapter 12 examining the link between being spanked and partner violence in adulthood, contribute to the criminogenic nature of spanking.

The adverse effects of spanking have been observed as early as the beginning of the second year of life. For example, Power and Chapieski (1986) found that toddlers whose mothers frequently spanked had a 58% higher rate of noncompliance with mothers' requests than did children whose parents rarely or never spanked. Among kindergarten children, Strassberg, Dodge, Pettit, and Bates (1994) found that those who were spanked that year had double the rate of hitting other children in school. Using children of widely varying ages, Straus (2001a, Chart 7.1) found that children in the National Family Violence Survey who experienced frequent spanking were twice as likely to severely assault a sibling as children of the same age who were not spanked that year. Analysis of another national survey found that, compared with children who were not spanked, those who were spanked the most were four times as likely to be delinquent (Straus, 2001b). Moreover, Chapter 12 on spanking and partner violence shows that the parents in that study who recalled having experienced corporal punishment during their early teens (about one half of the sample), were three times more likely to have hit their spouse during the previous 12 months.

Which is Cause and Which is Effect?

All of the studies just cited, however, used a research method that can only show that spanking is *correlated* with behavioral or emotional problems of children. These studies could not show that spanking *causes* those problems. It is just as plausible that the child's behavior problems caused the spanking. Our perspective is that there is a two-way causal process. This means that, although misbehavior causes spanking, when parents spank to correct misbehavior, it has the long-term effect of increasing the probability of aggression, noncompliance, and, as will be shown in Part IV, delinquency and, later in life, marital violence and other crime. Establishing whether this proposed boomerang effect is correct requires either experimental or longitudinal research that examines *change* in antisocial behavior subsequent to the spanking. The few longitudinal studies that had been completed prior to the study in this chapter did not measure change in children's behavior subsequent to spanking, so they did not permit inferring a cause-effect relationship (e.g., Simons, Burt, & Simons, 2008; Simons, Johnson, & Conger, 1994). Others, (e.g., Eron, Huesmann, & Zelli, 1991) included spanking in a scale measuring harsh disciplinary practices and therefore could not examine the effect of spanking per se. This problem continues to exist in many studies (e.g., Bender et al., 2007; Ehrensaft et al., 2003) that investigate spanking, but only as part of a harsh discipline scale.

Ethical and practical issues make it impossible to conduct experiments that randomly assign children to spanking or to non-spanking parents. However, longitudinal studies can follow children over time in their natural environments to see what happens in the months and years after they experience spanking.

Such studies can provide information about the effects of spanking, but only if the study measures *change* in behavior—that is, in the months and years subsequent to the spanking, did the child's behavior improve or get worse? Unfortunately, none of the longitudinal studies conducted up to 1997 measured change in children's behavior. Without such a control, even longitudinal studies that follow children for several years are unable to determine which is the cause and which is the effect. When a study finds that the more spanking a child experienced at Time 1, the more aggressive the child is at Time 2, this could reflect a situation in which parents were responding to a high level of aggression at Time 1. Because aggression is a relatively stable trait, it would not be surprising to find that the most aggressive children at Time 1 were still the most aggressive at Time 2. The most one can conclude from longitudinal studies that do not measure change in children's aggression is that the spanking did not reduce the level of that aggression.

The study in this chapter permitted us to overcome the causal direction problem because antisocial behavior was measured at the start of the study and then again two and four years later. This allowed us to determine whether spanking resulted in less, or more, antisocial behavior two years later. We tested the hypothesis that *the more parents spanked at Time 1, the greater the increase in children's antisocial behavior from Time 1 to Time 2.*

Sample and Measures

Sample

The sample consisted of the 807 children of women who were first interviewed in 1979 as part of the National Longitudinal Survey of Youth who were 6 to 9 years old when their level of antisocial behavior was measured. The data that is reported here was collected in three different waves, two years apart, which enabled us to examine the potential impact of spanking on antisocial behavior over time. For information on the sample and data see Giles-Sims (Baker, Keck, Mott, & Quinlan, 1993; Giles-Sims et al., 1995; Straus, Sugarman, & Giles-Sims, 1997).

The information on spanking was obtained from observation by the interviewer of whether the mother hit the child during the course of the interview and from asking, "Did you find it necessary to spank your child in the past week?" Mothers who said they had spanked were asked: "About how many times, if any, have you had to spank your child in the past week?" We used these data to create a spanking scale that combined the observed and the interview measures. If the mother was observed hitting the child, it was counted as one instance of spanking and this was added to the number of times the mother reported spanking in the previous week. From this scale, we formed four categories of children: those who experienced no spanking (during the interview or the previous week) and those who experienced one, two, or three or more instances of being spanked.

Antisocial Behavior

The measure of child *antisocial behavior* consists of the following six behaviors: cheats or tells lies, bullies or is cruel or mean to others, does not feel sorry after misbehaving, breaks things deliberately, is disobedient at school, and has trouble getting along with teachers. The mothers were asked if, during the preceding three months, each of the behaviors was *not true* of that child (scored as 1), *sometimes true* (scored 2), and o*ften true,* (scored 3). The antisocial behavior score is the sum of the scores for these behaviors.

Three Other Methodological Problems

In addition to research that does not permit inferring whether spanking causes antisocial behavior, much of the existing research also fails to deal with one or more of three other methodological problems, each of which could undermine the validity of the results.

Overlap with other parental behaviors. What seems to be an effect of spanking could be a *spurious* relationship. A spurious relation is one that results from some other variable being the underlying cause. For example, if parents who spank also are harsh and rejecting, and lack warmth and affection, those characteristics rather than spanking itself, could be what explains the correlation of spanking with antisocial behavior. Many studies show that harsh and rejecting parents do tend to spank more (Herzberger, 1990; Pinto, Folkers, & Sines, 1991; Simons et al., 1994). However, parents who spank are not usually harsh and rejecting in other ways. Spanking is something done by good parents in the belief that it is necessary to correct misbehavior. Moreover, if parents who spank are harsh and rejecting, because over 94% spank toddlers, it would mean that over 94% of American parents are harsh and rejecting. That is very unlikely. Therefore, it is also unlikely that the harmful side effects of spanking are the result of these other parental behaviors rather than the result of spanking itself. Still, it is very important to analyze spanking within the context of parents' child rearing styles. This means that research must separate the effects of spanking from the effects of other parental behaviors. Two crucial aspects of parenting that have been identified in previous research are warmth and *cognitive stimulation,* which refers to interacting with the child in a way that encourages the child to think and understand (Maccoby & Martin, 1983). Emotional support is especially important to take into consideration because it is widely believed that, if spanking is done by parents who provide emotional support, use of spanking in moderation and as a backup rather than a first resort, is beneficial to children (Baumrind et al., 2002). To deal with this problem, the statistical analysis for this study took into account the level of emotional support and cognitive stimulation.

Overlap with sex of child and socioeconomic status. Another methodological problem can occur if the study does not take into account whether the child is a boy or girl and whether the family is low or high in socioeconomic status. With respect to sex differences, boys engage in more disruptive behavior, school truancy, and verbal and physical violence than girls (Cullinan & Epstein, 1982; Hyde, 1984; Maccoby & Jacklin, 1980). This may be one of the reasons parents are more likely to spank boys more than girls, as was shown in Chapter 2 and by Simons et al. (1994). Thus, part of the relationship between spanking and a child's antisocial behavior may reflect the fact that boys misbehave more and parents are more likely to spank boys to correct the misbehavior. This is what is known as *confounding* of the relationship between spanking and antisocial behavior with the sex of the child (Hoghughi, 1992). There is also the possibility that spanking has different effects for boys and girls. This is what is known as an *interaction* effect or a *moderator* effect. We, therefore, examined whether the relation of spanking to antisocial behavior is different for boys and girls.

A similar problem applies to socioeconomic status and racial or ethnic group because, as was shown in Chapter 1, low socioeconomic status parents and parents from some minority groups spank more (see also Bank, Forgatch, Patterson, & Fetrow, 1993; Giles-Sims et al., 1995; Sears, Maccoby, & Levin, 1957; Straus, 2001a). Children from low socioeconomic status families, moreover, have higher rates of antisocial behavior and delinquency (Bank et al., 1993; Feshback, 1970; Junger-Tas, Haen Marshall, & Ribeaud, 2003; Simons, Gordon Simons, & Wallace, 2004). These two factors together can present a methodological problem. It is especially important to investigate whether the effect of spanking differs by racial or ethnic group because it has been argued that, in the context of a community where spanking is the cultural norm, spanking does not carry the same harmful side effects. This is believed to be the case because children who are raised with different norms concerning spanking do not equate spanking with parental harshness or rejection (Gunnoe & Mariner, 1997; Larzelere, Baumrind, & Polite, 1998; Polite, 1996) and therefore suffer no ill effects.

Effect of age of the child. Spanking might have different effects at different child ages. For example, it is widely believed that spanking *toddlers,* if done in moderation, does not have harmful side effects (Friedman & Schonberg, 1996a), whereas spanking older children and teenagers is thought to interfere with the transition to adulthood and autonomy. However, there does not seem to have been any empirical research on this issue. Thus, the advice to spank only young children is based on cultural tradition rather than scientific evidence. It is at least equally plausible to argue the opposite—that spanking toddlers will have a greater effect because it occurs at crucial developmental stages. Indeed, the results of the study described in Chapter 10 show that the effect of spanking on mental development is greater for younger than older children. Because there are plausible grounds for expecting age differences, we repeated the preliminary analysis for children of three age groups: 3 to 5 years, 6 to 9 years, and 10 years and over. The preliminary results were parallel for all three age groups. As a consequence, for the reasons given in the section of the Appendix for this chapter, the final analysis was conducted only for children aged 6 to 9.

Correlation of Spanking with Antisocial Behavior

The data permitted computing correlations between the frequency of spanking and the child's antisocial behavior. Fifteen of the correlations are on the relation of spanking to antisocial behavior in the same year (contemporaneous correlations), and 15 examine the relationship of spanking at Time 1 to antisocial behavior two years later (time-lagged correlations). All 15 contemporaneous correlations, and all 15 time-lagged correlations found that the more frequently a mother spanked her child in the week she was interviewed, the more antisocial behavior that year and also two years later. (The correlation coefficients are in Straus, Sugarman et al., 1997.

Following the recommendation of Bruning and Kintz (1987), we investigated whether the size of the correlations differed by year of measurement or by the age and sex of the child. We found that, with only two small exceptions, the relation between spanking and antisocial behavior was consistent across all ages and all years of interviews, and across gender (see Straus, 1997, Table 1). The fact that spanking was correlated with antisocial behavior to about the same extent for 3- to 5-year-old children as for older children is very important. It suggests that, contrary to both popular and professional beliefs (Friedman & Schonberg, 1996a), spanking is just as harmful for toddlers as it is for other age groups.

Spanking and Change in Antisocial Behavior

For the reasons explained previously, ordinary correlations may be misleading. What seems to be an effect of spanking on antisocial behavior could really be the effect of some underlying variable such as socioeconomic status or lack of parental warmth. The most important limitation of ordinary correlations is that they provide no information to distinguish cause from effect. Does spanking cause antisocial behavior or does antisocial behavior cause spanking? To deal with these problems, we used the statistical method known as analysis of covariance. This controlled for differences in family socioeconomic status, sex of the child, and the extent to which the home provided emotional support and cognitive stimulation. Most important, it controlled for the amount of antisocial behavior at the start of the study. The results of testing the hypothesis with this method can determine whether there is a *change* in children's antisocial behavior two years later (i.e., subsequent to the year in which the spanking occurred and whether that change is in the form of an increase or a decrease in antisocial behavior). It can also determine whether there is an effect of spanking that is over and above the effect of family socioeconomic status, sex of the child, and the extent to which the home provided emotional support and cognitive stimulation.

Chart 6.1 graphs the results of the analysis of covariance. At the left side of the chart are the children whose parents did *not* spank them during the week studied in the first year of the study. Those children had an average *decrease*

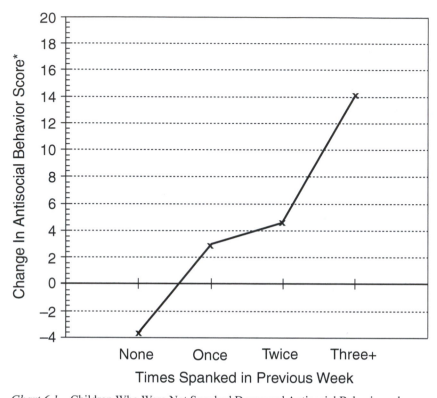

Chart 6.1   Children Who Were Not Spanked Decreased Antisocial Behavior, whereas Children Who Were Spanked Increased Their Antisocial Behavior Two Years Later

*Mean adjusted for T1 antisocial behavior, T1 cognitive stimulation, T1 parental emotional support, child gender, race, and socioeconomic status.

of four points on the antisocial behavior scale. Moving from left to right in Chart 6.1 to the children who were spanked once during the Time 1 week, shows that their antisocial behavior score increased by an average of two points. The children who were spanked twice also had about a two-point increase in antisocial behavior. The biggest change in antisocial behavior was for children spanked three or more times that week. Their antisocial behavior score increased by an average of 14 points. Thus, the more frequent the spanking in 1988, the greater the increase in antisocial behavior over the subsequent two years. Only among children who were not spanked the week before the Time 1 interviews did antisocial behavior decrease. The F tests and other statistics for these results are in Table 2 of Straus, Sugarman et al., 1997.

It is important to keep in mind that the terms *increase* and *decrease* describe change compared with other children in the study at each point in time. In absolute terms, the average amount of antisocial behavior decreases as young children mature (Tremblay, 2003). The way we measured antisocial behavior takes this average improvement in children's behavior into account because it measures how far above or below the average antisocial behavior of all children in the sample each child is at each time point.

Does the Context Make a Difference?

The results also provide information on whether the presence or absence of the variables we controlled affected the relation of spanking to antisocial behavior. As explained previously, it is widely believed that, if parents are loving and supportive, spanking does not have a harmful effect. When we investigated that possibility, we did not find a statistically significant interaction or moderator effect for emotional support. That is, spanking was associated with an increase in antisocial behavior among children whose parents were high in emotional support as well as among children of low-support parents. The fact that, even when there is lots of love and support, spanking is associated with an increase in antisocial behavior does not mean that love and support make no difference. Our study, like many others, found that the more supportive the parent, the lower the average level of antisocial behavior.

We did find that the relation of spanking to antisocial behavior was influenced by two other variables. Chart 6.2 shows that the tendency for spanking to be related to an increase in antisocial behavior two years later is stronger for boys than for girls, and Chart 6.3 shows that the relation between spanking and antisocial behavior is stronger for White children compared with minority children. Nevertheless, although the amount of increase in antisocial behavior associated with spanking may be smaller for girls and minority group children, both experienced an increase in antisocial behavior in proportion to the amount of spanking they had experienced two years earlier.

The result for minority group children is particularly important because many minority group parents believe that under the high crime conditions of inner city life, their children need (to use one of many euphemisms for spanking) "strong discipline" (Alvy & Marigna, 1987; Kohn, 1969; Peters, 1976; Polite, 1996; Young, 1970). Children growing up in those difficult circumstances no doubt need closer supervision and control, but these results suggest that attempting to do this by spanking increases rather than reduces the risk that children will get into trouble. Other studies that also found that the harmful effects of spanking apply in different cultural contexts are in Chapters 10 and 14. See also the review by Lansford (2010).

Summary and Conclusions

We found that the more spanking by the mothers in this sample, the greater the chances that two years later the child would have an *increase* in antisocial behavior. The tendency for spanking to be associated with an increase in antisocial behavior applies regardless of the extent to which parents provide cognitive stimulation and emotional support, and regardless of socioeconomic status, ethnic group, and sex of the child. These results are contrary to the idea

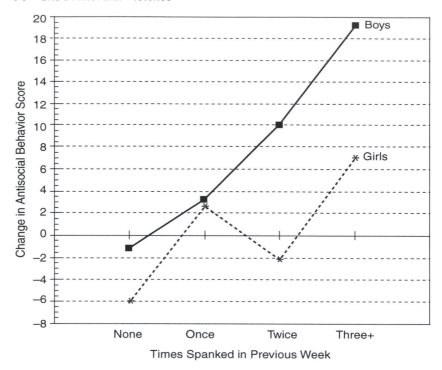

Chart 6.2   The Increase in Antisocial Behavior Associated with Spanking Is Much Greater for Boys than for Girls

*Mean adjusted for T1 antisocial behavior, T1 cognitive stimulation, T1 parental emotional support, child gender, race, and socioeconomic status.

that, if parents provide adequate warmth and cognitive stimulation, spanking will not harm children. Our results are also contrary to the idea that spanking works better among lower socioeconomic status families or in some minority families. Moreover, the findings are consistent across years (1986 to 1988, 1988 to 1990), across types of analysis (multiple regression and analysis of covariance), and for all three age groups (ages 3 to 5, 6 to 9, and 10 and over). The consistency across age groups is important because it contradicts the widespread belief, held by both the general public and professionals advising parents, that spanking is acceptable if confined to preschool-age children. As we noted in Chapter 2, the consensus statement from an American Academic of Pediatrics conference in 1996 permitted spanking for children age 2 to 6. If the results in this chapter, and those in Chapter 10 on spanking and cognitive ability, had been available at that time, the outcome of that conference might have been very different.

Another question that is often raised is, "Does only one spanking make a difference?" We found that the increase in antisocial behavior starts with children whose mothers spanked them only once during the week of the survey. This is

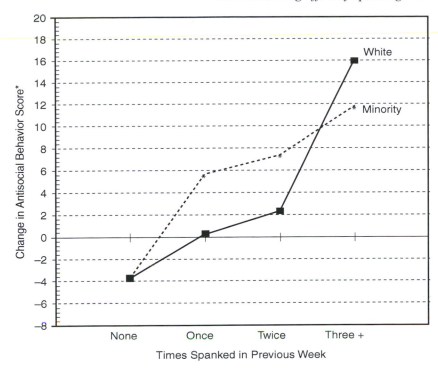

* Mean Adjusted For T1 Anti-social Behavior, T1 Conginitive Stimulation,
T1 Parental Emotional Support, Child Gender, Race, And SES.

Chart 6.3   Spanking Increases Antisocial Behavior by Both White and Minority Children, but the Effect Is Slightly Less for Minority Children

*Mean adjusted for T1 antisocial behavior, T1 cognitive stimulation, T1 parental emotional support, child gender, race, and socioeconomic status.

consistent with the results of studies by Larzelere and Grogan-Kaylor. Larzeler (1986) found "there is no evidence that a threshold frequency of spanking is necessary before it begins to influence child aggression" (p. 31). Grogan-Kaylor (2004) found that even relatively infrequent spanking is associated with an average increase in antisocial behavior compared with children whose parents did not spank to correct misbehavior.

Since the study in this chapter was done, there have been at least 14 other longitudinal studies that have found that spanking is associated with a subsequent increase in maladaptive behaviors. Chapter 19 reviews those that examined whether spanking is associated with an increase in the probability of antisocial behavior and crime.

It is important to understand the implications of the phrase "an average increase." When there is an average effect, it means that there will be children for whom the effect of spanking is greater than the average effect and children for whom the effect is less than the average. Or putting it another way, spanking does not always lead to an increase in antisocial behavior. As explained in Chapter 1, the effect of risk factors such as spanking is always in the form of an increased probability of the harmful effect, not a one-to-one relationship. A well-established example of a risk-factor effect is heavy smoking. About one third of heavy smokers die of a smoking-related disease (Matteson et al., 1987). But this high mortality rate also means that two thirds of very frequent smokers can point out that they smoked more than a pack a day all their life and have not died from a smoking-related disease. Similarly, most adults who were spanked can say, "I was spanked a lot and I'm OK." Although those who say these things are factually correct, the intended implication that smoking or spanking are safe is not correct. The correct implication is that such individuals are one of the "lucky ones." Thus, although most children who are spanked will not be high in antisocial behavior, that does not mean that spanking is harmless—just as the fact that most heavy smokers do not die, it does not mean that smoking is harmless.

The chapters that follow, and much other research, show that the behavior problems associated with spanking are not confined to aggression and other antisocial behavior. In addition, these studies, like the present chapter, reveal a *dose-response* to spanking, starting with even one instance. The *effect size* for one instance is small, but it exists. The more frequent the spanking, the greater the probability of behavior problems. Taking the whole range of spanking as measured by this study, a rough estimate of the potential for reducing antisocial behavior can be obtained by comparing the change in antisocial behavior scores for children who were not spanked in the past week with scores of children who were spanked 3 or more times in the past week. The score on the antisocial behavior scale of the children who were spanked 3 or more times is 18-points higher than the none group. The 6- to 9-year-old children in the 3-or-more-times group, who are 10% of the children in the study, would have had the greatest chance of improved behavior if their parents had not spanked them. In addition, because Chart 6.1 shows that even one instance of spanking in the previous week is associated with an increased risk of antisocial behavior, an additional 19.8% of children could benefit by a reduction in spanking from once to never, and 14.1% could benefit by a reduction from twice to once in a week. This comes to a total of 44% of the children in this national sample whose antisocial behavior could have decreased if their parents did not spank them or spanked them less often.

7   Impulsive Spanking, Never Spanking, and Child Well-Being

Impulsive behavior consists of acts carried out with little or no forethought or control, hot-tempered actions, acting without planning or reflection, and failing to resist urges (Hoghughi, 1992; Lorr & Wunderlich, 1985; Monroe, 1970; Murray, 1938). Parents may spank impulsively, or they may follow the recommendations of some advocates of corporal punishment such as Baumrind, Larzelere, and Cowan (2002) who find spanking acceptable if done as well-regulated spanking, that is, in a calm and collected way. Others believe in striking while the iron is hot. John Rosemond, the author of best-selling books on child rearing says that he believes in "spanking as a first resort; spanking in anger" (Rosemond, 1994a).

Violence is the use of physical force to cause pain or injury (Gelles & Straus, 1979). Corporal punishment of children (spanking) is a legal form of violence, provided it causes only pain and not lasting physical injury and is for purposes of correction and control. The child who is spanked impulsively experiences physical attacks as part of one of the most crucial social relationships in their lives. As these experiences become internalized, they provide a model for the child's own behavior. Thus, impulsive spanking may be an important risk factor for impulsiveness in the child. This process may be an important one for understanding the development of criminal behavior. The criminogenic nature of impulsiveness has been shown in a number of studies, including a longitudinal survey of 411 London boys that demonstrated that "low intelligence, an impulsive personality, and a lack of empathy for other people are among the leading individual characteristics of people at risk for becoming offenders" (Farrington & Welsh, 2006, page V). Studies by Aucoin, Frick, and Bodin (2006) and Olson, Sameroff, Kerr, Lopez, and Wellman (2005) found that the more spanking experienced by children, the higher their scores on a measure of impulsiveness. But because neither study distinguished between parents who spanked impulsively and those who did not, this correlation might reflect the part of the sample whose parents spanked impulsively. We believe that regardless of whether it is carried out impulsively or in a planned way, spanking increases the probability of antisocial behavior by the child. We also believe

Vera E. Mouradian is the coauthor of this chapter.

that this effect is even greater when the spanking is impulsive because, in that situation, spanking models not only violence but also impulsiveness. The study described in this chapter addressed the following questions:

- What percent of children were never spanked?
- When parents spank, how often do they spank impulsively?
- Are mothers who spank often more likely to do so impulsively?
- Is spanking related to impulsivity and antisocial behavior in children, even when the spanking is *not* done impulsively?
- Is spanking more strongly related to impulsivity and antisocial behavior in children when the spanking is impulsive than when it is planned?
- Are children who were never spanked less impulsive than those who have ever been spanked?
- Does maternal warmth and nurturance moderate the relationship of spanking to child antisocial and impulsive behavior?

Impulsive Spanking and Child Behavior Problems

It has been 60 years since Sears et al. (1957) found that spanking by parents was associated with a less well-developed conscience and higher levels of aggression in children. Some argue that the relationship between spanking and aggression by children depends on whether spanking is used impulsively or in a controlled way (Dobson, 1988; Friedman & Schonberg, 1996a; Larzelere, 1994), reflecting a belief that only impulsive spanking has harmful side effects. Others, however, recommend that parents spank in anger (e.g., Rosemond, 1994a, 1994b), and many parents have told us that to do otherwise is cold-blooded. This discussion raises two questions. One question is to what extent parents spank impulsively. The other question is whether spanking in general, or only impulsive spanking, is associated with child behavior problems. These questions are examined by reviewing previous research and then by presenting new research findings.

Prevalence of Impulsive Spanking

Only three studies were found that provided data on the prevalence of impulsive spanking, and even these two did not use the term *impulsive* to describe their findings. However, their definitions are consistent with what we are calling impulsive spanking: spanking little or no forethought or control, hot-tempered actions, without planning or reflection. Carson (1986) studied 186 parents in a small New England city. Her findings can be interpreted as showing that about one third of those parents spanked impulsively. Holden and Miller (1997) differentiated between instrumental spankers and emotional spankers. Emotional spankers felt irritated, frustrated, and out of control when spanking their children. They constituted just under one third of the sample of 90 parents who used spanking. In addition to these two studies of actual incidents of spanking, we located two other studies that provide an indication of the potential for parents to use spanking impulsively. A Canadian national survey (Institute for the Prevention of Child Abuse, 1989) found that 80% of parents said that, at least on rare occasions, they came close to losing control when disciplining their children. A study by Frude and Goss (1979) found that of 111 mothers, 40% were worried that they could lose control and possibly hurt their children. A third and longitudinal study of 132 parents from a southwestern urban region examined the context in which spanking occurs (Vittrup & Holden, 2010; Vittrup, Holden, & Buck, 2006). The authors found that almost a third (29%) of parents reported feeling angry while they were spanking, which could also be related to impulsivity.

Effects of Impulsive Spanking

A search of electronic databases did not locate studies of specific effects of impulsive spanking on children. However, two of the three studies just cited provide some indirect evidence of the relation of impulsive spanking to specific child behaviors. Holden and Miller (1997) found that emotional spankers were less likely to believe that spanking would result in achieving their goals for the child, such as immediate compliance, good behavior, and respect for authority. Similarly, Carson (1986) found parents who spanked when they lost control tended to be more likely to see spanking as ineffective. Therefore, parents seem to believe that the impulsive administration of spanking undermines its effectiveness. In addition, impulsivity implies lack of consistency in punishment, and inconsistent punishment has been found to be associated with lower levels of parenting self-efficacy (Acker & O'Leary, 1988).

There are theoretical grounds for expecting adverse effects of impulsive spanking on children. First, we could expect that impulsivity in the parent would provide a model of impulsivity for the child. Impulsivity in children has been found to be associated with conduct disorders and antisocial behavior, among other problem behaviors (Hoghughi, 1992; Olson et al., 2005; Schweinle, Ickes, Rollings, & Jacquot, 2010). Moreover, impulsivity in the form of low self-control is the core explanatory variable of the general theory of crime (Gottfredson & Hirschi, 1990; Rebellon, Straus, & Medeiros, 2008).

A child who experiences impulsive spanking may come to believe that the punishment results from the characteristics of the parent, rather than for the child's good. When spanking is perceived as parent-centered, it may be more likely to create resentment and anger, undermining the parent-child bond that is critical to preventing antisocial behavior (see Chapters 8 and 9). Impulsive spanking may also be more stressful for children, because it is less predictable and associated with more negative parental emotion. In other words, erratic spankings by an angry parent are probably more stressful for the child than spankings that follow some kind of consistent guidelines (e.g., every time a child throws a ball inside the house after repeated commands to stop).

Effects of Never Spanking

At the other end of the spanking continuum from impulsive spankers are parents who *never* spank. These parents are important to furthering our understanding of the effects of spanking on children. It is widely believed that spanking is sometimes necessary and that without it, children's behavior will become out of control and increasingly antisocial. Although the results of the study presented in the previous chapter demonstrate that spanking increases the probability of antisocial child behavior, they do not refute the prediction of those who believe that never spanking would be harmful because that sample did not include a group who *never* spanked. The no-spanking group in that study were mothers who did not spank in the previous week. But there are 51 other weeks in the year, to say nothing of previous years. The data presented in this chapter permitted us to study the children of mothers who never spanked, as well as those who spanked impulsively

The concerns that parents who never spank will lack effective control and that their children will have behavior problems were put forward at a community meeting in one of the cities where the present study was conducted. The meeting was held to discuss a proposed community initiative to end or reduce spanking. One of the parents attending said, "If you nuts have your way, we're going to be a town with kids running wild!" At the same meeting, those wanting a community-wide effort to reduce or end spanking made exactly the opposite prediction. They argued that, on average, children who are never spanked will have lower rates of delinquency and fewer psychological problems in childhood and as young adults.

The importance of this controversy cannot be overestimated. Some of the most sophisticated defenders of spanking, such as Baumrind and Larzelere (e.g., Baumrind et al., 2002) deny that they approve of spanking. But they say that spanking is a safe and necessary backup. As a consequence, the most crucial test, for both opponents and advocates of spanking, focuses on the children of parents who never spank. However, there does not seem to have been a study conducted that compared never-spanked children with those spanked very rarely. This is a crucial missing link in the research on spanking because spanking only as a backup is the advice, not just of Baumrind and Larzelere, but of almost all the pediatricians and parent educators with whom we have discussed this issue. Although most are now against spanking, they are unwilling to say that children should *never* be spanked.

The data for this study enabled us to identify children in the sample who were never spanked. As a consequence, we can make a start on resolving this critically important issue. Four hypotheses were tested:

1. The more spanking used by the mother, the greater the child's impulsiveness and antisocial behavior.
2. The more impulsive the spanking, the greater the child's impulsiveness and antisocial behavior.

3.   Spanking is associated with antisocial behavior and impulsiveness by the child only when spanking is impulsive.

4.   Children who were never spanked have the lowest levels of antisocial behavior.

Sample and Measures

These hypotheses were tested using data on a representative community sample of mothers of 1,003 children, aged 2 to 14, living in two counties in Minnesota. The data were obtained in 1993 by telephone interviews with the mothers. The children were primarily from two-parent families (95.1%). They were about equally divided between boys (54%) and girls (46%), and their mean age was 8.6 (median 9). The mean and the median age of the mothers was 37. They had been married an average of 13.9 years and had a median of two children living at home (mean = 2.5). Consistent with census data on the socioeconomic composition of these two communities, the sample was almost entirely Caucasian, and 31% of the mothers and 35% of the fathers were college graduates. Additional information on the sample is in Straus & Mouradian (1998).

Measures

Spanking. The mothers were asked how often in the past six months they had spanked, slapped, or hit the child when the child "does something bad or something you don't like, or is disobedient." The response categories, which are taken from those used in the Conflict Tactics Scales (Straus et al., 1998; Straus & Mattingly, 2007), were never, once, twice, 3 to 5 times, 6 to 10 times, 11 to 20 times, and more than 20 times.

   Children who were never spanked were identified on the basis of two questions that asked the mother the age at which spanking was first used and the age at which spanking was used the most. If the mother responded to both of these questions that she never spanked her child, we classified the child as not having been spanked. We used these data to classify the children into the following categories: never (189 children); not in the past six months (408 children); once in the past six months (98); twice in the last six months (81 children); 3 to 5 times (86 children); and 6 or more times (71 children). Thus, even in this low spanking community, only 20% of the children had never been spanked.

Other discipline. We measured non-corporal punishment discipline by asking the mothers how often in the past six months, when the child had done something bad, had done something the mother did not like, or had been disobedient, that she "Talked to him or her calmly about a discipline problem, sent him or her to his or her room, or made him or her do 'time-out,' took away something, or took away some privilege like going somewhere." Response categories were never, once, twice, 3 to 5 times, 6 to 10 times, 11 to 20 times, and more than

20 times. Response categories were transformed to the midpoints of the category (3–5 = 4, 6–10 = 8, 11–20 = 15, more than 20 = 25) and were summed. The resulting non-corporal punishment intervention scale scores ranged from 0 to 75 with a mean of 26.6 and a standard deviation of 19.6. The alpha reliability was .71. The scores were grouped into the following four categories for use in the ANOVAs: 15 times or less frequently (*n* = 326), 16–30 times (*n* = 244), 31–45 times (*n* = 196), and more than 45 times (*n* = 167).

Antisocial behavior by the child. Antisocial behavior was measured by asking the mother about 11 behaviors that involved acting out against other people including the child's family, teachers, and peers. Eight of the items were asked regardless of the age of the child: How often in the past six months the child was cruel or mean to other kids, a bully; cruel, mean to, or insulting to the mother; in denial of doing something he or she really did; hitting a brother or sister; hitting other kids; hitting you or other adults; damaging or destructive to things; and stealing money or something else. The remaining three items depended on the age of the child. Mothers of preschool-age children (2 to 4) were asked how frequently their child "refuses to cooperate; repeats misbehavior after being told not to do it; and misbehaves with a baby sitter or in day care." Mothers of school-age children were asked how frequently their child "disobeys you; is rebellious; and has discipline problems at school." The response categories for all items were: 0 = never, 1 = rarely, 2 = sometimes, and 3 = frequently. The alpha reliability for this scale was .81.

Child impulsiveness. This was measured by two items asking how frequently in the previous six months the child had "temper tantrums, hot temper" and "acts in unpredictable, explosive ways, impulsive." These items were chosen to reflect two often-cited features of impulsivity: acting quickly without apparent thought or a lack of planning, or failing to resist urges (Hoghughi, 1992; Lorr & Wunderlich, 1985; Murray, 1938) and being quick or hot-tempered (Hoghughi, 1992; Monroe, 1970). Response categories for these items were: 0 = never, 1 = rarely, 2 = sometimes, and 3 = frequently. The item scores were transformed to Z scores and summed. The alpha reliability score for this scale was .56. Scale scores were normalized and transformed into ZP scores. The correlation between the child antisocial behavior scale and the child impulsiveness scale measure was .60. Although this is a substantial correlation, 64% of the variance is not shared, leaving open the possibility that the findings on child impulsiveness could differ from those for antisocial behavior. In fact, we expect that impulsive corporal punishment will be more strongly related to child impulsiveness than to antisocial behavior because that relationship could reflect modeling, which is a more direct linking process than the processes which might bring about a relationship with antisocial behavior, such as anger and resentment.

Control variables. The analyses controlled for five characteristics of the families and the children that might influence the relationship between spanking and child behavior problems: the mother's nurturance, the age of the child, the child's sex, the family's socioeconomic status, and the child's level of problem behavior. The *interaction* or *moderating effect* of these five variables was also tested using analysis of covariance. The tests for interaction provide data on whether the effect of spanking is different when one of these five variables is present or absent, or low versus high. An example of a test for an interaction effect is the analysis of the widely held belief that spanking is not harmful when it is done by loving parents. We tested that theory in the previous chapter and in the chapter on the link between spanking and risky sex in adulthood (Chapter 9) and found that the harmful side effects of spanking were present even for children with warm and supportive mothers. The implications for the relation of spanking to crime and violence in society are discussed in Chapter 19.

The Question of Causality

In the previous chapter, we pointed out that if a study finds a correlation between spanking and child behavior, this could mean that the spanking is affecting the child's behavior or that the child's behavior is eliciting spanking. We believe that both are true. That is, misbehavior can lead parents to spank, but if parents do spank, the longitudinal studies, such as the studies on child antisocial behavior (Chapter 6), mental ability (Chapter 10), adult crime (Chapter 15), and several other studies summarized in Chapter 19, have found that spanking tended to make children's behavior worse. We can draw that conclusion because the longitudinal studies included information on the child's behavior at the time of the spanking and then two years later, making it possible to determine whether the problem behavior decreased or increased among children who were spanked. All of the longitudinal studies conducted to date have found that, on average, spanking makes children's behavior worse.

The study described in this chapter did not have follow-up data on the children. However, we were able to take other steps to control for the level of misbehavior that led the parents to spank. We developed a scale to measure the extent to which the mother used discipline methods other than spanking, such as deprivation of privileges, explaining, and time-out. Use of this scale is based on the assumption that parents would not engage in these disciplinary interventions if there were no misbehavior (as perceived by the parent). Therefore, it is plausible to assume that the frequency of these disciplinary interventions reflects the extent of the child's misbehavior. To the extent that this is correct, the nonviolent interventions scale controlled for the misbehavior that led to the corporal punishment.

Prevalence of Spanking and Impulsive Spanking

Prevalence of Spanking

Consistent with all other studies, such as the one on the use of corporal punishment in the United States (Chapter 2), we found that the younger the child, the larger the proportion of mothers who hit their child during the previous six months:

- 59.3% of mothers of children aged 2 to 4
- 45.8% of mothers of children aged 5 to 9
- 20.5% of mothers of children aged 10 to 12
- 14.4% of mothers of children aged 13 to 14

These are high rates, but they are much lower than those found for other representative samples of American children (see Chapter 2 and Giles-Sims et al., 1995; Straus, 2001a). Part of the reason for the lower rate of spanking may be because this study asked about spanking in the previous six months, as compared with the previous year for the other studies. It may also reflect the fact that the study was done in the state of Minnesota, which is a state that has long had a social and cultural climate that is favorable for children. Ever since the Annie E. Casey Foundation started annual publications that compared states on 10 indicators of child well-being, Minnesota has been in the top group. In the 2006 ranking, Minnesota ranked fourth in the nation (Annie E. Casey Foundation, 2006). Minnesota is also a state with a high average level of education, and it is the only state in the United States that has required every county to collect a tax to pay for parenting education. Perhaps most directly related to the relatively low rate of spanking for the mothers in this study is that one half lived in a city that had a Positive Parenting community-wide program to end the use of spanking sponsored by the Minnesota Cooperative Extension Service.

Relation of Spanking and Impulsive Spanking to Child's Antisocial Behavior

Chart 7.1 shows that the more spanking by the mother, the greater the antisocial behavior by the child. This is the same result as was shown in the previous chapter for children in a national sample. However, this study goes beyond the previous chapter in two important ways. The first advance is that it provides data on impulsive spanking. Chart 7.2 shows that impulsive spanking is even more strongly related to antisocial behavior than is spanking in general. The analyses of covariance used to obtain the results in these two charts are in Straus (1998, Tables 1 and 2).

The second advance over the study in the previous chapter is that it identified children who were *never* spanked. This enabled an important issue to be investigated for the first time in any study of spanking. This is whether there is a difference between children whose parents spanked only very rarely and those who did not spank at all. Both Chart 7.1 and 7.2 show that the never-spanked group at the left side of the chart had much less antisocial behavior than any other group, including the second group: children whose mothers did not spank at all in the past six months but had spanked previously. Three of the other five variables we examined were also significantly related to antisocial behavior: (1) the more nurturing the mother, the lower the child's antisocial behavior, (2) girls had lower antisocial behavior scores than boys, and (3) the more nonviolent discipline, the higher the antisocial behavior. This is probably

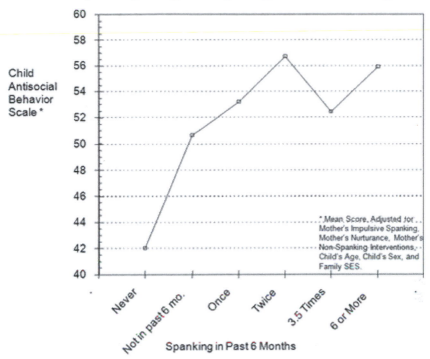

Chart 7.1 The More Spanking, the More Antisocial Behavior

because nonviolent discipline like spanking tends to occur in response to the amount of antisocial behavior.

Context Effects

The analysis for this study was done in a way that investigated whether the effect of spanking depends on whether the spanking was impulsive. The results showed that:

- The relation of spanking to antisocial behavior was greatest for the children whose mothers were most impulsive in using spanking—those who spanked impulsively one half or more of the time (upper line of Chart 7.3).
- The children in the never-spanked group had the lowest antisocial behavior. Thus, any amount of spanking, even when it occurred prior to the past six months, was associated with greater antisocial behavior than that by children of mothers who never used spanking.
- Among mothers who reported only rare impulsive spanking (dotted line in center of Chart 7.3), all five comparisons with children who never experienced spanking showed that the never-spanked children had lower antisocial behavior scores. This means that when there was any impulsive

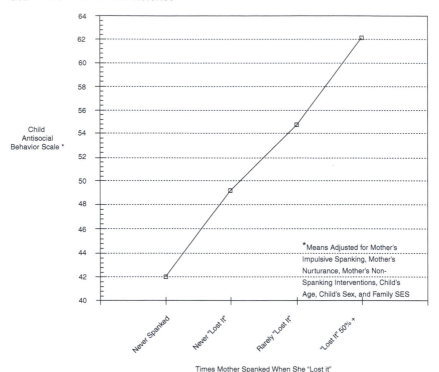

Chart 7.2   The More Impulsive Spanking, the More Antisocial Behavior

spanking in the past, even though there was none in the past six months, or when there was even occasional impulsive spanking, it is associated with more antisocial behavior than by children of mothers who never spanked.

• The solid line at the bottom of Chart 7.3 is for children of mothers who reported no impulsive spanking. This line shows that, even when there was no impulsive spanking, spanking is associated with more antisocial behavior. The bottom line in Chart 7.3 shows a decrease in antisocial behavior for the two highest levels of spanking. However, because mothers who never spank impulsively also are infrequent spankers, there are very few children in those two categories. As a consequence, the seeming decrease is not statistically dependable—see footnote to Table 1 in Straus (1998), and we do not think any importance should be attached to that seeming decrease with more spanking.

We also investigated whether the effect of spanking and impulsive spanking depends on one or more of the five other variables listed in the Hypotheses section. The only one of these five that made a difference was the amount of nurturance provided by the mother. With the exception of one data point, within each level of nurturance, the more spanking and the more impulsive the spanking, the higher

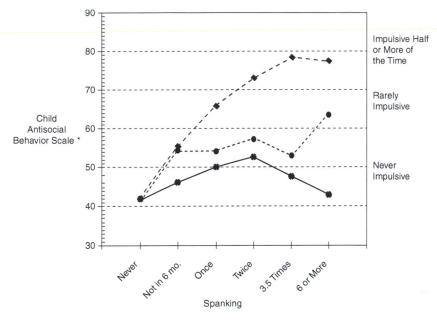

Chart 7.3 Spanking Is Most Strongly Related to Child Antisocial Behavior When Spanking Is Impulsive

*Means adjusted for mother's impulsive spanking, mother's nurturance, mother's non-spanking interventions, child's age, child's sex, and family socioeconomic status.

the average antisocial behavior. Thus, although children of nurturing mothers had lower antisocial behavior scores, spanking still had an important adverse effect.

Child's Impulsive Behavior

The three previous charts are about antisocial behavior by the child. In this section, the focus is on impulsive behavior by the child. Chart 7.4 shows that the more spanking, the more impulsive the behavior of the child. Chart 7.5 shows that the more impulsive the spanking, the more impulsive the child. For impulsive spanking, there is an almost one-to-one increase in child impulsiveness as the mother's impulsive spanking increases, and the differences are large.

The dashed line at the top of Chart 7.6 shows that the relation of spanking to impulsive behavior by the child is greatest when mothers use spanking impulsively half or more of the time. For children of these mothers, even one instance of spanking in the prior six months was strongly associated with children being much more impulsive than among children who did not experience spanking during the six month referent period or who were never spanked.

Among mothers who only rarely were impulsive when spanking, the dotted line in the center of Chart 7.6 shows that as spanking increases, there is

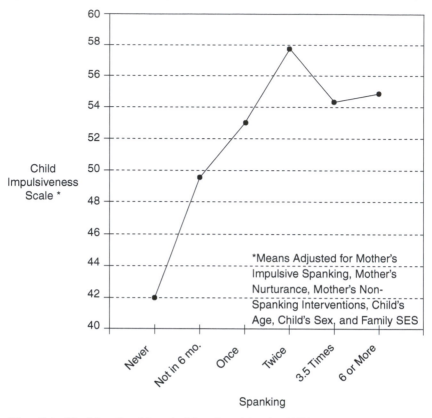

Chart 7.4   The More Spanking, the More Impulsive the Child

a step-by-step increase in child's antisocial behavior. For the most part, any spanking, past or present, was associated with more child impulsiveness than for children in the never-spanked group.

The relation of spanking to impulsiveness of children was weakest, but still present for children of mothers who spanked nonimpulsively (solid line at the bottom of Chart 7.6). As the frequency of spanking increased, impulsiveness increased, but only up to the "twice in the last six months category" of spanking, and then decreased. These decreases were not statistically dependable because there were very few cases in those two groups of children and are best regarded as chance occurrences.

Do the other five variables affect the relation of spanking to impulsive behavior by the child? The statistical tests found that the sex of the child and the socioeconomic status of the family made a difference in the relation of spanking to children's impulsiveness. There was a stronger relation between spanking and impulsive behavior by boys than by girls. Although the statistical analysis showed a significant interaction of family socioeconomic status with spanking, we were unable to identify a meaningful difference between low and

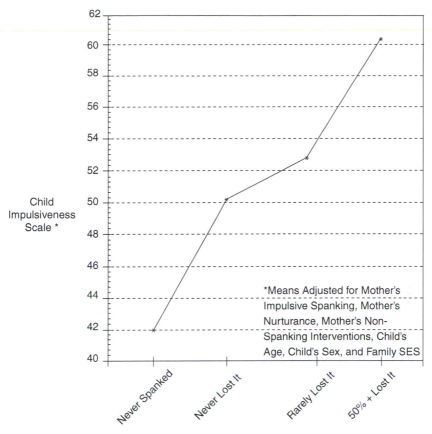

Chart 7.5 The More Impulsive Spanking, the More Impulsive the Child

high socioeconomic status families in the relation of spanking to impulsive behavior by children.

Summary and Conclusions

This study found that the more spanking is used, and the more impulsive it is, the more likely children are to be impulsive and antisocial, even after controlling for five other variables that could influence the effects of spanking. These results cast serious doubt on the recommendation of a conference of pediatric and other child behavior specialists that endorsed the use of spanking with children age 2 to 6, if done by loving parents (Friedman & Schonberg, 1996a). If this view were correct, we should have found that spanking was related to child misbehavior only among older children, and only among children with mothers who were less nurturing. Instead, the results of this study show that

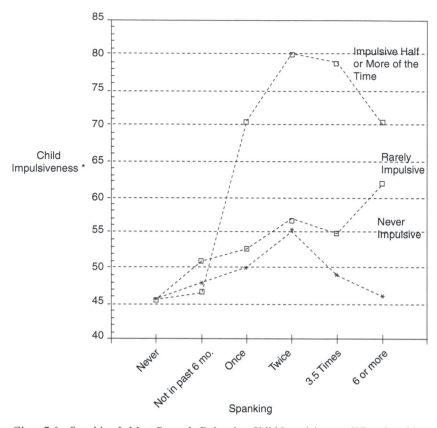

Chart 7.6   Spanking Is Most Strongly Related to Child Impulsiveness When Spanking Is Impulsive

*Means adjusted for mother's impulsive spanking, mother's non-spanking interventions, child's age, child's sex, and family socioeconomic status.

the tendency for spanking to be associated with more antisocial behavior and impulsiveness by the child applies to all age groups, regardless of the level of maternal nurturance—see Straus and Mouradian (1998) for tables giving the detailed results of the analyses of covariance.

Although the relationship between spanking and child behavior problems is weaker for children of mothers who were not impulsive spankers, it was strong enough for there to be a statistically dependable relationship between spanking and child behavior problems, even when spanking is not done impulsively.

Limitations and Strengths of the Study

One type of limitation is the fact that this study measured only two aspects of spanking: frequency and impulsiveness, and there are a number of other aspects needed for a complete understanding of spanking. For example, since conducting the study in this chapter, we developed the Dimensions of Discipline Inventory (Straus & Fauchier, 2011), which includes measures such as the degree to which explanation and support accompany spanking, as well as measures of eight other methods of correcting misbehavior.

The most important limitation of this study is that the findings are based on cross-sectional, rather than longitudinal or experimental, data. We attempted to take into account the fact that spanking is typically a response to child misbehavior by using a scale to measure nonviolent discipline as a proxy for child misbehavior. The results showed that spanking, and especially impulsive spanking, was associated with more child antisocial behavior and impulsiveness regardless of the level of misbehavior that led to the spanking. We interpret this as evidence that when spanking is used in addition to other disciplinary strategies, it tends to make things worse. This interpretation is strengthened by the findings from the longitudinal studies on child behavior (Chapter 6), cognitive ability (Chapter 10), crime in adulthood (Chapter 15), and other longitudinal studies summarized in Chapter 19 and Straus (2001c). These studies found that the more parents respond to misbehavior at Time 1 by spanking, the greater the *increase* in undesirable behavior from Time 1 to Time 2.

This study also has two unique strengths. The first is that, rather than treating spanking as present or absent, or differentiating only on the basis of the chronicity of spanking, the study took into account another of the many other dimensions of spanking—whether it was done impulsively.

A second unique feature of this study is that it identified children who, at least according to the mother, had never experienced spanking. It is particularly important to learn about children who have not been spanked because it is so widely believed that spanking is sometimes necessary (see Chapter 18) and that if parents are not prepared to spank as a backup when other methods have not worked, the child will grow up being out of control. Thus, the inclusion of a never-spanked group in this study begins to fill a void in the literature. It can be considered a starting point for addressing individual and societal concerns about the effects of ending *all* spanking. With these strengths and weaknesses in mind, what can be concluded from this study?

The findings suggest that spanking and impulsive spanking increase the risk of children developing a pattern of impulsive and antisocial behavior. Moreover, we believe that spanking, especially impulsive spanking, are part of the etiology of the high level of violence and crime in society because about one half of parents used spanking impulsively at least some of the time and because the long-term risks associated with corporal punishment have been demonstrated by the longitudinal studies in this book and the many other longitudinal studies listed in Chapter 19.

At present, parents of toddlers who do not spank make up a small but growing portion of the population (see Chapters 2 and 17). What will happen when, as seems likely, no-spanking becomes more widespread? That is likely to happen because of the changes in society described in the concluding chapter.

By 2011, 30 nations have chosen to follow the Swedish example and the recommendations of the European Union and United Nations by enacting laws against spanking by parents. Will it produce a generation of antisocial and out of control children as believed by those who think that spanking is sometimes necessary? The results in this chapter and the experience in Sweden described in Chapters 19 and 20 suggest that the opposite is more likely. The decrease in youth crime and drug abuse in Sweden since passage of the no-spanking law is consistent with that implication.

8   The Child-to-Mother Bond
and Delinquency

There are a number of ironic aspects of spanking. One of the most frequent occurs when a parent spanks a child for hitting another child—which they are more likely to do than for most other misbehaviors. A national survey of 1,012 parents asked what punishment these parents would consider appropriate for three types of misbehavior. For ignoring a request to clean up their room 9% thought spanking was appropriate, for stealing it was 27%, and for deliberately hurting another child 41% approved of spanking (Kane-Parsons and Associates, 1987; see also Sears et al., 1957). The irony is that when parents hit a child to correct the child's hitting, they are inadvertently modeling the very behavior they want the child to avoid. This is one of reasons for the almost complete consistency between studies like those in Part IV and by many longitudinal studies documented in Chapter 19, which have found that the more spanking used by parents, the greater the physical aggression by the child.

Studies that have found that spanking is associated with an increased probability of property crime as a child or adult (Grogan-Kaylor, 2004) are less easily understood than is the link between spanking and aggression. Except for the relatively rare parents who themselves engage in criminal acts, modeling is probably not an important part of the process linking spanking and delinquency. If it is not modeling, what social and psychological processes could account for the link between spanking and delinquency? The study in this chapter was designed to provide data on one of several possible processes. This is the possibility that, when parents spank, it tends to undermine the bond between child and parent, and the weakened bond in turn makes the child less receptive to parental guidance and more vulnerable to peer pressure and other factors that increase the probability of delinquent acts. In this chapter, we address the following questions:

- When spanking is used, does it weaken the bond between a child and his or her parents?
- If the parents who spank show warmth and support, does this avoid weakening the child-to-parent bond?

Kimberly A. Hill is the coauthor of this chapter.

- Do children whose parents correct misbehavior by spanking engage in less or more delinquent behaviors?
- If spanking is done by warm and loving parents, does it override the tendency for spanking to be related to an increased probability of delinquency?

Does Spanking "Teach Him a Lesson"?

The caning of an American teenager in Singapore in the 1990s (Elliott, 1994) received national headlines and public discussion. It brought to the surface the widespread belief in the United States that spanking reduces delinquency. Many letters to the editor and comments on talk shows argued that if parents would go back to the good old-fashioned paddle, there would be less delinquency. The research evidence, however, suggests that the opposite is more likely. For example, in this book:

- Chapter 6 showed that the more spanking used by parents, the greater the probability that the child's antisocial behavior would become worse. However, this study was for young children and for antisocial behavior rather than statutory delinquency.
- The five studies in Part IV all found that spanking was associated with an increased probability of crime later in life as an adult.

A few of the other studies include:

- A longitudinal study by Grogan-Kaylor (2005), which found that, after controlling for six other variables such as family income and cognitive stimulation by the mother, spanking was associated with an increase in antisocial behavior by the child, and that this applied across racial and ethnic groups.
- Welsh (1978) found that almost all the delinquent children in his sample had experienced a great deal of spanking by their parents.
- A study that followed up a large sample of boys from a high-risk area for 35 years found that spanking was associated with an increased probability of conviction of a serious crime as an adult (McCord, 1997).
- Straus (2001a, p. 108) found that, even after controlling for a number of other family characteristics, including socioeconomic status and whether there was violence between the parents, the more spanking the parent reported using, the greater the probability of the child being delinquent.
- Gove and Crutchfield (1982) found a number of parenting variables to be related to delinquency, including spanking, and that after controlling for all other variables, spanking remained significantly related to delinquent behavior.
- Conger (1976) and Rankin and Wells (1990) found that high parental punishment is associated with higher levels of juvenile delinquency. However, their measures of parental punitiveness included non-corporal punishment and yelling at the child. As a consequence, they do not provide direct evidence that spanking *per se* is related to delinquency.

- Simons, Lin, and Gordon (1998) found that adolescent boys who had experienced spanking were more likely to hit a dating partner, even after controlling for a number of factors such as parental involvement and support.

These are just a few of the 88 studies reviewed by Gershoff (2002). Forty-nine of the studies tested the hypothesis that corporal punishment is associated with an increased probability of physical violence and antisocial or criminal behavior as a child and as an adult; of these, 97% found that corporal punishment was associated with an increased probability of physical violence, antisocial behavior, and crime. This degree of consistency of results is extremely rare in any field of science, and perhaps even rarer in child development.

Nevertheless, many of these studies have important limitations. In addition, there are a few well-designed studies that found no relationship between spanking and delinquency (e.g., Agnew, 1993; Simons et al., 1994). Therefore, one purpose of this chapter was to reexamine this issue by testing the hypothesis that spanking is associated with delinquency. The main purpose, however, was to test the theory that one of the reasons spanking increases the probability of delinquency is because spanking undermines the bond between children and parents.

The Child-to-Parent Bond and Delinquency

Spanking and other forms of corporal punishment may stop a specific undesired behavior at the moment, but in the long run, it may teach children to avoid particular behaviors only when they are in the presence of a parent or other authority figure who can impose a penalty, or some other circumstance where the probability of punishment is high. Obviously, that leaves a great deal of opportunity to engage in delinquent and criminal acts. As children grow older, they become less subject to parental observation and, in adolescence, they are usually too big to control by physical force. When this happens, avoiding delinquent behavior is largely dependent on the child having internalized behavioral standards (i.e., on the development of conscience).

Two aspects of spanking are likely to interfere with development of such internalized standards. First, as just noted, spanking places the focus on behaving correctly as a means to avoid punishment, rather than on behaving correctly in order to follow principles such as honesty, courtesy, compassion, prudence, and responsibility—the cognitions and emotions that together make up conscience. When parents spank to teach these principles, children do learn them, but we believe it is despite the spanking, not because of it. There is also a greater risk that some or all of what the parent wants to teach will be inadequately learned because fear and anger interfere with learning (see Chapter 10). The same moral instruction *without spanking* is likely to be more effective in facilitating a well-developed conscience.

A second aspect of spanking that interferes with the development of conscience is the tendency of spanking to weaken the bond between child and parent (Azrin & Holz, 1966; Barnett, Kidwell, & Leung, 1998; Bugental, Johnston,

New, & Silvester, 1998; Mulvaney & Mebert, 2010; Parke, 1969). A strong child-to-parent bond is important because when there is a bond of affection with the parent, children are more likely to accept parental rules, restrictions, and moral standards as their own. These ideas are central to the social control theory of delinquency (Akers & Sellers, 2008; Hirschi, 1969). This theory links delinquent behavior to a weak social bond with parents and with other key institutions of society, such as the church, schools, and the workplace. The central idea of the social control theory is that law-abiding behavior depends, to a considerable extent, on the bond between a child and persons and organizations that represent the moral standards of society. A bond with parents refers to ties of affection and respect that children have for a parent. Hirschi argued that the bond or attachment to parents is the most important variable insulating a child against deviant behavior. It enables the child to internalize the rules for behavior and develop a conscience. The stronger the bond with the parents, the more likely children are to rely on internalized standards learned from parents when tempted to engage in a delinquent behavior (Hirschi, 1969, p. 86).

Hirschi's research and many empirical studies since then have found a link between a weak parent-child bond and juvenile delinquency. To take just four of these studies, Hindelang (1973) replicated Hirschi's study using rural adolescents and found that a weak bond to parents is also significantly related to juvenile delinquency in that environment. Wiatrowski and Anderson (1987) found that the weaker the bond with parents, the higher the probability of delinquency. Rankin and Kern (1994) found that a bond to both parents provides more insulation from delinquency than does a bond with one parent. Eamon and Mulder (2005) studied 420 Hispanic children and found that each increase of one point on the 15-point scale of parent-child attachment was associated with a 9% decrease in the probability of the child being in the high antisocial behavior category.

The relationship between the child-to-parent bond and delinquency is likely to be moderated by other variables, that is, to be contingent on other variables. Seydlitz (1990) found that the relation of some aspects of the bond with parents to juvenile delinquency depends on the age and gender of the adolescent. Several studies have also found an indirect relationship between bonds with parents and delinquency. For example, Agnew (1993) found that a weak bond with parents is associated with an increase in anger or frustration and an increased likelihood of association with delinquent peers, which in turn increases the likelihood of juvenile delinquency. Warr (1993) found that part of the reason for the link between bonding and delinquency occurs because a close child-to-parent bond inhibits forming delinquent friendships. Marcos and Bahr (1988) found both a direct link between bonding and drug abuse and an indirect link through the relation of bonding to greater educational attainment, conventional values, inner containment (the ability to withstand pressure from peers), and religious attachment.

Although there is a large body of evidence showing a link between weak child-to-parent bonds and delinquency, there does not seem to have been a study investigating whether spanking weakens the child-to-parent bond. In fact, Hirschi himself doubts that it does (Hirschi & Gottfredson, 2005). This study was designed to help fill that gap in the chain of evidence linking spanking and delinquency.

Spanking and the Child-to-Parent Bond

If spanking is typically carried out in the hope of raising a well-behaved and law-abiding child, what could explain why so many studies have found that spanking is instead associated with delinquency? Given the many studies just reviewed showing that a weak child-to-parent bond is associated with delinquency, it is plausible to suggest that one of the reasons for the relationship between spanking and delinquency is that spanking undermines the bond between parent and child.

If spanking and physical abuse are conceptualized as low and high points on a continuum of violence against children, a link between spanking and attachment to parents can be inferred from a number of studies that show that physical abuse has an adverse effect on child-to-parent attachment.

- Lyons-Ruth, Connell, Zoll, and Stahl (1987) compared 10 maltreated infants, 18 non-maltreated high-risk infants, and 28 matched low-income controls on the Ainsworth Strange Situation test and found less adequate infant attachment among the maltreated children. (The Strange Situation experiment examines the attachment between very young children and parents.)
- Crittenden (1985) studied 73 mother-infant dyads referred by the welfare department and found that infants who were abused showed an avoidant or ambivalent pattern of attachment, and adequately treated infants showed a secure pattern of attachment.
- Kinard's (1980) review of the literature on child abuse and emotional problems identified other studies showing that child abuse is associated with weak attachment.

Spanking children may be at the low end of the same continuum of parent-to-child violence as physical abuse, but it is also different. Spanking and other forms of corporal punishment are legal and socially approved parent behaviors and, in many communities, are expected parent behaviors (see Chapter 17 and Alvy, 1987; Carson, 1986; Walsh, 2002). Walsh, for example, found that in the previous six months, 61% of a sample of 1,003 mothers of children age 2 to 4 in two Minnesota counties had been advised to spank. Moreover, the children themselves accept the right of parents to spank—but they also resent it (Willow & Hyder, 1998). Similarly, when Cohn and Straus (Straus & Donnelly, 2001a, p. 149) asked 270 students at two New England colleges for their reactions to "the first time you can remember being hit by one of your parents" and also the most recent incident, 42% checked that they "hated him or her" from a list of reactions. Similar views were expressed by the 8- to 17-year-old children in a study by Saunders and Goddard (2010). Rohner, Kean, and Cournoyer's (1991) study of children in St. Kitts is particularly relevant because the right and the obligation of parents to spank is strongly embedded in the culture of that society, and many of the children shared this cultural belief. Despite that, research by Rohner and colleagues of children in St. Kitts, West Indies (Rohner et al., 1991) and research in a poor biracial Southern community in the United States (Rohner, Bourque, & Elordi, 1996) found that spanking was associated with feelings of rejection regardless of whether the children accepted the cultural belief that spanking is appropriate. Feeling rejected by a parent is close enough to a weak child-to-parent bond to suggest that is one of the processes explaining why spanking undermines the child-to-parent bond.

We believe that each spanking chips away at the bond between parent and child. Although a single instance will rarely undermine the bond, Chapters 2 and 10 show that a single instance, ever in a child's lifetime, is very rare. The typical pattern is about 3 times a week for toddlers, and for one half of American children it continues, although with lower frequency, for another six years. These repeated *chips* cumulatively weaken the strength of a parent-child bond. That does not mean that all children who are spanked have a weak bond with their parents, only that a larger percentage of these children than non-spanked children will have a weak bond (see the section in Chapter 1 on "Risk Factors: The Real Meaning of Social Science Results").

Although the studies we reviewed provide a plausible basis for the theory that spanking is related to delinquency, because it undermines the bond between children and parents, the evidence is far from definitive. For example, Baumrind et al. (2002) argue that what seems to be the effect of spanking is really the result of the combination of a lack of parental warmth and nurturance combined with very frequent or severe spanking. The effects of spanking may also depend on the age of the child and the socioeconomic status of the family. For example, as noted previously, it is widely believed that spanking harms only older children (Friedman & Schonberg, 1996a). The research described below, although it is also not definitive, can at least rule out these plausible rival interpretations.

Hypothesis

The studies and theories just reviewed led to the hypothesis that spanking is associated with delinquency because spanking is associated with a reduction in the bond between child and parent, and the weakened bond is in turn associated with an increased level of delinquency.

Sample and Measures

The data for this chapter come from interviews with the random sample of 1,003 mothers of children age 2 to 14 in two small cities and their surrounding counties in Minnesota described in the previous chapter and in Straus (1998). The analysis of the link between spanking and bonding is based on all 915 children for whom complete data was available. The part of the study that examined the link between spanking and delinquency used only the 411 children age 10 to 14 because the concept of delinquency is primarily appropriate for children this age or older.

Measures

Spanking. The mothers were asked how often they spanked, slapped, or hit their child in the past six months: none, once, twice, 3 to 5 times, 6 to 10 times, 11 to 20 times, or more than 20 times, and a parallel question on how often their husband or partner had spanked, slapped, or hit the child in the past six months. We summed these two items to obtain the measure of spanking.

Child-to-mother bond. We used a scale consisting of two items believed to reflect the aspect of child-to-parent bond that Hirschi identifies as effectual identification. The mothers were asked how often in the past six months their child showed affection or closeness toward them, and how often their child did things to please them. The response categories were: none = 0, rarely = 1, sometimes = 2, and frequently = 3. These two items were combined to form the child-to-mother bond scale. It should be noted that this scale is based on interviews with mothers. Thus, the scale measures the mother's perception of the child's behavior. This may be a less adequate measure than one based on the child's report. If so, it would mean that the results to be presented probably underestimate the relationship between spanking and the child-to-mother bond.

Delinquency. We asked the mother about the extent to which the child was rebellious; cruel or mean to other kids, a bully; cruel, mean to, or insulting to her (the parent); damaging or destructive to things; hitting other kids; hitting her or other adults; having discipline problems in school; stealing money or something else; drinking or using drugs; hanging out with kids who get into trouble; having school problems; and getting into trouble with kids he or she hangs around with. The response categories were: never = 0, rarely = 1, sometimes = 2, and frequently = 3. The scale is the sum of the scores for these 12 behaviors and could range from 0 (never for all 12) to 36 (frequently for all 12). A limitation of this measure is that mothers do not know about all delinquent behavior. As a consequence, the results may underestimate the relationship between spanking and delinquency. The alpha coefficient of reliability for the delinquency scale is .79.

Support and nurturance provided by the mother. Many other things could affect the relation of the child-to-mother bond and delinquency and some of these were controlled when we tested the hypothesis that spanking weakens the bond and that a weaker bond is part of the explanation for the link between spanking and delinquency. One of the most important of these other variables is the amount of support and nurturance provided by the mother. To investigate the role of nurturance, we used a scale composed of three questions about the mother's behavior toward her child in the past six months, whether she: comforted and helped him or her when the child had some kind of problem; hugged or kissed the child or did something else to show love; or talked to the child about things that bothered the child. The response categories were: 0 = never, 1 = rarely, 2 = about one half the time, 3 = usually, and 4 = always or almost always. The responses were summed to create the nurturance scale, with the possible range of scores between 0 and 12. Because of the small number of cases with scores below 7, scores of 4 through 7 were combined into one category.

Control variables. The analysis also included three demographic variables: gender, age of child, and socioeconomic status. Each of these variables is known to be related to spanking and delinquency, so leaving them uncontrolled could result in spurious findings. We also did an analysis to find out if the relation between spanking and delinquency is different among boys than among girls.

Spanking, Bonding, and Delinquency

Chart 8.1 shows the tendency for spanking to be associated with higher delinquency that has been found in many previous studies. Considering that spanking is used to correct misbehavior and, at the same time, intended to encourage

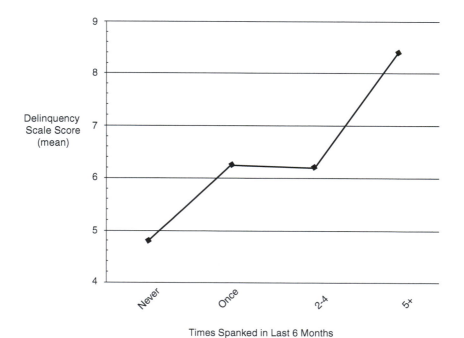

Chart 8.1   The More Spanking, the More Delinquency, Even after Controlling for Nurturance, Age, Gender of the Child, and Socioeconomic Status

correct behavior, the question of why it seems to do the opposite needs to be answered.

Chart 8.2 provides a start to answering that question. Reading from left to right, it shows that the more spanking by the mothers in this study, the weaker the bond of the child to the mother. Chart 8.2 begins to provide part of the explanation of why spanking is associated with more rather than less delinquency. The results in this chart suggest that it is because spanking undermines a bond to parents that, as we explained earlier, is extremely important for moral development and for avoiding criminal behavior.

Defenders of spanking such as Baumrind and Larzelere agree with the importance of the bond between child and parents for the development of conscience. They do not, however, think that spanking itself undermines the bond between parent and child. They propose that the weak bond is because some of the parents who spank are also cold and harsh parents. According to them, the inclusion of these parents with all other parents who spank explains the relationship. Chart 8.3 shows that the more nurturing the mother, the stronger the child-to-mother bond. As a consequence, to conclude that there is something

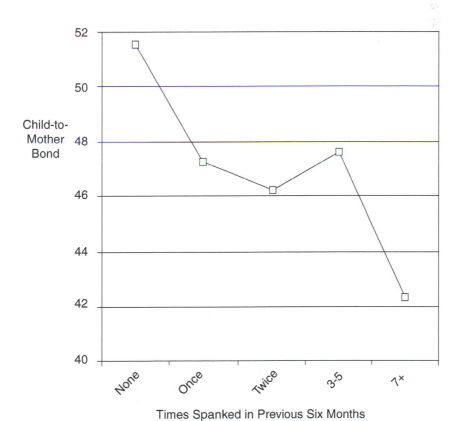

Chart 8.2   The More Spanking, the Weaker the Child-to-Mother Bond

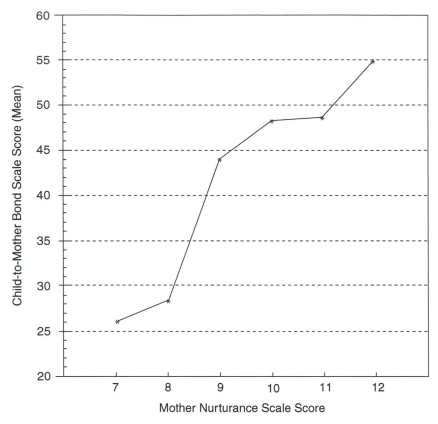

Chart 8.3   The More Nurturing the Mother, the Stronger the Child-to-Mother Bond*
*Controlling for spanking, age, gender of the child, and socioeconomic status.

about spanking itself that explains the link between spanking and a weak child-to-parent bond requires controlling for the amount of nurturance by the parents, and this is what we did, as explained in the next section.

Does a Weak Child-to-Parent Bond Help Explain the Link between Spanking and Delinquency?

We used a statistical technique called path analysis to test the theory that a weakened child-to-parent bond resulting from spanking is one of the processes that explain why so many studies have found that spanking is a risk factor for delinquency. Chart 8.4 summarizes the results of the path analysis we conducted to test that theory (see Appendix for the details). Each of the arrows or paths in Chart 8.4 indicates a relationship that was hypothesized and was found to apply to this sample of children. An important aspect of Chart 8.4 to keep in mind is that the paths represent relationships that hold after controlling for all

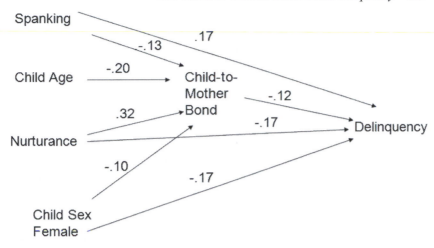

Chart 8.4   Paths to Delinquency

the other variables in the chart. That is, each is over and above the effects on delinquency of all four other variables in the analysis.

Two paths bear most directly on the theory that a weakened child-to-parent bond is one of the reasons spanking is associated with an increased probability of delinquency. The first is the path with a coefficient of −.13 going from spanking in the upper left to child-to-mother bond in the middle. The second is the path with a coefficient of −.12 going from child-to-mother bond to delinquency. The negative coefficient of −.13 in the path from spanking to child-to-mother bond shows that, among the children in this study, the more often they were hit by their parents, the weaker the child-to-mother bond. The −.12 path from child-to-mother bond to delinquency means that the stronger the child-to-mother bond, the less delinquency. In short, as hypothesized, spanking weakens the child-to-mother bond, and because the bond has been weakened, it cannot have the protective effect that it would have otherwise.

The path at the top of Chart 8.4 with a coefficient of .17 shows that spanking, in and of itself, has a direct relation to delinquency, even when controlling for all four of the other variables. This means that, in addition to the five variables we investigated, there are other processes that are set in motion by spanking that make children more vulnerable to delinquency, which we did not include in this study. For example, we found that spanking is associated with an increased chance that the child will be impulsive (Chapter 7), and that spanking is related to lower mental ability and lower school achievement (Chapter 10). Impulsiveness and doing poorly in school both increase the risk of delinquency (Farrington & Welsh, 2006). In addition, spanking is related to low self-esteem (Coopersmith, 1967), more feelings of alienation (Straus & Gimpel, 2001), and a higher level of anger and rage (Tsang, 1995). These are plausible intervening processes because each can increase the probability of delinquency. They were not included in the statistical analysis for this chapter because those variables were not available for this particular sample. They may be what accounts for the upper path in Chart 8.4.

The path with a value of .32 from nurturance to child-to-mother bond shows that the more nurturing the mother, the stronger the bond. It is the largest path in this chart, which means that nurturing behavior by the mother has more influence on the child-to-mother bond than any of the other variables. The −.17 path from nurturance to delinquency shows that the more nurturing the mother, the less delinquency. These results are consistent with many other studies that have found that warm and positive parenting is associated with a lower risk of delinquency.

The path from being a girl to delinquency (−.17) at the bottom of Chart 8.4 is consistent with many studies showing that girls are much less likely than boys to engage in delinquent behavior. Finally, the −.20 path from child's age to child-to-mother bond shows that older children have a weaker bond to their mothers than do younger children.

Does the Relation of Spanking to Bonding Depend on Other Variables?

It is widely believed that if spanking is used by warm and nurturing parents and is restricted to preschool-age children, it has no harmful side effects (Friedman & Schonberg, 1996a). One of the advantages of a path analysis such as in Chart 8.4 is that each path represents a result that is in addition to the effect of all the other factors. As a consequence, we can say that both spanking and parental nurturance have their own separate relationship to delinquency; or put somewhat differently, spanking is related to delinquency regardless of the age of the child and the nurturance of the parent (in this study, the mother).

Because the question of whether the adverse effects of spanking are really just a reflection of insufficient parental warmth and support, we also tested the interaction of spanking with parental nurturance. This determines if the relation of spanking to the child-to-mother bond and delinquency depends on the extent to which the mother is warm and loving. The analysis did not find a contingent effect that is statistically dependable. Keeping the limitations of cross-sectional data in mind, this indicates that, even when used by highly supportive parents, spanking is linked to a weakened bond and higher delinquency. This is an extremely important result because it contradicts the almost universal belief in many societies that if spanking is used by warm and loving parents, it does not have harmful side effects.

Similarly, we found that the relationship of spanking to child-to-mother bond was parallel for boys and girls, but the relationship was stronger for boys. For both boys and girls, the more spanking, the weaker the child-to-mother bond. This is in addition to the finding that the bond of boys to mothers is, on average, lower than the bond of girls to mothers. The combination is likely to be part of the explanation for the higher delinquency rate among boys.

Summary and Conclusions

The results show that:

- The more spanking used by mothers, the lower the child-to-mother bond. The results in Chapter 9 for an entirely different sample show the same tendency for spanking to weaken the bond between children and parents.
- The tendency for spanking to be associated with a weak child-to-mother bond applies to children whose mothers were high in nurturance as well as those with low-nurturance mothers.
- The lowered child-to-mother bond associated with spanking is one of the processes linking spanking and delinquency.
- The analysis controlled for nurturance by the mother. Thus, it is unlikely that the underlying link between spanking and delinquency is explained by lack of nurturance.

One of the important results of this study is the parallel, but opposite effects of spanking by mothers and nurturance by mothers. Both spanking and parental nurturance have an indirect effect on delinquency. Both are related to the bond between the children and their mothers in this sample, but in opposite directions. Spanking is associated with a weaker bond, and nurturance with a stronger bond. So, by weakening the bond, spanking is associated with an increased probability of delinquency, whereas by strengthening the child-to-mother bond, nurturance is associated with a decrease in the probability of delinquency. In addition to these indirect effects on delinquency, spanking and nurturance have about the same direct effect on delinquency (the path coefficients are .17 for both), but in the opposite direction.

The relationship between child-to-mother bond and delinquency, although significant, is not very large. This is consistent with the principle that delinquency determined in multiple ways, and therefore a single risk factor cannot have a strong relationship. To take a simple example, the data on child-to-parent bonds in this study included only the child-to-mother relationship. Based on Rankin and Kern (1994), who found that a bond to two parents provides more insulation from delinquent behavior than attachment to one parent, it is likely that there would be a stronger effect if the study had also been able to include data of the child-to-father bond.

Some Cautions

The results should be interpreted with caution because they are based on cross-sectional data and depend entirely on the report of the mothers who were interviewed. As noted, there is also no information on the bond of the children in the study to their fathers. The limitation of cross-sectional data is an especially important limitation because the relationship between spanking and delinquency could reflect the fact that parents use spanking in response to delinquency (i.e., that delinquency causes spanking). We believe that is what happens. However, we also believe that using spanking, although it may work in the immediate situation, is counterproductive in the long run. That is what was found by the longitudinal studies in the chapters on child behavior (Chapter 6), mental ability (Chapter 10), adult crime (Chapter 15), and several other longitudinal studies described in Chapter 19. These studies followed up children to examine the long-term effects of spanking and found that when parents use spanking to correct misbehavior, it boomerangs and is associated with a subsequent increase in problem behavior. As a consequence, we discuss the findings from that perspective and focus on the processes that make spanking counterproductive in the long run, even though spanking may work in the immediate situation.

Other Processes Linking Spanking and Delinquency

The focus of this chapter emphasizes the notion that one of the reasons why spanking is related to more, rather than less, delinquency is the tendency of spanking to undermine the child-to-parent bond, which in turn makes the child more vulnerable to delinquent influences. As pointed out previously, there are many other variables that are related to both child-to-parent bonds and to delinquency. For example, this chapter shows that there is a strong relationship between maternal nurturance and child-to-mother bonding. Thus, parenting strategies to insulate a child from delinquency must include far more than just not spanking. It must also include warm and nurturing interaction with the child. But this does not mean that the combination of warmth and avoiding spanking are sufficient. For example, studies of other aspects of the control theory of delinquency indicate the need to establish clear standards and rules, and to monitor the child's behavior and enforce these rules. Without clear rules and standards for behavior, children can interpret warmth and absence of spanking as parental approval for whatever a child does. In respect to physical aggressiveness by the child, for example, Sears et al. (1957) found that children of parents who avoided spanking were less aggressive to other children, but only if the parents also had clear rules about not hitting others.

It is also crucial to keep in mind that a strong bond to parents will only decrease delinquency if the parents exemplify socially legitimate behavior. A strong child-to-parent bond can *increase* the probability of deviant behavior if the parents exemplify antisocial and criminal behavior. This is illustrated by the research of Jensen and Brownfield (1983) who found that attachment to non-drug using parents decreases the likelihood of adolescent drug use, whereas attachment to drug-using parents increases the likelihood of the child's drug use. Similarly, Foshee and Bauman (1992) found that among the children of smokers, the stronger the attachment, the more likely the child was to smoke.

Finally, we want to stress that physical assaults in the form of spanking are only one mode of punitive child rearing. The Dimensions of Discipline Inventory (Straus & Fauchier, 2011), for example, measures three punitive methods of correcting misbehavior (corporal punishment, verbal/psychological aggression, and deprivation of privileges), five nonpunitive methods (diversion, explain/teach, ignore misbehavior, monitoring, reward), and one that combines punitive and nonpunitive methods of correction (penalty tasks and restorative behavior). Psychological attacks on a child in the form of yelling, nagging, scolding, swearing at the child, demeaning the child, or frequent *grounding* for long periods are as highly or more strongly correlated with delinquency than physical attacks on a child (Briere & Runtz, 1988; O'Hagan, 1993; Vissing, Straus, Gelles, & Harrop, 1991). One of the probable reasons for such findings is that these approaches, like spanking, undermine the bond of children to parents and, therefore, the ability of parents to supervise and influence the child.

Many factors affect the relationship between spanking and delinquency. The evidence in this chapter, however, (as well as in the next chapter), suggest that the tendency of spanking to weaken the child-to-parent bond is an important part of the process leading from spanking to an increased, rather than a decreased, probability of delinquency.

9   Spanking and Risky Sex

The consequences of unprotected sex, such as unwanted pregnancy and sexually transmitted diseases, may be greater for youth than for adults because these events can drastically alter a young person's entire life trajectory. This possibility strikes understandable fear in the hearts of parents and concern on the part of the nation. The actions taken based on those fears and concerns, however, can be counterproductive, such as when the promotion of sexual abstinence denies youth information and access to contraceptives (Kirby, 2002). In families, parental fear and anxiety over sexual activity may lead parents to lash out physically to control sexual behavior, such as slapping a child for engaging in activities that might have involved sex. This can be counterproductive because, as shown in the previous chapter, the side effects include weakening the child-to-parent bond, and this can decrease the influence parents have and, therefore, increase rather than decrease the probability of risky sex—sexual behavior that puts a young person at greater risk for an unwanted pregnancy or a sexually transmitted disease.

Research on the etiology of risky sex has found that it is related to experiencing childhood sexual abuse (Messman-Moore, Walsh, & DiLillo, 2010) and childhood physical abuse (Elliott, Avery, Fishman, & Hoshiko, 2002). Elliott found that girls ages 14 to 17 who experienced physical violence from parents had a 3.5 times greater rate of risky sex. However, that study used a measure of violent parent-child interactions that included a broad range of violent acts in addition to corporal punishment. A 30-year follow-up study of abused children (Wilson & Widom, 2008) also found that abuse was related to risky sex. It is possible that the relationship between broad measures of physical abuse and risky sexual behavior also applies to spanking, even though spanking is a culturally approved form of parental violence.

Although there has been a great deal of research on the side effects of spanking, we did not find any empirical studies that examined whether spanking was associated with an increased probability of risky sex. This chapter presents the results of two studies that did investigate whether there is a link between spanking and risky sex. Perhaps more important, both also investigated

Rose A. Medeiros is the coauthor of Study 1 in this chapter.

processes that might explain why spanking is related to risky sex. Thus, using these two separate studies, we addressed the following questions.

Questions Addressed

Study 1: Risky Sex by High School Students

- How frequent is risky sex among a sample of high school students?
- Were the students who were spanked more likely to have risky sex?
- If spanking is linked to risky sex among high school students, is it because spanking is associated with one or more of the following:
  - Weakened child-to-parent bond
  - Reduced self-esteem
  - Lower academic achievement
  - Increased risk of sexual victimization
  - Traditional gender roles
  - Low self-control
  - Approval of violence

Study 2: Unprotected Sex by University Students

- Are university students who were spanked in childhood more likely to have risky sex?
- Is spanking associated with a child who is low in self-control and high in violence approval?
- Are low self-control and high approval of violence part of the explanation of why spanking is associated with an increased probability of risky sex?

Study 1: Risky Sex by High School Students

We began the research in this chapter by drafting a causal diagram that included the variables and links just discussed, as well as a number of others. Then we looked for a data set that included as many of the variables of interest and related variables as possible. By a stroke of luck, we found such a data set in our own backyard. It was a study of students in the Durham, New Hampshire high school. This study was conducted at the request of parents and students to provide information that might help address the concerns about teen pregnancy and sexually transmitted diseases mentioned in the introduction to this chapter. The study was intended to provide information on a variety of student health-related behaviors (i.e., substance use, drinking, etc.) and serve as a baseline for future programs intended to encourage healthy behavior by students.

The sample consisted of 440 students in the 9th through 12th grades of a single high school in New Hampshire. This school is located in a university community and serves an almost all-White, high-average-education population. The students were surveyed during the 1992–1993 school year. The sample included equal numbers of males and females and approximately equal numbers of students from each grade level. Most students were 16 or 17 years old. A little over two thirds lived with both parents. Eleven percent lived with a parent and a stepparent. About one third of students said they had average grades of B+ or better, and about an additional third of students reported a grade average of B or B–. About one quarter of students received average grades of C or C+, and less than 10% received grades that averaged lower than a C.

The Child-to-Parent Bond

What especially drew us to this sample was that it included a measure of alienation from parents, which is the opposite end of the continuum from a close child-to-parent bond. If there is a link between spanking and risky sexual behaviors, it is not necessarily traceable to a single incident of being hit as a teenager. Parents who slap a child who has failed to come home at a reasonable hour probably had used spanking for years when the child was younger. As a consequence, as evidenced by the results in Chapter 8, the child-to-parent bond may have been weakened. If spanking interferes with the quality of parent-child relationships as was shown in that chapter, it suggests that spanking will be linked to an increased probability of children engaging in problematic behaviors, including risky sex. This is because a weakened bond between children and parents decreases the influence of parents in setting standards for many problematic behaviors (Akers & Sellers, 2008; Hirschi, 1969). The results of several studies are consistent with this theory because they find that a weak parent-to-child relationship is related to an increased probability of sexual intercourse during the teenage years (Danziger, 1995; Metzler, Noell, Biglan, Ary, & Smolkowski, 1994; Moore, 1998; Resnick et al., 1997) or a pregnancy at an early age (Danziger, 1995; Pick & Andrade Palos, 1995).

A weakened parent-to-child bond may also be linked to risky sex by less direct but still important processes. For example, as was shown in the previous chapter, spanking is associated with an increased probability of delinquency. Numerous studies have found that delinquent children tend to associate with delinquent peers (Hirschi, 1969; Matsuenda & Anderson, 1998), and other research shows that associating with delinquent peers increases sexual risk taking by adolescents (Metzler et al., 1994). Thus, spanking may also be linked to risky sex because spanking is associated with an increase in delinquent peers, which then may then lead to an increased likelihood of risky sexual behavior.

Measure of Risky Sex

Risky sex can be broadly defined as sexual activities that increase the likelihood of two life-altering events: pregnancy and contracting a sexually transmitted disease. Because of the negative impact of both sexually transmitted diseases and childbearing on adolescents' lives and development, any behavior that increases the likelihood of these events can be considered risky. Frequently used measures of risky sex include: age at first intercourse (Danziger, 1995; Murray, Zabin, Toledo-Dreves, & Luengo-Charath, 1998; Pick & Andrade Palos, 1995), number of sexual partners (Lucke, 1998; Metzler et al., 1994), and nonuse of contraception (including condoms; Kowaleski-Jones & Mott, 1998; Lucke, 1998; Metzler et al., 1994; Pick & Andrade Palos, 1995). The items used to measure risky sex in this chapter are consistent with the literature on risky sex; this study does, however, include more items than was typical of studies in our literature review. Rather than relying on just one indicator of risky sex, nine behaviors were used to create a measure of risky sex.

- Ever had sexual intercourse
- Age at first sexual intercourse
- Number of sex partners
- Frequency of condom use
- Frequency of birth control pill use
- Frequency of the use of other contraception
- Number of times respondent has purchased condoms in the past year
- Number of times the respondent has had sex in the past year
- Whether or not the respondent has had or caused a pregnancy

The more of these nine indicators a student reported, the higher the score on the risky sex scale. (Further information on the scale is in the Appendix.)

Prevalence of Spanking

Just over two thirds of these high school students reported that their parents had spanked at some point in their life (see Appendix Table A9.1). This is a high percentage, but it is also a much lower percentage than the 90% to 98% found in Chapter 1 and those typically found by surveys of college students (Berger, Knutson, Mehm, & Perkins, 1987; Bryan & Freed, 1982; Deley, 1988; Graziano et al., 1992). The difference may stem from the fact that New England is the region with the lowest rates of use and approval of spanking (Flynn, 1994, 1996b), and the fact that the students are from a high school serving a university community with parents who, on average, tend to have a high level of education. Even allowing for these regional and community characteristics, because ages 2 to 4 are peak ages for spanking, it is likely that at least some of the almost one third of students who reported never experiencing spanking did in fact experience some spanking, but were too young at the time to recall the experience.

The peak age of spanking reported by these students was around 8 years of age. Again, that is likely influenced by the fact that few people remember events that happened when they were only 2 to 4 years old, which are the ages when the most parents report using spanking (see Chapter 1). On average, spanking for this sample ended around age 10, which is two or three years younger than the national figure. During the year they were spanked the most, these students reported that it occurred an average of 2.9 times a year by their father and 2.8 times a year by their mother. This is an atypically low frequency of spanking. As in other studies, boys were spanked slightly more often than girls (3.0 versus 2.7 times) by their father, but reported the same average number of incidents of spanking by their mother.

For the analysis, students were divided into five groups. Those who reported experiencing no spanking were the first group (39% of the sample). Those who reported spanking were divided into quartiles based on their score on the spanking scale. Group 2 consisted of the one quarter of students who experienced the least spanking. Each consecutive quartile group experienced increasing duration and frequency of spanking. On average, the students in category five (those who experienced the most spanking) were spanked until almost 13 years of age (until 12.6 years old by mother and 12.8 years old by father) and were older the year they were spanked most often (10.5 years). The frequency of spanking in the year that they were spanked the most was about 4 times by their father and about 3 times by their mother.

Prevalence of Risky Sexual Behavior

Almost one half of students (42%) reported having had sexual intercourse at least once. This is very close to the national average for 2009 of 46% (Centers for Disease Control and Prevention, 2010b). The percentages for boys and girls were quite similar. The average age for first having sex was about 14.5 years old. Of the students who reported having had sex, the average number of partners was three. The average number of times they had sex in the past year was 31.5, with males reporting a slightly higher number than females (33.5 versus 29.5). Except for the fact that boys reported somewhat more frequent sex, the sexual behavior of the boys and the girls in this sample was remarkably similar, as was also found by the 2009 Youth Risk Behavior Survey (Center for Disease Control and Prevention, 2010b). Students who had sexual intercourse typically had been in their current dating relationships longer (an average of 11 months versus an average of 3 months).

Of the students who had sex at least once, 17% had never used a condom, 58% had never used birth control pills, and 83% had never used *other* contraceptives. These categories were not mutually exclusive, and there is overlap between them. The mean number of times that they purchased condoms in the past year was 2.7. Only 8% had never used any form of contraception. This is a remarkable figure because it means that almost all sexually active students in this school (92%) had used contraception at least once.

Despite the high use of contraception, 8% of the students who had sex experienced pregnancy, but they were not necessarily the students who had never used contraceptives. This included 5.3% of boys who said they had impregnated a sexual partner and 10.4% of girls who reported having been pregnant. This large difference in pregnancy rate may have occurred for a number of reasons; for example, the male partner may not have known because the female partner did not disclose the pregnancy to the boy who was responsible, the sexual partners of some of the girls who became pregnant may have attended a different school, or they may have no longer been in high school.

Links between Spanking and Risky Sex

Chart 9.1 graphs the relationship of the score on the spanking scale to the risky sex scale. It shows that students who experienced the most spanking (the two groups at the right of the chart) also had the highest risky sex scores. Statistical tests comparing those two groups found that, after holding constant

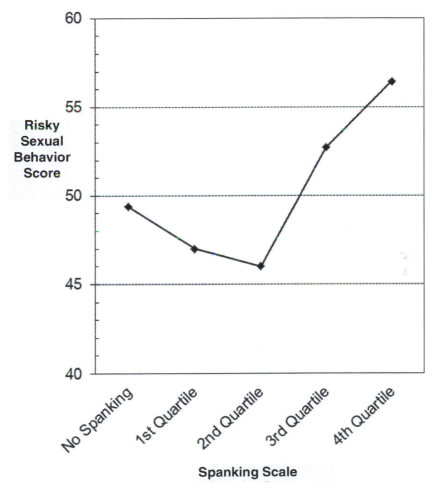

Chart 9.1 Students Who Experienced the Most Spanking Were Most Likely to Engage in Risky Sexual Behavior

the sex of the student and socioeconomic status of the student's family, students in the two groups who experienced the most spanking had risky sex scores that were higher than students who experienced little or no spanking (Groups 1, 2, and 3).

Chart 9.1 shows that spanking is related to risky sex, but it does not provide information on the process that could explain why spanking increases the probability of risky sex that was discussed in the introduction to this chapter. For example, spanking might be related to risky sex if spanking weakens the bond to parents. To investigate these issues, we used a method called structural equation modeling. The data that were available made it possible to examine five explanations for the relation of spanking to risky sex. We used this method to test the theory that spanking is associated with an increased probability of the following five variables, each of which in turn is associated with an increased probability of risky sex.

- Alienation from parents
- Lower school performance
- Belief in traditional gender roles
- Sexual victimization
- Low self-esteem

Information on the measures used to obtain the data on these five variables is in the Appendix. It should be noted that the data on sexual victimization was obtained by questions that are more applicable to victimization by peers rather than molestation by an adult or incest.

Paths from spanking. Chart 9.2 shows the interrelationships among the variables included in our study. We had expected spanking to be related to all five variables in the center of Chart 9.2 and to sexual risk taking at the right side of the chart. However, only some of those hypothesized relations were found. The heavy black arrows in Chart 9.2 show that spanking is directly related to beliefs in traditional gender roles and to alienation from parents. Because alienation from parents is very similar to a weak child-to-parent bond, these results confirm those reported in the previous chapter—that spanking is associated with a weakened child-to-parent bond. The present findings suggest that spanking increases the probability of alienation from parents (.46), which in turn is associated with an increased probability of risky sex (.57). These are the largest coefficients in the model.

Sexual victimization, self-esteem, and risky sex. The findings for this sample also show, as expected, that students who had been sexually victimized (i.e., had a sexual behavior forced on them) were more likely to engage in risky sex (see Appendix for the measure of sexual victimization). It is important to note that, although having been sexually victimized may lead to risky sex, it is also possible that engaging in risky sex increases the probability of being sexually victimized.

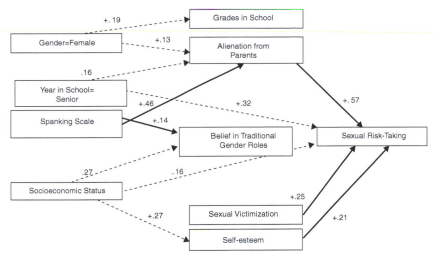

Chart 9.2 Paths from Spanking to Risky Sex

The results for self-esteem are the reverse of what was predicted. The arrow from self-esteem to risky sex indicates that high self-esteem is linked to more risky sex when all other variables are controlled. But when only self-esteem and risky sex are examined, without controlling for other variables, self-esteem is linked to less risky sex. At the time this study was planned, we were aware only of studies showing that self-esteem is associated with positive outcomes in many spheres of life (e.g., Covington, 1989; Rosenberg, Schooler, & Schoenbach, 1989). Since then, however, two critiques of the research on self-esteem have been published disputing the idea that self-esteem has across-the-board benefits. They point to research showing that high self-esteem can be associated with more problem behavior (Baumeister, 2001; Baumeister, Heatherton, & Tice, 1993; Emler, 2002). These reviews suggest that some people with very high self-esteem may not engage in enough self-appraisal of their behavior. This hypothesis might help to explain our unexpected finding that higher self-esteem was linked to more risky sex. Although some of the results may be difficult to understand, the key result from Study 1 is that spanking is associated with an increased probability of alienation from parents, and alienation from parents, in turn, is associated with an increased probability of risky sex.

Study 2: Unprotected Sex by University Students

Study 2 was designed to test two hypotheses. Both hypotheses test the idea that the more spanking experienced as a child, the greater the probability of risky sex as a young adult. The difference between the two hypotheses is in the process or mechanism that could explain why spanking is associated with risky sex later in life. The first hypothesis is that spanking leads to low self-control, and that low self-control is associated with risky sex. This hypothesis is based on assuming that risky sex tends to be an impulsive act that is more likely to occur when there is low self-control.

Our second hypothesis was that spanking is associated with approval of violence, and that the more violence approval, the greater the probability of coercing a partner into sex without a condom. This hypothesis reflects the fact that we measured risky sex as the percent who reported one or more instances in which they said they, "Made my partner have sex without a condom." This is both a measure of sexual coercion and risky sex because it is about coercion to engage in a risky sexual behavior. The question is from the sexual coercion scale of the revised Conflict Tactics Scales (Straus, Hamby, Boney-McCoy, & Sugarman, 1996).

The sample was composed of the 14,252 university students who participated in the International Dating Violence Study and were in a romantic relationship. This is the same sample as was analyzed for Chapters 3, 13, and 16. A detailed description of the study, including the questionnaire and all other key documents and previous publications is available on the website (pubpages.unh.edu/~mas2) and from the Inter-university Consortium for Political and Social Research where the data file has been deposited. Most of the data were obtained by administering a questionnaire during regularly scheduled classes. The analyses either controlled for gender or were conducted separately for male and female students.

Corporal punishment was measured by a question from the Personal and Relationships Profile (Straus et al., 2010), "When I was less than 12 years old, I was spanked or hit a lot by my mother or father," with the following response categories: 1 = strongly disagree, 2 = disagree, 3 = agree, and 4 = strongly agree. The measure of self-control was a six-item scale described in Rebellon et al. (2008). For the present study, we used a cutoff score of the lower boundary of the top fifth of the sample as the criterion measure of high self-control. Violence approval was measured by the eight-item violence approval scale of the Personal and Relationships Profile (Straus et al., 2010). High violence approval participants were those in the top scoring fifth of the sample.

Relation of Spanking to Risky Sex

Chart 9.3 shows that the more a student was spanked before age 12, the greater the likelihood that he or she would insist on having sex without a condom. It also shows that this relationship applies to both men and women.

Chart 9.4 provides the results of the test of the two hypotheses about the processes or mechanism that might explain why having been spanked is related to this aspect of risky sex. The numbers on the path arrows are the percentages by which the variable at the left are associated with an increased or decreased probability of the variable at the right. These are based on a logistic regression analysis that also controlled for the age and sex of the student, education of the mother and father, length of the dating relationship, and the score on a scale to measure a tendency to avoid disclosing socially undesirable characteristics (the

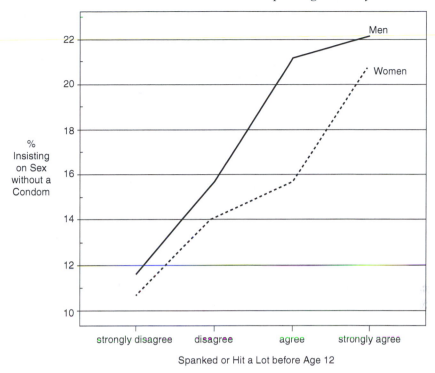

Chart 9.3   The More Spanking, the Greater the Percent Who Insisted on Sex without a Condom

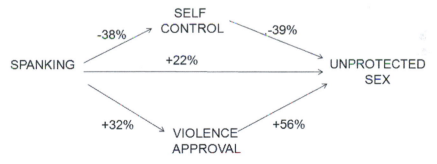

Chart 9.4   Links between Spanking as a Child and Unprotected Sex by University Students

limited disclosure scale of the Personal and Relationships Profile (Straus et al., 2010; Straus & Mouradian, 1999). High self-control and high violence approval students are those in the high scoring fifth of the samples. The middle arrow in Chart 9.4 shows the same relationship as was graphed in Chart 9.3—that the more spanking, the greater the probability of insisting on sex without a condom. The additional contributions of the results in Chart 9.4 are the path arrow at the top and the bottom of Chart 9.4. They indicate two of the processes that explain why spanking is related to risky sex.

Self-control. The top left path of Chart 9.4 shows that spanking is associated with a 38% *reduction* in the percentage of students who were high in self-control. This relationship is shown in more detail in Chart 9.5. The top right path of Chart 9.4 shows that high self-control is associated with a 39% *decrease* in the percent who insisted on sex without a condom. This relationship is shown in more detail in Chart 9.6. Thus, spanking is related to insisting on sex without a condom in part because spanking is associated with a lower probability of high self-control.

Violence approval. The lower left path in Chart 9.4 shows that spanking is associated with a 32% *increase* in violence approval. This relationship is described in more detail in Chart 9.7. The lower right path of Chart 9.4 shows that violence approval is associated with a 56% increase in insisting on sex without a condom. This relationship is shown in more detail in Chart 9.8. Thus, spanking is related to sex without a condom in part because spanking is associated with an increased probability of approving violence in some circumstances. See Chapters 5 and 12 for other studies that found that the more spanking, the more approval of violence.

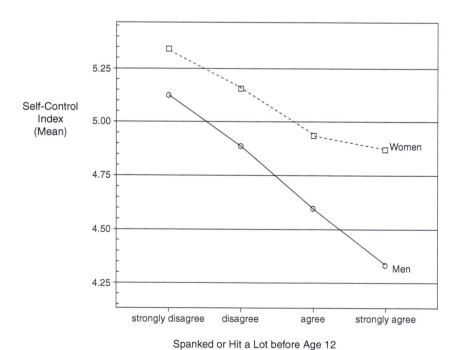

Chart 9.5　The More Spanking, the Lower the Self-Control as a Young Adult

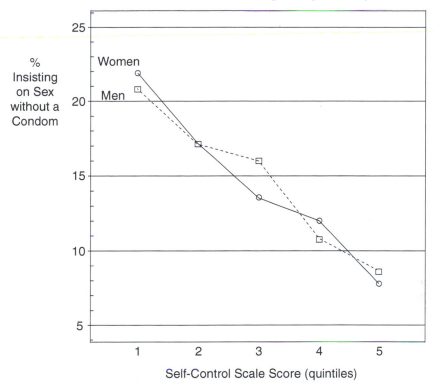

Chart 9.6 The Higher the Self-Control, the Lower the Percent Who Insisted on Sex without a Condom

Summary and Conclusions

The results of the two studies described in this chapter show that spanking is associated with an increased probability of risky sex by adolescents and young adults. Despite a very different sample, a different source of data, and different measures, the results of Study 1 also confirm what was found in the previous chapter—that spanking weakens the parent-child bond. The tendency of spanking to undermine the parent-child bond helps to explain why spanking is linked to problems such as antisocial behavior (Chapters 6 and 7), delinquency (Chapter 8), lower academic achievement (Chapter 11), and crime (the chapters in Part IV).

Other Paths from Spanking to Risky Sex

Although we examined several processes that could explain why spanking is related to risky sex, there are other important influences on sexual behavior that are affected by spanking and need to be investigated in future research. The studies in Part III of this book show that spanking slows cognitive development and lowers academic achievement. Low academic achievement has been shown

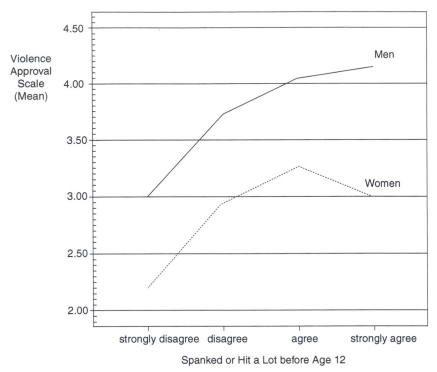

Chart 9.7   The More Spanking, the Higher the Violence Approval as a Young Adult

to be associated with risky sex (Abma, Driscoll, & Moore, 1998; Murray, 1938; Resnick et al., 1997) and adolescent pregnancy (Scaramella, Conger, Simons, & Whitbeck, 1998). Further, Coopersmith (1967) found that spanking is associated with low self-esteem, and low self-esteem is associated with decreased use of contraception (Kowaleski-Jones & Mott, 1998). For young women, low self-esteem has been found to be associated with an increased risk of pregnancy (Berry, Shillington, Peak, & Hohman, 2000; Kowaleski-Jones & Mott, 1998).

Although our results demonstrate that spanking is associated with risky sex, it must be remembered that these data are cross-sectional, so we cannot draw conclusions about the direction of causality. However, the fact that most spanking tends to occur before the age at which risky sex occurs makes a causal relation plausible. On the other hand, the fact that spanking occurs before the risky sex does not rule out the possibility that the relationship between spanking and risky sex is spurious, that is, caused by a third variable that is associated with both. For example, parents who are under great stress may be more likely to spank and also less likely to exercise guidance and supervision over their adolescent children. It may be the stress variable that explains both more spanking and less adequate guidance.

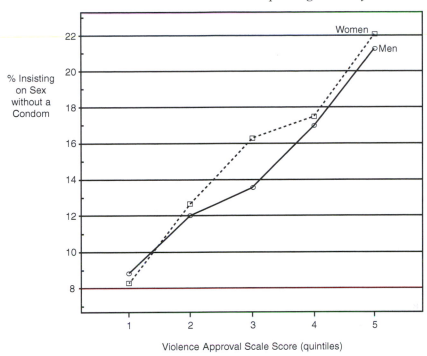

Chart 9.8   The More Approval of Violence, the Higher the Percent Insisting on Sex without a Condom

But the case for believing that spanking *causes* the harmful side effects found by these two studies, and the many other correlational studies published during the last 30 years, rests on new evidence obtained from the growing number of longitudinal studies conducted since 1997—the year the first studies were published that showed that spanking is associated with a subsequent change for the worse in the child's behavior (Chapter 6 and Gunnoe & Mariner, 1997). The longitudinal studies in the chapters on child antisocial behavior (Chapter 6), mental ability (Chapter 10), and adult crime (Chapter 15) controlled for the misbehavior that presumably elicited the spanking, and found that spanking was associated with a subsequent increase in the problematic behavior. Chapter 19 summarizes many other longitudinal studies that have found that spanking is associated with a subsequent increase in the probability of physical aggression, antisocial personality, and crime as a child and as an adult.

In addition to identifying an additional important correlate of spanking, the two studies in this chapter provide another example of why it is difficult or impossible for parents to see the harmful effects of spanking—because it is linked to behaviors that do not occur until years after most parents have ceased to use spanking and behaviors of which parents might not even be aware.

Part III

Spanking and Human Capital

10 Mental Ability

A guest opinion editorial in *The New York Times* in 2011 advocated spanking (Williams, 2011). The reader reaction was mostly critical and opposed spanking. This is the opposite of the reader response to the *Time* magazine article described in Chapter 1. The *Time* article summarized a study showing that spanking was associated with an increase in children's antisocial behavior. The letters to the editor of *Time* were almost entirely defenses of spanking, and many dismissed the research as junk science. Perhaps the antispanking letters to *The New York Times* compared with the pro-spanking letters to *Time* was a reflection of the characteristics of readers of *The New York Times*. It could also be the tendency for more people who disagree with an article to write a letter to the editor than those who agree with the article.

Regardless of the explanation, one of the letters to *The New York Times* that favored spanking was particularly relevant for this chapter. The writer said: "I'll never forget watching a woman trying to reason with a two-year-old, explaining all the reasons not to do something. At two, the child does not have the capacity for critical reasoning, but he or she understands a swift spank on the bottom." We doubt that a swift spank on the bottom, without explanation or some other means of conveying what specifically was wrong, will teach the child right and wrong, and it may teach entirely wrong lessons, such as "Mommy doesn't like me." Moreover, not explaining to a child is a form of cognitive deprivation. Research shows that talking to an infant or toddler is associated with enhanced mental ability. That research suggests that the more parents talk to a child, including talking to infants, the larger their vocabulary and the more different type of words they use (Huttenlocher, Waterfall, Vasilyeva, Vevea, & Hedges, 2010). Presumably this is because these are formative ages for the development of neural connections in the brain (Blakeslee, 1995; Dawson & Fischer, 1994). This has implications for understanding the side effects of spanking because, as the letter just quoted indicates, more spanking usually means less talking to a child and less talking to a child can result in less brain development. This line of thinking led us to look into the following questions that are addressed in this chapter.

Mallie J. Paschall is the coauthor of this chapter.

- What process might link spanking and mental ability?
- Is there any evidence from previous research that spanking adversely affects mental development?
- What percent of children age 2 to 4 and 5 to 9 were spanked during the two sample weeks, and how many times per week were they spanked?
- Is spanking associated with a subsequent change in the child's mental ability, and does this apply to toddlers as well as school age children?
- Do contextual factors, such as socioeconomic status and whether mothers are loving and supportive, affect the relation of spanking to mental development?
- Do the adverse effects of spanking apply as much to toddlers as to older children?
- What are the theoretical and policy and practice implications of the results of this study?

Processes that Could Link Spanking and Mental Ability

Less Verbal Interaction

As suggested in the previous paragraph, when parents spank or slap a child's hand for touching a forbidden object, they are less likely to engage in cognitive methods of behavior control, such as explaining to the child why the object should not be touched. Of course, they usually do both, but some parents have told us that they spank because they don't have time for all that explaining stuff, and many think that just a quick swat will take care of things. The reduction in talking to a child by parents who spank could also come about if, as other parents have told us, they believe that you can't reason with a two-year-old. For these parents, spanking often replaces reasoning and explaining. The other side of the coin is more clear because the less spanking used by a parent, the more verbal interaction is needed to teach and correct the child. The increased level of verbal interaction may enhance the growth of neural connections in the brain, and with it the child's mental development.

Spanking and Stress

In addition to limited verbal interaction, spanking could adversely affect mental ability through other processes. Being slapped or spanked by someone 2 or 3 times the size of the child, and from which there is no escape, is a frightening and threatening event that many children experience as highly stressful (Saunders & Goddard, 2010; Turner & Finkelhor, 1996; Willow & Hyder, 1998). For some parents, fright and fear is an explicit part of their discipline strategy. A father recently told us that he wants his son to fear him so that he will obey. "Respect will come later," he said. Relatively few parents are this explicit about fear. But regardless of whether it is intentional, when parents spank, they are using fright as a means of teaching. Ironically and unfortunately, fear and fright can result in cognitive deficits such as erroneous or limited coding of events and diminished elaboration (Heuer & Reisberg, 1992; Perry, 2006). The physiological arousal from being hit by a parent tends to narrow the range of cues in the environment to which the child is sensitive (Bruner, Matter, & Papanek, 1955; Easterbrook, 1959).

There is now evidence that spanking is associated with adverse changes in brain structure. Bugental et al. (2003), Bugental, Schwartz, and Lynch (2010), and Tomoda et al. (2009) found that the 34% of infants in their study who were spanked "showed high hormonal reactivity to stress." They concluded that "the hormonal responses shown by infants may alter the functioning of the hypothalamic—pituitary—adrenal (HPA) axis in ways that, if continued, may foster risk for immune disorders, sensitization to later stress, cognitive deficits, and social-emotional problems" (p. 237).

Moreover, to the extent that spanking is experienced as stressful, it is a stress that, for many children, continues for several years. Those who defend spanking typically approve of spanking only with young children, for example, ages 2 to 6 (see the consensus statements and personal statements in Friedman & Schonberg, 1996b). In addition, as shown in the chapters on spanking and the child-to-mother bond (Chapter 8) and risky sex (Chapter 9), spanking tends to undermine the attachment and bond between the child and the parent and reduce a child's motivation to learn from parents. Whatever the intervening processes, if spanking influences mental ability, it has broad implications because as shown in Chapter 2 on spanking in the United States, at least one third of U.S. children are hit as infants and over 90% as toddlers, and for one third, it continues into the early teenage years.

Previous Research

Both physical abuse and spanking are acts of physical assault. A key difference is that, by definition, spanking does not cause physical injury. However, the difference between spanking and physical abuse is not as large as one would gather from newspaper stories. News articles are almost always about physically injured children, whereas empirical research has found that most physical abuse cases dealt with by Child Protective Services also do not involve an injury serious enough (Trocmé, MacMillan, Fallon, & De Marco, 2003) to require medical treatment. Spanking and physical abuse are also similar in that both increase the probability of psychological injury. For psychological injury, the difference is that the effect size of physical abuse (the probability of psychological damage occurring) is much smaller for spanking, but still present. For example, Strassberg et al. (1994) found that both physical abuse and spanking were associated with more aggressive behavior observed in kindergarten. Spanking was associated with twice the number of acts of physical aggression compared with the children who were not spanked six months earlier. But physical abuse was associated with 4 times as many physically aggressive acts. A study by Afifi, Brownridge, Cox, and Sareen (2006) of a U.S. nationally representative sample found that spanking was associated with 2.2% more cases of externalizing problems such as antisocial personality, whereas physical abuse was associated with 15.3% more cases. Thus, the adverse effect of spanking was much less, but still present. As a consequence, the results of studies showing that maltreatment at an early age can have enduring negative effects on a child's brain development and function (Craig, 1986; Kinard, 1999; Teicher, Andersen, Polcari, Anderson, & Navalta, 2002; Widom, 1989) can also apply to children who experience spanking, but with a lower probability of it happening.

A possibly tragic aspect of cultural beliefs about spanking is reflected in the advice given to parents by many professionals such as pediatricians and child psychologists. It is the belief that spanking is acceptable if restricted to early childhood. For example, a *consensus statement* drawn up at the conclusion of a conference on corporal punishment sponsored by the American Academy of Pediatrics, recommended limiting spanking to children between 2 and 6 years old (Friedman & Schonberg, 1996a). However, there is no research evidence for that recommendation. It is a part of folk beliefs about spanking, even though put forth by professionals. Contrary to this folk belief, the risk of psychological damage from spanking may be greatest in early childhood. We found that the increase in antisocial behavior that occurred subsequent to spanking applied to toddlers as well as older children (Chapter 6). This chapter investigates whether that also applies to a slower rate of mental development for toddlers as well for older children.

Hitting children at a young age may be worse than hitting them when they are older because the neural connections in the brain are being formed more rapidly by young children. Another reason why hitting young children may be the worst possible age is that spanking is associated with a weakened bond to the mother, as shown in Chapter 7 on impulsive spanking and child well-being and Chapter 8 on spanking, the child-to-mother bond and delinquency, and by Afifi et al. (2006) and Coyl, Roggman, and Newland (2002). If the ages below 6 are the most crucial for developing bonds of attachment to the parent, the weakened bond may reduce a child's motivation to learn from the parent who is hitting them.

Studies Suggesting that Spanking Might Adversely Affect Mental Ability

There are several studies that found spanking to be related to characteristics that are related to mental ability. A study by Bodovski and Youn (2010) of a large, nationally representative sample of U.S. elementary school students measured spanking when the children were in kindergarten. They found that spanking in kindergarten was associated with lower 5th-grade math achievement even after controlling for many other variables such as parental depression, parental warmth, and racial or ethnic group. These results bear on the issue of this chapter because one of the causes of poor math ability is low IQ.

A study of a national sample of American adults found, even after controlling for the education and occupation of the respondent's parents and other potential confounds, that the more spanking, the lower the probability of the study participant being in the top fifth of the occupational and income distribution for the United States (Straus & Gimpel, 2001). The next chapter presents the results of a study of another nationally representative sample of U.S. adults and found that the more spanking experienced, the lower the percentage who graduated from college.

A unique natural experiment was studied by Talwar, Carlson, and Lee (2011). They compared the *executive functioning* of children in two West African private schools: one high in use of corporal punishment and one non-punitive. Executive function is an umbrella term for mental processes such as planning, problem solving, verbal reasoning, and mental flexibility. Both schools served high-education families. The study controlled for verbal IQ. In kindergarten, the children did not differ in executive functioning. By Grade 1, however, the children in the punitive school had lower executive functioning scores (i.e., they had fallen behind the growth in executive functioning of the children in the school without corporal punishment). Although this study was of corporal punishment by teachers, not parents, we believe the same processes are involved in spanking by parents.

Studies of Spanking and Mental Ability

We found six studies that examined the relation of disciplinary practices to standard measures of mental ability. Bayley and Schaefer (1964) studied the children in the Berkeley Growth Study whose mental ability had been tested at frequent intervals from birth to age 18 (approximately 25 boys and 25 girls). From age four on, especially for boys, the more punishment was used, the lower the mental ability. However, the adverse effect on mental ability may not have been the result of spanking because their measure of punishment was not restricted to spanking.

Smith and Brooks-Gunn (1997) studied 715 low birth weight children. Discipline was measured at 12 and 36 months. The Stanford Binet intelligence test was administered at 36 months. They found that the children who experienced harsh discipline had the lowest IQ, even after controlling for many socioeconomic factors, including birth weight, neonatal health status, ethnic group, mother's age, family structure, mother's education, and family income. One limitation of this study is that the harsh discipline measure included scolding the child. Therefore, it is not possible to separate out the effect of spanking alone. Another limitation is that there was no Time 1 measure of mental ability to enable testing whether spanking at Time 1 was followed by a subsequent decrease in IQ scores.

Power and Chapieski (1986) interviewed and observed the interaction of 18 upper middle class mothers with their 12- to 15-month-old children. They compared children whose mothers relied on spanking with children whose mothers rarely or never spanked. The outcome measure of interest was children's score on the Bayley infant development scale when the children were tested at an average age of 21 months. The mental ability of the small proportion of children whose mothers rarely or never spanked, averaged 20 points higher than the rest of the children. Two limitations of this study are the small number of cases and lack of differentiating "rarely" spanking from "never."

Aucoin et al. (2006) compared children who experienced no corporal punishment over approximately a 2-week period, those who had experienced mild levels of corporal punishment (i.e., 1 or 2 instances), and those who had experienced high levels of corporal punishment (i.e., 3 or more instances), and found differences between groups in IQ. Children in the low corporal punishment group scored significantly higher on a brief measure of intelligence than children in the high corporal punishment group. Although the statistical analysis did not control for family income, race, or gender, the groups did not differ significantly on these variables.

Two recent and comprehensive studies provide the most definitive evidence on the extent to which spanking harms the development of mental ability. A study of a sample of 2,573 low-income, White, Black, and Mexican American children ages 1 to 3 (Berlin et al., 2009) found that, after controlling for a number of other variables, spanking at all three ages predicted lower Bayley mental development scores at age 3. Another longitudinal study found similar results. This study examined an urban U.S. national sample of 779 children (MacKenzie et al., 2011). It found that frequent spanking by mothers at age 3 was associated with a large subsequent decrease at age 5 in the probability of the child being high in cognitive ability relative to other children as measured by the Peabody Picture Vocabulary Test. This study controlled for 30 other variables, including child characteristic variables such as low birth weight and difficult temperament, maternal and family characteristics such as mother's age at the time of the child's birth, and pre-natal risk variables such as substance abuse during pregnancy. This may be more than in any other study of the effects of spanking and included variables that are particularly relevant for child mental ability such as maternal depression, maternal intelligence, and an observational measure of the extent to which the home environment was cognitively stimulating. This study is also important because it provides information on the belief that the adverse effects of spanking do not apply in cultural contexts where it is the norm, such as among Blacks. This study, like most of those summarized in Chapter 14 on cultural context effects, found that the adverse effects of spanking on mental ability applied to Black children as well as Hispanic and White children.

The findings of these studies lead us to hypothesize the following:

1. Spanking is associated with lower mental ability relative to other children of the same age.

2.   When data is analyzed over a 4-year time period, spanking at Time 1 is associated with an average decrease in mental ability at Time 2, relative to other children of the same age.
3.   The decrease in mental ability is greater for preschool-age children (age 2 to 4) than for children age 5 to 9.

Sample

The sample consists of the children of women who were first interviewed in 1979 as part of the National Longitudinal Survey of Youth (see Chapter 6 for a description of the sample). At the start of the study in 1979, the women were 14 to 21. Starting in 1986, those women who had children were interviewed periodically about child rearing practices and behavior problems of their children. This included 806 children age 2 to 4 and 704 children age 5 to 9 whose mental ability was tested. Additional information on the characteristics of the sample is in (Straus & Paschall, 2009).

We studied two groups of children because each can help address a different issue. The younger group was studied because the theory underlying this study is most applicable to young children because the development of neural connections is greatest for infants and toddlers. If that is the case, the adverse effects of spanking should be greatest for the younger children. In addition, the effect of what the parents do may be greater for younger children because, on average, they have fewer nonfamily experiences that could be related to mental ability (e.g., school experiences) than older children. We studied the second group of children so that we could replicate the hypotheses with children who were age 5 to 9 at Time 1. Many parents continue spanking into this age range (see Chapter 2). Also, the American Academy of Pediatrics (Friedman & Schonberg, 1996a) advises against using spanking with children older than 6, implicitly because they believed that spanking of older children is more likely to result in harm than is spanking of preschool-age children. If that is correct, it suggests that the adverse effects of spanking on mental ability should be greater for the 5- to 9-year-old children than for the 2- to 4-year-old children.

Measures

Mental Ability

For both age groups, mental ability was measured at both Time 1 and four years later at Time 2—using at Time 1 as many of the following tests as were appropriate for each age child: body parts recognition, memory for locations, and motor and social development. At Time 2, mental ability measure was the Peabody Individual Achievement Tests (PIAT) for math and reading recognition (see Baker et al., 1993, p. 3043). The scores from the mental ability measures were transformed so that the resulting scores indicate how far above or below the average level of mental ability each child was relative to other children in this study of approximately the same age (see Straus, 2009a).

Spanking

Spanking was measured during one sample week in 1986 and again in 1988 using two types of data. The first is observation by the interviewer of whether the mother spanked or hit the child during the course of the interview. The second was two interview questions: "Did you find it necessary to spank your child in the past week?" Mothers who said they had spanked were asked: "About how many times, if any, have you had to spank your child in the past week?" We used these data to create a scale that combined the observed behavior and mothers' reported behavior for Time 1. If the mother was observed hitting the child, it was counted as one instance of spanking in addition to any that the mother reported as having occurred in the past week. Next, we grouped the children into four categories: (1) those who experienced no spanking in either of the two weeks, (2) those who experienced either one, (3) two, or (4) three or more instances. The fact that a score of zero identifies children who were not spanked in either of the two sample weeks over a 2-year time span, makes it plausible to consider the zero group as children for whom spanking was extremely rare, or in some cases, nonexistent. However, the spanking scale used for this study does not eliminate the possibility that the children in the zero category experienced spanking on rare occasions.

Control Variables

Because many other things that influence mental ability may also be correlated with spanking, it is necessary to take those other influences into account to pin down the effect of spanking. To do this, analysis controlled for the amount of cognitive stimulation and emotional support by the mother. Cognitive stimulation was measured by the Home Observation for Measurement of the Environment Short Form (Caldwell & Bradley, 1984). This includes questions and observations on whether the mother read to the child or whether the mother helped the child learn colors, numbers, shapes, or the alphabet; and how many books the child had of his or her own. Emotional support was measured by behaviors such as how often the child had dinner with both parents, whether the mother caressed or kissed the child, and whether the mother's voice showed positive feeling toward the child. See Straus & Paschall (2009) for additional information on these measures.

Other variables controlled for this study included the child's birth weight, child's age, child's ethnicity, child's gender, number of children of the mother in the home, mother's age at child's birth, mother's education, and if the father was living with the mother at Time 1.

Prevalence and Frequency of Spanking

- Only 6.6% of the 2- to 4-year-old children were not hit at all in either of the two sample weeks; thus 93% were hit at least once in those two weeks. This is almost identical to the 94% of parents who reported hitting children in this age group in our national survey of U.S. children (Chapter 2).
- The percent of 5- to 9-year-old children who were not hit is much greater, but more than one half (58.2%) were spanked in that period.
- Almost one half of the 2- to 4-year-old children were hit 3 or more times in those two weeks.
- Mothers of children age 2 to 4 years who had spanked in the past week, did so an average of 3.6 times that week. One third of the mothers spanked 4 or more times, and 12.8% spanked 7 or more times that week.
- The mothers of children age 5 to 9 who had spanked in the past week reported doing so an average of 2.5 times that week.

As pointed out in Chapter 2 on spanking in the United States, these may be low estimates because spanking is used so frequently and is taken for granted as being sometimes necessary. As a consequence, parents do not realize how often they do it. One indication of the taken-for-granted nature of spanking children is that, among the children who were 26 months old at Time 1, 18% of the mothers hit the child *during the interview.* Although we cannot be sure of the number of times these children were hit, it is clear that they experienced a lot of spanking.

Spanking and Development of Mental Ability

We hypothesized that spanking slows the rate of further mental development. Therefore, we should find that 4 years down the road, the more children who were hit by their parents, the more likely they are to fall behind the average for children their age. To test this, it was necessary to have data that could determine if spanking is associated with *change* in mental ability, and specifically, whether the more spanking experienced, the slower the growth of mental ability. The results of testing this hypothesis are presented in Chart 10.1 and, in more detail, in Straus and Paschall (2009). Chart 10.1 shows that the 2- to 4-year-old children who were not spanked gained an average of 5.5 points more than the average child, and the 5- to 9-year-old children gained an average of almost 2 points more than the average child.

At the other extreme of the spanking categories, the 2- to 4-year-old children who were hit 3 or more times in the two sample weeks neither gained nor lost relative to other children their age. This is consistent with the fact that they are the typical children in this age group, for whom we found that 48 were hit 3 or more times. Thus, 2- to 4-year-old children who experienced 3 or more instances of spanking were typical of all children in the nation in respect to both being spanked and growth in mental ability.

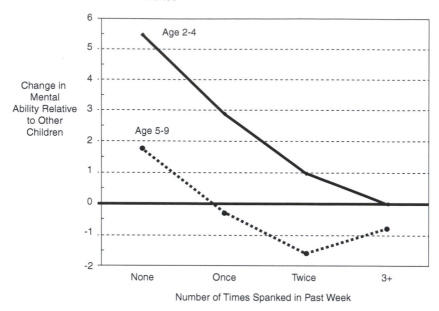

Chart 10.1   The More Spanking, the More the Child's Mental Ability Fell Behind that of Other Children Four Years Later

For children age 5 to 9, the statistical norm for spanking was quite different. Instead of most children that age being hit 3 or more times in those two weeks, as was true of the younger children, only 15% of the 5- to 9-year-old children were hit 3 or more times in those two weeks. The relation of spanking to mental ability, however, was similar to the results for the 2- to 4-year-old children. The mental ability of the children whose parents did not spank in either of the two sample weeks was greater than the children who were hit even once in those two weeks. They gained an average of almost 2 points more than the average child. On the other hand, the 5- to 9-year-old children who were hit once neither fell behind nor gained compared with other children. In other words, their score stayed at about 100. The 5- to 9-year-old children who were hit 2 or more times in those two weeks fell slightly behind the average child in mental ability in the 4 years following the initial testing.

To understand these results, it is important to realize that the decreases shown in Chart 10.1 do *not* mean that spanked children became less smart. Unless there is some developmental impairment, all young children become much smarter than they were 4 years earlier. A mental ability score of 100 indicates a score at the average for children of the same age. To maintain a score of 100 over a 4-year period, a child's ability must increase during those years at the average rate of increase. Thus, the decreases associated with spanking do not indicate an absolute reduction in mental ability, only that spanking is associated with failing to keep up with the average development of mental ability.

Does the Harmful Effect of Spanking Depend on the Social Context?

As noted earlier, on the basis of both theory and the results of empirical research, there are grounds for expecting that the effect of spanking depends on the presence or absence of other variables, or as it is sometimes put, the effects of spanking may be *context specific*. In order to examine this, we considered spanking in combination with other variables in this study. Chart 10.1 shows that the adverse effect of spanking is greater for toddlers than for early school-age children. We examined each of the other child and family characteristics available for this sample to see if they reduced or exacerbated the relation of spanking to mental ability. For example, it is often claimed that spanking is not harmful in a sociocultural context where it is the norm, such as among Blacks (see Chapter 13). We tested this idea and found that the results for Blacks parallel those for Whites. Spanking was found to be related to a slowing of mental ability development among both Blacks and Whites and also among each of other nine parenting and demographic context variables.

Is "Just Once" Harmless?

Defenders of spanking believe it is harmless if done only rarely. They do not indicate how often rarely is, so their belief cannot be tested exactly. For this study, the best approximation to only rarely was the children who were spanked only once in the two sample weeks. We consider this rare for U.S. parents because only 10.5% of the children in this sample were spanked this rarely. We compared the 6.6% of the children who were not hit at all during the two sample weeks with the 10.5% who were hit only once, those hit twice, and those hit 3 or more times. The mental ability of children of mothers who hit them even once in these two weeks was slower than the development of the children whose mothers did not hit them at all. However, the difference was just short of the usual standard for being statistically dependable for either the 2- to 4-year-old children ($p = .062$) or 5- to 9-year-old children ($p = .057$).

Summary and Conclusions

This study investigated the extent to which mothers spanked in large national samples of children age 2 to 4 and 5 to 9. It tested the hypothesis that spanking experienced by these children is associated with slower development of mental ability over a 4-year period.

Prevalence of Spanking

Ninety-three percent of the mothers of children age 2 to 4, and 58% of mothers of children of the 5- to 9-year-old age group spanked in the two-week referent period. These prevalence rates are consistent with the other studies cited in the introduction to this chapter. Among those who spanked, it occurred an average of 3.6 times per week. This figure is consistent with the average of 2.5 times per week for toddlers found by Holden, Coleman, and Schmidt (1995), provided one takes into account that these authors studied college-educated mothers who tend to spank less than mothers with less education (Day et al., 1998). If the average of 3.6 per week is extrapolated to a year, it results in an estimated 187 instances per year per child. This is at least 10 times higher than the average number of times based on studies that ask parents about the number of times they spanked in the past year (the method used for Chapter 2). We suggest that the much lower chronicity of spanking (frequency of spanking among those who spanked) found by studies that use a 1-year recall period occurs because, for many parents, spanking is such an everyday and taken-for-granted occurrence that parents do not realize how often they use it. This interpretation is consistent with findings from a pioneer study by Goodenough (1931) that found that when mothers used a diary to record their disciplinary tactics, the chronicity of spanking was 6 times greater than when the figure was based on recall during an interview.

We believe that the public and most service providers and social scientists do not realize the high prevalence and how chronic spanking is in the lives of U.S. children. We further suggest that misperception of the extent of spanking is an example of *selective inattention* (Dexter, 1958) by members of a society in which spanking is the norm (Straus & Mathur, 1996). Selective inattention may be one of the mechanisms that enables our society to continue to support spanking because it avoids the necessity of facing up to the fact that almost all children are hit, and most are hit frequently. Without the information on prevalence and frequency, the results about the effects of spanking could be dismissed as applicable only to atypical, high-spanking parents. Indeed this was a basis used by defenders of spanking to dismiss the general applicability of the results reported in Chapter 6 on spanking and children's antisocial behavior; spanking increases rather than decreases antisocial behavior of children (Ambati, Ambati, & Rao, 1998).

Relation of Spanking to Development of Mental Ability

Although almost all U.S. children experience at least some spanking, the differences in how often mothers spank provided sufficient variation in the use of spanking to test the hypothesis that the more spanking experienced by a child, the slower the development of mental ability. The results from this study are consistent with the hypothesis. We found that 2- to 4-year-old children who experienced no spanking in either of the two sample weeks gained an average of 5.5 more mental ability points over the next 4 years than children whose mothers spanked. Similarly, children in the 5- to 9-year age group, whose mothers did not spank in either week, gained an average of about 2 points more than children whose mothers spanked. Conversely, for both age groups, spanking was associated with a decrease from Time 1 to Time 2 in mental ability test score.

These findings remained, even after adjusting statistically for 10 variables that could be the real underlying causes of the link between spanking and slower development of mental ability. This includes the child's birth weight, child's age, child's ethnicity, child's gender, number of children of the mother in the home, mother's age at child's birth, mother's education, mother's cognitive stimulation with the child, mother's emotional support, and if the father was living with the mother at Time 1. In addition, the results of our analysis are probably minimum estimates of how closely spanking is related to slower development of mental ability because of the relatively low reliability of cognitive testing of children as young as those in this sample at Time 1.

Contextual effects. The question of whether there are circumstances or contexts that make spanking appropriate has been the subject of much debate. For example, it has been argued that if parents are loving and supportive, children will know parents are spanking them for their own good, and spanking will have no adverse effect. Given the debate and theoretical importance of contextual effects, we tested the interaction with spanking of the 10 variables listed in the previous paragraph. These analyses indicate whether each of the 10 made a difference in the degree to which spanking is related to the development of mental ability. For example, if mothers are loving and supportive, is there still a harmful effect of spanking? The answer is yes there is. Or, more generally, none of the 10 tests of moderator effects found that these variables either mitigated or enhanced the relation of spanking to mental ability. The lack of any context effects indicates that the relation of spanking to slower development of mental ability applies even when done by loving and attentive parents, even when it occurs among a sector of the population with cultural norms that approve of spanking such as Blacks, among children of low and high socioeconomic status, etc. These results can also be interpreted as showing that spanking has a unique harmful effect, that is in addition to the effect of the 10 variables that were statistically controlled.

The fact that none of these 10 variables mitigated the tendency for spanking to be related to slower development of mental ability does not mean that these variables have no effect on mental ability. Table 3 in Straus and Paschall (2009) shows that many of them were related to the child's mental ability. For example, the more children in the family, the lower the average mental ability. This result is consistent with much other research on the effect of number of children (Blake, 2011). Many readers will find this implausible, just as many will find it hard to believe that spanking lowers mental ability. They might say "I was spanked and my IQ is 120" or "I was one of five children and my IQ is 120." To understand the results on the relation of spanking or number of children to mental ability, it is necessary to understand that almost all social science and medical research results are typically in the form of risk-factor relationships rather than one-to-one relationships. See the section of Chapter 1, Risk Factors: The Real Meaning of Social Science Research.

Limitations

Although we studied a large and nationally representative sample of children, controlled for many potential confounds, and examined many contextual effects, there are limitations to keep in mind. The data are more than 20 years old, and many changes in parent practices have probably taken place during this period. However, as shown in the chapters on the prevalence of spanking in the United States (Chapters 2 and 17), there has been virtually no change in the use of spanking children of the ages of those in this study. Moreover, the issue of this study is not the prevalence of spanking but the effect of spanking on children. That is likely to be the same even if spanking had decreased. Second, this study did not have a method for screening out severe forms of corporal punishment that might be considered physical abuse. Thus, it is possible that some of the parental reports of spanking might actually have been in the form of physical attacks that are severe enough to be physical abuse rather than legal spanking. Third, because this is a longitudinal study, the measures of mental ability had to be different at Time 1 and Time 2 in order to be age-appropriate. We took this into account by standardizing the scores so that for each testing, the scores indicate how much above or below the average of the children tested at that time point. Fourth, the relatively small effect size of spanking needs to be kept in mind. If future studies confirm the findings of this study, it means an average gain of about 5 points for children who do not experience spanking. For an individual child, a 5-point gain in a 100-point mental ability test is good but, given measurement error, not a major difference. Nonetheless, it is a well-established principle in epidemiology that reducing a widely prevalent risk factor with small effect size, such as spanking, can have a much greater impact on public health than reducing a risk factor with a large effect size, but low prevalence, such as physical abuse (Rose, 1985; Rosenthal, 1984, p.131). An example showing the greater effect in reducing antisocial behavior of ending spanking than of ending physical abuse is given in the concluding chapter.

Fifth, the children who were not spanked in either of the two sample weeks could have been spanked in the other 50 weeks of the year. Similarly, children who experienced 1 or 2 instances of spanking in the two-week sample period may have experienced much more spanking on a regular basis. Finally, no data on the behavior of the fathers is available for these children, and the measure of the mother's emotional support is minimal.

Perhaps the most important limitation of the study is that we did not control for the Time 1 level of behavior problems or externalizing behavior. Research indicates that children with low IQ scores also often have externalizing behavior problems and impulsivity, which may in turn lead to a higher likelihood of spanking. Therefore, it is possible that those with lower IQs had more behavior problems that lead to more spanking, rather than spanking leading to lower IQ. That is why the longitudinal studies that did control for Time 1 behavior

(Chapters 6, 10, and 15, and the longitudinal studies reviewed in Chapter 19) are so important.

Implications for National Level of Mental Ability

A review of data on mental ability found an increase in scores on many different intelligence tests in a number of countries (Neisser, 1997). The evidence compiled by Neisser and others leaves little doubt that intelligence test scores have been increasing, and that the increase is not an artifact of the tests used. What is in doubt is why this has occurred. Neisser identifies a number of plausible contributing factors. For example, there is abundant evidence that children of educated parents obtain higher scores on intelligence tests (Flynn, 1999; Neisser et al., 1996). Because the level of education of parents has been increasing worldwide, this is likely to be an important part of the explanation. Another strong possibility is that nutrition levels have been improving because better nutrition is associated with greater mental ability (Rizzo, Metzger, Dooley, & Cho, 1997).

Chapter 4, which shows that the more children in a family, the higher the probability of spanking, suggests another change that could be contributing to the increase in IQ. Around the world, birth rates have been declining. That means less use of spanking around the world. Therefore, as shown in this chapter, less spanking means a higher *average* IQ. It does not mean that everyone is smarter. The section of Chapter 1, Risk Factors: The Real Meaning of Social Science Results, explains how that could be correct if, as is probably the case, most readers of this book were spanked as children and do not suffer from low IQ.

Reductions in spanking and its replacement by cognitive forms of correction might also explain part of the worldwide increase in IQ. When parents spank less, they tend to use more cognitive methods of correction. They also tend to shift away from the idea that children should be seen and not heard. Explanation, rather than the fear of being spanked, becomes the reason the child should engage in socially appropriate behavior. If this theory is correct, and if there has been a worldwide decrease in spanking, then that decrease could have contributed to the worldwide increase in scores on mental ability tests. We do not have data on change in spanking to test that theory. However, we do have data on national differences in spanking and national differences in IQ for 32 nations. An analysis of this data (Straus, 2009a) found a tendency for the larger the percent of children under 12 who were spanked, the lower the national IQ ($r = .21$). The correlation with IQ of or slapping and spanking older children was much higher ($r = .43$). However, with a sample of only 32, after introducing controls for such variables as the level of economic development and the average education, the regression coefficient was not statistically dependable. These results suggest that future research with a larger sample of nations might provide more definitive evidence that prevalence of spanking in a nation is associated with a lower national IQ. However, for a definitive test, there needs to be data on change in the percent spanked to see if, when that decreases, IQ goes up.

Policy Implications

Although a smaller percent of parents of older children in the United States now spank, almost all U.S. parents continue to spank and slap toddlers (see Chapters 2 and 17). There is a cruel irony to this because both the theoretical basis and the findings of this study suggest that it is precisely at early stages of development that avoiding spanking and using cognitive modes of correction may be most beneficial for the development of mental ability (Doyle, Harmon, Heckman, & Tremblay, 2009). Moreover, it is even more ironic that most defenders of spanking have reformulated their position to oppose spanking of older children and accept spanking of toddlers (Friedman & Schonberg, 1996a). It is ironic because that is precisely the age group this study suggests is most vulnerable to adverse effects on mental ability. Moreover, there are many studies that, although they did not compare age groups, have found serious adverse effects of spanking for toddlers. The combination of our findings on mental ability and the many other studies showing that spanking toddlers is harmful suggest that media and educational programs explicitly focused on not hitting *toddlers,* and making clear the benefits of avoiding spanking could help bring about a national increase in mental ability, as well as many other benefits that are discussed in this book. That includes less crime because, as Farrington and Welsh (2006) conclude from their own and other longitudinal studies, low intelligence is one of the leading individual level risk factors for crime. It may be one of the mechanisms that explains the links between spanking and crime shown in Chapters 12 through 15 and 19.

11 College Graduation

One of our previous studies analyzed a large and nationally representative sample of American adults and found that the more spanking they experienced as a child, the lower the probability of being in the top fifth of the U.S. occupational and economic achievement distribution (Straus & Gimpel, 2001). This relationship remained valid even when controlling for other family characteristics that overlap with parents spanking, such as the educational level and race or ethnic group of the parents. That is, spanking made a unique contribution to lowering a child's chances of being in the top fifth. Many people thought the results were implausible, perhaps in part because that study provided no empirical data on the processes that explain why spanking is related to lower occupational achievement and income. The previous chapters in this book suggest some of the possible processes, including impulsivity (Chapter 7), lower mental ability (Chapter 10), an increased probability of antisocial behavior and delinquency (Chapters 6, 7, and 8), and crime as an adult (all the chapters in Part IV).

Depression is also likely to interfere with academic achievement. The next chapter shows that, as in at least 14 other studies, spanking is associated with an increased probability of depression. Examples of such studies include (Afifi et al., 2006; Bordin et al., 2009; Leary, Kelley, Morrow, & Mikulka, 2008; Turner & Muller, 2004). The study in Chapter 9 found that spanking is associated with an increased probability of risky sex. This is relevant because risky sex as a high school student means an increased probability of a teenage birth, which in turn risks completion of high school and of going on to higher education, especially for girls. Each of these adverse effects of spanking is related to low academic achievement. Therefore, it seems plausible that one of the reasons spanking is associated with lower occupational and economic achievement is that spanking reduces the probability of college graduation. The research reported in this chapter examined that issue. Specifically, we present data on the following questions:

- Is spanking associated with a lower probability of college graduation among two large and nationally representative samples of U.S. adults?

Anita K. Mathur is the coauthor of this chapter.

- Does that relation of spanking to college graduation apply to both men and women?
- Has the relationship of spanking to college graduation become stronger or weaker during a 10-year period in which there was a large increase in the percent of the U.S. population who attended college?
- Does the relation of spanking to college graduation apply after taking into account four family characteristics that might be the underlying cause: the education of the parents, race or ethnic group, violence between the parents, and the age of the participants in the study?

We did not find any study of the relation of spanking to college graduation. However, two studies are relevant. A study by Bodovski and Youn (2010) of a large, nationally representative sample of U.S. elementary school students measured spanking when the children were in kindergarten. They found that spanking in kindergarten was associated with lower 5th-grade math achievement even after controlling for many other variables such as parental depression, parental warmth, and racial or ethnic group. Poor academic achievement in 5th grade is associated with a lower probability of completing higher education. A longitudinal study by Margolin, Vickerman, Oliver, and Gordis (2010) found the spanking was associated with an increased probability of academic failure in the 5th grade. This study is particularly important because it is longitudinal. Many parents spank when a child gets failing grades in school in the hope that fear of being spanked again if there is no improvement will motivate the child to work harder and avoid failing again. This study shows that, although failing in school may have prompted some of the incidents of spanking, the effect was to increase rather than decrease the chances that the child will have failing grades again. These two studies are relevant to the issue of the relation of spanking to college graduation because the same processes that result in spanking being related to poor academic achievement in 5th grade, could also apply to lower educational achievement later in life.

A college degree is a direct and strong predictor of high occupational level and income. As a consequence, it is important to determine if spanking is related to a reduced probability of graduating from college. If so, not graduating from college could be another effect of spanking that could help explain why our previous study found that spanking is associated with lower economic and occupational achievement. A college degree is particularly important in a post-industrial society because it is almost a prerequisite for being in the top fifth of the income distribution. If college gradation is virtually a prerequisite, a crucial step in the process of understanding the link between corporal punishment and economic achievement is determining whether corporal punishment is related to the probability of college graduation. We, therefore, tested the hypothesis that *the more spanking experienced, the lower the probability of college graduation.*

Sample and Measures

Sample

We used data on two large and nationally representative samples to test the hypothesis just stated: the 1975 and 1985 National Family Violence Surveys. The 1985 survey is briefly described in Chapter 4. Both studies are described in more detail in Straus and Gelles (1986). Testing the hypothesis with two different samples a decade apart can provide greater confidence in the findings than either one by itself in the results, if the results are similar.

The data for this study are 25 and 35 years old. Does that mean they are outdated and not worth analyzing? They certainly are outdated as far as the percent of men and women who graduate from college. The percentages are now much higher. But the purpose of this study is not to find out what percent of men and women graduate. That is easily found in the annual Statistical Almanac of the United States. Rather, the purpose of the study is to test the theory that spanking is associated with a lesser chance of graduating from college. If the results show that spanking was related in 1975 and again in 1985, that is likely to still be the case.

Measure of Corporal Punishment

The extent of corporal punishment was assessed by asking the adults who participated in the survey, "I'd like to ask you about your experiences as a child. Thinking about when you were a teenager, about how often would you say your mother or stepmother used physical punishment like spanking or slapping or hitting you? Think about the year in which this happened the most." The response categories were never, once, twice, 3 to 5 times, 6 to 10 times, 11 to 20 times, and more than 20 times. The question was repeated for corporal punishment by fathers. The responses to the two questions were added to obtain a measure of how many times the respondent experienced corporal punishment. This variable was then grouped into seven categories ranging from never to 30 or more times.

Asking about spanking or slapping in the early teenage years, however, means depending on the ability and the willingness of the study participants to recall these events. However, there is empirical evidence indicating that adults' recall of events in childhood can provide a valid measure (Coolidge, Tambone, Durham, & Segal, 2011; Fisher, Bunn, Jacobs, Moran, & Bifulco, 2011; Morris & Slocum, 2010). Another limitation is that the measure is about spanking during the teenage years. This raises the possibility that the data would apply to only a small and atypical group of children who were being hit at as teenagers. That turns out to not be the case. More than one half of the respondents reported being hit as a teenager. This percentage is roughly consistent with what we reported in the chapter on spanking in the United States (Chapter 2) for a national sample of U.S. parents. Almost 40% of the parents of children age 13 and 14 were still spanking or slapping. The percentage of the study participants for this chapter who were hit when they were 13 and 14 is very likely to be higher than that because they represent earlier generations than in the chapter on spanking nationwide (Chapter 2). For those generations, being hit by their parents when they were age 13 to 14, rather than being a small and possibly deviant group of families, probably represent a typical child of their generation. In fact, for those interviewed in 1975, almost two out of three reported one or more incidents of being hit by parents when they were in their early teenage years (Straus et al., 2006).

A decade later in 1985 when the second survey for this chapter was conducted, the prevalence rate had dropped substantially. But even the 1985 figures indicate that just over one half of that sample of adults in the United States that year (52%) said they had been spanked or slapped as a teenager (Straus, 2001a). Moreover, among those who were hit during their teenage years, it was not usually a rare event. The average was 8 times in the year they were 13 and 14, and the median was 5 times (Straus, 2001a).

Men and Women

Women not only have now achieved parity with men in college enrollment but, in recent years, have considerably higher rates of college enrollment and degrees granted than men (U.S. Bureau of the Census, 2011, Table 226). The two national samples for this study, however, were interviewed in 1975 and 1985 and, on average, were college students years before they were interviewed. They, therefore, represent earlier generations of college students when more males than females graduated from college. In either case, if spanking makes a difference in college graduation and if boys are hit more than girls, it is important to examine the relation of spanking to college graduation separately for men and women. We, therefore, repeated the analysis for men and women in the 1975 and the 1985 samples, making four tests of the theory that spanking is associated with a reduced probability of college graduation.

College Graduation

Those who participated in the study and had 4-year college degree or higher were coded as 1 and all others as 0. Among the 1975 sample, 28% of the men and 16% of the women were college graduates. For the 1985 sample, it was 31% of the men and 20% of the women who were college graduates.

Are Other Variables the Real Cause?

When we tested the hypothesis that the more spanking, the lower the probability of graduating from college, we took into account four other variables that are known to affect the probability of graduating from college. Because these four variables are also correlated with spanking, they could be the underlying cause of a relationship between spanking and completing college. One of the four controls was violence between the parents of the study participant. As shown in Chart 5.7 in Chapter 5, which addresses violence approval and spanking, and in Straus, Gelles, and Steinmetz (2006), Silverstein et al. (2009), and Taylor, Lee, Guterman, and Rice (2010), parents who hit each other are more likely to hit their children. In addition, witnessing violence between parents has been found to be associated with a number of social and psychological problems (Davies, DiLillo, & Martinez, 2004; Holden, Geffner, & Jouriles, 1998; Kitzmann, Gaylord, Holt, & Kenny, 2003; Straus, 1992). As a consequence, unless violence between the parents is controlled, the results for college graduation might merely be showing the harmful effect of growing up in a family where the parents are violent to each other.

Another variable that needs to be controlled is the age of the respondent. The percent of the population who attend college has been increasing each decade and the percent of school-age children who were spanked has been decreasing. Unless the age of the respondent is held constant, this combination could result in statistics seeming to show that spanking is associated with a lower chance of graduating from college, but which really only shows the effects of these two trends.

Third, there is a large amount of research showing that the more educated the parents, the higher the chances the child will complete college. Better-educated and higher socioeconomic status parents also spank less (see Chapter 2 and Taylor, Lee et al., 2010). As a consequence, to rule out the possibility that a relationship of spanking to college graduation is really the result of better-educated parents spanking less, we controlled for parent education.

Finally, race or ethnic minority parents are more likely to spank their children are less likely to complete college. As a consequence, both the race and ethnic group of the parents was controlled in these analyses.

Other Measures

Violence between parents. Study participants were asked, "Now thinking about the whole time you were a teenager, were there occasions when your father/stepfather hit your mother/stepmother or threw something at her." If the response was yes, respondents were asked how often that happened and presented with the same response categories as was used for the question on corporal punishment. The same questions were repeated for whether the mother had hit the father. A code of 1 was assigned if either parent was reported as having hit the other and zero if not. Depending on the year of the survey and whether the information was obtained from interviews with male or female study participants, from 13% to 16% of the participants reported one or more physical assaults between their parents.

Age. Age was controlled because, as explained previously, the parents of older study participants were part of a generation that was less likely to be college graduates and more likely to spank.

Parent's education. The education of the parents of the study participants is related to whether the study participants complete a college degree. Education of parents is also related to the frequency of using corporal punishment, as shown in the chapter on spanking in the United States (Chapter 2) and by Giles-Sims et al. (1995). The 1975 survey included information on the education of each parent of the study participants. A two-item parental education index was computed by adding the number of years of education completed by the father and mother of the participants in the 1975 survey.

Ethnic group. Disadvantaged ethnic groups have substantially lower average education and income than Whites, making it important to control for ethnic group when relating corporal punishment to college graduation. The 1975 study did not include enough minority group respondents for a reliable analysis of ethnic groups. However, the 1985 study oversampled Blacks and Hispanic Americans. This permitted taking minority ethnic groups into account by coding. Blacks, Hispanic Americans, and Native Americans were coded as 1 and Whites as 0. Seventeen percent of the study participants identified themselves as one of these racial or ethnic groups.

Corporal Punishment and College Graduation

The left side of Chart 11.1 shows the relationship between spanking and the percent who graduated from college in the 1975 sample, and the right side shows this relationship in 1985. The dotted lines are the actual graduation rates, and the solid lines are the relationship predicted on the basis of the statistical analysis that controlled for other possible causes of educational attainment such as the educational level of the parents. (See the Appendix for the variables controlled and their effects.) It was important to control for these variables because, to take the example of parent's education, more educated parents spank less and the children of more educated parents do better academically. Despite these controls, both the 1975 and the 1985 charts show that the more spanking, the lower the percent who graduated from college. Both charts also show that this relationship applies to both men and women.

Although spanking was associated with a lower probability of graduating from college for both men and women, in 1975 the adverse effect was greater for men than for women. For men, each increase of one category of the spanking categories was associated with an 11% decrease in the probability of graduating from college, whereas for women, each increase in the spanking scale was associated with an 8% decrease. A decade later, although more men than women continued to attend college, there was no difference between men and women in the adverse effect of spanking on the chances of college graduation. For both men and women, each increase of one unit in spanking was associated with an 8% decrease in the probability of college graduation for both men and women. Perhaps the increase in gender equality, including

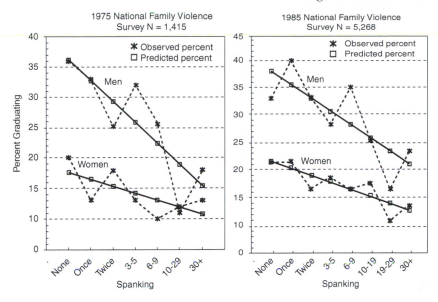

Chart 11.1 The More Spanking as a Teenager, the Lower the Percent Who Graduated from College

more women attending college, had something to do with the adverse effects of spanking becoming more gender-equal.

Other Variables Related to College Graduation

Our focus in this chapter on the relation of spanking to college graduation does not mean that other variables are unimportant as determinants of college graduation. The other independent variables, although they were included in the analysis as controls, are also interesting in their own right. Moreover, Table A11.1 in the Appendix shows that some, such as the education level of parents and violence between the parents, have a much stronger relation to college graduation than spanking. Although other variables have a stronger relationship, controlling for them did not erase the adverse effect of spanking. Moreover, controlling for these other variables shows that spanking had a unique effect, over and above the effect of parent's education and violence between the parents. In addition, Appendix Table A11.2 confirms what has been shown by many studies: That position in society, not just individual ability or family experiences such as spanking, is related to the probability of completing a college degree. Thus:

• Children from low-education families in these two studies, as in the nation as a whole, were much less likely to graduate from college. This applies to both men and women (see Appendix).

- Minority men in the 1975 survey were less than one half as likely as White men to have graduated from college. Minority women were about one third less likely than White women to have graduated from college. Thus, although minority women were more likely than minority men to graduate from college, compared with Whites, they were also less likely to be college graduates.
- Women, in this sample, as in the nation as a whole at the time the participants in this study were college age, had lower rates of college gradation than men.
- To our surprise, after controlling for the other variables, we found that violence between the parents was not related to college graduation in any of the four replications.

Summary and Conclusions

We tested the hypothesis that spanking is associated with a reduced chance of graduating from college in four different samples: nationally representative samples of men and women interviewed in 1975 and in 1985. All four analyses found that spanking was associated with a lower probability of college graduation. These analyses controlled for variables that could be the underlying real reasons spanking is associated with a lower probability of college graduation: educational level of the study participants' parents, ethnic group of the family in which the participant grew up, physical violence between the respondent's parents, and the age and sex of the study participant. The study found that after taking account of the effect of these control variables, spanking makes an additional independent contribution to predicting college graduation. Nevertheless, there could be other variables that need to be controlled to provide more confidence in the conclusion that spanking is associated with a reduced chance of college graduation.

It would be especially important to control for parental warmth and supportiveness and cognitive stimulation, as we have done in other chapters, because spanking might be just one way in which lack of parental involvement, warmth, and support manifest themselves. It could be a lack of warmth and support by parents who spank, rather than the spanking itself, that is the problem. We do not agree because, although harsh parenting and lack of warmth are correlated with spanking, it is not a strong correlation. Most warm, loving, and involved parents also spank. Probably most parents believe they do it out of love and concern for the child. In fact, for the sample of mothers studied to examine the effect of impulsive spanking (Chapter 7), there was a tendency for more nurturing mothers to spank slightly *more* than less nurturing mothers. Moreover, we controlled for parent support and warmth in four other chapters: those that studied the relation of spanking to child antisocial behavior (Chapter 6), impulsiveness (Chapter 7), delinquency (Chapter 8), and mental ability (Chapter 10). The results can be summarized by saying that, when data was available to control for positive parental behaviors such as explaining and warmth and supportiveness, the controls reduced the size of the link between spanking and child behavior problems, but spanking continued to have the harmful side effect studied. In addition to controlling for other variables, longitudinal studies are needed to provide a stronger basis for concluding that spanking is one of the causes of failing to complete a college degree. We were able to do longitudinal studies for three of the chapters in this book, and a number of other longitudinal studies are described in Chapter 19. The three longitudinal studies in this book found that spanking led to more antisocial behavior (Chapter 6), slower development of cognitive ability (Chapter 10), and an increased probability of crime as an adult (Chapter 15). The study in this chapter, although it is not longitudinal, is consistent with those studies in finding that spanking is associated with an increased probability of a harmful effect. Other chapters suggest some of the processes that explain why spanking is related to lower educational attainment, such as antisocial behavior as a child (Chapter 6), impulsiveness and lack of self-control (Chapter 7), and slower development of cognitive ability (Chapter 10). In addition, still other research has found that spanking is associated with alienation (Straus & Gimpel, 2001) and depression (Chapter 12 and DuRant, Getts, Cadehead, Emans, & Woods, 1995; Straus, 2001a). Finally, college graduation requires a self-directed commitment to learn, but in our opinion, spanking teaches obedience more than self-direction.

Whatever the processes that link spanking to a lower probability of completing higher education, the results in this chapter are another of the many cruelly ironic aspects of spanking. Many parents spank if the child comes home with poor grades, as in the example of a 13-year-old boy in Texas who did badly on a test. His teacher told the boy he was going to paddle him, in the same fashion as his father did to him. He then hit the boy twice with a large wooden paddle (Harrison, 2011). The irony of course is that the paddling probably decreased, rather than increased, the chances that the boy will do better on the next test. Although this book is about spanking by parents, corporal punishment by teachers probably has parallel adverse effects. A study by Talwar, Carlson, and Lee (2011) compared children in the first grade in two private schools in a West African country. Both schools served families who lived in the same urban neighborhood, and the parents were largely civil servants, professionals, and merchants. One school used corporal punishment and the other did not. They found that the children in school that used corporal punishment performed significantly worse in tasks involving *executive functioning*—psychological processes such as planning, abstract thinking, and delaying gratification. These are all characteristics needed for college graduation.

Both the research in this chapter and the results in previous chapters on the relation of spanking to characteristics that are inimical to completing a college degree, make it reasonable to conclude that spanking is associated with a decreased *probability* of college graduation. It is important to also keep in mind that a decreased *probability* means just that. That is, this adverse side effect actually affects only a minority of spanked children, just as only a minority of heavy smokers die of a smoking related disease (see the section on Risk Factors Relationships in Chapter 1). It is important to also keep in mind that this study also provided data on some many other life experiences and characteristics that influence academic achievement. Spanking is only one of these harmful experiences and not nearly as important as being the child of low-education parents or parents who physically assault each other. If we want more children to complete higher education, we need to move toward a society in which everyone is educated and no one assaults their partner and no one assaults their child under the guise of discipline.

With those qualifications in mind, our finding that spanking is associated with a decreased probability of graduating from college has important theoretical and practical implications. One theoretical implication is based on studies that show that low-education parents tend to spank more often than middle class parents (see Chapter 2 and Giles-Sims et al., 1995; Socolar & Stein, 1995; Straus, 2001a, Chart 4). Ironically, although parents spank to raise children who will follow rules and who will do well in school, the results of our research suggest that spanking may be a mode of discipline that more often has the opposite effect. If that is correct, it is as we said a cruel irony because more spanking, and with it less use of cognitive modes of correction, by low-education parents makes it particularly difficult for the children of the poor to attain a level of education that will enable them to surmount their difficult life circumstances and the economic and social barriers to upward social mobility.

Part IV
Spanking and Crime

12 What Explains the Link Between Spanking and Assaulting a Partner?

A substantial body of research, including the chapters in Parts II and III, has found that spanking or corporal punishment experienced as a child is associated with a broad range of serious behavior problems of children and adolescents. The chapters in this part of the book extend the inquiry to crime as an adult. This chapter and the next chapter are about the links between spanking and physically assaulting a romantic partner or spouse. Chapters 14 and 15 are about the relation of spanking to a broad range of criminal acts. Chapter 16 is about the relation of spanking to forcing sex on a partner. In the concluding part of the book, Chapter 19 summarizes the results of many studies of the relation of spanking to crime, with an emphasis on cross-cultural and longitudinal research. The questions to be addressed in this chapter include:

- What has previous research found about the link between being spanked as a child and later in life assaulting a marital or dating partner?
- What is the relationship of spanking to depression as an adult, to approving of violence, and to marital conflict?
- Are depression, approving violence, and marital conflict processes or mechanisms that explain why spanking is associated with an increased probability of assaulting a partner?
- Does the relation of spanking to assaulting a partner apply when the study controls for things that could be the underlying causes?
- Does the relationship between having been spanked as a child and assaulting a partner apply to assaults by women as well as men?
- Do the results apply to both minor assaults such as slapping a partner and severe assaults such as punching or choking a partner?
- What are the policy and practice implications of the results of the study reported in this chapter?

Carrie L. Yodanis is the coauthor of this chapter.

Spanking and Assaults on Partners

Studies over the last 35 years have found that spanking is related to physically assaulting a partner. Gelles (1974) studied 80 families and found that adults who had been spanked frequently as a child (at least monthly) had a higher rate of assaulting a partner than those who had not been hit. Carroll (1977) studied 96 couples and found that "36.6% of those who had experienced a high degree of parental punishment reported assaulting a spouse compared to 14.5% of those who had not." Other studies found similar results. Johnston (1984) studied 61 abusive men and 44 nonabusive men and found that spanking was related to both minor and severe spouse abuse. Kalmuss's (1984) analysis of a nationally representative sample of 2,143 American couples found that being slapped or spanked as a teenager more than doubled the probability of husband-to-wife and wife-to-husband assaults.

Straus and Kaufman Kantor (1994) studied a second nationally representative sample and found that spanking was a significant risk factor for assaults on wives, even when other potentially influential variables, such as socioeconomic status, gender, age, witnessing violence between parents, and alcohol use, were controlled. Finally, a longitudinal study of high school boys (Simons et al., 1998) found that the more spanking these boys had experienced, the more likely they were to hit a dating partner. The Simons et al. (1998) study is important because it controlled for the level of misbehavior that presumably led to the parents spanking when the boys were younger. This is critical because, as noted in previous chapters, parents tend to spank in *response* to misbehavior. Therefore, if a study does not control for the level of misbehavior in adolescents, it may reflect preexisting aggressive and antisocial tendencies of the boys who were spanked, rather than the effect of spanking.

The research showing that spanking is associated with an increased probability of physical assaults against a partner is consistent with many studies that have found that spanking is related to physical aggression against other children and to other behavior problems. This includes the studies on spanking and child behavior problems in Part II, the other chapters on the relation of spanking to adult violence and crime in this part of the book, and the studies reviewed by (Gershoff, 2002).

The Linking Processes

Previous studies have found that spanking is associated with physically assaulting a partner. But those studies do not show *why* spanking is associated with an increased probability of physically assaulting a partner. This chapter presents the results of investigating three of the many possible processes that could explain what produces the link between spanking and violence against a partner. The three *mediating* processes are:

- Corporal punishment teaches that it is morally correct to hit to correct misbehavior and that carries over to relationships between adults.

- Corporal punishment limits development of nonviolent conflict-resolution skills that results in a high level of conflict with partners and, therefore, a higher probability of violence.
- Corporal punishment increases the probability of depression, which in turn increases the probability of aggression.

The Morality of Violence

Although physically assaulting a partner is a criminal act, American culture actually tolerates and legitimizes such acts in various ways. National surveys show that at least one quarter of the population approves slapping a spouse under some circumstances (Gelles & Straus, 1988; Greenblat, 1983; Moore & Straus, 1995; Simon et al., 2001; Straus et al., 2006; Straus, Kaufman Kantor, & Moore, 1997). When asked for an example of such a circumstance, by far the most frequently mentioned circumstance was sexual infidelity (Greenblat, 1983, pp. 243–246). Among the university students studied for Chapter 13 on spanking and partner violence in 32 nations, the rates for approving of a husband slapping his wife under some circumstances ranged from 26% to 45%, and the rates for approving of a wife slapping her husband ranged from 65% to 82%.

These attitudes are partly a carryover from a previous historical era when husbands did have the legal right to *physically chastise* an *errant wife* (Calvert, 1974). American courts began nullifying this common law principle in the 1870s, but it has survived in American culture and in the informal culture of the criminal justice system. To take just one of thousands of examples, a New Hampshire judge, when sentencing a man who stabbed his wife, admonished him by saying—"if you had just slapped her, you wouldn't be here today" (Darts & Laurals, 1993). The multitude of ways in which the actions and inactions of the criminal justice system continued to legitimize partner assault has been documented for at least a generation (Straus, 1976). There has been remarkable progress since then, largely due to the efforts of the women's movement. Instead of advising police officers to avoid interfering in domestic disturbances, (International Association of Chiefs of Police, 1967), most police departments now require or recommend arrest (Buzawa & Buzawa, 2003; Sherman, Schmidt, & Rogan, 1992).

The reasons for the persistence of norms permitting marital violence are multiple and complex. This chapter examines the hypothesis that one of the explanations is spanking by parents. Because parents who spank or slap a misbehaving child are doing so with community approval and act in the belief that spanking is sometimes necessary for the child's own good, spanking teaches children the unintended lesson that hitting is a morally correct way of dealing with misbehavior. That lesson can then be carried over to also apply to the misbehavior of an intimate partner.

Social learning theory suggests that one of the ways children learn to use and value violence is by observing and modeling the behavior of their parents (Bandura, 1973). We think this is especially likely to happen if the violence they observe is in the form of spanking a misbehaving child because, as just noted, doing so is socially approved behavior. A 1998 survey of a nationally representative sample of U.S. adults found that 73% believe spanking is a necessary part of child rearing (Ellison & Bradshaw, 2009). Thus, when parents spank to correct and teach, it is accompanied by an unintended hidden curriculum. One of the hidden lessons in that curriculum is that violence can be and should be used to secure good ends—that is, it teaches that violence is morally justified, not just in the extreme of self-defense, but when dealing with persistent misbehavior in ordinary human interaction (Wolfe, Katell, & Drabman, 1982). Another lesson stems from the fact that most parents hit a child only after trying other methods of correction and control. From this, children learn that violence is permissible "when other things don't work" (Straus et al., 2006, pp. 103–104).

Parents assume that these lessons about the morality of hitting someone who misbehaves and "won't listen to reason" will be applied when their child is an adult, only to hitting a child who misbehaves. Studies of children show, however, that children who are spanked tend to apply these principles to interaction with other children who misbehave toward them (see Chapter 6 and Simons & Wurtele, 2010). This chapter builds on that research by investigating the possibility that the lessons learned persist into adulthood and dating and marital relationships. This possibility arises because it is almost inevitable that, sooner or later, a partner will misbehave and not listen to reason as the partner sees it. As one woman put it, "I punch guys for the same reasons people 'discipline' their children. I've got expectations in love, and I want him to improve" (Connell, 2002).

These research results and theories led to the following hypotheses:

Hypothesis 1: The more spanking experienced, the greater the probability of believing that there are circumstances when one would approve of hitting a partner.

Hypothesis 2: Individuals who believe that it is sometimes permissible to hit a partner are more likely to actually hit their partner than those who do not.

Truncated Development of Conflict-Resolution Skills

Another process that we investigated to try to understand what might explain why spanking is associated with an increase in physically assaulting an intimate partner starts from the assumption that the more parents rely on spanking to deal with misbehavior, the lower the child's skills will be in nonviolent problem solving. This is partly because, as was shown in Chapter 10 on spanking and cognitive ability, spanking slows cognitive development. An even more direct relationship may occur because each time parents spank, it denies the child the opportunity to observe, participate in, and learn nonviolent modes of influencing the behavior of another person. These modes include explaining, negotiating, compromising, and modifying their own behavior to adapt to the situation. As one parent we spoke to put it, in explaining why she spanked, "I don't have time for all that." Based on this line of reasoning, we hypothesized that:

> *Hypothesis 3: The more spanking experienced, the greater the probability of inadequate skill in managing conflict and, therefore, a higher probability of unresolved conflicts with partners.*
>
> *Hypothesis 4: A high level of conflict, in turn, is associated with an increased risk of violence (as shown in Straus et al., 2006, Chart 13).*

The data available for this chapter let us test the fourth hypothesis because it includes a measure of the presumed consequence of a lack of such problem-solving skills: a measure of unresolved marital conflict.

Depression

Still another process that might explain why spanking is linked to assaulting a partner identifies depression as a *mediating* variable (also known as an *intervening* variable). A mediating variable refers to a characteristic or a process that, if supported by the statistical analysis, provides at least part of the explanation for the link between the hypothesized cause variable and the effect variable.

Depression was included in the theory we tested because of the results from two related lines of research. The first line of research shows that spanking is associated with being depressed as an adult. Straus (1995a) and Straus and Kaufman Kantor (1994) found that, after statistically controlling for six risk factors (e.g., witnessing parents assault each other and a low socioeconomic status), individuals who were slapped or spanked frequently during adolescence were twice as likely to experience severe depressive symptoms and suicidal ideation when they were adults. There are at least 13 other studies that have found that spanking is associated with an increased probability of depression, including: Afifi et al. (2006), Bordin et al. (2009), DeVet (1997), DuRant et al. (1995), Fergusson, Boden, & Horwood, (2008), Harper, Brown, Arias, & Brody (2006), Holmes & Robins (1988), Leary et al. (2008), Spencer (1999), Turner & Finkelhor (1996), Turner & Muller (2004).

A second relevant line of research has found that depression is associated with an increased probability of hostile and aggressive behavior toward others. Although depressed individuals are typically thought of as passive and motivationally deficient, a growing body of research suggests that depression is often associated with aggression, especially in the form of uncontrolled violent outbursts against others (Berkowitz, 1993). The co-occurrence of depression and aggression among children (Garber, Quiggle, Panak, & Dodge, 1991) as well as adults, led Berkowitz (1983, 1993) to speculate that depressive symptoms may be linked to hostility or violence against a partner. This speculation is confirmed by the results of studies focusing specifically on domestic violence. For example, one study found that domestically violent males are more than twice as likely (45% versus 20%) to report symptoms of clinical depression than nonviolent males (Julian & McKenry, 1993). The differences remained even when race, quality of the marital relationship, life stress, and alcohol use were controlled for statistically. Further, Maiuro, Cahn, Vitaliano, Wagner, and Zegree (1988) found that 67% of men who assaulted their wives were clinically depressed compared with 34% of young men who assaulted nonfamily members, and 4% of nonassaultive men (see also Tolman & Bennett, 1990).

The link between depression and partner assault has not yet been adequately explained and most likely represents a complex, reciprocal relationship with a number of other characteristics of each of the partners and of their relationship. Some researchers (Maiuro et al., 1988; Tolman & Bennett, 1990), however, have suggested that individuals who are depressed may resort to physical violence to help deal with feelings of helplessness that frequently accompany depression. In the case of marital relationships, an individual may act aggressively toward his or her partner in an effort to reestablish control over a discordant marital relationship that is in jeopardy of dissolving. Additionally, enduring patterns of low self-esteem and personal insecurity, or fears of abandonment, may predispose some individuals to respond aggressively to perceived threats of loss of the relationship.

Postulating that depression serves as a precursor to spousal aggression does not contradict the fact that depression can also be a consequence of being assaulted by a partner, as was shown by Stets and Straus (1990). We believe there is a bidirectional relationship and that depression is both a cause and a consequence of partner violence.

These theories and research results led to the following hypotheses:

Hypothesis 5: The more spanking experienced, the greater the probability of depression.

Hypothesis 6: Depression, in turn, increases the probability of violence against a partner.

Sample and Measures

We used path analysis to test the theory that spanking is related to assaulting a partner because spanking is associated with an increased probability that the child will grow up to approve of violence, have a marriage with a high level of conflict, and be depressed. Each of these three problems, in turn, is associated with an increased probability of hitting a partner. We tested this theory separately for men and women to allow for the possibility that the effects of spanking might be different for men and women and because it is widely believed that assaults on partners by women have a different etiology than assaults on partners by men (Cascardi & Vivian, 1995; Medeiros & Straus, 2006; Navaro, 1995; Straus, 2009c; White & Smith, 2009).

Sample

The sample used to test the theory consisted of 4,401 participants in the 1985 National Family Violence survey (2,557 women and 1,844 men). This sample is briefly described in Chapter 10 on number of children and spanking and in more detail in Straus & Yodanis (1996) and the Appendix. This is a nationally representative sample, not a sample selected because of involvement in some type of violence. The study participants were interviewed as adults about whether they were slapped or spanked when they were adolescents. For the generation who were adults at this time of this survey in 1985, being hit when they were adolescents was far from a rare event. Just over one half of American parents at that time hit early adolescent children, and they did so an average of 8 times a year (Straus & Donnelly, 1994). The high prevalence and chronicity of corporal punishment of adolescents in this nationally representative sample is important because it indicates that, despite the fact that the data are on early adolescence, the results are broadly applicable to that generation and are not restricted to a small number of families in which there was an abnormally high level of violence.

Measures

More detailed statistical information about the following measures are in Straus and Yodanis (1996).

Corporal punishment. Corporal punishment was measured by asking each study participant, "Thinking about when you, yourself, were a teenager, about how often would you say your mother or stepmother used physical punishment like slapping or hitting you? Think about the year in which this happened the most." The response categories were never, once, twice, 3 to 5 times, 6 to 10 times, 11 to 20 times, and more than 20 times. We asked a parallel question about corporal punishment by the participant's father. Empirical research and socialization theories of parent-child relationships have noted that mothers and fathers spend unequal time, perform unique parenting roles, have different interactions, and form dissimilar relationships with their children (Demo, 1992; Peterson & Rollins, 1987). The effects of parental use of corporal punishment may also be different depending on whether it is done by the father or the mother. To find out, we examined the effects of fathers' and mothers' use of corporal punishment separately.

A limitation of this measure is that it depends on the ability and the willingness of the study participants to recall these events. Fortunately, as we noted in the previous chapter, there is empirical evidence indicating that adults' recall of events in childhood can provide a valid measure (Coolidge et al., 2011; Fisher et al., 2011; Morris & Slocum, 2010). Further, the adult recall questions focused on adolescence because asking adults about corporal punishment at earlier ages would be less accurate. Finally, readers should note that *never* experiencing corporal punishment meant that it was never experienced during the teenage years; respondents could have experienced corporal punishment before they were teenagers, but that was not the focus of this question.

Assaults between partners. Assaults between partners was measured using the original Conflict Tactics Scales (described in Straus, 1979; Straus et al., 1996).

Violence approval. Violence approval was measured using two questions, "Are there situations that you can imagine in which you would approve of a husband slapping a wife's face?" and "Are there situations that you can imagine in which you would approve of a wife slapping a husband's face?" The response categories were 1 = strongly disagree, 2 = disagree, 3 = agree, and 4 = strongly agree.

Unresolved conflict. Unresolved conflict in the respondent's marriage or other relationship was measured by questions about how often the respondent and the spouse or partner disagreed on five issues: managing the money; cooking, cleaning, or repairing the house; social activities and entertaining; affection and sexual relations; and issues about the children. The response categories were 0 = never, 1 = sometimes, 2 = usually, 3 = almost always, and 4 = always.

Depression. Depression was measured using four questions from the Psychiatric Epidemiological Research Instrument (Dohrenwend, Askenasy, Krasnoff, & Dohrenwend, 1978): "Have you been bothered by feelings of sadness or worth?," "Have you felt very bad and worthless?," "Have you had times when you couldn't help wondering if anything was worthwhile anymore?," and "Have you had times when you felt completely hopeless about everything?" Respondents were asked to report how often this happened within the past year: never = 0, almost never = 1, sometimes = 2, fairly often = 3, and very often = 4. More information about this variable can be found in Straus (1995a).

Controls

The analysis included controlling for the following factors that might influence the results: age of the participant (to control for generational differences), socioeconomic status of the ethnic group, and the witnessing of violence between parents. To make the results more readily understandable, the charts in this chapter do not include the paths from the control variables. The results for those paths and more information about the measures and statistical methods used for this chapter are in Straus and Yodanis (1996).

Interrelation of Depression, Conflict, and Approval of Violence

Up to this point, the discussion treated each of the three processes that might explain the relation of spanking to physically assaulting a partner separately.

However, attitudes about the legitimacy of hitting a partner, conflict resolution skills, and depression are likely to work *together* to increase the likelihood of partner assault. This perspective is based on research showing that marital conflict and depression are linked (Beach, Sandeen, & O'Leary, 1990; Julian & McKenry, 1993; Maiuro et al., 1988). As for links with approval of violence, although we have not found previous research showing a connection between approval of violence and marital conflict and depression, such a connection is plausible as the cognitive aspect of the link between marital conflict and depression. The results of examining the relation of these mediating variables to each other revealed the following:

- *Depression and marital conflict.* Women with a high level of depression were about 3.4 times more likely to have a high level of marital conflict, and men with a high depression score were about 2.5 times more likely to be in a relationship with a high level of conflict. It is important to keep in mind that, because this is a cross-sectional study, it is just as plausible to interpret this result as showing that a high level of conflict is associated with an increased probability of depression, or that there is a bidirectional relationship and perhaps also an escalating cycle.
- *Depression and approval of marital violence.* Women with a high depression score were 1.7 times more likely to approve of marital violence. For men, there was no relationship between depression and approval of hitting a partner.
- *Marital conflict and approval of marital violence.* Men who approved of slapping a partner under some circumstances were 2.5 times more likely to be in a relationship characterized by high levels of conflict. For women, there was no relationship between conflict and approval of hitting a partner.

The difference between the findings for men and women might reflect gender differences in socialization and conflict management. To be more specific, these findings may reflect the tendency of men to externalize problems in the form of aggression and of women to internalize problems in the form of depression (Kramer, Krueger, & Hicks, 2008; Maschi, Morgen, Bradley, & Hatcher, 2008).

Relationship Between Spanking and Assaulting a Partner

The arrows in Chart 12.1 show the connections between the variables that were found to be statistically dependable. The numbers on each of these paths indicate the percent by which an increase of one unit of the variable at the start of the path is associated with an increase or decrease in the probability of the variable at the end of the path. The detailed tests of significance are in Straus and Yodanis (1996).

A. Assaults by Men (N= 1,844)

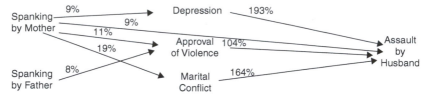

B. Assaults by Women (N= 2,557)

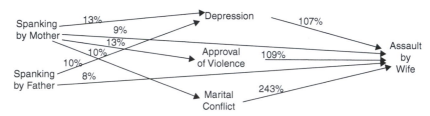

Chart 12.1   Three of the Processes Explaining the Link between Spanking and Assaulting a Partner

Direct Links between Spanking and Assault

Spanking by mothers. The upper section of Chart 12.1 (Part A) summarizes the results for assaults by male partners, and the lower section (Part B) summarizes the results for assaults by female partners. In the chart for assaults by men, the 9% on downward sloping arrow in the middle that goes from Spanking by Mother on the left to Assault by Husband on the far right indicates that each increase of one category in the seven-category measure of having been spanked or slapped by a mother is also associated with a 9% increase in the odds of a man assaulting his partner. The comparable arrow in Part B (the lower half of Chart 12.1) shows the same link between spanking or slapping by mothers and *women* assaulting their male partners.

Spanking by fathers. The results for Spanking by Father in Part A does not show a direct path from Spanking by Father to Assault by Husband because a statistically dependable relationship was not found. On the other hand, the chart for women (Part B) does show a direct path from Spanking by Father to Assault by Wife. The arrow from Spanking by Father to Assault by Wife shows that for each increase of one category in the spanking or slapping scale, there is an 8% increase in the probability of a woman physically assaulting her partner. In short, spanking or slapping by a mother is associated with an increased probability of later hitting a partner for both men and women, but spanking or slapping by a father is only related to *women* hitting their partner. However, as will be shown in the next section, spanking has similar indirect effects leading to physical assaults against a partner by both men and women.

The Mediating Mechanisms

The main issue addressed by this study is the theory that part of the explanation for the link between spanking and assaulting a partner is that spanking increases the probability of depression, approval of violence, and marital conflict. The paths from having been spanked or slapped to these three variables in the middle of both Part A and B of Chart 12.1 show the results of investigating three processes that might explain why being spanked or slapped by parents is associated with assaulting a partner.

Depression. One hypothesized process that might help explain the link between having been spanked or slapped by parents and physically assaulting a partner is that spanking or slapping increases the probability of depression. The paths from Spanking to Depression in both parts A and B of Chart 12.1 show that, for men and for women, the more spanking by mothers, the more likely both men and women are to have symptoms of depression. For women, but not for men, this also applies to spanking by fathers. The 193% on the path from Depression to Assault in Part A of Chart 12.1 shows that men in the high-depression group were almost 3 times more likely to have assaulted a partner in the previous 12 months than other men. The same path in Part B of Chart 12.1 shows that women in the high-depression group were just over twice as likely (107% increase) to have physically assaulted a partner than were other women.

Approval of violence. Another process that might explain why spanking is associated with an increased probability of assaulting a partner is that spanking increases the probability of approving violence. For this study, that was measured by whether the study participant agreed that there are circumstances when they might approve of a husband slapping his wife and a wife slapping her husband. Because a central theme of this book is that spanking is a fundamental cause of violence in the family and in society, we graphed that relationship in detail. Chart 12.2 shows that spanking or slapping is related to approval of violence by men, even when there was no violence between their parents as well as when there was. This does not mean that witnessing assaults between parents is unimportant. The fact that the line for men who witnessed this type of violence is higher on the graph shows that witnessing violence is also associated with even more approval of violence. Men who both witnessed physical assaults between their parents and were hit by their parents as an adolescent have the highest level of approving a husband slapping his wife. Almost identical results were found for women.

Returning to Chart 12.1 in Part A, there are paths on this issue for Spanking by Father and for Spanking by Mother. For men, the 11% on the path going from Spanking by Mother to Approval of Violence indicates that each increase

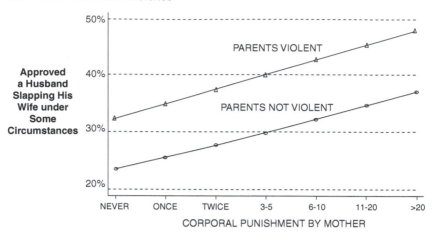

Chart 12.2   The More Spanking Men Experienced, the Higher the Probability They Will Approve of a Husband Slapping His Wife

* "Approve" was measured as the percent who did not strongly disagree that "I can think of a situation when I would approve of a husband slapping a wife's face."

of one point on the seven-point spanking or slapping scale is associated with an 11% increase in the probability of approving a husband slapping his wife. The 8% on the path from Spanking by Father to Approval of Violence shows that each increase of one unit in the measure of having been spanked or slapped as a teenager is associated with an 8% increase in the probability of approving the slapping of a partner. Part B of Chart 12.1 shows that for women, spanking by mothers, but not spanking by fathers is associated with a greater probability of approving a wife slapping a husband. For women, the 13% on the path in Chart 12.1 from Spanking by Mother to Approval of Violence indicates a somewhat stronger tendency for spanking or slapping by a woman's mother to be linked to approving slapping a husband. However, for women, we did not find a statistically dependable relationship between Spanking by Father and Approval of Violence. For women, spanking by fathers was related to an increased probability of depression.

The paths in Part A going from approval of violence to assault shows that men who agreed there are circumstances when they would approve of a husband slapping his wife are about twice as likely to actually hit their partner than are other men. Similarly, Part B shows that women who agreed that there are circumstances when they would approve of a wife slapping her husband were about twice as likely (109% increase) to have physically attacked their partner in the previous 12 months. These findings are consistent with the theory that spanking teaches the moral legitimacy of hitting someone who misbehaves, and this in turn increases the probability of actually physically assaulting a partner who misbehaves as that partner sees it.

Marital conflict. The paths from Spanking by Mother to Marital Conflict in Parts A and B of Chart 12.1 show that the more spanking by mothers, the more likely both men and women are to report high marital conflict. However, there is no path from Spanking by Father to Marital Conflict because we did not find a statistically dependable relationship for this path. The paths from Marital Conflict to Assault in both Parts A and B of Chart 12.1 show that high marital conflict was associated with men being 164% more likely to assault a partner and women being 243% more likely to assault a partner. These results are consistent with the theory that spanking and assaulting a partner are related because spanking restricts a child's opportunity to learn nonviolent modes of conflict resolution and, therefore, increases the probability of a high level of marital conflict, which in turn is associated with an increase in the probability of physically attacking a partner.

Do the Results Apply to Severe Assaults?

We also investigated the possibility that the results just presented might be different if the outcome variable was *severe* assaults; that is assaults involving attacks with objects, punching, and choking. These are acts, such as kicking and punching, that are associated with a greater risk of causing injury than slapping, shoving, and throwing things (see Straus & Yodanis, 1996), for information on the severe assault scale.) The results for severe assaults were similar to those just reported. The analysis for men found that depressive symptoms, violence approval, and marital conflict were associated with an increased probability of severely assaulting a female partner. Spanking or slapping by mothers, however, was not associated with severe assaults by men. The analysis for women found that depressive symptoms, violence approval, marital conflict, and spanking by mothers were associated with an increased probability of severely assaulting a male partner. Spanking or slapping by the fathers of these women, however, was not associated with an increased probability of severe assaults by women.

Other Variables Related to Assaulting a Partner

The five variables included in the analysis as controls are also of interest in their own right. The tables in Straus and Yodanis (1996) show that:

* Having grown up in a family where there was violence between their parents was associated with an increased probability of depression, approval of slapping a partner, marital conflict, and actually assaulting a partner.
* The probability of approving violence and actually assaulting a partner decreases with age. This is consistent with other studies of crime, including assaulting a partner (Suitor, Pillemer, & Straus, 1990).
* Higher socioeconomic status was associated with a *lower* probability of both the men and women in this study, being high in depression, approving

the slapping of a partner, experiencing marital conflict, and actually assaulting a partner.
- Minority ethnic group respondents in this study had a higher probability of marital conflict and assaulting a partner.

Summary and Conclusions

This chapter tested a theory about some of the processes that bring about a link between spanking and physically assaulting a partner in a marital or cohabiting relationship. The processes investigated are three of the adverse side effects of spanking: depression, attitudes approving violence, and marital conflict (which we used as proxies for deficits in conflict-resolution skills resulting from the use of corporal punishment). Our theory is that spanking is associated with an increased probability of each of these, and each in turn is associated with an increased probability of assaulting a partner. The results of the analyses from a nationally representative sample of married or cohabiting partners were largely consistent with this model. We found that spanking in adolescence was associated with an increased probability of:

- Experiencing depression as an adult
- Approving violence against a spouse
- A high level of marital conflict

In turn, each of these effects of spanking was associated with an increased probability of physically assaulting a partner. Thus, at least part of the association between spanking and adult spousal assaults is explained by these three variables. Moreover, these links were found for both men and women regardless of age, socioeconomic status, ethnic group, and whether or not the participants in the study grew up in a family in which there were assaults between their parents. Thus, spanking had a unique effect that was in addition to the effect of the control variables.

The Dose-Effect of Spanking

Defenders of spanking believe it is not harmful if it is used only rarely. To address this, we examined differences between participants in this study who were never hit, hit only once, hit only twice, hit 3 times, etc. Those analyses showed that each increase in spanking of an adolescent, *starting with just one instance,* was associated with an increase in approval of violence and actual violence toward a partner. Harmful effects for rare spanking are shown in the chapters on spanking and children's antisocial behavior, the outcomes associated with impulsive spanking (Chapters 6 and 7), and the other four chapters in this part of the book and in Straus (1994, Chart 7–2, 2001a) and in a study by Turner and Finkelhor (1996). Turner and Finkelhor used data from interviews with children age 10 to 16. They found that even one or two instance of spanking at those ages was associated with an increase in stress in children.

Some Limitations

Although the analysis controlled for a number of possible sources of spurious findings, some limitations of the research need to be considered to properly evaluate the findings. First, the effect of spanking might have occurred because some of the participants who experienced spanking might also have experienced more serious violence in the form of physical abuse. If so, that probably accounts for part of the effects on the participants who experienced frequent spanking. It is unlikely to explain the effects of low and moderate amounts of spanking because those participants were unlikely to have been victims of more severe physical attacks. In addition, studies by MacMillan et al. (1999); Straus and Kaufman Kantor (1994); Straus and Donnelly (2001a); Vissing et al. (1991); and Yodanis (1992) were able to exclude abused children and, after excluding them, each of those studies found that spanking continued to have significant harmful side effects such as those reported in this chapter.

Another limitation is that the spanking data were obtained by asking the study participants about being hit by their parents when they were adolescents. This raises several problems. Those who were hit at that age might be an unrepresentative sample. However, as reported earlier, more than half of the cohort in this study recalled being hit at the age. Thus, corporal punishment of early adolescents was typical of the U.S. population of that time. Since then, the percent of early adolescent children who are slapped or spanked has decreased. The data are, therefore, dated in respect to the prevalence of spanking, but as we pointed out earlier, this does not necessarily affect the relationship between spanking and later assaulting a partner. Another problem is that adults' recall data can be biased. However, it is not necessarily biased, as shown by studies such as (Coolidge et al., 2011; Fisher et al., 2011; Morris & Slocum, 2010). Nevertheless, participants in the study who hit their partners might perceive and report their parents as more violent than those who did not assault their partner. Although that is a concern for the study in this chapter, there are studies that do not depend on recall. These include the chapters on spanking and child behavior (Chapter 6), impulsive spanking (Chapter 7), the child-to-mother bond (Chapter 8), and spanking and adult crime (Chapter 15). Strassberg et al. (1994), Gershoff et al. (2010), and Taylor et al. (2010) all found that spanking is associated with subsequent violence. It is unlikely that, 20 years later, the study participants can accurately recall how many times they were hit. As a consequence, we view this as an ordinal measure that indicates who was hit more than others, not a measure of the actual number of times. Finally, most of those who were not spanked in their early teenage years were probably spanked at earlier ages. Thus, the results do not refer to those who were spanked and those who were not. They mostly refer to those for whom spanking continued into the early teenage years. One implication of this limitation is that the results shown may be minimum estimates of the effects of spanking because the most of the group who were not spanked in their early teenage years experienced the spanking earlier.

Finally, this was not a longitudinal study that controlled for misbehavior that led to the spanking. As a consequence, unlike the three longitudinal studies in this book and the longitudinal studies listed in Chapter 19 on spanking and its implications for societal-level crime and violence, the relationships found may reflect the effects of the maladaptive characteristics of the study participants who hit their partner, rather than the effects of spanking.

Policy Implications

To the extent that these cross-sectional findings can be interpreted as reflecting a causal relationship between spanking and assaulting a partner later in life, eliminating or reducing spanking can contribute to reducing marital violence. This is because, although spanking has declined in the United States, at least one third of American parents continue to hit early adolescent children (see Chapter 2).

Reducing or ending spanking may also make an indirect contribution to ending marital violence through its effect on the way the criminal justice system deals with partner violence. Police and prosecutorial policies intended to reduce partner violence have often been weakly implemented (Garner & Maxwell, 2009). It is possible that the link between spanking and approval of slapping a partner may be one of the factors underlying this weak implementation. The attitudes of police, prosecutors, and judges, like most other Americans, may reflect violence-justifying effects of spanking. That may be part of the reason the criminal justice system so often fails to act against all but the most egregious cases of marital assault. To the extent that criminal prosecution in cases of partner violence is an effective policy, ending spanking in child rearing could contribute to ending the de facto institutional practices that tolerate violence between marital, cohabiting, and dating partners.

The results in this chapter also suggest that a reduction in spanking could have a beneficial impact on one of the most pervasive forms of psychological distress—depression. Close to 15% of the population will experience an episode of major depression at some point in their lives (Substance Abuse Mental Health Services Administration, 2005). Moreover, mood disorders account for more usage of mental health services than any other psychiatric disorder and are responsible for the majority of all attempted and completed suicides (Boyer & Guthrie, 1985; Charney & Weissman, 1988). Thus, in addition to the association of spanking with physical assaults, the severity of the consequences associated with depression also underscores the need for professionals working with parents (such as nurses, parent educators, and pediatricians), to inform parents about the harmful side effects of spanking and help them avoid using spanking.

13 Assault and Injury of Dating Partners by University Students in 32 Nations

The previous chapter showed that spanking is associated with an increased probability of physically assaulting a partner. It also provided information on some of the processes or mechanisms that could explain why spanking is related to assaulting a partner among couples in a large and nationally representative of U.S. households. The research described in this chapter extends the examination of the link between spanking and assaulting a partner by examining these questions:

- What percent of university students in 32 nations physically assaulted a dating partner in the previous year?
- Does the link between spanking and physically assaulting a partner found for U.S. couples in the previous chapter apply to dating relationships of university students in 32 nations?
- What is the effect of being in these 32 different national social contexts on the prevalence of attitudes favoring slapping a partner and actually assaulting a partner, and the relationship of spanking to those attitudes and behaviors? That is, when the percent of the students in a national context who were spanked a lot is large, is there a correspondingly large percent of students who:
  - Approve of slapping a partner?
  - Actually assaulted a partner?
  - Injured a partner?

Information on the extent to which physical violence in university student dating relationships result in physical injury is important because we think that many people believe that acts of violence between dating couples is rarely serious or dangerous.

National Differences in Dating Partner Violence

There is an important difference between this chapter and the previous chapter in the method of research. This chapter presents the results of a cross-national

Emily M. Douglas is the first author of this chapter.

comparative study in which the issue is the potential effect of the national context on violence in couple relationships. To do this, we used data on the percent in each of the 32 nations of university students who experienced corporal punishment and the percent in each nation of students who had attitudes favorable to hitting a partner under certain circumstances, the percent in each nation who actually assaulted a partner, and the percent who assaulted seriously enough to physically injure their partner. The underlying theoretical reason for the focus on nations is to find out if *social settings* where there is a high rate of violent socialization of children in the form of spanking also tend to be social settings where there is a high rate of physically assaulting a dating partner.

Assaults on Dating Partners

Student Rates versus General Population Rates

As high as the percent of married couples who engage in physical assaults is (see previous chapter), numerous studies have found even higher high rates of physical assault on dating partners by university students. The typical results show that from 20% to 40% of students physically assaulted a dating partner in the previous 12 months (Archer, 2000, 2002; Katz, Washington Kuffel, & Coblentz, 2002; Sellers, 1999; Sugarman & Hotaling, 1989). The dating couple rates are 2 to 3 times greater than the rates typically found among representative samples of American households, and both the household and the dating couple assault rates are many times the rate of assaults known to the police. Assaults known to the police are reported as rates per 100,000 population, whereas assaults between couples are so prevalent that percentages (the rate per 100 couples) are more appropriate.

The much higher rate of assault by university students than in surveys of households is probably because most students are much younger. The average age of university students is about 20, whereas the average age of community samples of couples is about 40. The long established *age-crime curve* refers to the fact that most crimes, and especially violent crimes, peak in the late teens or early twenties and then decline rapidly. That is clearly the case for the crime of assaulting a partner. The rates decline from a peak of over 30% for the late teens to less than one half that at about age 40 (Straus & Ramirez, 2007; Suitor et al., 1990). Most of the dating violence studies have been in the United States and Canada. As noted previously, one of our objectives was to determine the extent to which these monumentally high assault rates are found among students in other national settings around the world. If high rates of physical assaults against dating partners are found to be characteristic of university students in most or many countries, it adds urgency to research which can help explain why so many students engage in this type of behavior.

Hypotheses

Like any form of violence, assaulting a partner has multiple causes. For purposes of this book, we investigated whether the prevalence of corporal punishment is one of them. The specific hypotheses we tested are:

The higher the percentage of students in a nation who are spanked as children, the higher the percent of students who:

- *Approve of a husband slapping his wife and a wife slapping her husband*
- *Assaulted a dating partner*
- *Injured a dating partner*

Sample and Measures

Sample

The hypotheses were tested using data on assaults perpetrated against dating partners by university students who participated in the International Dating Violence Study in 32 nations. The study and the sample are described in Chapter 3 on the worldwide prevalence of spanking and in (Rebellon et al., 2008; Straus, 2008b, 2009b). We analyzed data on the 14,252 of the 17,404 students in the study who were in a romantic relationship. Of the 32 nations, there were two in Africa, seven in Asia, thirteen in Europe, four in Latin America, two in the Middle East, two in North America, and Australia and New Zealand.

Measures

Spanking. Spanking was measured by asking the students whether they agreed or disagreed that: "I was spanked or hit a lot by my parents before age 12" and "When I was a teenager, I was hit a lot by my mother or father." The response categories were: strongly agree (1), agree (2), disagree (3), and strongly disagree (4). Anyone who did not strongly disagree was considered to have been spanked as a child. This is based on assuming that if their parents had not spanked or hit a lot they would choose strongly disagree. We tested that assumption before proceeding by computing the correlations of these variables with approval of a husband hitting his wife under some circumstances. Each pair of correlations compared counting anyone who chooses any response, except strongly disagree, as having been spanked with correlations using agree or strongly agree as the criterion. All the correlations were higher using not strongly disagree as the criterion for having been spanked.

The question asks about being spanked or hit *a lot* because of evidence that a lot is the typical experience in the United States, and perhaps in most of the other nations in the study. Studies that measured how often toddlers were hit have found an average to 2 to 3 times a week (Giles-Sims et al., 1995; Holden et al., 1995; Stattin et al., 1995). One study found that even at age 6, 70% of children were hit once a week or more (Vittrup & Holden, 2010).

Approval of partner violence. Two questions were used to measure approval of violence against a partner: "I can think of a situation when I would approve of a husband slapping a wife's face" and "I can think of a situation when I would approve of a wife slapping a husband's face." The response categories for these questions were the same as for the spanking question. The cut points were again the percentage of students at each nation who did not strongly disagree. And again, exploratory analyses found stronger correlations using this cut point than with other possible cutting points.

Measures of partner violence. Physical assault and injury were measured by the revised Conflict Tactics Scales or CTS2 (Straus et al., 1996). In the past 25 years, the Conflict Tactics Scales have been used in hundreds of studies in many nations, but especially in economically developing nations because it is part of the World Health Organization sponsored studies of maternal health. It has demonstrated cross-cultural reliability and validity (Archer, 1999; Straus, 1990a, 2004; Straus & Mickey, 2012). For this chapter, we used the CTS2 scales measuring physical assault and physical injury, and the subscales for severe assault and severe injury. As in previous studies using the CTS with general population samples, most of the assaults and injuries were in the minor category. Because severe violence may be a unique phenomenon with a different etiology, (Straus, 1990c; Straus, 2011; Straus & Gozjolko, in press) all analyses were conducted for the overall rates of partner violence, and then repeated for the rates of severe violence.

Physical assault. The CTS2 uses five behaviors to measure minor assault, for example, slapping a partner. For severe assault, there are seven behaviors, for example, punched or choked a partner. The *overall* rate of partner assault is the percent in each nation who perpetrated any one or more of the 12 acts.

Injury. There are five CTS2 items to measure injury inflicted on a partner, such as "Having a sprain, bruise, or cut after a fight with a partner" (a minor injury item) and "Needed to see doctor because of a fight with a partner."

The scales for assault and injury were coded 1 if any of the acts occurred in the past year and coded 0 if there were none. The data used for this chapter are the percentage of students at each nation with a score of 1, which is the percentage who assaulted or injured a dating partner. The reliability for the overall physical assault scale for the samples in this study was .88. For the injury scale, the alpha coefficient was .89.

Moderator and control variable. Because the etiology and the effects of assaulting a partner may be different for men and women, we used gender as a moderator variable by repeating all analyses for male and female students.

The analysis controlled for the score for each nation on the limited disclosure scale (Chan & Straus, 2008; Sabina & Straus, 2006; Straus et al., 2010; Straus & Mouradian, 1999). In research on self-reported criminal behavior, differences between nations could reflect differences in the willingness of people in different nations to report socially undesirable behaviors and beliefs as much or more than real differences in crime and criminogenic beliefs. For example, we found that the higher the score on the limited disclosure scale, the lower the percent who agreed that they could think of a situation when they would approve of a husband slapping his wife ($r = -.36$) and the lower the percent who said they had injured a partner ($r = -.21$). Scores of the students in each nation on the limited disclosure scale permit a statistical control for nation to nation differences in willingness to disclose such information. Without this control, the results could be spurious; that is, the correlations might reflect differences between nations in the willingness of students to self-report socially undesirable behavior and beliefs rather than differences in spanking.

Data Analysis

The analyses used a *nation-level* data file, in which the cases are the 32 nations, not individual students. The data for each case consists of summary statistics for the nation, such as the mean or the percentage of students with a certain characteristic. Separate data files were created for males and females, based on aggregating the data for the males and females in each site, and the analyses were replicated using those files.

Partial correlation analysis was used to test the hypothesized relationships of corporal punishment to approval of slapping a spouse, perpetration of physical assault against a dating partner, and injuring a dating partner. The analyses controlled for the age of the respondent, length of the relationships, social desirability, and socioeconomic status—and for analyses of the total sample, gender of the respondent.

Differences Between Men and Women and Between Nations

This section describes the percent of students at each of the 32 nations who were spanked as a child and as a teenager, the percent who approved of violence against a dating partner, and the percent who physically assaulted and injured a dating partner in the previous 12 months. For each of these beliefs and behaviors, we give the average percentage for all 32 nations, and also the nation with the lowest and the highest percent and the percent for the United States. The section below on differences between nations explains how to use Charts 13.2 to 13.7 to get a rough estimate of the percentages for each nation, and for men and women students.

Spanking before age 12. The percent of students who were spanked as a child ranged from 15% in the Netherlands to 75% in Taiwan. The average for the

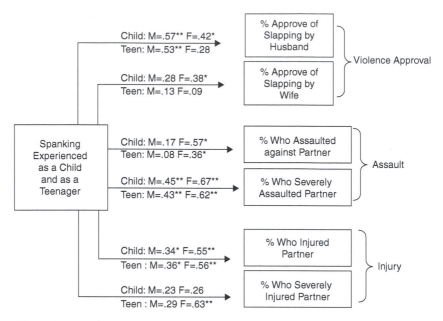

Chart 13.1 Nations Where Students Have Experienced More Spanking Tend to Also Be Nations Where a Larger Percent of Students Approve of Partner Violence, Assault a Partner, and Injure a Partner[a]

[a]M = Correlation for male student data. F = correlation for female student data.
*p < .05, **p < .01. Coefficients on each line are the partial correlations using nations as the cases (N = 32), controlling for mean limited disclosure scale score of each nation.

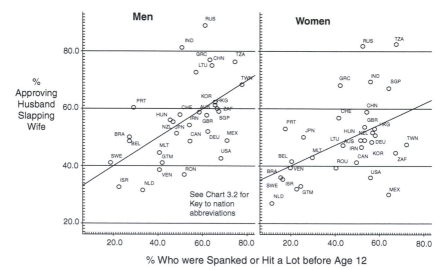

Chart 13.2 The Larger the Percent in a Nation Who Experienced Spanking *as a Child,* the Larger the Percent Who Approved a Husband Slapping His Wife

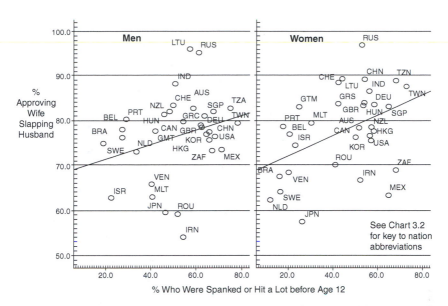

Chart 13.3 The Larger the Percent in a Nation Who Experienced Spanking *as a Child,* the Larger the Percent Who Approved a Wife Slapping Her Husband

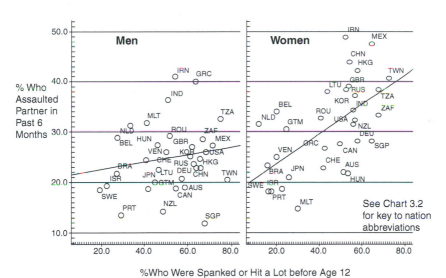

Chart 13.4 The Larger the Percent in a Nation Who Experienced Spanking *as a Child,* the Larger the Percent Who Assaulted Their Partner

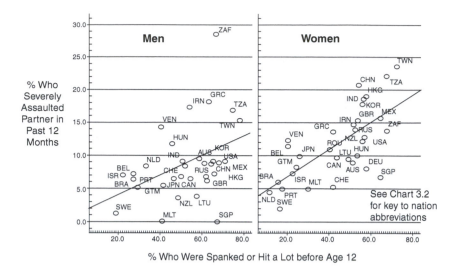

Chart 13.5 The Larger the Percent in a Nation Who Experienced Spanking *as a Child,* the Larger the Percent Who *Severely* Assaulted Their Partner

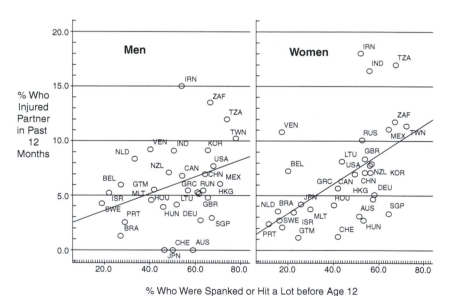

Chart 13.6 The Larger the Percent in a Nation Who Experienced Spanking *as a Child,* the Larger the Percent Who Injured Their Partner

See Chart 3.2 for the key to nation abbreviations.

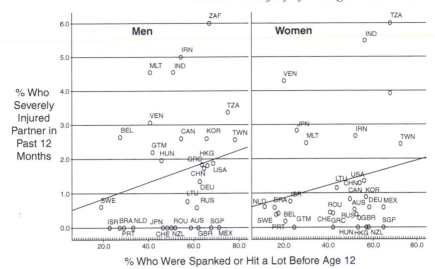

Chart 13.7   The Larger the Percent in a Nation Who Experienced Spanking *as a Child,* the Larger the Percent Who *Severely* Injured Their Partner

See Chart 3.2 for the key to nation abbreviations.

32 nations was 47%. Table 2 in Chapter 3 and Chart 13.2 give the percent for each of the 32 nations and also show that in almost all nations, boys were hit somewhat more than girls.

The 47% who experienced spanking as a child, as reported by the students in this sample, is almost certainly an underestimate for the children and families from the nations in this study. Among the U.S. students, for example, only 61% reported spanking before age 12, whereas Chapter 2 on spanking in the United States shows that 94% of the parents interviewed reported spanking toddlers at least once in the preceding year. The difference between 94% and 61% probably reflects at least three things. First, many people cannot remember much of what happened when they were toddlers (the peak ages for spanking). Second, the question asked about being spanked a lot, whereas the percent in Chapter 2 is for any spanking in the previous 12 months. Third, this is a sample of university students and, therefore, has relatively few from the lowest socioeconomic status households where spanking is most prevalent. These reasons for underestimating probably apply to students in all 32 nations. To the extent that the underestimate applies to all the nations, it means that the percentages can be used to rank the percent of students in the 32 nations who were spanked. That rank order is crucial for determining if the extent of spanking in a national context is associated with the percent who assaulted.

Teenagers. We had expected the percent of students who were hit as teenagers would be substantially lower than the percent who were spanked before age 12, in part because that is what our three national surveys of parents in the United

States have found (see Chapter 2). However, the percentages for the university students in this sample are lower, but not that much lower. They ranged from 10% hit as a teenager in the Netherlands to 66% in Tanzania, with the average for the 32 nations being 33%. This is lower than the 44% for being hit before age 12, but not nearly as much lower as we expected. As we found for being hit before age 12, the percent of boys in each nation who were hit by parents as a teenager was almost always slightly higher than the percent of girls who were hit as a teenager (see Chapter 3, Table 3.2).

Approval of husband slapping his wife. The students were asked whether they agreed or disagreed with "I can think of a situation when I would approve of a husband slapping a wife's face." The percent who did not strongly disagree that they could approve of a husband slapping his wife in some situations ranged from 28% in the Netherlands to 85% in Russia. The average for the 32 nations was 51%. Among U.S. students, 38% did not strongly disagree that they could approve of a husband slapping his wife in some situations.

Approval of a wife slapping her husband. The students were also asked the extent to which they agreed or disagreed with "I can think of a situation when I would approve of a wife slapping a husband's face." The percent who did not strongly disagree that they could approve of a wife slapping her husband in some situations ranged from 59% in Japan to 96% in Russia. The median for the 32 nations was 77%. Among U.S. students, 77% did not strongly disagree that they could approve of a wife slapping her husband in some situations.

The much higher percent of students who would approve of a women slapping her husband in some circumstance (median of 51%) than approve of a man slapping his wife (median of 77%) is consistent with several other studies (Felson, 2000; Felson & Feld, 2009; Gulas, McKeage, & Weinberger, 2010; Nabors, Dietz, & Jasinski, 2006; Simon et al., 2001; Sorenson & Taylor, 2005; Straus, 1995b; Straus, Kaufman Kantor et al., 1997). It is an indication of cultural toleration of a woman hitting her partner. Part of the explanation is probably public recognition of the greater potential for injury when men assault women (Greenblat, 1983). Regardless of why assaults by women are more accepted, that cultural acceptance is probably also one of the reasons that more than 200 studies have found higher rates of assault by female than male partners (Archer, 2002; Fiebert, 2010; Straus, 2008b, 2009c). Of course, many other variables also contribute to the high rate of assaults by women on male partners, for example, women are protected (up to a certain point) by chivalry norms (Felson, 2002; see also Straus, 1999; Winstok & Straus, 2011a).

Differences between nations. The approximate values for each nation of the variables in this study can be found by reading the values shown on the vertical and horizontal axes in Charts 13.2 to 13.7. For example, in Chart 13.2, the plot point for Israel (ISR) in the lower left of the panel for men shows that 33% of the male students in Israel did not strongly disagree that "I can think of a situation in which I would approve of a husband slapping a wife's face." On the other hand, when it comes to a wife slapping her husband, the plot point for Israel in Chart 13.3, shows that almost twice as many of the men (63%) did not strongly disagree that there are situations in which they might approve of a wife slapping her husband. As pointed out earlier, greater acceptance of a wife slapping her husband than the husband slapping his wife is consistent with several other studies.

Assaulting a partner. The percent who physically assaulted a partner in the previous 12 months differed greatly from nation to nation. For all assaults regardless of whether it was a minor assault like slapping or a severe assault like punching, the rates ranged from 17% in Portugal to 40% in Iran, and the average for the 32 nations was 30%. A rate in the range of 20% to 40% is typical of most studies of dating partner violence (Archer, 2002; Katz et al., 2002; Stets & Straus, 1990; Sugarman & Hotaling, 1989). Even the lowest assault rate in this study is still very high, compared with rates for other nonclinical populations. For example, it is about 3 times higher than the percent of married and cohabiting couples who physically assault (Gelles & Straus, 1988; Straus & Gelles, 1986; Straus & Smith, 1990).

Our finding that, in most of the 32 nations, female students were somewhat *more* likely than male students to have assaulted a partner is also typical of other studies of university students (Archer, 2002; Desmarais et al 2012; Straus, 2008b). The percent of male and female students in each nation who assaulted a partner in the previous 12 months is given in Straus (2008b) and can also be determined by reading the value for a nation in the vertical axis of Chart 13.6.

For *severe* assaults, the rates are of course much lower. The percent who severely assaulted a partner in the previous 12 months ranged from 1.8% in Sweden to 22% in Taiwan, and the average for the 32 nations was 11%. Among U.S. students, 11% reported severely assaulting a partner. Considering that these are severe assaults (roughly analogous to an aggravated assault in the U.S. legal system), these are extremely high rates.

Injured a partner. Although in this and more than 200 other studies (Desmarais et al 2012; Fiebert, 2010), as many or more female than male students assaulted a partner, the attacks by male students usually resulted in more injury than attacks by female students (Archer, 2000, 2002; Capaldi et al., 2009; Whitaker, Haileyesus, Swahn, & Saltzman, 2007). The typical finding is that women suffer about two thirds of the injuries. However, for this study, as in a few other studies, the difference was much smaller. The 6.9% of female students who were injured is only 15% higher than the 6.0% of male students who suffered an injury from an attack by a female partner. The results for severe injury show a larger difference: 1.6% of the women suffered a severe injury compared with 1.1% of the men, which is a 45% higher injury rate for women. For the U.S. part of the sample, the rates for any injury of students are 7.8% of women and 7.6% of men, which is only a 3% difference. For severe injury however, the rate of injury of U.S. women students was 46% greater than the rate of severe injury of male students (1.9% of women, 1.3% of men). These injury rates are roughly consistent with the rates for a nationally representative sample of U.S. couples (Stets & Straus, 1990).

Relationship between Spanking and Partner Violence

As astonishing and important as are the high percent of university students who approve of slapping a partner under some circumstances, and who actually assaulted a partner or inflicted injury, the crucial issue for this chapter is why these aspects of violence are so prevalent. Of course, there are many forces at work. The one we investigated for this book is whether nations in which spanking is more prevalent also tend to be nations in which there is a high rate of approving of slapping a partner and actually assaulting and injuring a partner. To find out, we computed the correlation of the level of spanking in each nation with each of the six aspects of partner violence described above, again, by nation, controlling for the score on the limited disclosure scale. The correlations are shown in Chart 13.1. Most of these correlations are large enough to be statistically dependable despite being based on only 32 cases. Because the link between having been spanked and assaulting a partner might be different for men and women, we ran the analysis separately for male and female students. In addition, the analysis controlled for nation-to-nation differences in reluctance to disclose socially undesirable beliefs and behaviors. Chart 13.1 summarizes what we found in the form of the correlations between spanking and each of the six aspects of partner violence studied. Charts 13.2 to 13.7 are scatter plots with the regression line showing the relation of the percent spanked in each nation to each of the six aspects of violence. They also indicate (with the aid of a ruler), the percentages for each of the 32 nations for each of these aspects of violence, separately for men and women. See the example presented earlier in the section on differences between nations.

Spanking before Age 12

The correlation coefficient of .57 on the top arrow in Chart 13.1 shows that the larger the percent of male students in a nation who were spanked or hit a lot before they were 12, the larger the percent who did not strongly disagree with the statement "I can think of a situation when I would approve of a husband slapping a wife's face." The correlation of .42 on that line is for women. It shows almost as strong a relationship between being spanked as a child and approval of a husband slapping his wife. Chart 13.2 lets the reader see which nations are low and high on spanking and approval of a husband slapping his wife. The trend line shows that the higher the percent of students in a nation who were spanked or hit a lot before they were 12, the higher the percent who approved of a husband slapping his wife under certain circumstances, and that this applies to both men (the left side of the chart) and women (the right side of the chart).

Spanking during the Teenage Years

The correlations on the underside of the top arrow in Chart 13.2 are for teenagers. For men, the correlation of .53 is almost as strong a relationship to approval of a husband slapping his wife as was found for being spanked as a young child. For the women in this sample, however, the correlation of .28 is not large enough to be statistically dependable when there are only 32 cases.

In Chapter 5 on approval of violence and spanking, we presented similar results, but for that chapter, the focus was on whether people who approve of slapping a wife are more likely to approve of spanking. We believe both are correct—that is, that spanking increases the probability of being inclined to violence (our interpretation of the results in this chapter) and that being inclined to violence increases the probability of spanking (our interpretation of the results in Chapter 5).

Spanking and Approval of a Wife Slapping Her Husband

The correlations on the top of and below the arrow leading to Approve of Slapping by Wife in Chart 13.1 show that the only statistically dependable result we found for the issue of whether spanking is related to approval of *a wife* slapping her husband was for women who were spanked or hit a lot before they were 12 years old. Even that correlation is smaller than the correlations for approval of husband slapping a wife. This was unexpected because, as shown earlier in this chapter, a larger percent of the students approved of a wife slapping her husband. Although only one of the four relationships is statistically dependable, the percent of men and women students in each nation, who approved of a wife slapping her husband under certain circumstances, are important descriptive statistics.

Spanking and Assaulting a Partner

Any assault. The percentages of men and women who assaulted a partner are given in Chart 13.4. The arrows leading to Assault in the center of Chart 13.1 give the partial correlations from testing the hypothesis that the higher the prevalence of spanking in a nation, the more likely students would be to physically assault a dating partner. Contrary to what we expected, for men we found no relationship between the percent in a nation who were spanked and physically assaulting a partner. However, for women, the larger the percent in a nation who experienced spanking, the larger the percent who physically assaulted a partner.

Severe assault. Most of the assaults in the Assault measure are minor, such as slapping or throwing something at a partner. Because severe violence may be a unique phenomenon with a different etiology (Straus, 1990c; Straus, 2011; Straus & Gozjolko, in press), we repeated the analysis using severe assaults such as punching and choking a partner. The correlations on the arrows to

Severe Assault against Partner are all large and statistically dependable. Thus, for both men and women, the percent in a nation who were hit by parents to correct misbehavior, either as a child or as a teenager, is related to an increased percent in who severely attacked a partner. Again, the link between spanking and severe assault on a dating partner is slightly stronger for the women in this study than for the men. The percentage in each nation who severely assaulted a partner in each nation is indicated in the vertical axis of Chart 13.5. See the example for Israel of how to find these percentages in the charts given in a previous section on differences between nations.

Spanking and Injuring a Partner

Any injury. Charts 13.6 show the percentages in each nation who injured a partner. The arrow leading to Injury in the lower part of Chart 13.1 shows that the larger the percentage of students in a nation who experienced spanking as a child, the higher the percentage who injured a dating partner. This relationship applies to both male and female students when the outcome variable is any injury.

Severe injury. When the outcome variable is severe injury to women, the results are similar in the sense that all four of the correlations are in the predicted direction, but only the correlation of .63 for the relation of corporal punishment as a teenager to severely injuring a partner is large enough to be statistically dependable. Although the correlation of spanking before age 12 with severely assaulting a partner is not strong enough to be statistically dependable, we included Chart 13.6 (the scatter plot for this relationship) because it shows the approximate percent of students in each of the 32 nations who severely injured a partner, including the fact that there are six nations in which 3% or more of the men severely injured a partner and four nations in which 3% or more of the women students severely injured a partner.

Summary and Conclusions

Although not all the correlations were statistically dependable, the general pattern is that nations where spanking is more prevalent tend to also be nations in which a higher percent of the students in this study approved of slapping a partner, actually physically assaulted a partner, and injured a partner. These societal-level results show that the link between spanking and violence applies not only to the characteristics of individual persons, but also to the national contexts in which the students in this study lived.

Limitations

Before drawing further conclusions from these results, some important limitations need to be mentioned. First the data is on university students and may be unique to that sector of the population of a nation. However, the results are consistent with those of other studies (including the preceding chapter), which have found similar relationships for representative samples. In addition, there is evidence that nation-to-nation differences found for these students corresponds to national differences in the same variables found by other studies. Evidence showing the validity of the International Dating Violence Study data is in Straus (2009b).

Another limitation is that about two thirds of the sample is female. We reduced the potential problems resulting from this limitation by conducting separate analyses for males and females.

The measure of spanking is another limitation because it is recall data. However, as we pointed out in a previous chapter, there is empirical evidence indicating that adult recall of events in childhood can provide a valid measure of childhood experiences (Coolidge et al., 2011; Fisher et al., 2011; Morris & Slocum, 2010). Another limitation of the measure is that it asks about having been spanked or hit a lot. As explained in the description of this measure, we think the phrase a lot fits the experience of most children. Nevertheless, the number of times the students had in mind for a lot is unknown, and it likely varies between students and sites. In addition, because the question asked about being spanked or hit a lot, it could be interpreted as a measure of physical abuse. Our opinion, however, is that this is not likely because, as pointed out earlier, the research shows that two or more times a week is typical. As a consequence, one would have to conclude that physical abuse is typical. Our opinion is that any spanking of children is abuse, but that is not the cultural or statistical norm in the United States or most other nations.

Finally, although we controlled for the score of each nation on the limited disclosure scale, because of the small sample size (32), we did not control for enough other variables to have more confidence that the results really reflect the effect of spanking, such as whether there was violence between the parents. However, the study in the preceding chapter did control for violence between the parents and found that spanking made a unique and additional contribution to explaining the occurrence of assaulting a partner.

Links between Spanking and Assaulting Dating Partners

Keeping these limitations in mind, the results support the hypothesis that the larger the percentage of persons in a social context who were spanked, the higher the prevalence of three aspects of violence in partner relationships: cultural norms tolerating or supporting hitting a partner, physically assaulting a dating partner, and assaulting severe enough to injure a partner. An unexpected finding is that the links between spanking and these three aspects of partner violence are stronger for women than for men. More than 200 other studies have found the percent of women who assault a partner is as high or higher than the percent of male partners who assault a partner (Archer, 2002; Desmarais et al., 2012). The results in this chapter on the stronger link between spanking and partner violence for women, when combined with the data showing high rates of spanking experienced by these women, may be part of the explanation for the high percentage of women who physically assaulted a partner.

Why Is Spanking Linked to Violence against a Partner?

Elsewhere in this book, we discussed and presented results on the relationship between spanking and antisocial and aggressive behaviors by individual persons. In this chapter, the issue included whether there is a similar relationship at the societal level. Is a society in which spanking is prevalent also likely to be a society in which other types of violence are prevalent? Levinson's study (1989) of the societies in the Human Relations Area Files, for example, found a correlation of .32 between the extent of corporal punishment used and the extent of wife beating. Levinson's findings, like those in this chapter, are consistent with the cultural spillover theory of violence (Baron & Straus, 1989; Baron, Straus, & Jaffee, 1988). The cultural spillover theory asserts that the more a society uses violence for socially legitimate purposes such as bringing up children or punishing criminals, the more individual citizens are likely to use violence for socially illegitimate and often criminal purposes. That is, violence in any sphere of life will tend to engender violence in other spheres of life (see Chapter 19 for a discussion of spillover of violence from one sphere of life to another). To the extent that this theory is correct, prevention of spanking will contribute to prevention of partner violence and vice versa. That is, as we noted earlier, it is also likely that the relationship between spanking and violence against a partner is bidirectional; that is, societies in which violence is prevalent are also likely to be societies in which children are brought up violently, that is, with the use of spanking.

Prevalence of Corporal Punishment in Adolescence

A previous study found that, for Americans who were adults at the time of this survey in 1985, being hit as an adolescent was not a rare event. Just over one half of American parents at that time continued corporal punishment into adolescence, and they did so an average of 8 times in the previous 12 months (Straus & Donnelly, 1994). The high prevalence and chronicity of corporal punishment of adolescents is important because it indicates that, despite the fact that the data is about early adolescence, the results are applicable to the majority of the participants; that is, they are not restricted to a small number of families in which there was an abnormally high level of violence.

Policy Implications

The research in this chapter revealed that despite considerable progress toward ending partner violence (Durose et al., 2005; Smithey & Straus, 2004; Straus, 1995b; Straus & Gelles, 1986), a large proportion of university students continue to physically attack a dating partner. To the extent that the results of this research are correct in identifying spanking as a risk factor for partner violence, further steps toward primary prevention of partner violence should include increased policy and programmatic efforts to end all use of spanking by parents.

The finding that the social context, as measured by the percentage of students who experienced spanking, is related to the percent of students who assaulted a partner calls for an expanded view of the processes linking spanking to criminal violence. It suggests the process involves more than the criminogenic effect of spanking on specific individuals who were hit by their parents. These results suggest that when a large percentage of the population are brought up violently, it may create a social climate that increases the probability of other kinds of violence by amplifying the effect of spanking, and perhaps by increasing the probability of violence by those who did not themselves experience a high level of spanking. If so, it strengthens the argument in Chapter 19 on spanking and societal-level crime and violence that spanking is part of the process that creates and maintains a violent society, and that one way to curb this violence is through public policy than bans all forms of corporal punishment, including so-called mild spanking.

14 Cultural Context and the Relation of Spanking to Crime

A disproportionate number of delinquent children in the United States are Black. Poverty, racism, and neighborhood violence are major parts of the explanation for the disproportionate number of Black delinquent children. However, the results of the studies in Part II and the other chapters in Part IV suggest that violent child rearing in the form of spanking is also part of the explanation. That idea has been heatedly rejected by most Blacks we have talked to, including Black social scientists such as Polite (1996). Obviously more research is needed. This chapter provides some of it by presenting results from an analysis of a nationally representative of U.S. households on the following questions:

* What is the theoretical basis for believing that the relation of spanking to crime is different for different race or ethnic groups?
* What has previous research found about the belief that spanking does not have harmful side effects in sociocultural contexts where it is the statistical or cognitive norm?
* What percent of Americans who were adults in 1985 were hit by parents when they were teenagers?
* Is there a link between having experienced corporal punishment as a teenager and the following nine aspects of criminal behavior and beliefs among Black and Hispanics as well as Whites?
  * Child aggression
  * Child delinquency
  * Assaulted a spouse in previous 12 months
  * Approval of a husband slapping his wife in some situations
  * Approval of a wife slapping her husband in some situations
  * Assaulted a nonfamily person in previous 12 months
  * Severely assaulted a child in previous 12 months
  * Drug use
  * Arrested in previous 12 months

Sean Lauer is the coauthor of this chapter.

- How consistent are the results of this study with those of 15 other studies examining whether the effects of spanking are mitigated by cultural norms supporting spanking?

Sociocultural Context Differences in the Effects of Spanking

Many Blacks, including some Black social scientists, believe that spanking not only corrects the immediate misbehavior but also helps make the child generally law abiding. They argue that spanking is part of the Black cultural tradition and that it is necessary to use strong discipline (usually a euphemism for spanking) to protect children in the difficult circumstances of inner-city life (Daniel, 1985; Ealey, 1980; Hampton, 1987; Harris, 1992; Ispa & Halgunseth, 2004; Polite, 1996; Taylor, Hamvas, Rice, Newman, & DeJong, 2011; Thomas & Dettlaff, 2011). There is also an important minority of Black social scientists who stress the unintended harmful effects of spanking—for example, Hampton (1987), Comer and Poussaint (1992), and Earls and colleagues (Molnar et al., 2003). They oppose spanking in any form. One has developed a parent education program, *Effective Black Parenting* (Alvy & Marigna, 1987), which explicitly argues that continued reliance on spanking is a dysfunctional carryover of patterns based on slavery.

Catholic schools have traditionally used corporal punishment. But by the spring of 2011, of the thousands of Catholic schools in the United States, only one continued to do so—St. Augustine's High School in New Orleans. This is an all-male and predominately Black school. Archbishop Gregory Aymond of New Orleans called on St. Augustine to end the practice and pointed out that no other Catholic school in the United States uses corporal punishment. The request was met with demonstrations by more than 500 students, parents, and other supporters of the school's use of corporal punishment. They contended that its discipline code and practices are the reason their young men are successful in life and their future careers. Rev. John Raphael, president of St. Augustine High School, said the controversy is not as much about the paddle as about the right of Black parents to discipline their children in the matter they see fit (Dequine, 2011).

Why Might Spanking Have Different Effects for Black Children?

Academic defenders of spanking by Black parents have used cultural relativity theory and adaptation to difficult life circumstances theory to argue that spanking may be beneficial for Black children.

Cultural relativity theory draws on the slavery experience and argues that under those circumstances it was a matter of life and death for Blacks and their children to be obedient. Misbehavior could even result in being sold. This brutal reality required unquestioned obedience of children that was achieved by spanking. To the extent that spanking remains an element of Black culture, children of parents who do *not* spank may perceive their parents as not caring or not loving, with all the negative consequences that flow from such feelings (Alvy, 1987; Kohn, 1969; Peters, 1976; Young, 1970).

Deterrence theory (Gibbs, 1975) is implicit in the perspective of Baumrind (1991a) and Belsky (1991). They argue that the dangers of ghetto life, although different from the dangers of the plantation, are equally lethal; for example, there is peer pressure to use drugs and participate in crime. Under those circumstances strong deterrents are needed to prevent children from succumbing to alcohol and drug abuse, violence, and other crime that surrounds them in the ghetto. A beating by parents when the child misbehaves is thought to provided that.

Bronfenbrenner (1985) and others present an argument that has much in common with social disorganization theory (Bursik, 1988; Faris, 1955). Because society, and especially the social circumstances of low-income minorities, has become increasingly unstable, there is a need for families to provide more structure and stability in the lives of their children, including a high level of engagement and firm discipline. Bronfenbrenner rejected spanking as part of the firm discipline, but others such as Baumrind (1972, 1991b, 1992a, 1992b, 1996; Baumrind et al., 2002) accept it.

Deater-Deckard and Dodge (1997) suggest that because spanking is considered appropriate and normal in Black families, it is delivered dispassionately and matter-of-factly rather than in the context of a rageful, out-of-control parent. To the extent that this is correct, spanking would not be accompanied by the psychological maltreatment, such as terrifying threats or emotionally abusive verbalizations, that much research has indicated has more pernicious effects on child development than spanking alone (Vissing et al., 1991). We have not located empirical research on the emotional tone or impulsivity of corporal punishment by Black parents, but there is research that can throw some light on the issue of the extent to which spanking and psychological aggression are linked among both Black and White parents. It is a nationally representative sample that included 792 White and 120 Black parents (Straus et al., 1998). We computed the correlation between spanking and psychological aggression for both groups of parents. The results showed a stronger link between spanking and psychological aggression among Black parents than among White (correlation for Black parents .75 and .51 for White parents; $p < .001$ for both correlations).

Deater-Deckard et al. (1996) and Gunnoe and Mariner (1997) found that spanking was associated with an increase in the child fighting in school for White children but not for Black children. Both emphasize this cultural context difference in discussing their results. However, using a composite scale to measure aggressive and antisocial behavior, both Gunnoe and Deater-Deckard also found that spanking was related to more aggressive and antisocial behavior for Black as well as for White children. In the Gunnoe and Mariner paper, the findings section includes only one brief sentence acknowledging that their study "replicates the Straus et al. findings" on the link between spanking and antisocial behavior regardless of ethnic group. The extensive discussion and conclusion sections omits mentioning the results showing that spanking at

Time 1 was associated with more antisocial behavior subsequently for children of all ages and all ethnic groups.

A similar discrepancy between the results and the discussion of the results occurred in a six-nation study of the effects of spanking (Lansford et al., 2005). The results section states that "in all countries higher use of physical discipline was associated with more aggression and anxiety." However, the final sentence of the article says that the findings "suggest potential problems in using physical discipline even in contexts in which it is normative." Thus, the unambiguous results have become something that is suggested by the findings, and only that spanking is a potential problem. The Duke University press release contradicted the actual results even more directly. It declared that, "A particular parenting practice may become a problem *only* if parents use it in a cultural context that does not support the practice" [emphasis added].

Given the competing theoretical arguments and the inconsistency in research on this important issue, there is a clear need for additional research. The study reported in this chapter was undertaken to provide some of the needed additional research, and specifically to test what can be called the Universal Harm Theory of spanking, that:

> *Regardless of cultural context, spanking is associated with an increased probability of violence and other crime, and drug abuse.*

The universal harm theory is in contrast to the cultural relativity theory that argues that spanking has no adverse effects (and many would argue has beneficial effects) if done in compliance with cultural norms that prescribe spanking to correct misbehavior.

Sample and Measures

The data for this chapter come from the second National Family Violence Survey (Gelles & Straus, 1988; Straus & Gelles, 1986) that included 2,557 mothers and 1,844 fathers of children under age 18 living at home. This is the same sample used for Chapter 12 on the link between spanking and assaulting a partner. Although the study in this chapter was mainly stimulated by the controversy over whether the adverse effects of spanking apply to Black children, Hispanic Americans were also analyzed because the contextual conditions of poverty, segregation, and dangerous high-violence neighborhoods also apply to many Hispanic families. In such neighborhoods, parents of all race and ethnic groups tend to spank more (Winstok & Straus, 2011b). The study oversampled minorities to provide enough cases to be examined separately

Measures of Spanking

Two measures of spanking were used. The first measure used adult recall data. It was obtained by asking the adult participants in the survey, "Thinking about when you yourself were a teenager, about how often would you say your mother or stepmother used physical punishment, like spanking or slapping or hitting you? Think about the year in which this happened the most. Never, once, twice, 3 to 5 times, 6 to 10 times, 11 to 20 times, more than 20 times." The second measure uses contemporaneous parent report data and will be referred to as *contemporaneous data*. It was obtained using the Conflict Tactics Scales to ask parents with a child under 18 living at home whether and how often they had spanked during the preceding year. The version of the CTS used for this study is very similar to the revised CTS used for Chapter 3 on spanking in the United States.

The Data on Crime

Using the adult recall data on spanking, we were able to test the relationship between having experienced spanking as a child and seven aspects of violence and crime later in life: assaults on individuals who are not part of their family, arrests, physical abuse of children, approval of a wife slapping a husband, approval of a husband slapping a wife, actually assaulting a partner, and drug use.

Using the contemporaneous data, we could test the relationship between spanking experienced by children as reported by their parents and two outcomes during childhood: aggressiveness and delinquency.

The above measures are described in the Appendix.

Control Variables

The data for this sample permitted us to control for several characteristics of the participants and their families. These are characteristics that might be the underlying reason for the relation between spanking and crime. For example, if there is a tendency for parents who are physically violent to each other to also hit their children more than other parents, a correlation between spanking and violence and other crime by their children might be due to the children having witnessed parents being violent toward each other rather than due to the child being spanked. As a consequence, the analyses using the adult recall measure of spanking controlled for:

- Whether the participants' parents were violent to each other
- The age of the participant
- Family socioeconomic status
- Gender of participant

The analysis using the contemporaneous data controlled for all of the above, as well as four additional variables:

- Number of children in the household
- Whether the spanking was by the mother or the father

- The amount of reasoning used by the parent when dealing with misbehavior by the child (see Appendix for details on the questions)
- Physical abuse

As a result of these controls, the statistics in this chapter show the *net effect* of spanking. The net effect is the degree to which spanking is related to crime *over and above* the relation to crime of the characteristics that were controlled.

In addition, it was also possible to control for the confounding of legal spanking with physical abuse by excluding from the sample children who experienced one or more of the items in the severe assault scale of the parent-child Conflict Tactics Scales (Straus et al., 1998). This could only be done, however, for the analysis using the contemporaneous data because no measure of physical abuse was available for the adult recall data sample.

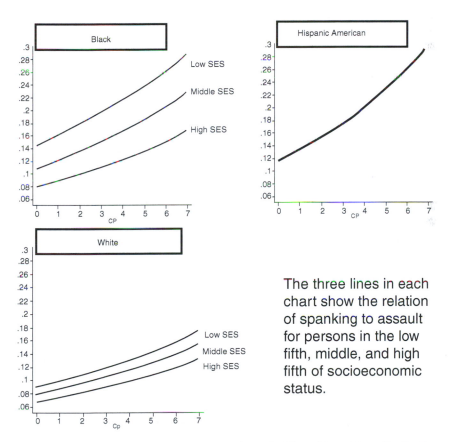

The three lines in each chart show the relation of spanking to assault for persons in the low fifth, middle, and high fifth of socioeconomic status.

Chart 14.1 The More Spanking, the Greater the Probability of Assaulting a Nonfamily Person

Corporal Punishment and Assault and Arrest as an Adult

Assault

Assaults of a nonfamily person. The parts of Chart 14.1 show that for all three ethnic groups, the more spanking experienced as an adolescent, the higher the probability that they had physically assaulted someone outside their family during the 12 months preceding the survey.

Each part of Chart 14.1 has three lines, one for each of three different socioeconomic status levels: low socioeconomic status (20th percentile, i.e., the bottom fifth), middle socioeconomic status (50th percentile), and high socioeconomic status (80th percentile, i.e., the highest fifth in socioeconomic status). These lines show the relation of spanking to the probability of assaulting someone other than a family member by study participants who are low, middle, and high in socioeconomic status. The lines in the charts for the lowest socioeconomic status group (the 20th percentile) are higher than the other lines, indicating a higher assault rate for the lowest socioeconomic status group. This is consistent with all other U.S. national data on assaults. More important, these results show that spanking as a child is associated with an increased probability of having assaulted someone during the year covered by this study, even though the effect of socioeconomic status is controlled because everyone in each group is in the same socioeconomic status group.

The detailed statistics in the Appendix indicate that, among Black men, each increase of one point in the spanking scale was associated with a 13% increase in the probability of assaulting a nonfamily person. An increase of 10% and 13% percent may seem to indicate that, despite being *statistically significant,* the effect size is small (i.e., that spanking does not strongly influence later behavior). However, those percentages mean an average increase of 10% and 13% associated with *each* step in the eight-interval spanking scale. Thus the cumulative effect of these step-by-step increases is substantial. For example, in the upper left section of Chart 14.1, the line for Blacks in the high socioeconomic status group starts at about 8% who assaulted among those who reported no spanking as a teenager and increases to about double that for those at the right side of the line who experienced the most spanking as a teenager. The upper line in the Black part of Chart 14.1 shows that among low socioeconomic status Blacks, the probability of assaultive behavior in the preceding 12 months increased from about 15% for those who did not recall any instance of having been hit by their parents as a teenager to almost double (30%) for those who reported 30 or more instances of having been hit by a parent.

The results are similar for Hispanic American and White men (increases of 13% and 10%, respectively). For women, the rate of assaults was much lower than for assaults by men, but the results show that spanking of girls is associated with a similar increase in the probability of women physically assaulting someone when they are adults.

The upper right part of Chart 14.1 shows that Hispanic Americans who experienced the most spanking had an assault rate that is 2.6 times greater than those who were not hit as a teenager. The three plot lines overlap so much that it seems as though there is only one line because, for the Hispanic Americans in this study, socioeconomic status was not related to assault.

Section C of the chart shows that for Whites, although on average the assault rates are lower than for the other two ethnic groups, those who experienced the most spanking were almost twice as likely to assault someone outside their family, as those who experienced the least spanking.

Arrest

The results from testing whether spanking is related to having been arrested during the year covered by this study were in the predicted direction (i.e., the more spanking, the greater chances of having been arrested). None of the relationships in these analyses, however, met the scientific standard for statistical dependability (statistical significance), and thus we cannot conclude that spanking is related to arrest based on this study. This may be a reflection of the small proportion who were arrested in the year covered by this study (3% of Blacks, 2% of Whites, and 1% of Hispanic Americans). Another problem was an error in asking about arrest. The phrase "for something serious" was supposed to be included in the question about having been arrested, but it was omitted and the error was not discovered until after the survey was administered and the data had been collected. Thus, an unknown proportion of the arrests may have been for traffic violations.

Corporal Punishment and Family Violence

Physical Abuse of Children

A previous analysis of this sample found that the more spanking or slapping experienced, the greater the probability of physically abusing a child in the year covered by this study (see Straus & Yodanis, 2001, for the results and for an analysis of the processes linking corporal punishment and physical abuse). That analysis, however, did not investigate whether the results applied to different racial or ethnic groups. The analysis for this chapter found a strong relationship between having been spanked and later in life physically abusing a child. We also found that this relationship applied to each of the three racial or ethnic groups. In fact, of the possible effects of spanking on the 12 aspects of crime and violence examined for this chapter, spanking had the strongest relation to physical abuse of a child. This is not surprising if one takes the view that physical abuse is part of a continuum that begins with spanking (Straus, 2000; Straus & Yodanis, 2001).

Spouse Assault

This section presents results for an aspect of crime and violence that we think of as *criminogenic attitudes* (i.e., attitudes that are related to or might increase criminal activity). We asked the participants in the survey a slight variation of the question used in the study of university students (Chapter 13), "Are there any situations that you can imagine in which you would approve of a husband slapping his wife's face?" The question was repeated for the approval of a wife slapping her husband's face. We found that in all three racial or ethnic groups, spanking is associated with an increased probability of the participant approving. For approval of a wife slapping her husband, the findings for Hispanic and Whites are similar, but the overall approval rates are higher, and the relationship between spanking and approval of a wife slapping her husband is stronger than for approval of a husband slapping his wife. Among Blacks, however, the relationship between spanking and approving slapping a wife was not statistically significant.

The next question is whether the link between spanking and attitudes approving violence against a partner translates into actually hitting a partner. The analysis in the previous chapter using the same sample and found that the more spanking experienced, the more approval of violence, and the greater the probability of having assaulted a partner in the previous year (Chapter 12). What the analysis for this chapter adds is whether spanking is a risk factor for partner assault in all three racial or ethnic groups.

Corporal Punishment and Drug Abuse

The hypothesis that, for both men and women, spanking is associated with drug use was supported. However, consistent with the cultural context theory, the association was not significant for Black males or Hispanic females.

Corporal Punishment and Child Delinquency and Aggression

For all three ethnic groups, the more spanking the parents reported using in the previous 12 months, the greater the probability that their child was classified as physically aggressive (see Appendix for the measure). For Hispanic and White children, but not for Black children, spanking was associated with an increased probability of delinquency.

Systematic Review of Cultural Context Effects

Studies of the effect of the cultural context on the relation between spanking and later maladaptive behavior are hard to compare and to arrive at a conclusion about what they show overall. First there are the usual problems making the studies difficult to compare such as differences in the type of research design, sample, the measures used, and the mode of analysis. Second, as documented in the introduction to this chapter, when reviewing the studies, some authors who favor spanking tend to focus on the studies that found no harmful effect. Similarly, some authors who are opposed to spanking tend to emphasize results and cite studies showing that the harmful effects apply to all children. A meta-analysis of the research on cultural context would be the best way to avoid this type of bias. Although we did not do a formal meta-analysis in the sense of a specified search for all available studies and computation of effect sizes under different conditions, we did do a systematic comparison. We located and tabulated the results of 17 studies that compared the side effects of spanking in different cultural contexts, one of which is the study in this chapter. Many of the studies reported more than one test of the effects of spanking in different cultural groups, or reported separate tests for different side-effect variables. For example, Lansford, Deater-Deckard, Dodge, Bates, and Pettit (2004) reported separate tests for children and adolescents and repeated these tests for different outcome variables of whether spanking was associated with harmful side effects for the child in different cultural contexts. As a consequence, these 17 studies provided results for 60 comparisons of cultural groups. To provide the basis for systematic analyses of these results, we created a table listing each of the studies. For each study, the table gives information on the sample, measures, and the results of comparisons of cultural groups provided by the study. Because the table is so long (27 pages), we created Table 14.1, which summarizes the results. The full table can be downloaded from the section on corporal punishment (pubpages.unh.edu/~mas2/).

Table 14.1 Percent of Cultural Context Comparisons that Found a Cultural Context Effect (This table is a summary of the detailed table in pubpages.unh.edu/~mas2/.)

Outcome Variable	Cultural Context Variables	Number of Comparisons	Found Context Effect	
			Number	Percent
Child Externalizing Behavior				
Aggression	Children's' perceived norm of corporal punishment	4	0	0%
Aggression	Mothers' perceived norm of corporal punishment	4	0	0%
Antisocial behavior	White versus Minority	1	0	0%
Aggression, antisocial behavior, delinquency, and externalizing behavior	White versus Black versus Hispanic American	8	2	25%
Antisocial behavior, conduct behavior, externalizing behavior, and fights at school	White versus Black	8	2	25%
All the above		25	4	16%

(Continued)

Table 14.1   (Continued)

Outcome Variable	Cultural Context Variables	Number of Comparisons	Found Context Effect	
			Number	Percent
Child Internalizing Behavior or Both Internal and External				
Anxiety	Mothers' perceived norm of corporal punishment	3	0	0%
Anxiety	Children's' perceived norm of corporal punishment	3	0	0%
Depression	Endorsement of corporal punishment	1	0	0%
Internalizing behavior	Black or not	1	0	0%
Internalizing behavior	White versus Black versus Hispanic American	2	0	0%
Internalizing and externalizing behavior	White versus Black versus Hispanic American	1	0	0%
All the above		11	0	0%
Adolescent and Adult Externalizing/Criminal Behavior				
Aggression, dating violence, externalizing behavior, general violence, police trouble, and school trouble	White versus Black	18	9	50%
Arrest, assaults on spouses, drug abuse, nonfamily violence, and severe assault on own children	White versus Black versus Hispanic American	8	1	17%
All the above		26	10	38%
All comparisons in the table		62	14	23%

The upper panel of Table 14.1 summarizes the results of 17 comparisons using as the outcome various aspects of antisocial behavior by the child. The total row for that section of the table shows that only 4 of the 25 comparisons found support for the theory that spanking is harmless in cultural contexts where spanking is the cognitive or statistical norms.

The center panel of Table 14.1 summarizes the results of 11 comparisons using as the outcome various aspects of child internalizing problems, and one study reporting results for a measure that combined internalizing and externalizing problems. None of the 11 comparisons supported the theory that spanking is harmless in cultural contexts where spanking is the cognitive or statistical norm.

The lower panel of Table 14.1 summarizes the results for 26 comparisons using as the outcome variable externalizing and criminal behavior by adolescents and adults. Ten of the 26 comparisons (38%) supported the cultural context theory that spanking is unrelated to crime in cultural contexts where spanking is the cognitive or statistical norm. However, caution is needed in interpreting these results because 7 of the 10 comparisons supporting the idea that cultural norms mitigate the harmful effects of spanking are from one study (Lansford et al., 2004).

Overall, 77% of the 60 tests contradicted the cultural context theory. However, the 23% of the comparisons that were consistent with the cultural context mitigation theory cannot be dismissed. Further research is necessary to try to identify why a cultural context effect was found in those studies. For example, because so many Blacks believe in spanking (see Chapter 5 and Ellison & Bradshaw, 2009; Flynn, 1996a; Straus & Mathur, 1996), spanking is virtually synonymous with discipline. In that context, no spanking may mean no discipline. If that is correct, in view of the research on the importance of parental monitoring and control for prevention of delinquency (Buker, 2011; Patterson, DeBaryshe, & Ramsey, 1989; Sampson & Laub, 1993), it is no wonder that spanking has no harmful effect, or even a positive effect, when no spanking tends to mean no discipline. This issue urgently needs further research. Such research could include data to test both the no spanking means no discipline explanation and the cultural legitimacy explanation.

Summary and Conclusions

The controversy over cultural context effects has sometimes become painful because it involves not only science, but also racial pride and the well-being of children, as was illustrated by the controversy about the use of corporal punishment in a Black New Orleans high school described earlier in this chapter. We think the balance is shifting away from corporal punishment by Blacks, even though slowly. For example, in 2011 a Black anti-spanking educational organization was founded (sparethekids.com/). They describe their mission as providing "Black parents, families and communities with a full range of alternatives to corporal punishment." Nevertheless, as illustrated by the principle of St. Augustine High School, many Black leaders continue to believe that efforts to end spanking are an imposition of middle class, White cultural values in the guise of science (Daniel, 1985; Ealey, 1980; Hampton, 1987; Harris, 1992; Polite, 1996). One of us experienced this personally after speaking to a meeting of mostly Black social workers. In the discussion period after the talk, a member of the audience said it was "racism in disguise—trying to ram white middle class values down our throats." This was followed by loud applause.

A frequent theme was that attempts to end the use of spanking will put Black children in even more danger than they already face. Our view is exactly the opposite. We believe that continued use of spanking by Black parents makes it even more likely that that their children will be violent, become victims of violence, and be trapped in the life of poverty and crime. This opinion is likely to outrage many who will point to the array of other criminogenic conditions faced by Black children, such as poverty and racism, and experiences correlated with poverty such as inadequate diet and failing schools. The need to address our conclusion that spanking is a criminogenic aspect of Black experiences in no way denies or subtracts from the importance of the problems just listed. It simply adds to the list.

On the optimistic side, spanking may be more amenable to change than other causes of crime such as poverty, racism, and failing schools. In addition, the evidence in Chapter 17 on trends in use of spanking found that Black support for spanking has declined, even though not as much as among Whites. As the average education of Blacks increases, that decline is likely to accelerate.

What was called the universal harm theory of spanking was examined by testing the hypothesis that spanking is associated with an increased probability of criminal beliefs and behavior regardless of racial or ethnic group. All together, 36 analyses were conducted using 12 measures of criminal beliefs and behavior to determine if spanking was related to crime by Blacks, Hispanic Americans, and Whites. The findings are mostly consistent with the universal harm theory because 35 out of 36 resulted in finding that spanking was associated with an increased odds of crime or criminal beliefs, and 29 of the 36 odds ratios were statistically dependable (see Appendix). The crucial issue for this chapter is whether the link between spanking and crime also applies to all three race or ethnic groups. The 36 analyses included examined the same set of 12 crime variables for each cultural group. Among Whites, 11 of the 12 tests found that spanking was related to crime. Among Blacks, it was 8 out of 12, and among Hispanics, 10 out of 12 tests found that spanking is related to crime.

These findings are noteworthy because, even though they are not based on longitudinal data, they are from a study that overcomes some of the limitations of many previous studies. First, the findings refer to large and nationally representative samples. Second, the analyses controlled for many potentially confounding variables. As a result of these controls, we know that adverse side effects of spanking manifest themselves regardless of socioeconomic status, gender of the parent doing the punishment, gender of the child, age at which spanking was used, number of children in the household, amount of reasoning used by the participant when dealing with misbehavior by the child, or physical violence between the participant and his or her spouse. In two thirds of the tests, they also apply to Blacks. For the relation of spanking to child aggressiveness and delinquency, it was also possible to exclude children who had experienced physical abuse, thus providing confidence that the relationship was not the result of the overlap between physical abuse and spanking.

Theoretical Implications

For the most part, the findings support the perspective of universal harm from spanking rather than the idea that the harmful effects of spanking are culturally relative. Universal harm does not mean that every child is damaged by being spanked. It is only a minority, just as only one third of heavy smokers die from a smoking related disease. See the explanation of risk factors in the concluding section of Chapter 1.

The findings can also be taken as lending some support for cultural relativity theory because the hypothesized links between spanking and crime were less consistently supported within the Black sample. On the other hand, such an interpretation would have to ignore the fact that a significant relationship between spanking and crime was found in two thirds of the tests for Black families and five out of six tests for Hispanic American families. Moreover, the weaker findings for the Black and Hispanic American samples might occur because the forces producing the high rates of substance abuse and crime in Black and Hispanic neighbors may be so powerful that it overwhelms the importance of whether parents spank.

Cultural relativity theory. There is an important aspect of the cultural relativity theory with which we agree. It is the idea that parental disciplinary methods that are appropriate for socializing a child to adapt to one type of society may not be appropriate in another society that has a different set of values and behavioral expectations. If, for example, a society emphasizes close adherence to rules more than it emphasizes individual initiative and creativity, parents need to emphasize obedience control. If the society is one in which physical fighting is needed for survival, either individual fighting or fighting as part of an army (as in ancient Sparta or certain nonliterate bellicose societies), spanking and harsh discipline are likely to prepare children for survival in such a society. The available evidence, however, suggests that this will be accomplished at the cost of more unwanted aggressive and violent behavior and psychological well-being (Lansford, 2010). Rohner et al. (1991) found that even in St. Kitts—a society in which the cultural norms strongly approve of spanking—the more spanking actually experienced, the higher the incidence of psychological problems such as low self-esteem, emotional instability, and emotional unresponsiveness. In Jamaica, another nation where spanking is the norm, Smith, Springer, and Barrett (2010) found that the overwhelming majority of adolescent respondents experienced spanking and that it was associated with adverse psychological and behavioral consequences.

Cross-cultural comparative studies show that societies that are high in use of spanking also tend to be high in frequency of warfare and violent interpersonal relationships (Lansford, 2010; Otterbein, 1974; Russell, 1972) including violence against spouses (Levinson, 1989). Lansford's review of the cultural context theory concludes that "Although corporal punishment is generally related to more behavior problems regardless of cultural group, this association is weaker in countries in which corporal punishment is the norm. Yet cultures in which corporal punishment is the norm also have higher levels of societal violence" (Lansford, 2010, p. 105).

In the context of a post-industrial society, deductions from cultural relativity theory lead to the opposite hypothesis than has been argued on the basis of the presumed cultural appropriateness of spanking. In a post-industrial society, children need experience in negotiation and cognitive methods of influencing others rather than experience in use of physical force to reach desired outcomes. To the extent that is the case, cultural relativity theory suggests that optimum socialization for life in such a society should emphasize reasoning and explanation and avoid spanking. Moreover, a high level of cognitive ability and higher education are critical for optimum adaptation to a post-industrial society, and the results in Part III of this book show that spanking hinders achieving those characteristics.

Social disorganization theory. Social disorganization theory leads to the proposition that, in the context of a high level of social disorganization, parents need to compensate for the lack of structure and social control by a more structured pattern of family relations and control than would be optimum in other settings in order to increase the probability of the child developing clear conceptions of right and wrong and avoiding demoralization. Neither our theoretical perspective nor the results of this study contradict that proposition. Our results do suggest, however, that a high level of supervision and control should not include control by hitting the child for misbehavior. In fact, as Sears et al. (1957) have shown, children are more likely to develop an internalized conscious and control if parents monitor.

Deterrence theory. This theory leads to the proposition that, because of the intense peer pressure to participate in substance abuse and crime faced by children living in poverty-stricken neighborhoods, to protect the child there need to be strong penalties for transgression and that this is best accomplished by spanking. However, deterrence theory also holds that for punishment to deter, the offender must *perceive* it as certain and severe. Neither of these applies to children at the age in which delinquency typically occurs because parents probably do not know about most of the child's transgressions. In addition, in the context of the fights and violence that pervade in neighborhoods where poverty is concentrated, being slapped by a parent, or even paddled with a hairbrush, may not be very severe.

Policy Implications

It would be unrealistic not to recognize that non-spanking could be a disaster if parents take it to mean being permissive and ignore a child's misbehavior.

Children do need firm but loving control, as exemplified in what Baumrind (1991b) calls an authoritative parenting style. That said, spanking is not a necessary part of Baumrind's authoritative type. Parents do not need to spank to be authoritative. If social norms change enough to prevent parents from spanking, some parents will give up trying to correct misbehavior, but that is likely to be rare because most parents are deeply committed to producing responsible children. If they stop spanking while continuing to use the same nonviolent methods of correction and control as before, the evidence in this book and many other studies suggest that they will be more effective parents just by leaving out the spanking. This is also the implication of four studies in Sweden (Durrant & Janson, 2005).

Another possible danger is that efforts to correct misbehavior will shift from physical aggression (spanking) to verbal aggression (attempts to cause psychological pain by insulting or depreciating the worth of the child). That would truly be disastrous because psychological attacks have more harmful psychological effects than physical attacks (Vissing et al., 1991). As a consequence, educational programs to end spanking must give equal weight to discouraging or ending verbal attacks on the child, or, as in the Swedish no-spanking law, avoiding all humiliating treatment of children.

There is a tragic irony in the belief, often found in poor urban neighborhoods, that spanking is necessary to bring up children to resist the drugs, crime, and violence. From a societal perspective, it is ironic because spanking is one of the bases of cultural legitimization of violence (see Chapter 5 and Baron & Straus, 1989; Straus, 1991). From a family-level perspective, spanking tends to undermine the very things parents, regardless of culture, most want—a child whose behavior is governed by internalized standards and "stays out of trouble." Instead, spanking teaches that force rather than reason prevail, that even good people (i.e., one's parents) hit others. Moreover, the use of spanking inhibits the development of internalized controls and conscience (Sears et al., 1957). As shown in Chapter 8 on spanking and the child-to-mother bond and Chapter 9 on spanking and risky sex, spanking also tends to undermine the bond between parent and child that is crucial if parents are to exercise influence that will protect children from drugs and crime once they are too big to spank.

15   Spanking High-Risk Children and Adult Crime

Part II, III, and IV of this book, especially the longitudinal studies in Chapters 6 and 10 and the longitudinal studies by others on the effects of spanking, such as the 16 longitudinal studies reviewed in Chapter 19 lead to the ironic conclusion that spanking to correct misbehavior, although it may halt the immediate misbehavior, is associated with an *increase* in subsequent misbehavior. Moreover, there is a remarkably high level of consistency between studies on the harmful effects of spanking. Among the 112 tests of long-term effects of spanking reviewed by Gershoff (2002), 108 or 96% showed that spanking was associated with later problematic behavior such as less moral internationalization, poor parent-child relationships, delinquency, and mental health problems.

Despite the mass of evidence just cited, when the outcome variable is crime as an adult, additional research is needed. One reason is that most of the previous research has investigated the relation of spanking to aggression and other antisocial and criminal behavior *of children*. Perhaps even more important, the few studies that investigated the link between spanking and adult crime have been limited by being cross-sectional studies or by an inadequate longitudinal design. Some longitudinal studies could not provide information about spanking *per se* because the spanking data was analyzed as part of a *harsh parenting* factor or index that included other undesirable parent practices such as psychological aggression against the child, for example, Eron et al. (1991). The aggression by these children later in life might be the result of the other adverse parent behaviors in the index. Other longitudinal studies, although they measured criminal behavior years after the spanking, did not control for the level of antisocial behavior that led the parent to spank at Time 1. Thus they could not determine if the spanking led to a subsequent *change*, for better or for worse. They are little better than cross-sectional studies in determining whether spanking *causes* the higher rate of crime later in life. Aggression and antisocial behavior tend to be persistent characteristics. Thus, the higher rate of crime could be another manifestation of the behavior problems that led the parents to spank.

Because antisocial behavior causes parents to spank, it is crucial to control for the level of antisocial or delinquent behavior at Time 1. Doing so allows a

John P. Colby, Jr. and Rose A. Medeiros are coauthors of this chapter.

researcher to determine if the link between spanking and antisocial behavior is because (1) when parents spank to correct antisocial behavior it actually increased the probability of antisocial behavior, (2) antisocial behavior on the part of children increases the probability of parents resorting to spanking, or (3) as we believe, both. Longitudinal research can determine this by measuring the level of antisocial behavior that presumably led to the spanking and then measuring the antisocial behavior later to see if, as most people believe, the spanking taught them a lesson and if those who were spanked are less likely to commit crimes or if, as we hypothesize, their behavior, on average, gets worse. Statistically, this is called the *causal order* problem. If experiments are not possible or practical, the best way of dealing with the causal order problem is probably to statistically control for the amount of antisocial behavior at Time 1. Doing that results in the measure at Time 2 being a measure of the amount of change in antisocial behavior and whether, as we said, the change is for the better or for the worse.

The few studies that have dealt with the causal order problem by controlling for the Time 1 antisocial behavior, which could have led the parents to spank such as the study in Chapter 6, have not investigated whether spanking is a risk factor for crime by adults. The longitudinal research reported in this chapter helps fill this gap because it provides data on some important questions:

- Is spanking to correct antisocial behavior as a child associated with an increase in the probability of adult antisocial behavior in the form of crime?
- Does the link between spanking as a child and crime as an adult apply to property crimes as well as violent crime?
- When parents are emotionally supportive and monitor the child's activities, does that mitigate the effect of spanking?
- Does a relationship between spanking and crime as an adult apply to women as well as men, and does it apply regardless of whether the child grew up in a high-risk situation as indicated by a low-education mother, being the child of a very young mother, not having a father present in the household, having many siblings, and having low emotional support and low parental monitoring of the child's behavior?

The sample for this study was deliberately designed to ensure that there are sufficient children in these high crime risk groups to enable an adequate statistical analysis.

Sample and Measures

Sample

The data for this chapter comes from the National Longitudinal Survey of Youth. That study oversampled minorities and low-income mothers in order to make it possible to have enough young adults from Black, Hispanic American, and low socioeconomic status backgrounds to investigate issues that are particularly important for these groups. Thus, it provides an opportunity to test the hypotheses that spanking is related to later criminal behavior among the very groups who are most committed to the idea that strong discipline (by which they mean spanking) is necessary to make sure that children resist the opportunities and pressures to engage in crime that are so often prevalent in their neighborhoods. In short, the theory underlying the research in this chapter is that spanking as a method of discipline, rather than protecting children from engaging in criminal activity, increases the chances of that happening.

The characteristics that led us to identify the 468 children studied as high-risk for later life crime were not just based on race or ethnicity, which were 51% Black and 21% Hispanic, but a number of risk factors for crime. These risk factors correspond with the characteristics in the Moore, Vandivere, and Redd (2006) Sociodemographic Risk Index. The average level of education of the mothers was less than a high school education—11 years, and the average age of the mothers at the time of the birth of the children in this sample was 17.3 years. Moreover, the father was present in the household at the time of interview for only 36% of the children. The average number of children in the household in 1986, when this data was collected, was high (3.6).

Measures

Spanking. Spanking was measured by interviews with the mothers when the children were between 8 and 13 years old. The mothers were asked, "Sometimes kids mind pretty well and sometimes they don't. About how many times, if any, have you had to spank your child in the past week?"

Crime. The data on crime were obtained by interviewing the children when they were between 18 and 23 years old. They were asked if, in the past 12 months, they had done any of the following 14 criminal acts:

Violent Crime

- Hurt someone badly enough to need bandages or a doctor
- Gotten into a fight at school or work
- Used force to get money or things from someone else
- Hit or seriously threatened to hit someone
- Attacked someone with the idea of seriously hurting or killing them

Property Crimes

- Taken something from a store without paying for it
- Other than from a store, taken something not belonging to you that was worth less than $50

- Other than from a store, taken something not belonging to you that was worth $50 or more
- Intentionally damaged or destroyed property that did not belong to you
- Tried to get something by lying to someone about what you would do for him or her (tried to con someone)
- Taken a vehicle without the owner's permission
- Broken into a building or vehicle to steal something or to just look around
- Helped in a gambling operation, like running numbers or books
- Knowingly sold or held stolen goods

The overall crime scale included all 14 items. The violent crime scale includes five items; the property crime scale includes nine. The scale score could range from zero (committed none of the 14) to 14 (committed all of the 14). There was no one who committed all 14. In addition, we created a subscale for violent crime that could range from 0 to 5, and a score for property crime that could range from 0 to 9.

The study participants were asked only if they had engaged in a specific behavior in the past 12 months, not the number of times they committed a criminal act. Thus, the scores represent the total number of different types of crimes they committed, rather than the number of crimes. There is evidence that the number of different types of crime is a better measure of criminality than the frequency of criminal acts (Sweeten, 2009).

Antisocial behavior. Antisocial behavior was the proxy for criminal behavior at Time 1. It was measured in this study by a six-item subscale of the National Longitudinal Survey of Youth behavioral problems scale. Parents were instructed, "As you read each sentence, decide which phrase best describes your child's behavior over the last three months." Parents were asked if each of the following were often true, sometimes true, or not true. "He or she cheats or tells lies"; "he or she bullies or is cruel or mean to others"; "he or she does not seem to feel sorry after he or she misbehaves"; "he or she breaks things on purpose or deliberately destroys his or her own or another's things"; "he or she is disobedient at school"; and "he or she has trouble getting along with teachers."

Controls. The data available enabled us to control for ten child and family characteristics that are associated with both spanking and with crime. These controls are very important because, if we find a relationship between spanking and crime, they might be the underlying reason for that relationship, not the effect of spanking *per se*. These variables are mother's education, mother's age when she gave birth to the child, child's race, child's gender, number of other children in the household, whether the child's father was present in the household, and parental emotional support and monitoring of child behavior. Each of these was used in two different ways: first, as control variables to see if the effect of spanking is in addition to those seven variables and to answer the question of whether spanking makes a unique contribution to explaining crime. We also used them as moderator variables to answer the question of whether the relation of spanking to crime applies to different levels or categories of these variables; for example, when parental warmth and support is high, is there a relation between spanking and crime or, among race or ethnic groups, is there a relation between spanking and crime within each of the groups (Black, White, Hispanic)?

Prevalence of Corporal Punishment and Crime

How Much Spanking and Who Does It

The children in this sample ranged from 8 to 13 years old the year when spanking was measured. This is well beyond the peak years for spanking documented in Chapter 2. Despite that, 29% were spanked during the week prior to the Time 1 interview in 1986, including 6% who were spanked 3 or more times that week. This is consistent with the ethnic or racial composition and the socioeconomic status of the sample. The Appendix gives other information on the use of spanking by the mothers in this sample.

Although mothers with less education and mothers with more children spanked more, the differences were not large enough to be statistically significant. This may be due to the limited education of most of the mothers in this sample. Slightly more than one half of the mothers (52.2%) had not completed high school, and only 13.5% of mothers had any education beyond a high school diploma. There was unexpectedly little difference between race or ethnic groups in spanking, probably because of the low average socioeconomic status of all the race and ethnic groups in the sample. There was also little difference in spanking by father's presence in the household, mother's age at the birth of the child, and the level of parental monitoring.

Of the seven characteristics of the children and families in this study, only the child's antisocial behavior was related to spanking strongly enough to be statistically dependable (see Appendix for statistical details). The average antisocial behavior scale score of the children who were not spanked in the seven days before the interview was 1.6. Among those who were spanked once in the past week, the average antisocial score was 2.4, and among those spanked twice or 3 or more times, the average antisocial scale score was 3.0 and 3.0, respectively. Thus, the more spanking, the more antisocial behavior or the more antisocial behavior, the more spanking. The simple cross-sectional analysis cannot tell us which causes which, or whether (as we believe), there is bidirectional causation. To find out, it is crucial to examine what happens subsequently. That is, when parents spank to correct misbehavior, does it teach the child a lesson in the sense of reducing the probability of subsequent misbehavior, or does it boomerang as was shown in Chapter 6, and as we investigated for this chapter, will it be associated with an increase rather than decrease in the chances of the child becoming involved in crime as a young adult?

Crime

When these children were interviewed as young adults, over one half of the males and almost one half of the young women reported having committed at least one crime in the previous 12 months. Specifically:

* 58.2% of the men and 45.2% of the women had committed at least one of the crimes
* 45.9% of the men and 27.1% of the women had committed a violent crime
* 50.5% of the men and 38.9% of the women had committed a property crime

These are extremely high crime rates, but they are consistent with the crime rates found by many other studies of self-reported crime, especially among of youth with similar sociodemographic profiles (Junger-Tas et al., 2003; Nettler, 1984; Thornberry & Krohn, 2000).

Corporal Punishment and Crime as a Young Adult

We examined the relationship between spanking and the three measures of crime: violent crime, property crime, and the combination, which we call the overall crime scale. Using the entire sample, although all three relationships were in the hypothesized direction (the more spanking, the more crime), none were large enough to be statistically dependable. When the hypotheses were tested separately for men and women, however, we found that for men, there were statistically dependable relationships between spanking and crime. For the overall crime scale, the regression coefficient was .20, for property crime it was .23, and for violent crime, .24. Chart 15.1 graphs these coefficients. These are substantial relationships, especially because they indicate a relationship of spanking to crime that is over and above 10 key risk factors for later criminal behavior, such as early antisocial behavior by the child and parental emotional support and monitoring of child behavior, and shows that for boys, spanking is related to later crime that is in addition to the effect of the 10 control variables. However, Chart 15.1 also shows that for the girls in this study, there was no relationship between spanking and later crime. The statistical details are in the section of the Appendix for this chapter.

In addition to controlling for six variables, we also looked into whether the relation of spanking to crime applies to different levels or categories of these variables; for example, when parental warmth and support is high, is there a relation between spanking and crime, and is there a relation between spanking and crime *within* all three race or ethnic groups (Black, White, and Hispanic)? We did not find any of them to make a statistically dependable difference. That is, the relation of spanking to crime that is graphed in Chart 15.1 applies regardless of the mother's education, race or ethnic group, amount of emotional support, and cognitive stimulation provided to the child. As we have seen, only the sex of the

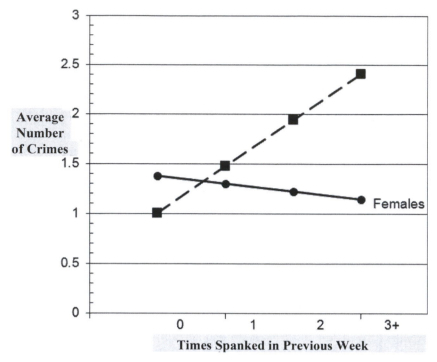

Chart 15.1　For Men, the More Times Spanked, the More Criminal Acts. For Women, There Is No Relationship*

*Controlling for mother's education, child's race, child's gender, number of other children in the household, whether the child's father was present in the household, the mother's age when she gave birth to the child, and parental monitoring of child behavior.

child made a difference: Spanking was related to later crime for boys but not for girls. The findings on the relation of spanking to crime applied to all the ethnic groups. This is particularly important because it contradicts the claim (discussed in Chapter 14) that spanking is harmless when it occurs in a cultural context in which spanking is the norm, such as in many poor Black neighborhoods.

Other Variables Related to Crime

Although we did not find that the other variables in the study affected the relation of spanking to crime, that does not mean those variables are not risk factors for crime. In this study, as in many other studies, the more monitoring by parents, the less total crime and the less violent crime. When we examined the relationship of the risk factors to crime separately for males and females, emotional supportiveness of the mother and having an older mother were associated with less violent crime for girls, but not for boys. For boys, Hispanic ethnicity was associated with the overall crime scale and monitoring the child's activities was associated with a lower probability of violent crime as an adult. (See Appendix for the statistical details.)

Summary and Conclusions

The characteristics of this sample of 8- to 13-year-old children provided an opportunity to examine whether the adverse effects of spanking apply to children from low socioeconomic status families, many of whom were ethnic minority children and lived in disadvantaged high-violence neighborhoods. These life circumstances are part of the explanation for the high rate of spanking (Winstok & Straus, 2011b), which we and others have found. The high level of spanking, despite the euphemism spanking, describes violent child rearing, and these data suggest it is another part of the explanation for the high crime rate we found for the young adults in this study. Moreover, these results are particularly noteworthy because they are based on a longitudinal study that controlled for 10 other variables that are associated with an increased probability of later criminal behavior. Thus, spanking, rather than helping to protect children from crime, is associated with an increased probability that they will later engage in criminal behavior.

Parents in high-violence neighborhoods tend to believe that immediate compliance is necessary because noncompliance may have dire consequences (Garbarino, Kostelny, & Barry, 1997; McLeod, Kruttschnitt, & Dornfeld, 1994; Staples & Johnson, 1993). Spanking does work in securing compliance in the immediate situation, but it is not more effective than nonviolent methods of correction, (Larzelere, Schneider, Larson, & Pike, 1996). However, parents do not know this, and cultural myths described in Chapter 18 and in *Beating the Devil Out of Them* (Straus, 2001a, Chapter 10) lead most U.S. parents to erroneously believe that spanking is more effective than other methods of discipline and is therefore sometimes necessary. That belief, in combination with the high priority parents in such neighborhoods give to immediate compliance (Kohn, 1977) compared, for example, with the ability to be self-directed, helps explain their high use of spanking. Instead, for the boys in this study, even after controlling for misbehavior that might have led parents to spank, spanking was found to be associated with an *increased* probability of crime as a young adult. For the girls, spanking was not associated with either an increase or a decrease in the probability of crime. Therefore, although spanking did not increase the probability of crime later in life by girls, neither did it help them avoid crime. In short, for boys (who are most at risk for criminal behavior), spanking was associated with a worsening of the antisocial behavior for which they were spanked as young children, and it did not protect girls in the sense that spanked girls engaged in less crime as an adult.

Our not finding a criminogenic effect of spanking for girls, was consistent with the results of the study by Boutwell, Franklin, Barnes, and Beaver (2011) described in Chapter 20. That study examined the combined effect of genetic heritage and spanking and found that the effect of spanking on child antisocial behavior applied only to boys. Boutwell et al. suggest that this is because of a genetic difference between males and females. One of several other possible explanations is routine activities theory (Cohen & Felson, 1979; Marcum, 2010; Osgood, Wilson, O'Malley, Bachman, & Johnston, 1996). Women are less likely to engage in activities that facilitate crime because they spend less time with men than men spend with men, and many more men than women commit crimes. Thus women are less likely to interact with and be influenced by a criminal person. In addition, women spend less time in locations such as bars and less time at certain types of sports such as boxing that are high in crime and are frequented by more persons prone to crime than other locations. A flip side of this gender difference is that the increasing equality of women and men in the good things in life also means women gain more equality in exposure to criminogenic situations and hence an increase in crime by women. Dawson and Straus (2011) tested this theory cross-nationally and found that the more gender-equal the nation, the closer the crime rate of women was to the crime rate of men. They also found that part of the lower male-predominance in crime in more gender-equal societies occurs because male crime rates are lower in gender-equal societies.

Limitations

It can be argued that using antisocial behavior as the Time 1 control for criminal behavior is not appropriate because it is qualitatively different than adult criminal behavior (Kandel, 1991). On the other hand, there is a growing body of research showing that early antisocial behavior is associated with later criminal behavior and violent behavior (Loeber & Farrington, 1995; Stouthamer-Loeber, Loeber, Huizinga, & Porter, 1997; Tremblay, 2006).

The measure of spanking used for this study was whether the child was spanked in the previous week. This gets more accurate information about spanking than a longer recall period (see Chapter 2), but it is also a limitation. It is not possible to differentiate between children who were never spanked and those who were not spanked during the seven days before the Time 1 interview. The latter group might include a substantial number of children whose parents do spank, but not on a weekly basis. Future research can deal with this limitation by using the new response categories by using the new response categories for the Conflict Tactics Scales (Moore, Straus, & Winstok,2013) which have also been used in the Dimensions Of Discipline Inventory(Straus & Fauchier, 2011). These make it is possible to have both the greater accuracy of asking about spanking in the past week and simultaneously determine how often spanking occurred in the other weeks of the year. They would also permit determining whether the never spanked fare better than children who were rarely spanked. It is possible that there is a threshold in the use of spanking, up to which point spanking does not result in maladaptive social and psychological outcomes for children. This is the belief of those who defend moderate use of spanking (Baumrind et al., 2002; Friedman & Schonberg, 1996a) but, except for the fact that the harmful effects of spanking are in the form of a *dose-response* (see, for example, Chapters 6, 7, and 10) that belief is based on cultural tradition rather than empirical evidence.

Another limitation is that there is no information on spanking by the fathers of these children. It was not practical to get that information for a number of reasons, but especially because two thirds of the children were in households where the fathers did not reside. Nevertheless, for the one third who were living with their father, this measure erroneously includes in the not-spanked group children who were not spanked by their mother, but were spanked by their father.

Implications of Study Findings

As pointed out in several chapters, the findings of most of the research showing a link between spanking and adult crime could be spurious because those studies did not control for the misbehavior that led parents to spank. Thus, the adult criminal behavior of the spanked children, rather than being an effect of the spanking could be just another manifestation of the tendency to antisocial behavior that led the parents to spank. The research reported in this chapter and in Chapter 6 (on the boomerang effect of spanking) and the studies reviewed in Chapter 19 makes that a less likely explanation because they controlled for antisocial behavior that might have caused parents to spank at Time 1.

The controls used for this study also included the amount of parental emotional support provided, cognitive simulation, and parental monitoring of the child's behavior. These are important protective factors. It is sometimes argued that what seems to be an adverse effect of spanking is really an effect of bad parenting. This study shows that, important as those protective factors are, after taking them into account, spanking still has a net effect; that is, spanking explains child-to-child differences in crime as an adult that are in addition to what is explained by the presence or absence of these protective factors.

Our results showing that the spanking is related to adult crime for children from low socioeconomic status families, many of whom were living in high-violence neighborhoods, does not contradict the fact that an important part of the explanation for crime by youth lies in the social setting—for example, living in areas of concentrated poverty, family and neighborhood disorganization, and the perception or reality of being locked out of legitimate employment (Sampson, Raudenbush, & Earls, 1997; Wilson, 1996). Nor does it contradict cultural explanations such as the code of the streets (Anderson, 1999). It adds one more risk factor to life circumstances that are already overflowing with risk factors for crime. Although respect for the cultural autonomy of racial and socioeconomic groups is an important principle (Polite, 1996; Rohner et al., 1996), when an element of that culture, such as spanking, even though undertaken with the intent of enhancing the well-being of children and protecting neighborhoods from crime, has the opposite effect, we believe the effort must be made to change that aspect of the culture.

16 Sexual Coercion and Sexual Assault

The chapters up to now have shown that corporal punishment by parents is associated with an increased risk of antisocial behavior and several types of crime. But why should something that parents do to produce a well-behaved child be associated with crime later in life? The chapter on the relation of spanking to physically assaulting a partner presented evidence on that issue. It showed that being spanked is a risk factor for physically assaultive behavior because spanking is associated with an increased probability of approving violence, depression, and conflicts with a partner.

This chapter also examines another possible linking process: Whether the relationship between spanking and crime occurs because spanking increases the probability of antisocial personality traits. This follows up what was reported earlier: That spanking has the long-run side effect of increasing the probability of the child developing antisocial personality traits and behavior (Chapter 6).

The chapter also takes into account two other victimization experiences— sexual abuse and neglect. The issue investigated is whether spanking, neglect, and sexual abuse are each uniquely associated with an increased probability of sexually coercing and sexually assaulting a partner. Although the study is about the relation of three kinds of victimization to sexual coercion, somewhat more attention is presented about spanking because spanking is the focus of the book. The questions to be addressed are:

- What percent of male and female university students engage in verbally coercing sex and physically forcing sex on a dating partner?
- Are being spanked and experiencing relatively minor forms of neglect, such as not being comforted when distressed, associated with an increased probability of antisocial traits and sexual violence, and does this apply to women as well as men?
- Are the effects of spanking and minor neglect unique in the sense of being in addition to the effect of having been sexually abused?

Manuel Gámez-Guadix and Scott Hershberger are coauthors of this chapter.

- Is part of the reason why spanking, sexual abuse, and neglect are related to sexual coercion because these three victimization experiences increase the probability of antisocial traits and behavior?

Prevalence of Sexual Coercion and Gender Differences

Sexual coercion is a widespread problem with deleterious short- and long-term consequences (Demaris, 2005; Kernsmith & Kernsmith, 2009; Temple, Weston, Rodriguez, & Marshall, 2007; Tewksbury, 2007). A number of terms in addition to sexual coercion are used to refer to the range of physical or nonphysical behaviors to coerce a partner into unwanted sexual activity. These include sexual assault, sexual aggression, sexual violence, sexual pressure, and date or acquaintance rape. Sexual coercion can be verbal coercion such as insisting on sex when the partner does not want to or threatening an unwilling partner to gain sexual contact against the partner's will. Or it can be physical coercion, which we will call sexual assault.

Research on sexual coercion has consistently found high rates in college and community samples (Basile, Chen, Black, & Saltzman, 2007; Dekeseredy & Schwartz, 1998; Dekeseredy, Schwartz, & Tait, 1993; Koss, Gidycz, & Wisniewski, 1987; Tjaden & Thoennes, 2000). Most of the studies have asked only about men sexually coercing women (e.g., Koss et al., 1987), although a growing body of literature has showed that women also sexually coerce (Anderson & Struckman-Johnson, 1998; Davies, 2002; Hettrich & O'Leary, 2007; Kar & O'Leary, 2010; Muehlenhard & Cook, 1988; Panuzio & DiLillo, 2010). There has also been considerable research on the etiology of sexual coercion, but again, primarily studies of male perpetrators.

The prevalence of perpetration of sexual coercion and assault *by men* has been widely researched and has been extensively reviewed (Hines, 2007; Spitzberg, 1999). Therefore, this review focuses on studies that present rates for both men and women in dating relationships. All these studies used student samples. Examples include a study by Struckman-Johnson (1988) that found that 10% of men and 2% of women in a sample of university students admitted to forcing a date into sexual activity at least once in their lifetime, including psychological pressure and physical tactics to engage in sexual intercourse, but the study did not provide separate rates for verbal coercion and sexual assault. O'Keefe (1997) found that 12.3% of male students and 3% of females reported forcing sex in their dating relationships, but this study did not specify what was meant by force. A study that did distinguish between verbally coercing and physically forcing sex is Poitras and Lavoie (1995). They found that

- 12% of males and 6.3% of females used verbal sexual coercion
- 0.3% of males and none of the females misused authority
- 2.3% of males and none of the females used alcohol or drugs
- 3.9% of males and 0.3% of females threatened to or used physical force

Hines and Saudino (2003) found that 29% of male and 13% of female university students reported one or more acts of sexual coercion including verbal and physical tactics in the previous 12 months. In short, these studies show that in relationships with acquaintances both men and women use a broad range of sexually coercive behaviors, but many more men than women do so.

Prior Victimization and Perpetration of Sexual Coercion

We decided to investigate the relation of spanking, minor neglect, and sexual abuse as a child or adolescent to sexually coercing or assaulting a partner because, on theoretical grounds and on the basis of the studies reviewed below, each of these three childhood maltreatment experiences could contribute a distinctive piece to the explanation of sexual coercion.

- Minor neglect can contribute to less moral internalization and less self-control, including control of aggression (see review below).
- Spanking can contribute examples of using physical force and violence to control the behavior of another person.
- Sexual abuse history can provide an example of coercion to obtain sex.

Together, we believe they are almost a perfect storm that increases the probability of sexual coercion. Moreover, in addition to these direct relationships, the three types of victimization increase the probability of antisocial traits and behavior, which then further increases the probability of sexual coercion.

Previous studies of the relation of childhood victimization to sexual coercion and assault have a number of limitations. For example, some studies combined several types of prior victimization into a single variable (e.g., Wolfe, Scott, Wekerle, & Pittman, 2001), thus providing no information on the separate effect of each type of childhood victimization. Most studies of sexual coercion have considered exclusively male samples. As mentioned previously, there are some studies of sexual coercion by women. However, because samples and measures differ from those used in studies of sexual coercion by men, they cannot accurately compare male and female prevalence rates and etiology. That requires studies that include both men and women in the same study, as in this chapter. Finally, many of the studies of the relation of prior victimization to sexual coercion examined the effect of only one type of victimization in isolation from other types (Loh & Gidycz, 2006). Because *poly-victimization* is common (Finkelhor, Ormrod, & Turner, 2007), research on a single type of victimization tends to overestimate the effect of that one type of victimization. There is a need to determine the relation of different forms of victimization to sexual coercion while controlling for each of the other types of victimization in order to estimate the unique effect of each. This chapter does that by considering the combined effect and the net effect of three childhood and adolescent types of victimization: neglect, spanking, and sexual abuse in a sample of men and women. In addition, because a number of studies have shown that antisocial traits and behavior are important in the etiology of sexual coercion by men against women (Knight & Sims-Knight, 2004; Malamuth, Linz, Heavey, Barnes, & Acker, 1995), we investigated the extent to which antisocial traits and behavior explains the link between earlier victimization and sexual coercion— that is, whether the relation of the three types of victimization (minor neglect, sexual abuse, and spanking) to sexual coercion occurs because they increase the likelihood of developing antisocial traits and behavior. The following sections review the research on the relation of the three types of victimization to sexual coercion.

Why Focus on Spanking and Neglect?

There has been little research on whether spanking a child and minor neglect (such as not helping a child experiencing a difficulty) are risk factors for sexual coercion. Perhaps this is because it has been presumed that spanking and minor neglect constitute a much less severe level of victimization than sexual abuse. However, there are important reasons to think that spanking and minor forms of neglect increase the risk of later sexual coercion.

One reason to focus on these presumably less serious types of victimization is the well-established public health principle that mitigating a frequently occurring risk factor with a low effect size (such as spanking a child) can result in a greater reduction in the prevalence of a disease than mitigation of a relatively rare risk factor with a large effect size, such as physical abuse (Rose, 1985). Thus, if spanking and minor neglect are found to be related to sexual coercion, reducing these two risk factors could be a major step in preventing sexual coercion because they are such prevalent forms of child victimization. This is because, as shown in Chapter 2 on the use of spanking in the United States, over 90% of toddlers are spanked. Similarly, studies of minor forms of neglect by parents such as failing to console a child who is sad or in physical pain, have found very high rates (Straus et al., 1998; Straus & Savage, 2005). A cross-national study of minor neglect in a large sample of university students used a scale of eight neglectful behaviors, such as "Did not comfort me when I was upset." It found that about one half of the students experienced one or more of eight neglectful behaviors, including 12% who reported two of the eight, and another 12% experienced three or more (Straus & Savage, 2005).

Neglect History and Sexual Coercion

Neglect is "behavior by a caregiver that constitutes a failure to act in ways that are presumed by the culture of a society to be necessary to meet the developmental needs of a child and which are the responsibility of a caregiver to provide" (Straus & Kaufman Kantor, 2005). We located only one study investigating the link between neglect and sexual coercion. DeGue and DiLillo (2004) found that a history of physical or psychological abuse was related to sexual coercion, but that a history of neglect was not. Nevertheless, there is both a theoretical and an empirical basis for hypothesizing a link between neglect and sexual coercion and assault.

Tremblay (2003) argues that a responsive parent and consistent discipline enable children to learn nonviolent strategies for achieving their goals and expressing anger. A child who does not have a responsive caregiver and consistent guidance may not adequately learn nonviolent strategies and, consequently, is more likely to engage in maladaptive coping strategies and an aggressive pattern of interaction (see also Chapple, Tyler, & Bersani, 2005; Gottfredson & Hirschi, 1994; Spitz, 1959). Consistent with this theory, a number of empirical studies have found that neglect constitutes a risk factor for aggressive and antisocial behavior (Chapple et al., 2005; Hildyard & Wolfe, 2002; Horwitz, Spatz Widom, McLaughlin, & Raskin White, 2001). There is also a study of the link between minor neglect and physical violence against a dating partner using the same measure of neglect as used for this chapter and found that even this relatively minor level of neglect experienced as a child was significantly related to assaulting and injuring a dating partner (Straus & Savage, 2005).

One can conclude from these studies that there is a large body of evidence showing that neglect is a risk factor for later aggressive and criminal behavior, including physical aggression against dating partners. Therefore, even though one study that investigated sexual coercion did not find a relationship between neglect history and sexually coercing a partner, we hypothesized that:

> *The more minor neglect experienced, the greater the probability of engaging in sexual coercion of a dating partner.*

Spanking and Sexual Coercion

The chapters in Part II and the previous chapters in this Part and Chapter 19 show that spanking is associated with an increased probability of antisocial behavior as a child and criminal behavior as an adult. Several mechanisms that might explain the association between spanking and aggressive antisocial and criminal behavior were identified in a review by Simons, Burt, and Simons (2008). According to social learning theory (Bandura, 1977), children spanked as a means of discipline learn through the example of this legal and morally correct behavior by their parents that aggression is a socially acceptable and effective means for getting others to do what you want. Consistent with this, in the United States and around the world, spanking is associated with an increased probability of physical violence against a marital or dating partner (Chapters 12 and 13).

Although spanking produces compliance in the short term, the studies in this book have found that the long-term effect is the opposite: Spanking increases the probability of deviance, including antisocial behavior. The association between spanking and antisocial behavior was found by the studies in the chapters on spanking and child antisocial behavior (Chapter 6), impulsive spanking (Chapter 7), spanking and the child-to-mother bond (Chapter 8) and a large number of studies reviewed in the chapter on spanking and societal-level rates of crime and violence (Chapter 19). Gershoff's meta-analysis (2002) included 40 tests of the hypothesis that spanking is associated with an increased probability of aggressive and delinquent behavior. Of nine tests of the relationship between spanking and subsequent abuse of the victim's own children or partner, all nine found the hypothesized relation.

Given the consistency of the research showing that spanking is related to aggression and crime, it is not surprising that it has also been found to be related to sexual coercion of women (DeGue & DiLillo, 2004; Malamuth, Linz, Heavey, Barnes, & Acker, 1995; Simons et al., 2008). On the basis of both theory and those empirical results, we hypothesized that spanking as a child is associated with an increased probability of perpetration of sexual coercion. Moreover, because Chapters 12 and 13 show that the relationship between spanking and assaulting a partner applies to both men and women, we hypothesized that:

Spanking experienced as a child is associated with an increased probability of sexual coercion by men and women in this study.

Sexual Abuse History and Sexual Coercion

Previous reviews have shown that experiencing sexual abuse is associated with a wide variety of problematic behaviors. Because previous reviews are available (Berliner & Elliott, 1996; Kendall-Tackett, Williams, & Finkelhor, 2001) and because of space limitations, we mention only studies that examined the relation of sexual abuse to sexual coercion. Loh and Gidycz (2006) found that men with a history of childhood sexual victimization were over 6 times more likely to perpetrate sexual assault as adolescents and adults. Lyndon, White, and Kadlec (2007) found that males who used force to gain sexual contact reported significantly more childhood history of sexual abuse compared with both men who used manipulation and men who reported engaging in only consensual sex. Sexual abuse history has also been found to be a predictor of perpetration of sexual coercion by women. Krahé, Waizenhofer, and Moller (2003), for example, found that the probability of sexual coercion of a male was 2.62 times higher for females who reported childhood sexual victimization than for females without a history of sexual abuse. Based on these results, we hypothesized that:

A history of sexual abuse is related to sexual coercion by both the male and female students in this study.

Antisocial Traits and Behavior and Sexual Coercion

The link between an antisocial orientation and sexual coercion against women has been extensively studied in both criminal and noncriminal samples of men (Abbey & McAuslan, 2004; DeGue & DiLillo, 2004; Knight & Sims-Knight, 2004; Malamuth et al., 1995; Simons et al., 2008). The related concept of psychopathy has also been found to be associated with sexual coercion (Hare,

Clark, Grann, & Thornton, 2000; Knight, 2006). These studies leave little doubt that antisocial traits and behavior are associated with sexual coercion by men but do not answer the question of whether this relationship also applies to women. We therefore tested the hypothesis that:

> *Antisocial personality and behavior is associated with an increased probability of sexual coercion by both the male and female students in this study.*

Sample and Measures

Sample

The sample for this study is from the International Dating Violence Study that also provided the data for the chapters on spanking in world perspective (Chapter 3) and spanking and partner violence among university students across the globe (Chapter 13), namely 14,252 university students in 32 nations. The study and the sample are described in Chapter 3 on the worldwide prevalence of spanking (in Rebellon et al., 2008; Straus, 2008b, 2009b). Most of the data were obtained by administering a questionnaire during regularly scheduled classes. Because this study is on issues in which gender differences are crucial, the analyses either controlled for gender or were replicated for male and female students.

Measure of Sexual Coercion

Sexual coercion and assault of a dating partner was assessed using the Sexual Coercion Scale of the revised Conflict Tactics Scales or CTS2 (Straus et al., 1996). Example items are: "Used threats to make my partner have sex" and "Used force (like hitting, holding down, or using a weapon) to make my partner have oral or anal sex." Participants who reported perpetrating one or more of the verbal coercion items in the past year were coded as 1, and all others as 0. The same procedure was used to identify participants who had committed a sexual assault by physically forced sex. Because research suggests that individuals who use nonphysical coercion to gain sexual contact differ in several ways from individuals who use physical force (DeGue & DiLillo, 2004; Lyndon et al., 2007), these two scores were used to create a Sexual Coercion Severity typology that enables separately analyzing verbal sexual coercion and physically forced sex. The typology classified each participant into one of three mutually exclusive categories: 0 = no sexual coercion, 1 = verbal sexual coercion without physical force, and 2 = physically forced sex.

Measures of Neglect, Sexual Abuse, and Spanking

The measures of minor neglect, sexual abuse history, and spanking are from the Personal and Relationships Profile (Straus et al., 2010; Straus & Mouradian, 1999). The response categories for the questions making up all the scales are (1) strongly disagree, (2) disagree, (3) agree, and (4) strongly agree.

Minor neglect. The Personal and Relationships Profile includes an eight item short form of the Multidimensional Neglectful Behavior Scale (Straus, Kinard, & Williams, 1995). It has two items to measure each of the four dimensions of neglectful behavior: cognitive ("My parents did not help me to do my best"), supervisory ("My parents made sure I went to school"), emotional ("My parents did not comfort me when I was upset"), and physical ("My parents did not keep me clean"). The scale was scored by adding all the items to which the participant agreed or strongly agreed. Thus, the scores indicate the number of different types of minor neglect experiences that each respondent experienced as a child. The Neglectful Behavior Scale has demonstrated good cross-cultural construct validity and reliability, with an overall alpha of .72 (Straus, 2006). For this study, the alpha coefficient of internal consistency reliability was .70 for males and .71 for females.

Spanking. The Personal and Relationships Profile includes the question "I was spanked or hit a lot by my parents before age 12." Participants responded using the 1 (strongly disagree) to 4 (strongly agree) categories described earlier.

Sexual abuse history. Sexual abuse was assessed using the eight-item sexual abuse history scale of the Personal and Relationships Profile. This scale includes questions on whether participants had experienced contact and/or noncontact sexual abuse by family members, peers, and/or nonfamily adults. The scale asks about two behaviors: "Made me look at or touch their private parts (sex organs), or looked at or touched mine" and "Had sex with me (vaginal, anal, or oral)." Each of them was asked for the following four situations: perpetration before age 18 by an adult family member, by another child in the family, by a nonfamily adult, and by nonfamily children. The total score was computed by adding the items to which the respondent marked agree or strongly agree. Thus, the score on the sexual abuse history scale corresponds to the number of different experiences of sexual abuse that each participant experienced as a child and/or adolescent, with a maximum of eight experiences. Strong internal consistency reliability was found for previous samples (Straus & Mouradian, 1999). For this study, alpha coefficient was .80 for males and .79 for females.

Antisocial Traits and Behavior

This scale is derived from the DSM-IV (American Psychiatric Association, 1994). Although the questions were derived from the DSM-IV definition of antisocial personality disorder, this scale was not designed as a diagnostic tool. Because the DSM-IV definition of antisocial personality disorder includes criminal behavior, both before and after age 15, the scale combines the nine antisocial personality traits scale and the criminal history scale of the Personal and Relationships Profile (Straus et al., 2010). Examples of the nine antisocial personality trait items are "I often lie to get what I want" and "I don't think about how what I do will affect other people"). Each of the four criminal behaviors are asked for "before age 15" and for "since age 15." Examples of the eight criminal history scale items are "Before age 15, I stole money from anyone, including family" and "Since age 15, I have physically attacked someone with the idea of seriously hurting them." The 17 items comprising both subscales were summed and divided by the number of items to obtain a mean antisocial traits and behavior score. The internal consistency reliability (Chronbach's α) was .82 for males and .81 for females. Information on the construct and concurrent validity of the antisocial traits and behavior subscale is in Hines and Straus (2007). To examine the extent to which medium and high levels of antisocial traits and behavior are associated with an increased probability of sexual coercion, we coded the antisocial traits and behavior scores into three categories: 1 = low antisocial traits and behavior (scores below the 25th percentile), 2 = medium antisocial traits and behavior (scores between the 25th and 75th percentile), and 3 = high antisocial traits and behavior (the top 25% of the distribution).

Control Variables

A relationship between spanking and sexual coercion might just reflect some underlying third variable. To take that into account, we statistically controlled for five other variables that could be related to both spanking and sexual coercion. Each of these is described in more detail in the Appendix.

Social desirability. The tendency of some participants in a study to minimize disclosure of socially undesirable behavior could lead them to underreport both spanking and sexual coercion and, therefore, create a spurious correlation. This was controlled using the limited disclosure scale of the Personal and Relationships Profile (Chan & Straus, 2008; Sabina & Straus, 2006; Straus et al., 2010; Straus & Mouradian, 1999).

Family socioeconomic status. Family socioeconomic status was controlled using a three-item scale based on the education of the student's father and mother and family income.

Age. Age was controlled because it is well-established that younger ages are associated with higher rates of violent crime, including partner violence (Stets & Straus, 1989).

Relationship length in months. It was important to control for the length of time the couple had been together because the longer the relationship, the greater the opportunity for sexual coercion to have occurred.

Prevalence and Gender Differences in Sexual Coercion

As has been found in previous studies, a high percent of students sexually coerced a partner. More male than female students sexually coerced a partner, but a substantial percent of women also engaged in sexual coercion. Statistically dependable gender differences were found for the verbal coercion scale and the physical coercion scale and for most of the items making up these scales (see Appendix for the tests of significance).

Verbally coercing sex was reported by 27% of the male students and 20% of the female students. Statistically dependable differences between men and women were also found in most of the verbal sexual coercion items: insisting on sex when the partner did not want to (males = 15.9%, females = 8.2%); threatening the partner to have sex (males = 1.4%, females = 0.8%); insisting on sex without a condom (males = 14.9%, females = 12.9%); insisting on oral or anal sex (males = 11%, females = 3.8%); and threatening the partner to have oral or anal sex (males = 1.2%, females = 1.1). Physically forcing sex was reported by 2.4% of the male students and 1.8% of the female students. Rates for the two specific items were: 1.3% of males and 1.0% of females used force to have sex, and 1.6% of the males and 1.0% of the females used force to have oral or anal sex. Thus, as in other studies that compared sexual coercion by men and women in the same study, both men and women engaged in sexually coercive behavior, but men predominate.

Tests of the Theory

Chart 16.1 summarizes the results of testing the theory that the causes of sexual coercion include having been spanked, and that the effect of spanking is in addition to the effects of having been sexually abused or neglected. Moreover, the theory also specifies that one of the reasons spanking is related to sexual coercion is because, as was shown in Chapter 6, spanking increases the probability of antisocial traits The lines in the chart (called paths) show the relation of each of the three risk factors to antisocial traits and the relationship of antisocial traits to sexual coercion.

Chart 16.1 gives only the most directly relevant results because, if the results for all the possible paths were included, there would be so many lines that it would be very difficult to read and understand. Therefore, only paths that are statistically dependable are in the chart, and the paths for the control variables are also not shown. However, the coefficients and tests of significance for all the variables are in the section of the Appendix for this chapter.

The numbers on each path are the amount by which each increase of one point in the variable at the left side of the path is associated with an increase in the variable at the right side of the path. These numbers are *odds ratios*. There are two odds ratios on each path: The one on the right is the odds ratios for women and the one on the left is the odds ratio for men.

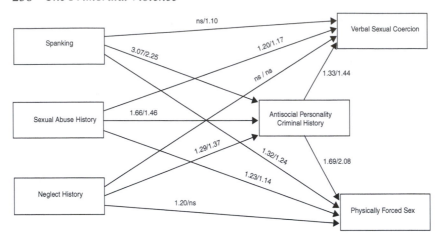

* Odds ratios on paths to Antisocial Personality are the odds of being in the High Antisocial category.

Chart 16.1   Spanking Is One of the Risk Factors for Sexually Coercing a Partner by Both Men and Women

Spanking

Verbal sexual coercion. The first of the two odds ratios on the path from Spanking (upper left) to Verbal Sexual Coercion (upper right) is marked as *ns* (not statistically significant) because, for male students, there was not a statistically dependable relationship between Spanking and Verbal Sexual Coercion. But for women, the second odds ratio of 1.10 indicates that each increase of one point on the four-point scale of spanking before age 12 is associated with increasing the odds of Verbal Sexual Coercion by the women in this study 1.10 times (i.e., a 10% increase in Verbal Sexual Coercion).

The paths from Spanking to Antisocial Personality Criminal History, and from there to Verbal Sexual Coercion show that Spanking is also associated with Verbal Sexual Coercion indirectly by increasing the odds of Antisocial Personality Criminal History (center box) by just over 3 times (odds ratio of 3.07) for males and just over 2 times (2.25) for females. The path from Antisocial Personality Criminal History to Verbal Sexual Coercion, in turn, shows that Antisocial Personality Criminal History is associated with increasing the odds of Verbal Sexual Coercion 1.33 times for males and 1.44 times for females. Thus, part of the reason spanking is associated with verbal sexual coercion is because spanking increases the probability of antisocial traits and behavior in general, of which sexual coercion is one example.

Physically forced sex. The diagonal path from Spanking to Physically Forced Sex shows that spanking is directly associated with an increased probability of Physically Forced Sex. The first of the two odds ratio on this path is for the male students. The 1.32 indicates that each increase of one point on the spanking measure is associated with a 33% increase in the probability of men physically forcing sex. The second odds ratio of 1.24 for female students indicates that each increase of one point on the spanking measure is associated with a 27% increase in the probability of the women in this study physically forcing sex.

The path from Spanking to Antisocial Personality Criminal History in the center of the chart indicates that spanking is also related to physically forcing sex, by increasing the probability of Antisocial Personality Criminal History, which in turn, is associated with increasing the probability of physically forcing sex by 1.69 times for males and by 2.08 times for females.

Charts 16.2 and 16.3 graph the relation of spanking to sexual coercion in more detail. The lines for men are higher in both graphs than for women because the men in this study engaged in more sexual coercion than the women. However, Chart 16.2 shows that for both men and women, the more spanking, the higher the percent who used verbal sexual coercion. Chart 16.3 shows that spanking is associated with an increased probability of physically forced sex by both men and women, but the increased probability is greater for the men.

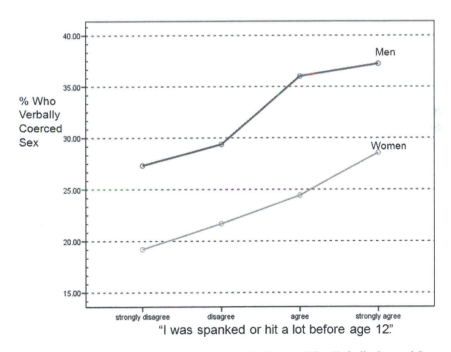

Chart 16.2   The More Spanking, the Greater the Percent Who *Verbally* Coerced Sex in the Previous 12 Months

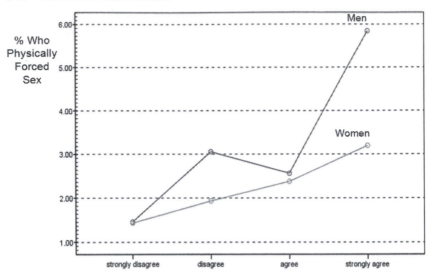

Chart 16.3   The More Spanking, the Greater the Percent Who *Physically* Coerced Sex in the Previous 12 Months

Sexual Abuse History

Returning to Chart 16.1, the paths from Sexual Abuse History to Verbal Sexual Coercion show that each increase of one point on the four-point Sexual Abuse History scale is associated with a 20% increase in the probability of verbal sexual coercion by men and a 17% increase in the probability of verbal sexual coercion by women.

Having been sexually abused is also associated with an increase in the probability of physically forcing sex. For men, each increase of one point of the Sexual Abuse History Scale is associated with a 1.23 times increase in men physically forcing sex, and a 1.14 times increase in women physically forcing sex.

Prior sexual abuse is also associated with sexual coercion indirectly through an increased probability of antisocial traits and behavior. Thus, as hypothesized, the more sexual abuse experienced, the greater the probability of both verbal and physical sexual coercion.

Neglect History

The *ns/ns* on the path from Neglect History to Verbal Sexual Coercion indicates that we did not find a direct link between neglect and verbally coercing sex. For physically forcing sex, the path from Neglect History to Physically Forced Sex shows that for men, each increase of one point in the Neglect History scale is associated a 1.2-time increase in the probability of physically forcing sex, but for women, the *ns* means that we did not find a relationship.

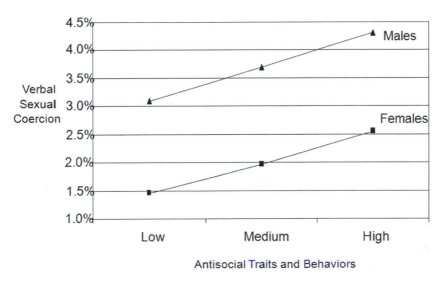

Chart 16.4 The More Antisocial Traits and Behavior, the Greater the Percent Who *Verbally* Coerced Sex in the Previous 12 Months

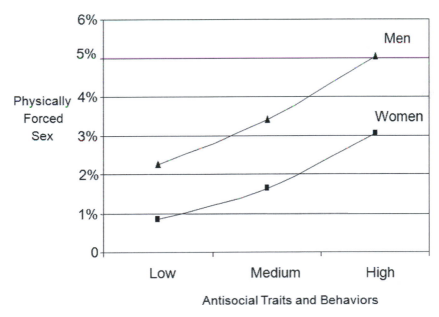

Chart 16.5 The More Antisocial Traits and Behavior, the Greater the Percent Who *Physically* Forced Sex in the Previous 12 Months

For both the men and the women in this study, neglect is indirectly related to physically forcing sex because, the paths from Neglect History to Antisocial Personality Criminal History show that neglect is associated with a 1.29-time increase in antisocial traits by men and a 1.37-time increase for women, and the path from antisocial traits to physically forcing sex shows that being high in antisocial traits and behavior is associate with a 1.62-time increase in the probability of men and a 2.08-time increase in the probability of women physically forcing sex.

Antisocial traits and behavior. Because antisocial traits and behavior appears to play such a central role in explaining sexual coercion by both men and women, we examined this relationship in more detail in Charts 16.4 and 16.5. These plot lines were computed with the value of all other variables controlled. Both charts show that although the probability of both kinds of sexual coercion is higher for male than for female students, antisocial traits and behavior is associated with a sexual coercion to about the same extent for both the men and women in this study.

Summary and Conclusions

We studied a large multi-nation sample of university students and, consistent with other studies, found high rates of verbally coercing sex and of physically forcing sex. To be more specific, 27% of the male students and 20% of the female students verbally coerced sex in the previous 12 months, and 2.4% of the male students and 1.8% of the female students physically forced sex during that period. Thus, as in other studies that compared sexual coercion by men and women in the same study (e.g., Banyard et al., 2007; Hines & Saudino, 2003; Kar & O'Leary, 2010; Panuzio & DiLillo, 2010), both men and women engaged in sexually coercive behavior, but the rates for men are higher. The data on physically forcing sex by women are difficult to interpret because the questions did not specify the specific acts of force used. Most of the instances may be manually or orally stimulating the male partner despite physical resistance, whereas forced sex perpetrated by males probably includes penetration attempts and actual penetration.

The results show that, with two exceptions, the relation to sexual coercion of the three risk factors we investigated (spanking, sexual abuse history, and neglect history) are parallel for men and women. The two exceptions are that spanking is related to verbal sexual coercion by women but not by men, and having been neglected as a child is related to physically forcing sex by men but not by women.

Tests of the Theoretical Model

The main objective of the study was to test the theory that the three types of child and adolescent victimization (spanking, neglect, and sexual abuse) are each independently associated with an increased probability of engaging in sexually coercive behavior later in life, both directly and because those victimization experiences increase the probability of the child developing antisocial traits and behavior, which, in turn, increases the probability sexual coercion.

Spanking. Frequent spanking of a young child was found to be an important risk factor for sexual coercion, both directly and because it increases the probability of antisocial traits and behavior. Experiencing frequent spanking was associated with a tripling of the probability of being high in antisocial traits and behavior for men and doubled the probability for the women in this study. In turn, antisocial traits and behavior significantly increased the likelihood of either verbal sexual coercion or physically forced sex for both males and females.

It is important to keep in mind that these results are based on a question that asks about experiencing a lot of spanking. Research shows that the harmful side effects of spanking take the form of a *dose-response* pattern (Gunnoe & Mariner, 1997; Straus, Sugarman et al., 1997). Therefore, the effect of only occasional spanking is likely to be much lower. Nevertheless, these results are consistent with the results of a meta-analysis of research on spanking (Gershoff, 2002), which found a large and unusually consistent body of research showing that spanking tends to *increase* the probability of deviant behavior and psychological problems. This includes the longitudinal studies in this book and those summarized in Chapter 19.

Sexual abuse history. For both men and women, a history of sexual abuse was associated with an increase in the probability of sexual coercion and of antisocial traits and behavior. Antisocial traits and behavior, in turn, was associated with a significantly greater probability of either physical or verbal sexual coercion. These findings are in keeping with past research that found that individuals with a history of sexual abuse are associated with an increased probability of antisocial and criminal activities (Herrera & McClosky, 2003; Swanston et al., 2003; Widom & Ames, 1994) and sexual coercion against men (Krahé et al., 2003) or women (Loh & Gidycz, 2006; Lyndon et al., 2007).

Neglect history. The hypotheses concerning experiencing mild forms of neglect as a child were only partly supported. Minor neglect was not significantly associated with a higher probability of Verbal Sexual Coercion. For male students in this study, but not for female students, even this level of neglect was associated with an increased probability of physically forcing sex. The results show that minor neglect is associated with an increased probability of being in the high antisocial traits and behavior category, which in turn is associated with either verbal sexual coercion or physically forced sex for both men and women. This is consistent with the studies reviewed earlier that found an association of neglect with partner violence and antisocial behaviors (see also Chapple et al., 2005).

Antisocial traits and behavior. The results underscore the importance of antisocial traits and behavior in understanding the association between victimization as a child or adolescent and sexual coercion by both men and women. Although the role of an antisocial orientation on sexual coercion has been demonstrated among men in previous studies (Abbey & McAuslan, 2004; Knight, 2006; Knight & Sims-Knight, 2004; Malamuth et al., 1995), the current results indicate that this applies to women as well. However, as in other studies, the rate of antisocial behavior was higher for the men in this study than for the women. In addition, effect size for the association of spanking and sexual abuse with antisocial traits and behavior is higher for the male students than for the female students. This is congruent with research that found that men abused as children are more likely than women who were abused to have antisocial behavior symptoms (e.g., Horwitz et al., 2001).

Limitations

Although this study avoided some of the limitations of previous research, such as restricting the study to male perpetration, failing to control for socially desirable response bias, examining a particular type of prior victimization in isolation from other types of victimization (i.e., not allowing for polyvictimization), and combining several types of victimization into a single variable, there are nonetheless a number of limitations to keep in mind when considering the conclusions and implications.

First, like much previous research on the origins of sexual coercion, the study participants were university students and the data on prior victimization depends on their willingness and ability to recall and report prior victimization. Second, because the rate of most crime, including sexual crime, peaks at about the age of university students, these studies may overestimate the prevalence of sexual coercion in the general population. On the other hand, the opposite bias may be present because university students tend to be from higher socioeconomic status families, and there is abundant evidence that parent-child violence and partner violence become less prevalent with increasing socioeconomic status (see Chapter 2 and for partner violence, Straus et al., 2006; Chapter 12; Straus et al., 1996). Moreover, as pointed out in the Methods section, the study used convenience samples. However, the risk factors for partner violence found in studies using convenience samples of students are almost identical to those found in community sample studies.

An important limitation is that the cross-sectional design does not permit concluding that the relationships found reflect a cause-effect sequence. This is particularly important in the case of spanking because that is something parents typically do to correct misbehavior. Thus, spanking, rather than being a cause of later antisocial traits and behavior, may be a consequence of early child behavior problems, which carries over into adulthood. However, there are at least seven longitudinal studies that show that although misbehavior does cause parents to spank and that spanking does result in cessation of the misbehavior at the time, in the longer run, the use of spanking boomerangs in the sense of increasing the probability of subsequent antisocial behavior (Straus, 2001a).

At least two of the measures have important limitations. The Neglect History scale measures relatively mild forms of neglect, and even students with high scores would be unlikely to be classified by child protective services as *neglected.* The item used to measure spanking has almost the opposite problem. As pointed out previously, the question refers to having been spanked or slapped a lot before age 12. Thus, the results may not apply to students who were spanked only occasionally. In addition, the question is defective in not using a more specific indication of frequency of spanking, as do the response categories of the parent-child Conflict Tactics Scales (Straus et al., 1998) and the Dimensions of Discipline Inventory (Straus & Fauchier, 2011).

Implications

Although stranger rapes are almost exclusively perpetrated by men, this study, like other studies (Banyard et al., 2007; Kar & O'Leary, 2010; Panuzio & DiLillo, 2010) found that, in partner relationships, women as well as men engage in both verbal and physical coercion of partners. That is an important finding for its practical implications and because it requires an alteration of the theory that sexual coercion and sexual assault are primarily motivated by and instrumental in maintaining male-dominance in relationships and in the society. The practice implication is that, even though men predominate in sexual coercion, it should not obscure the fact that women also engage in sexual coercion. Public service announcements and other educational efforts to prevent sexual coercion of partners need to be explicitly addressed to women as well as men.

Our results also contribute to the debate about whether spanking is harmful enough to be banned. They add to the already large and consistent body of evidence showing that spanking children is a risk factor for a wide variety of maladaptive conditions documented in other chapters and by Gershoff (2002). This study adds sexual coercion to the identified aggressive and criminal behaviors that are linked to spanking. Moreover, because having been sexually abused or neglected were controlled in the statistical analysis, the study shows that the effect of spanking is unique; that is, it is in addition to the effect of those two other types of victimization.

Because antisocial traits and behavior seem to be part of the explanation for the link between victimization and sexual coercion, further development of brief but effective methods of treating this disorder can contribute to preventing sexual coercion and sexual assault in couple relationships.

Programs directly focused on the prevention of rape, such as the date-rape prevention programs at many U.S. universities, are extremely important, even though the evidence on their effectiveness is mixed (Davis & Liddell, 2002; Gidycz et al., 2001). This suggests that prevention of sexual coercion and sexual assault also needs to address victimization experiences that have no obvious link to sexual coercion, such as spanking and neglect. Helping parents avoid spanking and avoid even seemingly innocuous forms of neglect could contribute to reducing sexual coercion because spanking and minor neglect are so prevalent in the lives of children and youth.

Finally, the results of this study provides another of many examples of the principle that humane treatment of children can have major benefits in creating more humane relationships in general, including sexual relationships between men and women.

Part V

Social Change and Trends in Spanking

17 The Decline in Spanking

Spanking and more severe corporal punishment to correct misbehavior by a child has been an almost universal part of the childhood experience of children throughout history (DeMause, 1984; Levinson, 1989; Montague, 1978; Newell, 1989). The results of our national survey on corporal punishment in the United States (Chapter 2), in 32 nations (Chapter 3), and in this chapter, show that this is still the case in most of the world. However, change has been taking place, and we will examine the available data to get a picture of the pace of the change. Some of the data are the results of surveys that asked about attitudes concerning spanking and provide information about cultural norms supporting spanking. We also present data on change in the actual use of spanking. Together, they provide a better understanding of trends in use of corporal punishment. To do this, the chapter pieces together several studies to investigate the following questions:

- To what extent has approval of spanking in the United States decreased since the late 1960s?
- To what extent is the decrease of the result of demographic changes such as the increase in the average level of education and to what extent is it a reflection of changes in cultural norms about the appropriateness and necessity of spanking?
- Do various sociocultural groups in American society, such as Blacks and Whites, differ in approval of spanking, and are there differences between groups in the degree to which approval of spanking has decreased?
- To what extent has the actual use of spanking decreased during this period?
- To the extent that there has been a decrease in spanking, does it apply to children of all ages, and specifically to toddlers as well as older children?

Anita K. Mathur is the coauthor of this chapter

Cultural Norms on the Necessity of Spanking

Interrelation of Social Organization and Cultural Norms

When a behavior is almost universally prevalent, there are likely to be cultural norms that encourage or at least legitimate that behavior. If changes in the organization of society bring about a change in behavior, such as families having fewer children which, as shown in Chapter 4 on family size and spanking, tends to result in less spanking, new norms are likely to emerge that justify and regularize the new pattern. For example, in the second half of the 20th century, as middle class married women increasingly engaged in paid employment, the norms that had previously disparaged paid employment by married women have been replaced by norms that favor it. The new norms almost require paid employment by married women, as they do for men.

Regardless of which occurs first, and despite many exceptions, over time cultural norms and actual behavior tend toward being consistent with one other. A recent example of cultural norms changing to reflect and facilitate change in the organization of society is the norms about unmarried cohabitation. As that has become more and more prevalent, the old stigma and pressures to marry have changed to accepting it as just one additional form of relationship. This was illustrated by the election in 2010 of Edward Miliband to be the head of the Labor Party in the United Kingdom and potentially the next prime minister. He is the father of two children living with his partner. A reporter interviewed residents of Pangbourne, a village of 2,900, how they felt about this. Only a minority in the village voted for his party in the last election and are, therefore, unlikely to be biased because of favoring him politically. The interviewees were just about unanimous in saying his cohabiting relationship was unimportant and some asserted that as a prescriptive norm, "None of that stuff bothers me, nor should it bother anyone" (Henley, 2010).

The shift to what is called a post-industrial economic system in many high economically developed nations is a major change in the economic organization of society, and we believe that these economic changes and the increases in education and other social changes that accompany economic development are some of the things that have produced the decline in spanking. The new economic order brought with it a change in the occupations of most people in economically developed societies. Employment in manufacturing has declined drastically, as has the demand for unskilled manual workers. The predominant occupations are now in services, management, the professions, and sciences. In 1950, 30% of U.S. workers were employed in manufacturing compared with less than 15% in 2008. In 2008 there were more choreographers (16,340) than metal-casters (14,880; Caldwell, 2008). These trends mean that an increasing percentage of the population needs to have interpersonal skills to cooperate, explain, and negotiate, and to be self-directed, autonomous, and creative. These are not skills that are fostered by spanking. When parents require unquestioning obedience and hit rather than explain to enforce it, they model an economic and social system that needs more obedient workers than self-directing workers, and that economic system is disappearing.

Kohn and others (Kohn, 1969; Kohn & Schooler, 1983; Pearlin, 1967; Straus, 1971) found that frequent use of spanking is associated with an emphasis on obedience rather than on reasoning, negotiation, and problem solving. Those parents also have less interest in the child going to college (Pearlin, 1967). Because each instance of spanking is a lost opportunity to learn cognitive, interpersonal negotiation, and managerial skills, there is a concordance between spanking and parental expectations for their child. The studies in Part III are consistent with that theory. These studies held many other things constant such as the parents education, supportiveness, and cognitive stimulation. One is a longitudinal study that followed up a large national sample of children and found that the more spanking, the more a child was likely to fall behind other children in development of mental ability (see Chapter 10).

The second study found that the more spanking, the lower the probability of graduating from college (see Chapter 11). Moreover, one of our previous studies found that, even among those who did graduate from college, spanking is associated with a lower probability of being in the top fifth of the U.S. occupation/income distribution (Straus, 2001a, pp.137–142). Of course, this does not mean that spanked children will not graduate from college. If that were the case, because as shown in research on corporal punishment throughout the United States (see Chapter 2), over 90% of U.S. parents spank toddlers, almost no one would graduate from college. It just means that a lower percent will graduate. (See the section in Chapter 1, Risk Factors: The Real Meaning of Social Science Research Results.)

Consistent with this theory about the links between the occupational structure of society and modes of discipline, Kohn (1969) found that parents who expected their child to go to college spanked less. He interpreted these results as *anticipatory socialization* by parents who expect their child to be employed in nonmanual work occupations. That is, when parents envision their child in roles where what is needed is cognitive ability, critical thinking, and negotiation skills rather than physical strength and compliance with the rigid routines of the assembly line, they tend to rely on cognitive more than physical modes of teaching and correcting. To the extent that theory is correct, the norms and practices of parents in the United States and other post-industrial societies should be moving away from the use of corporal punishment in child rearing. These characteristics of a post-industrial occupational system may be part of the explanation for a *moral passage* (Gusfield, 1963, 1981) that could eventually change the world from one in which almost all children are socialized by spanking to one in which this occurs for only a small minority of the population. Such a change would be part of the centuries-long "civilizing process" described in the concluding chapter.

Cultural Norms Supporting Spanking

Although cultural norms supporting spanking children may be changing, there is abundant evidence that these norms are still deeply rooted and pervasive in American culture (Greven, 1990; Straus, 2001d). One of the most fundamental ways in which cultural norms supporting spanking are expressed is in the criminal law on assault. In every U.S. state, hitting a child for purposes of correction or control is exempt from the crime of assault, usually with the provision that it must be limited to reasonable force (Davidson, 1997). In practice, numerous recent state supreme court decisions have ruled that this includes the right to hit with belts and paddles, provided the child is not physically injured (e.g., rulings by the supreme court of New Hampshire in 1992 and of Minnesota in 2008). In the Minnesota case (Olson, 2008), the father paddled his unruly son 36 times. In a unanimous decision, the court ruled that spanking a child is not necessarily abuse. The judges said they declined to rule that the infliction of any pain constitutes either physical injury or physical abuse, because to do so would effectively prohibit all corporal punishment of children by their parents and that they did not intend to ban corporal punishment. Nevertheless, the fact that these and other similar cases even got to a state high court is an important indicator of change.

In the 1960s, every state in the United States passed child protection legislation designed to protect children from physical abuse and to provide services for abused children. Ironically, in order to garner sufficient votes to pass these laws, it was typically necessary to include a provision declaring that parents continued to have the right to use corporal punishment (i.e., to hit children for purposes of correction and control). Thus, legislation intended to protect children from physical abuse contained provisions that further legitimated hitting children in the form of corporal punishment.

- Indiana provides an example of such legislation, where the state's definition of child abuse and neglect reads: "This chapter [on child abuse and neglect] does not limit: The right of the parent to use reasonable corporal punishment to discipline the child." (Indiana Ann. Code §§ 31–34–1–12; 31–34–1–14; 31–34–1–15)
- Similarly, Ohio's child abuse and neglect statute reads: "A child exhibiting evidence of corporal punishment or other physical disciplinary measures by a parent is not an abused child if the measure is not prohibited under Ohio state statute." (Ohio Rev. Stat. §§ 2151.03(B); 2151.031; 2919.22)
- South Carolina's child abuse and neglect statute also addresses corporal punishment. "The term child abuse or neglect excludes corporal punishment or physical discipline that: Is administered by a parent or persons in *loco parentis*; is perpetrated for the sole purpose of restraining or correcting the child; is reasonable in manner and moderate in degree; has not brought about permanent or lasting damage to the child; [and] is not reckless or grossly negligent in behavior by the parents. (South Carolina Ann. Code § 63–7–20)

The irony is that about two thirds of the cases of physical abuse that come to the attention of child protective services started out as spanking and then escalated into injury-producing attacks (Gil, 1970; Gonzalez, Durrant, Chabot,

Trocmé, & Brown, 2008; Kadushin & Martin, 1981; Trocmé, Tourigny, MacLaurin, & Fallon, 2003; Straus, 2000, 2008a).

Cultural norms supporting spanking are also documented by public opinion surveys asking respondents whether they approve of spanking. A 1968 survey commission by the National Commission on the Causes and Prevention of Violence found that 94% of the population approved of spanking a child who misbehaves (Stark & McEvoy, 1970). There may be no other aspect of child rearing except provision of basic physical necessities on which almost everyone agrees. In addition, the normative support for spanking goes well beyond mere permission to hit children. It is a morally correct and expected action. The question asked in the 1968 survey was whether they thought that spanking was sometimes necessary. Parents who do not spank are often thought of as bad parents whose children will grow up wild. That these are true cultural norms with expectations for conformity to the norm is shown by two studies. Carson (1986) found that non-spanking parents come under considerable pressure to spank from relatives, friends, and neighbors who questioned the adequacy of their parenting. Walsh (2002) studied the 998 mothers in our research on impulsive spanking (Chapter 7) and the child-mother bond (Chapter 8) and found that a majority of parents who do did spank were advised to do so. In the six months before being interviewed for the study, 61% of the mothers of children age 2 to 3 were advised to spank their child 1 or more times, and 52% of mothers of children age 13 to 14 were given the same advice.

Change in Approval of Spanking

The surveys of attitudes toward spanking that have been completed since the late 1960s have found both decreases and, despite that, continuing high rates of approval. The percentage who approve of spanking also varies considerably from study to study, probably because the questions used and the samples are so different. Therefore, these studies cannot be compared to determine if there has been a change in support for spanking. For example, a 1975 survey of a national sample of parents found that 77% believed that slapping or spanking a 1-year-old who misbehaved is normal and necessary (Straus et al., 2006). A survey of pediatricians published in the 1990s found that 77% supported spanking (White, 1993). These figures although a decade apart cannot be used to estimate change in attitudes because they used different questions and studied different populations. Nevertheless, the changes in the nature of U.S. society and the antispanking laws passed in many other nations led to the following hypothesis:

- Hypothesis 1: The percent of the U.S. population who believe that spanking is necessary has declined since 1968.

For this chapter, we also examined whether public approval of spanking decreased as result of demographic changes in U.S. society rather than because of a change in the cultural norms. For example, the percent of college graduates in the United States has been increasing tremendously. College graduates are less favorable to spanking. Therefore, the large increase in the percent of college graduates should result in less approval of and less spanking. A similar effect might result from the increase in the average age of the population. If people become less favorable to spanking as they mature, the overall level of approval could decrease when there are more older people in the population. However, that might not be the case because older persons are not only more mature, they also represent a previous historical setting that was favorable to spanking and that might produce the opposite result. To find out the extent to which such demographic changes explain the decrease in the percent who approve of spanking, we tested a second hypothesis about change in the public approval of spanking:

- Hypothesis 2: The decrease in approval of spanking will still be present after controlling for six demographic variables.

If hypothesis 2 is confirmed, it is plausible to infer that the decrease reflects a change in cultural norms rather than a change in the demographic composition of the population.

The Seven Surveys

These two hypotheses could be tested because there are publicly archived data files for seven surveys that used the identical or very similar question to determine the approval of spanking. All seven surveys used nationally representative samples of adults and collected data on the six sociodemographic variables that were included in the analysis for this chapter: the age of the respondent, income, education, gender of the respondent, and race. The samples, which together had 6,794 participants, are:

- **Survey 1** is a 1968 national survey, designed and conducted for the National Commission on the Causes and Prevention of Violence. It studied 1,160 adults (Stark & McEvoy, 1970).
- **Surveys 2–6** are the General Social Surveys for the years that included the question on spanking (1986, 1988, 1989, 1990, and 1991). (Davis & Smith, 1992).
- **Survey 7** is the survey that provided the data on corporal punishment in the United States in Chapter 2.

Six of the seven studies obtained data on approval of spanking by asking, "Do you strongly agree, agree, disagree, or strongly disagree that it is sometimes necessary to discipline a child with a good hard spanking?" A somewhat different question was used in the 1968 survey that asked: "Are there any situations that you can imagine in which you would approve of a parent spanking his or her child assuming the child is healthy and over a year old?" Respondents in this survey could answer only yes or no, rather than choose from four response categories. We tried to make the data from studies that used four response categories somewhat more equivalent by combining strongly agree and agree into agree, and combining disagree and strongly disagree into disagree. Thus, the data for all seven studies classifies the respondents as either agreeing or disagreeing. Nevertheless, some of the difference between the 1968 study and the other six studies may be a result of the difference in the wording of the question.

Trends in Support of Spanking

Chart 17.1 shows that the belief that spanking is sometimes necessary decreased from 94% in 1968, to 65% in 1994. Another survey asked the same question in 1999 and found a further decrease in the approval of spanking to 55% (Children's Institute International, 1999). In one generation, approval of spanking seems to have gone from something almost everyone in the United States thought was necessary to a bare majority. Of course, 55% is still a majority. However, other surveys since then suggest that the decrease to 55% may not be accurate. The decrease to 55% is inconsistent with more recent results from the General Social Survey to be discussed later. Nevertheless, using just the data up to 1994, the decrease from near unanimity to 68% represents an important social change, especially when one views it as a change in support

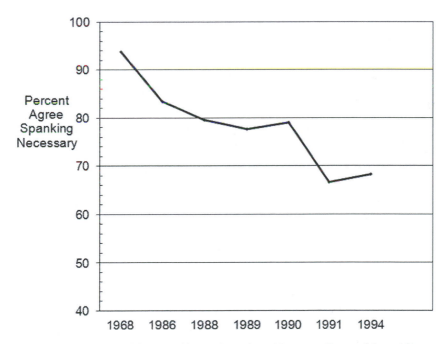

Chart 17.1   The Belief that Spanking Is Sometimes Necessary Dropped from Almost Everyone in 1968. However, in 1994, Two Thirds Still Thought Spanking Was Necessary

for a cultural norm that has existed for thousands of years and which is the law in every state of the United States.

Chart 17.1 originally had two trend lines. The line shown has been adjusted to control for the six demographic variables. There was another line showing the percentages before adjusting for the control variables. Because controlling for changes in the demographic composition of the population made almost no difference and the lines overlapped in a way that made the chart more difficult to read, the line for the raw data is not included in Chart 17.1 More important, the fact that the two trend lines are almost identical, indicates that the decrease from 1968 to 1999 represents a change in cultural norms rather than a change in demographics because the controls adjusted the data to take into account changes in the demographics.

Group Differences in the Trend

Another purpose of analyzing the seven surveys was to find out the extent to which various sociocultural groups in U.S. society differ in the approval of spanking, and if there are differences between groups in the trend over the 31-year period of the study. The evidence from other studies on group differences in the approval of spanking is contradictory. The 1968 survey by Stark and McEvoy (1970) found no difference on any of the demographic variables such as educational level. However, Flynn (1994) analyzed the 1988 General Social Survey and found that approval of spanking varied among different regions of the United States. The West, Midwest, and the South had more favorable attitudes toward spanking than the Northeast. Flynn also found that Blacks are more likely than Whites to favor spanking, and that low education, being male, and being young were also associated with a greater likelihood of approving of spanking. Why did Flynn find differences between regional and other groups, and Stark and McEvoy did not? Perhaps it is because in 1968, almost everyone (94%) thought spanking was necessary. That creates what is called a statistical ceiling effect because there is little room for group differences. The decline in approval of spanking since 1968 may have reduced the ceiling effect. If so, the even further decreases in approval of spanking should allow for more differences between demographic groups. We investigated this by examining the pattern of change over time within each group. Doing that uncovered some clues to explain the potential differences between groups in approval of spanking.

Gender. Chart 17.2 shows that from 1968 to 1994, approval of spanking decreased among both men and women but with a somewhat greater decrease for women. among 1968 almost everyone believed that spanking was necessary (95% of women and 92% men). By 1994 the slightly more women than men had reversed, and fewer women than men approved of spanking (61% of women versus 76% of men). This suggests that men have held on to the old values concerning spanking somewhat more than women.

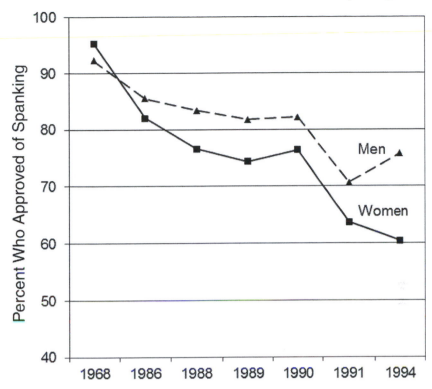

Chart 17.2   The Decrease in Approval of Spanking Has Been Greater for Women than for Men

Ethnic group. Three race or ethnic groups were compared: Whites, Blacks, and other. Overall, in 1968, there was little difference in the percent who approved of spanking. Over 90% of all three groups thought spanking was necessary. The trends in approval of spanking for each ethnic group in Chart 17.3 reveal large decreases in approval of spanking for both Whites and others over the 26-year period. For Blacks, the decrease in approval of spanking was much less than for the other ethnic groups—14 percentage points for this period, compared with 26 percentage points for Whites and 32 percentage points for the other category.

Region. Chart 17.4 shows that in 1968 there were almost no differences between regions. At that point in U.S. history, almost everyone, regardless of region believed that spanking was sometimes appropriate. Over the 26 years covered by this study, residents in all four regions decreased in the approval of spanking. Nevertheless, Southerners generally had the highest rate of approval of spanking at each time point, and the decrease was less than in other

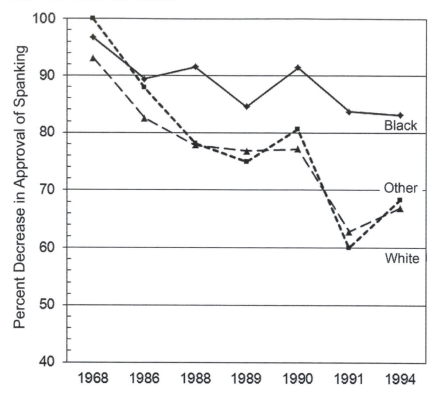

Chart 17.3   The Decrease in Approval of Spanking Has Been Greater among Whites and Other Ethnic Groups than among Blacks

regions from 1968 to 1994. The South decreased only 21 percentage points whereas the Northeast decreased a total of 35 percentage points from 1968 to 1994. The regions thus grew more different from each other in the proportion approving spanking mainly because the South did not decrease as much as other regions.

Age. As expected, the rate of approval of spanking was greatest for older respondents because they were socialized in a cultural climate that was more approving of spanking. However, the differences were not as large as we expected. When age is divided into five categories (from the youngest fifth in each survey to the oldest fifth), the maximum difference between any two age groups was only 6%. All five age groups followed the general downward trend.

Income and education. No relationship was found between income and approval of spanking. When income, like age, was divided into five categories (lowest fifth to highest fifth within each study), all five income groups followed

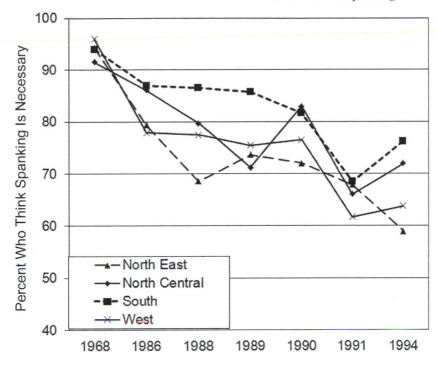

Chart 17.4   Difference between Regions in Approval of Spanking Increased because in 1968 Almost Everyone Approved

a similar downward trend in approval of spanking from 1968 to 1994. Education, on the other hand was strongly related to less approval of spanking. The respondents in each survey were divided into quartiles: the quarter of each survey with the least education, the two middle quarters in education, and the quarter with the highest education. All four educational groups decreased in approval of spanking over the 26-year period, but the highest education group decreased the most. As with the other demographic characteristics, in 1968, almost everyone approved of spanking and education made little difference. By 1994, the highest education group had a lower rate of approval than the other education groups.

Trends in Approval of Spanking since 1994

The General Social Survey continued asking the same question on whether spanking is sometimes necessary in surveys up to 2010. Chart 17.5 extends the trend line to that date. We expected that the decline shown previously in Chart 17.1 would continue or even accelerate. Instead, the percentages in Chart 17.5 for the years since 1994 show a remarkable cessation in the downward trend

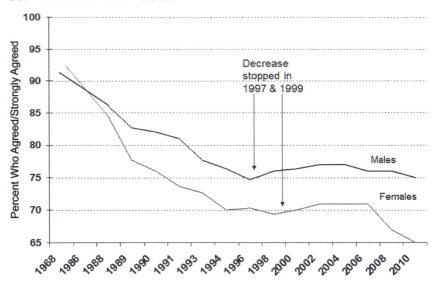

Chart 17.5   Percent of U.S. National Samples Who Agreed or Strongly Agreed that "A Good Hard Spanking Is Sometimes Necessary" (General Social Survey for all years except 1968. Moving Average 3 per year.)

of public opinion about the necessity of spanking. Instead of a continued large decrease with each survey, there has been almost no change since the mid 1990s. Just over 70% of the U.S. adult population continues to believe that "a good hard spanking is sometimes necessary." Research is needed on why the decrease has not continued. A similar cessation of the rapid decline in approval of spanking was found by Gallup/ABC News surveys (Pinker, 2011, p. 436). We suggest that part of the explanation follows from the results showing that almost all parents continue to hit toddlers, even though as shown in Chart 17.7, they now hit toddlers less often. It may be an example of the principle explained in the introduction to this chapter: cultural norms both influence and also reflect what people actually do. That is, because over 90% of U.S. parents spank toddlers, the cultural norms and beliefs about spanking continue to reflect that aspect of what parents do. Or putting it another way, it may be that U.S. parents are reluctant to believe that what they did was not necessary.

Trends in Spanking

Almost three quarters of U.S. adults may believe in the necessity of spanking sometimes, but what percent actually spank and has that changed? There are many indications that the actual use of spanking is decreasing. There are two studies that provide data on the extent to which this has occurred. The first are the annual surveys conducted between 1988 and 1999 by *Prevent Child Abuse*

America. Those surveys found that during just that decade, the percentage of parents who spanked in the past year decreased by one third (Daro & Gelles, 1992). This decrease is consistent with the theory outlined in the first part of this chapter—that parents tend to socialize children in ways that will help them fit into the social environment that the parent thinks the child will experience as an adult. Specifically, these children face a post-industrial society where self-direction and cognitive and interpersonal skills are needed for more and more of the available jobs. However, the Prevent Child Abuse America surveys did not provide data on the age of the child. As a consequence, we do not know if the decrease was for across the board or more for children of certain ages. Data on trends for each age group is important because, as found in our study about the use of corporal punishment in the United States (Chapter 2), the percent of spanking ranges from almost all parents of toddlers to a small percentage of parents of older teenagers.

Fortunately, we were able to examine the trend in spanking for children of different ages using data from three studies of nationally representative samples of parents: the National Family Violence Surveys conducted in 1975 and 1985 (Straus, 1990d) and the survey conducted for us in 1995 by the Gallup Organization that provided the data about the prevalence of corporal punishment in the United States (Chapter 2). The three studies used three somewhat different versions of the Conflict Tactics Scales to measure the use of corporal punishment. However, the question on spanking was the same in all three surveys. This enabled us to test the hypothesis that spanking has decreased over these three time periods. The question asked the parents whether they had spanked or slapped the child with their open hand in the past year and how often. The percentages who spanked will be lower than in other reports on these three studies, including the Gallup study (Chapter 2), because those reports were based on the full Conflict Tactics Scales, which also asked about methods of corporal punishment such as use of a belt or hairbrush.

Chart 17.6 shows that in 1995, 74% of the parents of 2- to 4-year-old children said they had spanked or slapped the child in the past year. This is only a small decrease (12%) from the 83% who spanked in 1975. On the other hand, spanking 9- to 12-year-old children decreased by 31% from 1975 to 1995, and for teenage children it decreased by 56%. In the next chapter, we suggest an explanation for how it can be that, for older children, approval of spanking and actual spanking decreased to one third or one half of what it had been in 1975, whereas during this same period almost all parents continued to hit toddlers. Why was there so little change in spanking younger children during the same period that cultural norms supporting spanking declined so precipitously, and when actual use of corporal punishment with older children also decreased at what may be a historically unprecedented pace? That chapter also suggests what would be needed to produce the same decrease for young children as has occurred for older children.

On the other hand, quite a different picture emerges when the criterion for change is *how often* parents who spanked did it. Chart 17.7 shows that the

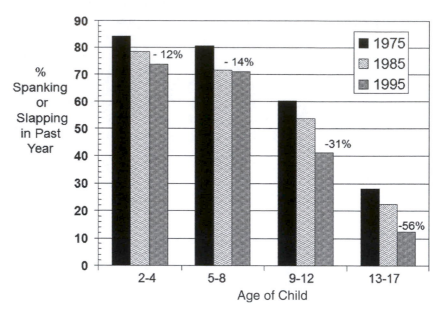

Chart 17.6 Spanking and Slapping Has Decreased Tremendously since 1975 for "Tweens" and Teens, but Very Little for Toddlers and Younger Children

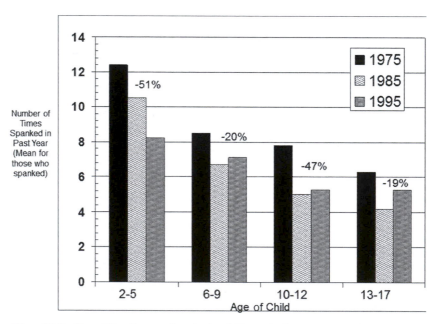

Chart 17.7 How Often Parents Spanked and Slapped Also Decreased since 1975, the Most Decrease Was for Toddlers

Data from national surveys conducted by Murray A. Straus and colleagues. University of New Hampshire (//pubpages@unh.edu/~mas2).

biggest decrease was for toddlers and the smallest decrease in how often parents spanked or slapped was for teenagers. What this boils down to is that although there was little change in the percent of parents who hit toddlers, how often they did it dropped by 51%, whereas the opposite was found for parents of teenagers. There was a big decrease in the percent of parents who hit teenagers, but those few who did it in 1995 hit almost as often as in 1975.

Spanking in 2006

Although we were not able to analyze a more recent national survey of parents using the same question on spanking and slapping as was used in 1975, 1985, and 1995, the 2006 Harris Youth Survey included a question we suggested. This provided recent and nationally representative data based on the responses of 1,213 children age 8 to 17. The participants were asked:

"In the past year, that is, since about this time last year, about how many times did your mother or your father (or whoever was taking care of you that year) use physical punishment, like spanking, slapping or hitting you? Once; twice; 2 to 5 times; 6 to 10 times; 11 to 20 times; more than 20 times; not in the past year, but it has happened before; never."

The data from the Harris Youth Survey cannot be used to infer change from 1995 to 2006 because the measure was not the same as in the surveys in Chart 17.6. In addition, the participants in the study were children rather than parents. There may be differences between parents and children's willingness to disclose or ability to remember instances of spanking. If children disclose or remember more instances, the positive side is that the Harris Youth Survey data probably provides a more complete picture of the extent to which corporal punishment is used than do parents. Chart 17.8 shows that over 40% of children age 8 to 10 said that they had been spanked or hit during the previous year. This is a high percentage, but it is much lower than the approximately 65% of children that age in the 1995 survey (see Chapter 2, Chart 2.1). Unfortunately, because of the differences between the Harris survey and the 1995 survey, it does not necessarily mean a decrease in corporal punishment. For older children, the percentages are also lower than a decade previously, but still very high. In 2006, almost one quarter of early teenage children and about one out of seven children age 17 and 18 were hit by their parents during the year of the study.

A study by Vittrup and Holden (2010) provides further evidence that, despite decreases, spanking remains both the statistical and the cognitive norm. They studied the parents of 108 children aged 6 to 10 living in a large city in Texas and also the children. According to the parents, 71% spanked their children at least once in the past week. According to the children, 82% of the 108 had been spanked in the past year. This is about the same percentage as shown in the Gallup study on the prevalence of corporal punishment in the United States in 1995 (Chapter 2). Of the 6-year-old children, 70% reported being spanked at least once a week, 36% were spanked 1 to 2 times per month or once

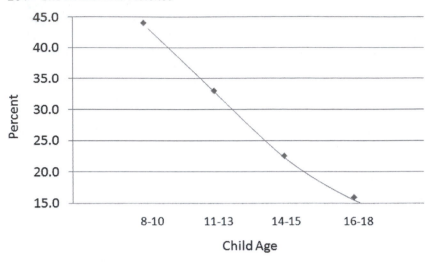

Chart 17.8   The Percent of School-Age and Teenage U.S. Children Spanked or Hit in 2006 Remains High

a week, and 20% spanked 2 or more times per week. A study by Taylor and colleagues (Taylor, Lee et al., 2010) found that two thirds of 3-year-old children were spanked at least once in the previous month by one or both parents.

Finally, the study by Zolotor, Runyan, Chang, and Laskey (2011) described in Chapter 2 found that 82% of the parents of children age 3 to 5 had spanked or slapped the child with an open hand that year. This is less than the 94% reported in Chapter 2 for our 1995 national Gallup survey, but not a lot less. Zolotor et al. themselves compared their results with our study on corporal punishment in the United States (Chapter 2) and with our 1975 and 1985 national surveys. They concluded that between 1975 and 2002, 18% fewer children were slapped or spanked by a caregiver and that this decrease was primarily for the older children.

Trends in Europe

Several nations in Europe have enacted legal prohibition of corporal punishment by parents. Bussman, Erthal, and Schroth (2011) studied changes in five of those nations. In Sweden in the 1950s, 94% of parents spanked, and one third did it at least daily (Stattin et al., 1995). One can infer from this that almost all Swedish parents did it at least once a week. By 1995, the percentage of parents who had spanked decreased to 33%. A 2003 study found no further decrease in the percentage who had ever spanked but found a tremendous reduction in the percentage who spanked once a week or more—to only 4% (Durrant, Rose-Krasnor, & Broberg, 2003). In Germany, surveys of nationally representative samples of children aged 12 to 18 in 1992 and

2002 found large decreases, especially in the most severe forms of corporal punishment (Bussman, 2004).

- Light slap in the face decreased from 81% to 69%
- Severe slap in the face decreased from 44% to 14%
- Beaten on the bottom with a stick decreased from 41% to 5%
- Beaten to the point of bruising decreased from 31% to 3%

Decreases of that magnitude are not likely to have occurred in response to a law passed in 2000, especially because the law was not known to 70% to 75% of the population. These remarkable decreases probably reflect changes in German culture and social organization as much or more as the law banning spanking. Nevertheless, analysis of the trends in Sweden led Bussman to conclude that an unambiguous legal prohibition accelerates the change.

Summary and Conclusions

Approval of Spanking

In 1968, 94% of the U.S. population believed that spanking was necessary. Except for the obligation to provide for the basic physical needs of a child, it is hard to think of any other aspect of child rearing on which there was such consensus. The percent who believe that spanking is sometimes necessary decreased steadily until the late 1990s. However, since then, it has remained at just over 70% until the most recent survey (2010).

Decline in Consensus on Spanking

One thing that is consistent in the recent General Social Survey results and other results in this chapter is that there are important differences between sectors of the population in believing that spanking is sometimes necessary: more men than women, more low education than better educated, and more Blacks than Whites. These groups also differed in the rate of decrease. Because some groups in the population have changed faster than others, it has ended the former national consensus on the necessity of spanking. The different rate of change has produced a widening gulf in attitudes toward the appropriateness of spanking children. For example, approval of spanking by men has decreased, but less than approval by women. Therefore, in contrast to the results for 1968, men are now stronger supporters of spanking than women. As a result, there are likely to be more couples who disagree about the necessity of spanking, and that disagreement could affect marriages as well as children.

Although approval of spanking in the South decreased since 1968, the decrease was smaller than in other regions of the United States. As a result, even though support for spanking declined in the South, the South has remained more favorable to spanking than other regions. Similarly, approval of spanking by Blacks declined, but less than in other ethnic groups. As a result, the Black-White difference in the belief that spanking is necessary has become larger than ever. Approval of spanking declined less for people with lower education and for older age groups. These differences in the rate of change have resulted in subcultural group differences in U.S. society in respect to spanking that did not exist or were minimal only a generation ago. In 1968, there were no differences because almost everyone (94%) believed in the necessity of spanking. The findings of the research in this book suggest that this change will have great benefits for children and for society. At the same time, the discrepancies created by differences in the extent to which different parts of the population have embraced the change can create or increase conflict over whether to spank, such as exists between fathers and mothers and Blacks and Whites. It is an example of the principle that all social change, no matter how beneficial, also has costs.

Is There a Backlash?

A decrease from 94% who believe spanking is sometimes necessary to the current 70% indicates both a major social change and persistence in the belief that spanking is necessary. It means that the cultural norm specifying that parents should spank when necessary, although no longer nearly unanimous, continues. In addition, what was a consensus on the necessity of sometimes spanking has become a widening gap between sectors of society. A change in a cultural norm about a family behavior that is as deeply embedded in peoples' beliefs about what is right can be a problem. It is one element in the much talked about *culture wars*. It may have given rise to a backlash against the movement to bring up children more humanely. An indicator of the backlash may be that child protective service agencies, which have responsibility for enforcing the legislation intended to protect children from physical and other abuse, have come under attack on the grounds that they prohibit spanking, even though that is not the case in any state in the United States. Legislation placed before the Florida legislature in the spring of 1994 would have prohibited child protective services from ruling that a child had been abused if the only evidence was that the parents used corporal punishment, and the child exhibited welts or bruises. The bill was passed overwhelmingly but was vetoed by the governor. However, the reason for the veto was not a disagreement with the purpose of the bill; it was because the governor believed it would create administrative problems (Hollis & Currie, 1994; Neal, 1994).

The seeming backlash and the widening gulf between socioeconomic status groups with respect to spanking is a source of concern. Ignoring these problems could interfere with the transition to new cultural norms that forbid any spanking. It could exacerbate class and race conflict if efforts to end spanking are seen as an attempt to control and limit the lives of the underprivileged. Such a perception would be a cruel irony because as we have previously noted in this book and in a previous study (Straus & Gimpel, 2001), violent socialization in the form of frequent spanking reduces the probability of upward social mobility. The greater adherence to spanking by low socioeconomic status groups suggests that the shift away from spanking among the majority, and the lesser change among low socioeconomic status groups, could have important consequences for class and race differences. We believe spanking by low socioeconomic status parents has and will continue to retard efforts to create a more equal society because, as this book and much other research shows, spanking is one of the reasons that the children of the poor have lower IQ, have a higher probability of being physically aggressive, have more psychological problems, and have more crime as adults. The social class gap could increase if low socioeconomic status parents continue to be frequent spankers and higher socioeconomic status parents continue to spank less and less.

In evaluating these conclusions, it is important to keep in mind that we said "increases the *probability*." Most children who are spanked a lot will not experience lower IQ than they would have otherwise, but an avoidable percentage will. This is the same sort of relationship as the link between smoking and dying of a smoking-related disease. As we pointed out in the introductory chapter to this book (Chapter 1) and elsewhere, one third of heavy smokers will suffer that ultimate harmful side effect. But that same statistic means that most heavy smokers will not die of a smoking-related disease. (See the section in Chapter 1 on Risk Factors: The Real Meaning of Social Science Research Results.)

The additional handicap imposed on children of low socioeconomic status suggests that although the efforts to end spanking need to be directed at all parents, there needs to be an even stronger effort for the low-income and low-education sectors of society. That includes many Blacks. Leaders of the Black community, including Black academics, need to be at the forefront of that effort. For academics, a needed focus is research on the most effective way to communicate the information about the effectiveness and side effects of spanking to different socioeconomic and cultural groups.

Variations in Trends in Spanking

The trend in respect to the use of spanking in the United States, like the trend in approval, presents a mixed picture. Among teenagers, the percent hit by parents is about one half of what it was in 1975. For children age 9 to 12, it has declined by about one third. However, spanking and slapping *toddlers* remains almost universal. That is a cruel age difference because the study of the adverse effects on spanking on IQ in Chapter 10 found that the harmful side effect of spanking is greatest at that age. However, that may not be true for all side effects of spanking. Finkelhor's (2008) Developmental Perspectives Model of child victimization argues that the age of maximum sensitivity to a form of victimization can depend on the nature of the developmental task. It may be different for attachment, control of aggression, peer relationships, or learning to defer gratification in favor of presumably larger later rewards.

The most vulnerable age for each of these is unknown. But what is known is that the advice to confine spanking to preschool-age children, whereas an improvement over no age limitation is based on folk-wisdom rather than research evidence.

The huge and almost entirely negative reaction described in Chapter 1 to a *Time* magazine article in April 2010 on *The Long-Term Effects of Spanking* could be interpreted as a backlash against the growing professional advice to avoid spanking when possible. An alternative interpretation of what seems to be a backlash is that it may be more a dying gasp by those who have always believed in the necessity of spanking. In the past, they did not have to defend the use of spanking because, as shown in Chart 17.1, the necessity of spanking was a belief shared by close to 100% of the U.S. population. Not only is that no longer true, but the advocates of spanking may eventually become a beleaguered minority. An indicator of the emerging cultural shift was a 2006 episode of the immensely popular television show *Desperate Housewives*. It pilloried one of the characters for spanking. A similar manifestation of the changing cultural landscape is the TV show, *Supernanny*. In her first book, Jo Frost, the supernanny of the show did not rule out spanking. But late in 2006, the U.S. edition of *Supernanny* devoted an episode to the effort of *Supernanny* to help a mother stop spanking.

The Confusion of a Culture in Transition

The cultural norms and practice of spanking are in a state of transition. Part of the inconsistency between studies and between the trends for younger and older children probably reflects that. The question used for this chapter to measure the approval of spanking requires a more complete rejection of spanking than has been achieved so far in the United States. It asks study participants whether they agree or disagree that spanking is sometimes necessary. To answer "disagree" means that the person believes children should *never* be spanked. Our guess is that, if the survey question were about whether spanking should be avoided as much as possible, most people in the United States, and especially the college educated, would now agree. The era in which spanking was thought to build character and prepare the child for the hard knocks of life is mostly gone. But an era in which children should *never* be spanked has not yet arrived in the United States. It has arrived in Sweden and, as will be shown in the final chapter, which discusses the notion of a world without spanking, the process is well underway in other nations. Our estimate of the current situation is that, in the United States, most people including most professionals concerned with children such as pediatricians, psychologists, and parent educators, are opposed to the use of spanking. However, they also believe it is sometimes necessary. An example we hear over and over is when a child runs out into the street or repeatedly commits the same misbehavior. Although *never* spanking is not currently the norm in the United States and most other nations, we believe it will eventually become the norm in all nations. Of course, there will always be some parents who spank, just as there will always be some parents who do not use seat belts.

As pointed out at the start of this chapter, the change is part of the transition to a post-industrial economic order, which as argued in the concluding chapter, is part of a process of social evolution that, since the late middle ages, has reduced person-to-person violence (Eisner, 2003; Elias, 1978; Pinker, 2011; Straus, 2001d). In our opinion, the social organizational and cultural evolution that has reduced other types of violence will eventually make spanking or slapping a child as offensive, morally and legally, as slapping a wife or husband.

18 Why Everyone Spanks Toddlers and What to Do About It

The previous chapter provided evidence that, even though almost three quarters of Americans believe that spanking is sometimes necessary, a growing number are opposed to spanking and think it should be avoided. Paradoxically, however, almost all parents of toddlers in the United States continue to spank, as shown in Chapter 2. Similarly, a survey of the disciplinary practices and attitudes of 1,000 parents in Northern Ireland found that the majority of parents have negative attitudes toward physical discipline. Nonetheless, many of the parents continued to spank despite the fact they do not believe it to be effective (Bunting, Webb, & Healy, 2010).

The belief that spanking should be avoided may be even more true of professionals who provide information to parents, such as child psychologists, parent educators, nurses, pediatricians, and social workers. However, few of these professionals directly advise parents not to spank, and even fewer advise parents to *never* spank. And as was shown in Chapter 1, about one third had actually advised parents *to* spank in the previous 12 months (Knox & Brouwer, 2008). An article in *American Family Physician* (Banks, 2002) argued that other methods of discipline are more effective and cites numerous studies that have linked negative outcomes to spanking. However, the article also says that "spanking is inappropriate in children younger than 18 months" (Banks, 2002, p. 1450). This implies that it is appropriate for children over the age of 18 months, and there is nothing in the article that says it should never be used with children of any age.

The studies presented in the last parts of Chapter 2 and the previous chapter found that this high percentage of parents who spank young children has continued into the 21st century. As we pointed out in the conclusion to the previous chapter, it seems that, although Americans now believe that spanking should be avoided, most also continue to believe that it may sometimes be necessary when other methods have not served to correct repeated misbehavior, and they act on that erroneous belief. This contradiction between not favoring spanking yet using spanking has also been shown internationally by a 35-nation study (UNICEF, 2010). Given these paradoxical discrepancies, this chapter addresses the following questions:

- What explains the discrepancy between what professionals who advise parents believe and what they actually advise and the discrepancy between what parents believe and what they do?
- What are the implications of that explanation of the discrepancy for advising parents about spanking?
- Should parents be advised to *never* spank under any circumstance, and given the current research evidence, is such advice ethical?

The predominant approach is now to help parents use an *alternative* strategy rather than spanking. We prefer to say nonviolent discipline because referring to those methods of correction and control as alternatives implies that the basic method is spanking. Regardless of the terminology, advice to never spank, no matter what circumstance, is avoided by all but a few pediatricians and parent educators. The analysis will suggest a paradoxical aspect of focusing exclusively on nonviolent alternative discipline techniques rather than a clear never spank message: It unwittingly contributes to *perpetuating* the use of spanking.

The Three Paradoxes

It is important to identify the conditions that explain why almost everyone spanks toddlers because that can contribute to understanding disciplinary strategies and to developing methods to help parents shift to nonaggressive discipline strategies. Three paradoxes about spanking provide a framework for explaining why almost everyone spanks toddlers and what to do to change that.

Paradox 1: Approval of Spanking Has Decreased, but Spanking Toddlers Has Not

Most aspects of corporal punishment have decreased in major ways in the last generation. The previous chapter showed that the percent of parents who hit adolescents has also dropped by 56% for children age 13 and over and by 31% for children age 9 to 12, but only by 12% for children age 5 to 8 and 11% for children age 2 to 4. The positive side of this is the 56% decrease for teenagers. The troublesome part is that, despite the decrease, about one out of seven teenage children continue to be hit by parents. In addition, as we have pointed out repeatedly in this and previous chapters, despite these major steps away from corporal punishment, at least 90% of parents of toddlers spank. Moreover, other studies show that parents who spank toddlers did so an average of about 3 times a week (Berlin et al., 2009; Giles-Sims et al., 1995; Holden et al., 1995; Vittrup & Holden, 2010). Obviously, we need to understand why parents who don't believe in spanking continue to hit toddlers and do it so frequently.

Paradox 2: Professionals Opposed to Spanking
Fail to Advise Parents to Never Spank

Many pediatricians, nurses, developmental psychologists, and parent educators we talk to are now opposed to spanking, at least in principle. But there is evidence that, despite being against spanking, all but a small minority of professionals continue to believe that spanking may sometimes be necessary and advise parents to spank when necessary (Burgess et al., 2010; Schenck et al., 2000). The main reason for this contradiction may be that they believe that spanking works when other methods do not. For example, Marjorie Gunnoe, a psychologist who has done research on spanking, responded to a reporter who asked about her recent study: "I think of spanking as a dangerous tool, but then there are times when there is a job big enough for a dangerous tool" (Black, 2010). In other words, spanking is acceptable if it is used as a last resort. Another explanation is that social scientists, like other Americans, subscribe to the cultural myth that when loving parents spank to correct misbehavior, it is harmless if done in moderation, whatever that is. It is like the courts, until about 1870, upholding "physically chastising an errant wife," provided it is done in moderation (Calvert, 1974).

When we have suggested to pediatricians, parent educators, or social scientists that it is essential to tell parents to *never* spank or use any other type of corporal punishment, with rare exception, this idea has been rejected. This is because many clinical child psychologists now believe that, although spanking is not desirable, it is sometimes necessary. Many academic developmental psychologists believe that the important thing is the overall pattern of parenting, not one behavior such as spanking (Baumrind et al., 2002; Parke, 2002). That is like saying that, in nutrition research and clinical advice, there is no point to focus on just one element, for example Vitamin C, because the important thing is the overall pattern of nutrition. A closely related objection to focusing on spanking is the belief that the problem is not spanking *per se,* but the overlap of spanking with harsh and incompetent parenting. The latter is not very plausible because over 90% of parents spank toddlers, although with greatly different frequency. Therefore, harsh and incompetent parents could only be the real cause of the harmful side effects of spanking if over 90% of parents were harsh and incompetent.

Rebecca Socolar, a leading behavioral pediatrician, told one of us she does not advise parents to never spank because that would turn off parents, and she would lose the opportunity to help them in other ways. Many professionals who advise parents have the same belief. Still another objection to advising parents to never spank is based on the assumption that some parents don't know what else to do or lack the verbal skills to effectively use cognitive correction. If so, preventing such parents from spanking could be harmful to children because they lack other means of fulfilling a parent's obligation to correct misbehavior.

One of us has been told many times in discussions with parent educators, child psychologists, and pediatricians that advising parents to never spank is a negative approach, and that a positive approach is needed, by which they mean teaching parents nonviolent disciplinary strategies. Teaching nonviolent strategies is very desirable. However, it is not a precondition for ending spanking because parents already use many other means of correcting misbehavior. As pointed out earlier, for most parents spanking is a last resort mode of discipline. If they stuck to the other methods consistently and left out the spanking, that alone would usually make them more effective parents.

The cumulative effect of these objections is to say nothing about spanking or to avoid making a recommendation (see Chapter 1). Widely used parenting programs such as Parent Effectiveness Training (Gordon, 2000) and STEP (Dinkmeyer & McKay, 2008) provide nonviolent alternatives to spanking but are silent on spanking itself. Fortunately, this is slowly changing. A pioneer in this change was Penelope Leach. Her book *Your Baby and Child* (Leach, 1977) had six pages on never hit. In several editions, it has sold two million copies worldwide. It is widely believed to be influential, but for years was the only widely read book giving this advice to parents. Since then, although they are still the exception, an increasing number of books for parents, parent education programs, and guidelines for professionals, advise never, under any circumstance, to spank a child. Examples of programs that directly advise never spanking for which there is empirical studies of effectiveness, including randomized control trials for some, include:

- The Baby College (http://www.hcz.org/programs/early-childhood)
- Early Start Program (Fergusson, Grant, Horwood, & Ridder, 2005)
- Effective Black Parenting (Alvy & Marigna, 1987)
- Family Nurturing Program (Palusci, Crum, Bliss, & Bavolek, 2008)
- Nurturing Parenting Programs (Bavolek, 1992–2006)
- Parent-Child Interactive Therapy (Chaffin et al., 2004)
- Parent Management Training (Patterson, 1995)
- Parent Training (Beauchaine, Webster-Stratton, & Reid, 2005; Webster-Stratton, 1984)
- Play Nicely Video (Scholer, Hamilton, Johnson, & Scott, 2010)
- Social Development Program (Hawkins & Haggerty, 2008)
- Tipple P (Markie-Dadds & Sanders, 2006; Prinz, Sanders, Shapiro, Whitaker, & Lutzker, 2009)
- VIPP-SD Program (Van Zeijl et al., 2006)

Both the movement away from spanking and a key limitation of that movement are illustrated by the publication of the "Guidelines for Effective Discipline" of the American Academy of Pediatrics (1998). This statement took years of controversy and negotiation to achieve and was an important step forward. Nevertheless, it also reflects the problem that is the focus of this chapter and that helps explain why almost all parents of toddlers continue to hit them. It recommends that parents avoid corporal punishment. However, as pointed out in Chapter 1, in order to obtain sufficient support for this guideline to be approved, it carefully avoids saying *never* spank. The difference between advising parents to avoid spanking and advising them to never spank may seem like splitting hairs. Unfortunately, the typical sequence of parent-child interaction that eventuates in spanking suggests that, for the reasons to be described later, in the absence of a commitment to *never* spank, even parents who are against spanking are likely to spank toddlers.

Paradox 3: Focusing Exclusively on Teaching "Alternatives" Results in Almost Everyone Spanking

The paradox that focusing exclusively on alternatives to spanking rather than on recommending never spanking results in almost everyone spanking, grows out of the combination of two factors:

- The high short-run failure rate of all methods of correcting and controlling the behavior of toddlers (see below).
- The myth that spanking works when other things do not.

When toddlers are corrected for a specific misbehavior (such as for hitting another child or disobeying), the recidivism rate according to one study is about 50% within two hours and 80% within the same day (Larzelere, 1996). As a consequence, on any given day, a parent is almost certain to find that so-called alternative disciplinary strategies such as explaining, deprivation of privileges, and time-out, do not work. They do not know that Larzelere found that spanking had the same two-hour and same-day failure rate. As a consequence, when the child repeats the behavior, because our culture teaches that spanking works when other things have failed, parents turn to spanking. The result is the infamous statistic: over 90% spank toddlers.

As shown in the previous chapter, about 70% of Americans believe that spanking is sometimes necessary. A generation or two ago, about that many probably believed that spanking was not only sometimes necessary, but that it was good for children. Today, although we do not know of a survey on this, we think that most Americans now also believe that spanking is something to be avoided. The contradiction between believing that it is best to avoid spanking and the belief that it is sometimes necessary is partly an example of the inconsistencies that occur when a society is changing. However, we think the contradiction is even more the result of the deeply entrenched belief that spanking works when other methods do not. That belief is why even parents and pediatricians who "do not believe in spanking" also believe that spanking is sometimes necessary, and why so many parents who are opposed to spanking spank. The same situation existed in Sweden 40 and 50 years ago. Surveys in the 1960s found that 45% thought that spanking was not a good thing to do, but 95% spanked toddlers (Modig, 2009). As described in our concluding chapter, Sweden resolved the contradiction by its 1979 law making spanking illegal and by a massive public information effort. Surveys in Sweden in recent years have found that only 10% approve of spanking, and only 11% spank (Modig, 2009).

Consistency is Confounded with Spanking

An important difference between spanking and other disciplinary strategies is that, when a child repeats a misbehavior for which he or she was spanked, parents do not question the effectiveness of spanking. The idea that spanking works when other methods of correction do not is so ingrained in American culture that, when the child repeats the misbehavior an hour or two after a spanking (or sometimes a few minutes later), parents fail to perceive that this indicates that spanking has the same high failure rate as explaining and deprivation of privileges. They spank again and then again, for as many times as it takes to ultimately secure compliance. Repeating the spanking or any other method of correction as many times as necessary is the correct strategy because consistency and perseverance is what it takes for a child to learn. However, spanking parents attribute the improved behavior to the spanking, not to the consistency and perseverance in correction. What they and most parents do not know is that, given the same consistency and perseverance with a recalcitrant child, non-spanking methods would not only also work, but work better (Beauchaine et al., 2005; Capaldi & Eddy, 2000; Patterson, Reid, & Dishion, 1992) and not have the long-term harmful side effects documented in previous chapters.

Because these three paradoxes are rooted in cultural myths about spanking, it is necessary to consider the research evidence on the two most directly relevant of those myths about spanking: the myth that spanking may sometimes be necessary because it works when other methods do not and the myth that spanking is harmless if done by loving parents (see Straus, 2001a, for other myths about spanking).

The Myth that Spanking is Harmless

The chapters in Parts II, III, IV, and the chapters that follow provide abundant evidence that spanking has serious and often lifelong harmful side effects. The meta-analysis of 88 studies by Gershoff (2002) analyzed 117 tests of the hypothesis that spanking is associated with harmful side effects such as aggression and delinquency in childhood, low empathy or conscience, poor parent-child relations, and as an adult, health problems such as depression, crime, and antisocial behavior. Of the 117 tests, 110 or 94% found results indicating a harmful effect. This is an almost unprecedented degree of consistency in research findings in any field of science, and perhaps even more unprecedented in social science. A number of these studies controlled for parental warmth and other context factors, as was done for the research in this book, and showed that spanking is harmful even when done by loving parents.

Most of the studies reviewed by Gershoff were cross-sectional, thus, it is plausible to interpret the relationships as showing, not the harmful effects of spanking, but that misbehavior, delinquency, and mental illness cause parents to use spanking to deal with those problems. That interpretation has become dramatically less plausible since 1997. At least 14 studies since then, including three in this book and others summarized in the next chapter, mark a watershed change. These are prospective studies that take into account the child's misbehavior at Time 1 as well as whether the parents spanked. They examine the *change* in behavior subsequent to the spanking. These studies, therefore, provide evidence on two opposite views about the effect of responding to the misbehavior by spanking. One view is that the appropriate use of spanking not only stops the misbehavior, but also results in the child ultimately becoming better behaved. We have called this the "teach them a lesson they won't forget" view of spanking. The other view is that, on average, spanking increases the probability of antisocial behavior and other problems. We call this the *universal harm theory* because we believe it applies in all nations and cultures.

The idea that spanking teaches children a lesson they won't forget is a deeply ingrained part of American culture. The other view is that, although spanking usually does stop the misbehavior in the immediate situation—in the longer run—it results in an *increased* probability of misbehavior, a lower IQ and educational progress (Part III), and an increased probability of antisocial and criminal behavior (Parts II and IV). We have called this a boomerang effect. Consistent with the 94% of agreement between the studies reviewed by Gershoff, the 18 longitudinal studies presented or reviewed in this book, all found harmful effects. All were based on community samples of children, and none of them depended on adults recalling what happened when they were children. All controlled for many variables (see the list in Chapter 1) such as socioeconomic status and parental warmth and support that could be the *real cause* of the link between spanking and crime and other antisocial behavior as an adult. These studies found that, on average, spanking was associated with a post-spanking increase in many forms of antisocial behavior and crime.

The Myth that Spanking Works When Other Methods Fail

The idea that spanking works when other methods are not successful may be the most prevalent of the 10 myths that perpetuate spanking about spanking described in Straus (2001e). As pointed out previously, even people who "do not believe in spanking" on philosophical grounds or because of the evidence of harmful side effects, tend to think that spanking works when other methods have not served to correct the problem. For example, Dr. Lewis R. First, when Director of Child Protection at Children's Hospital, Boston, stated that he was opposed to corporal punishment but also said, "if a child repeatedly runs into traffic, for example, you may want to play the big card" (Lehman, 1989). This seeming contradiction probably occurred because, for Dr. First, protecting the safety of the child was even more important that avoiding spanking. But it can only be more important for the safety of children because it is based on the mistaken assumption that spanking works when other things do not.

Immediate, Short-Term, and Long-Term Effectiveness of Spanking

To adequately examine the effectiveness of spanking it is important to distinguish between effectiveness in three time periods: in the immediate situation, in the short run (the next few hours or days), and in the long run (months or years subsequent to the misbehavior that was corrected). This is summarized in Chart 18.1.

Parents can easily observe that spanking does usually work in the immediate situation. Nonviolent discipline methods also usually work in the immediate situation, including just telling the child "No. Stop that." The child is very likely to stop, at least for the next few minutes. More generally, nonaggressive discipline techniques, starting with saying "No" and explaining why the child should or should not do something, moving a child, separating quarrelling siblings, and/or using time-out are just about as likely to stop misbehavior such as fighting, at least for a time. If all of these techniques are effective in the immediate situation, the question then becomes, which techniques are more effective in the short run such as the next few hours and in the long run. The following sections discuss research that has examined the effectiveness of spanking across these two time periods.

The short run. The most definitive evidence that spanking is no more effective than other modes of discipline is from experimental studies that randomly assigned spanking as one of the means of correcting a child who leaves the time-out chair before the time is up. Experiments by Roberts and colleagues (Day & Roberts, 1983; Roberts, 1988; Roberts & Powers, 1990) demonstrated that spanking was *not* more effective than other methods of training a child to remain in time-out for the specified time. An example of a nonviolent method

Effects and Side Effects	Spanking	Nonviolent Discipline
Immediate Effectiveness	High	High
Short-Term Effectiveness (Hours, Days)	Low	Low
Long-Term Effectiveness (Months, Years)	Makes Worse	High
Side Effects	Harmful	Beneficial

Chart 18.1   Effectiveness and Side Effects of Spanking Compared with Nonviolent Discipline

of teaching time-out is what they call the escape-barrier method. For this method, a child who breaks time-out is placed in a room with a waist-high piece of plywood held across the open door for a period of only one minute while the parent is standing there. The barrier method required an average of eight repetitions before the children were trained to stay in time-out by themselves. When spanking was used, it also required an average of eight repetitions. Thus, spanking did not work any better than other methods in getting a child to observe time-out. Not only did a single spanking fail to fix the problem, the spanked children engaged in more disruptive behavior (such as yelling and whining) before achieving compliance. In short, with the same degree of consistency and persistence, spanking is as effective but not more effective, than other methods that are applied as consistently.

An essential element in accounting for success in correction and control of toddlers is repetition and consistency. Almost nothing works, including spanking, without it. As previously pointed out, a difference between spanking and nonviolent methods of correction is that spanking parents tend to spank over and over until the child conforms. For example, a study by Bean and Roberts (1981) of parents who used spanking to secure compliance with the child remaining in time-out found that the average number of spankings was 8.3 and the median was 3.5. The median session lasted 22 minutes. Thus, the children in this group were spanked once every 3 minutes until the child did comply. They then attribute the improved behavior to the spanking, not to persistence and consistency in correction.

Just the opposite tends to happen when parents use so-called alternatives, which we prefer to call nonviolent discipline. When the misbehavior almost inevitably reoccurs, instead of repeating the correction, the repetition of the misbehavior is attributed to the lack of effectiveness of the nonviolent correction rather than to the lack of persistence and consistency in applying nonviolent correction. The experiments just described show that when parents are equally persistent, nonviolent methods are equally effective.

Spanking for disobedience and fighting. Another study that found that spanking is not more effective used data provided by mothers of 40 children age 2 to 3 (Larzelere, 1996). The researchers asked the mothers to keep a discipline record for a set number of days. The mothers wrote the nature of the misbehavior and the type of corrective measure that was used. The results were similar to the experiments on teaching children to observe time-out. They showed that, with toddlers, *all* methods of discipline, including spanking, had a high short-term failure rate as measured by the number of hours until the child repeated the misbehavior. The recidivism rate for misbehavior by the toddlers was about 50% within two hours. For a few children, the misbehavior was repeated within two minutes. By the end of the day, 80% had repeated the misbehavior.

Chart 18.2 compares four discipline scenarios from this study in respect to the average number of hours until a repetition of the misbehavior occurred. An effective discipline method is one that not only stops the behavior but also teaches the child to not do it again. Therefore, the longer the time before the misbehavior reoccurs, the more effective the method. Using this measure of effectiveness, Chart 18.2 shows that the four discipline types had about the same degree of effectiveness. Corporal punishment, either alone or in combination with reasoning, worked no better than reasoning alone, non-corporal punishment alone, reasoning, and corporal punishment. The statistical tests showed that the differences between methods were not statistically dependable.

The long run. Parents have the long-run effect in mind when they say that spanking will teach the child a lesson he won't forget. Unfortunately, the evidence in Parts II and IV and Chapter 19 shows that the long-run net effect is more often to increase rather than decrease the probability of antisocial behavior and crime. What many children don't forget is the aspect of spanking that parents do not think about, and if they did would want the child to forget—that their parents hit them, that hitting is morally correct, and that love and violence go together.

In some cases, that link between love and violence results in sadomasochistic sexual preferences. This is not a new idea. Rousseau (1928) attributed his

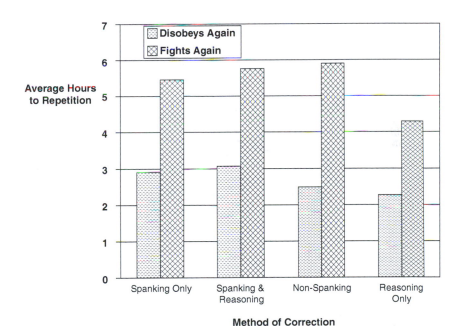

Chart 18.2   Spanking Does Not Deter Repeating the Misbehavior Any Longer than Non-Spanking
2,853 instances of disobedience and 785 instances of fighting by 40 children age 2 to 3, from Larzelere et al. (1996).

need to be spanked in order to become sexual aroused to being spanked as a child. Gibson (1978), Greven (1990), Krafft-Ebing (1895), Money (1986), and Money and Lamacz (1989) also argued that being spanked as a child can lead to an adult interest in sexual activities that incorporate pain and humiliation similar to those experienced at the hands of loving parents. A study of 455 university students found that the more spanking experienced as a child, the greater the percent who enjoyed being spanked or tied up as part of sex (Straus & Donnelly, 2001a).

A simple test of the idea that spanking teaches a lesson children won't forget comes from interviewing the representative sample of 1,003 mothers in two Minnesota counties (see Chapters 7 and 8). The mothers were asked what was the last misbehavior for which they had spanked their child. They were then asked if they had previously spanked for that misbehavior. Seventy-three percent said they had previously spanked for that misbehavior. This is a 73% failure rate, which is probably typical. However, parents do not perceive having to spank again as indicating that spanking has failed. But when a nonviolent method of discipline needs to be repeated, they do perceive it as having failed. We suggest that the dual standard for judging spanking and judging nonviolent modes of discipline is the result of the deeply ingrained cultural myth that spanking is the most effective method of discipline, and that it works when other methods have not worked.

A study by Power and Chapieski (1986) observed 18 mothers interacting with their 14-month-old child. They recorded the children's response to requests by the mother. Given the age of the children, all of these had to be relatively simple requests, such as "come here" and "put that down." The children whose mothers rarely or never spanked, failed to comply with the mother's requests in 31% of the interactions, whereas the children whose mothers relied on spanking as a disciplinary technique failed to comply in 49% of the interactions observed. Thus, spanking was associated with a 58% *greater* rate of misbehavior. Even at this early age, spanking was, on average, less effective in teaching a lesson the child will not forget than non-corporal disciplinary strategies.

Although the Power and Chapieski study involved only 18 children and neither this study nor the Minnesota study were experimental or prospective studies, when combined with the Roberts et al. experimental studies, the longitudinal studies in this book and those reviewed in the next chapter, and with many other studies, the weight of the evidence indicates that the idea that spanking works when other methods fail is a myth. In the short run, spanking does stop the misbehavior, but no more effectively than nonviolent modes of correction and control. In the long run, the results of the longitudinal studies on antisocial behavior of children (Chapter 6), crime as an adult (Chapter 15), and the longitudinal studies summarized in the next chapter show that spanking *increases* the probability of antisocial behavior by children and crime as an adult more often than it decreases antisocial and criminal behavior. Just as important for evaluating the effectiveness of spanking, we do not know of any studies in a peer-reviewed journal that found that spanking results in better behaved, better adjusted, or smarter children.

Why Spanking is No More Effective than Other Methods in the Short Run and Less Effective in the Long Run

The presumption that spanking is the most effective disciplinary technique is such a deeply embedded part of the culture of most societies, that it is necessary to explain why this obvious truth is untrue.

The Short Run

As we have said previously, we do not doubt that spanking will, on average, stop misbehavior in the immediate situation. However, as the research just reviewed shows, it has just as high a failure in the short run, that is, over the next few hours or days. Why isn't spanking different and more effective in teaching a lesson that lasts even a few hours or days?

Toddlers have limited ability to control their own behavior. The studies reviewed show that all methods of discipline, including spanking, have a high failure rate with toddlers. It takes a great deal of time and many repetitions for a young child to internalize standards of behavior (Tremblay, 2003, 2006). This biologically built-in limitation applies to spanking as well as other modes of discipline.

Spanking interferes with cognitive functioning. Being slapped or spanked is a frightening and threatening event that arouses strong negative emotions such as humiliation, sadness, and anger. Children also experience spanking as highly stressful (Saunders & Goddard, 2010; Turner & Finkelhor, 1996; Willow & Hyder, 1998) Fright, stress, and other strong negative emotions can result in cognitive deficits such as erroneous or limited coding of events and diminished elaboration (Bugental et al., 2010; Heuer & Reisberg, 1992; Meerum Terwogt & Olthof, 1989). To the extent that spanking arouses such emotions, the child is less likely to learn from the spanking than correction by other methods. Moreover, it can evoke resentment and weaken the bond between the child and the parent as shown in Chapters 8 and 9. When the bond between child and parent is weak, parents are less likely to be role models for the child and less likely to be able to influence the child, which may be part of the explanation for the long-term boomerang effect of spanking.

Spanking does not provide an explanation of the problem. Another reason spanking may be less effective is because toddlers and infants may not understand the reason for being hit. Imagine a toddler who is pushing food off a high-chair tray. The parent says "Stop that!" When the child does it again, the parent slaps the child's hand. A toddler does not think of pushing food off the tray as dirty or creating a mess and may not understand why he or she is being hit. The same principle applies, and perhaps more strongly, to being spanked for doing something that is potentially dangerous, such as touching a food mixer while helping a parent bake a cake. The child whose hand is slapped for doing that may come away with the idea that the danger is the parent because the child only experiences the hurt imposed by the parent and not the potential pain from the food mixer. If there is learning when the child's hand is slapped, it comes primarily from the parent also explaining why the child should not push food off the tray or should not touch the mixer. The learning that occurs is despite the spanking, not because of it, because on average, being hit is stressful and interferes with cognition and learning.

The Long Run

In addition to being no more effective in the short run, the research evidence in this book, and much other research, shows that in the long run, spanking is less effective than nonaggressive means of correction. Again, because American cultural beliefs are that spanking is more effective and therefore can and should be used when other modes of correction have failed, and that it will "teach him a lesson he won't forget," it is necessary to explain why, on average, the opposite is true.

Less well-developed conscience. Some of the earliest evidence on why spanking is less effective in the long run was a study of 379 five-year-old children by Sears, Maccoby, and Levin (1957). They found that spanking was associated with a less adequately developed conscience. Spanking teaches a child to avoid misbehavior if one of their parents is watching or will know about it, rather than avoiding misbehavior because the parents have explained why some things are right and others wrong. When parents explain, children will gradually come to understand and accept these standards, and they are likely to remain in effect in situations when no parent is present, and probably also for life. Proponents of spanking, of course, believe that this is what spanking accomplishes, but Sears, Maccoby, and Levin and others since then have found the opposite.

Weakens child-to-parent bond. Although most children accept the legitimacy of parents spanking, most children also resent it and feel angry with their parents for hitting them. Many even say they hated their parents for doing it (Straus, 2001a, p. 154; Willow & Hyder, 1998). Because spanking or other legal corporal punishment often continues for 13 years (Chapters 2 and 17), bit-by-bit, this anger and resentment chips away at the bond between parent and child (Chapters 8 and 9). A strong child-to-parent bond is important because children are more likely to accept parental restrictions and follow parental standards if there is a bond of affection with the parent. A strong bond facilitates internalizing the rules for behavior and developing a conscience. Many empirical studies have found a link between a weak parent-child bond and juvenile delinquency (Hindelang, 1973; Hirschi, 1969; Rankin & Kern, 1994; Wiatrowski & Anderson, 1987). The weakening of the child-to-parent bond that tends to result from spanking is also part of the explanation for the research showing that children who are spanked tend to have a less well-developed conscience. Children who harbor fear or resentment against their parents as a result of spanking may be less likely to internalize the parent's standards of behavior, and thus less likely to apply them when the parent or another authority figure is not present.

Feasibility of external control diminishes with age. The long-term effectiveness of spanking is also low because, from school-age on, children are increasingly out of sight of the parents. Hence, reliance on external controls such as spanking puts a child at increased risk of misbehavior because, as a child grows older, the feasibility of external controls diminishes. In addition, after a child has reached a certain size, anecdotal evidence suggests that many parents would like to still use spanking but cannot because the child is too big. By this, they often mean that it is no longer physically possible, not that it is no longer appropriate. Whatever the reason, as shown in a previous chapter, the prevalence of corporal punishment decreases as the child grows older (Chapter 2). Therefore, to the extent that parents have depended on spanking as a last resort, they are increasingly left without one.

Decreased opportunity to acquire cognitive and social skills. When parents spank and also explain why they are spanking, it reduces the adverse effects of spanking, but it does not eliminate them (Larzelere, 1986). However, many parents spank first. For example, one mother we interviewed told that she has three little kids and does not have time for "all that explaining stuff." She said she needed something that "works quickly." One leading advocate of spanking advises:

"Spank as a first resort? That's right. Spontaneously. As soon as you see that the child is losing control or as soon as the child commits whatever completely outrageous act (e.g., spitting on an adult). Whack" (Rosemond, 1994a, p. 210).

More generally, and also more importantly, as we suggested in Chapter 12 to explain the link between spanking as a child and conflict with marital partners later in life, to the extent that a parent spanks, either as a first resort or a last resort, it denies the child an opportunity to observe, participate in, and learn conflict resolution strategies that are important in many life situations. This is true even though the parent may have already explained because children require many repetitions to acquire these complex cognitive and social skills. Therefore, rather than spanking when the child repeats the misbehavior, the explanation and other modes of correction need to be repeated. We believe that when parents do not spank and enforce the rules by explaining and creating appropriate alternatives and compromises, their children are more likely to themselves acquire and use these vital skills. This is possible because, contrary to what many believe, even toddlers can understand directives from their parents and comply with the instructions that they receive (Hakman & Sullivan, 2009; Knudsen & Liszkowski, 2012; Owen, Smith Slep, & Heyman, 2009).

The research evidence from the studies in this book, and the studies we review, shows that children who are not spanked are, on average, better behaved. That does not mean that all unspanked children are better behaved, just as not all spanked children behave badly. As pointed out in the section of Chapter 1 on Risk Factors: The Real Meaning of Social Science Research Results, those results mean that nonviolent discipline increases the *probability* of good behavior, and spanking increases the *probability* of subsequent bad behavior, but fortunately does not guarantee it. As we pointed out in Chapter 1, the results reported in this book are analogous to the results on heavy smoking. Heavy smoking increases the probability of death from a smoking-related disease. One third of heavy smokers will die from a smoking-related disease, which also means that two thirds will not. Similarly, the research cited in this chapter showing that spanking increases the probability of a weak child-to-parent bond, less well-developed conscience, lower IQ, and crime later in life means that more spanked children will have these problems, but like most heavy smokers, most will not.

Why is Spanking Perceived as More Effective than It Is?

The studies show that spanking is no more effective than nonviolent discipline techniques. If these are the scientific facts and the facts of daily experience, why do parents and professions believe that spanking when necessary is so effective? We have already suggested part of the explanation. This section examines that question more systematically. A number of different processes probably come together to produce the false belief.

Selective Perception of Effectiveness

One process is selective perception. Even though every parent can observe the short-run high failure rate of spanking, few perceive it. The selective perception results from the cultural belief and expectation that spanking is more effective. They perceive the need to repeat the spanking, but they do not perceive it as indicating that spanking has failed. But when a child misbehaves and the parent explains and the child does it again, the repetition is attributed to the ineffectiveness of explaining to a young child. As the time-out experiments mentioned previously show, repetition of spanking does result in compliance, but these same experiments also show that repetition of just putting the child back in the time-out chair is equally effective and is accompanied by less disruptive behavior such as crying, yelling, and whining.

Emotional Gratification

Another part of the explanation for perceiving spanking as more effective than it is, may be because spanking can be emotionally gratifying, just as acting out of impulse can be gratifying (Toch & Adams, 2002). When a child misbehaves and repeats the misbehavior and the parent is angry and frustrated, hitting the child may be emotionally rewarding. It is not that parents enjoy spanking their children. Few do. But when parents are frustrated with their child, spanking the child allows the parent to perceive themselves as really taking the situation in hand, being in control, and therefore relieving some of the frustration.

Confusion with Retribution

Another part of the explanation for the belief in the superior effectiveness of spanking, despite the evidence that it is not the most effective, is the idea of just desserts (i.e., the belief children should *pay* for their misbehavior). This may even be the case among parents of infants, because many believe that their infants can and do act with intention or on purpose (Feldman & Reznick, 1996). Retribution is an end in itself that is quite different than effectiveness. However, retribution is also believed to act as a deterrent that will reduce the probability of further misbehavior. As a consequence, retribution is probably often confused with deterrence. Physically attacking another child is usually regarded as a moral offense, and this may be why it is the most commonly occurring misbehavior for which Sears, Maccoby, and Levin (1957), a Parents magazine survey (Lehman, 1989), and studies by Catron and Masters (1993) and Holden et al. (1995) all found that parents were more likely to use spanking to correct their child hitting another child than to correct most other kinds of misbehavior.

Long-Term Effects Are Not Observable

Finally, spanking is perceived as more effective than it is because parents have no way of observing for themselves that spanking increases the probability of many social and psychological problems such as slower mental development, school problems, delinquency, and depression and crime as an adult. They can see that when they spanked, in most instances it stopped the bad behavior. Moreover, if later problems such as school failure or serious crime occur, parents are unlikely to think the delinquency occurred because of the spanking. We suggest that the reverse is more likely: If a child is delinquent, most Americans will think that the delinquency occurred *despite,* rather than because of spanking. Many will think that it shows that she should have spanked more. The only way parents can know about the harmful effects of spanking is by being informed of the results of the research showing the harmful side effects. Unfortunately, as shown in the introductory chapter and in Douglas and Straus (2007), social scientists are not giving them that information, not even in child development or child psychiatry textbooks.

Beneficial Versus Harmful Side Effects

Chart 18.1 summarized the evidence on the effectiveness of spanking as compared with other discipline strategies. The first two rows of the chart summarize what has just been discussed: That in the immediate situation, the effectiveness of both spanking and nonviolent correction are high, but in the subsequent short run, the effectiveness of both is low. The difference between spanking and nonviolent discipline are in the next two rows. The third row summarizes what is in much of this book: The long-term effect of spanking is to *increase* the probability of antisocial behavior and many serious and sometimes lifelong problems such as crime and depression. The last row of the chart is based on the results of numerous other studies on side effects (as summarized in Gershoff, 2002) requires no additional comment.

All methods of discipline are likely to have side effects; that is, they result in behaviors by the child that were not necessarily part of the behavior that the parent intended to influence. The side effects of spanking documented in Parts II, III, and IV and the meta-analysis by Gershoff (2002) are overwhelmingly behaviors that parents would not want if they had been able to choose. The side effects of nonviolent modes of discipline tend to be beneficial. An example is the previously mentioned research by Sears, Maccoby, and Levin (1957), which found that spanking was associated with a less well-developed conscience. Presumably, parents who did not spank used cognitive methods of correction, and one side effect is developing a stronger conscience. Another is greater cognitive ability, as suggested by the results in Chapter 10.

When parents use hitting as a method of discipline, the side effect is an increase in the probability of a child who does a lot of hitting. Similarly, when parents consistently use explanation and reasoning as a means of correcting and influencing the child, the side effect is likely to be a child who uses and may insist on explanation and reasoning. In the short run, this can be a problem because a child who uses and expects a reason and an explanation for everything can be exasperating, even infuriating. However, whereas that behavior may be exasperating from a child, it represents exactly the kind of behavior that most parents want to see in their child as an adult.

Summary and Conclusions

This chapter described three paradoxes about spanking: approval of spanking has decreased, but spanking toddlers has not; professionals opposed to spanking fail to advise parents to never spank; and focusing exclusively on teaching alternatives results in almost everyone spanking.

These paradoxes reflect the almost inevitable contradictions that arise when the social organization and the culture of a society are undergoing change. Because the research presented elsewhere in this book indicates that it is in the best interest of children and of national well-being to hasten the shift to nonviolent methods of child rearing, the conclusion we suggest about how to deal with paradoxes and contradictions is to focus on an unambiguous policy of: Never hit a child as a way to correct misbehavior.

Why Never Spank Must Be the Advice to Parents

Spock and Rothenberg (1992), and now defenders of spanking such as the Baumrind, Larzelere, and Cowan (2002), and Gunnoe (2009), advise parents to avoid spanking if they can. That seems like sensible advice. But, it is not. The problem is the clause "if they can." Remember the research shows that 80% of toddlers will repeat a misbehavior for which they were corrected within the same day. As a result, almost all parents who accept this advice will end up spanking because no matter what they do, the child is likely to repeat the misbehavior. Therefore, they will incorrectly conclude that they can't avoid spanking. They will think they found that the nonviolent discipline method did not work, but what they are really seeing is the low ability of toddlers to control their behavior. Parents do not know, because social scientists and professionals advising parents have not told them, that all methods of correcting the behavior of a toddler, including spanking, have the same low level of one-time success. Moreover, because of the myth that spanking is harmless when done by loving parents, they will not be strongly motivated to avoid adding a spank or two to their disciplinary practices. They fall back on the myth that spanking works when other methods have failed, not realizing as we said, that all methods of discipline have a high failure rate with toddlers. This set of circumstances is what led 94% of our national samples of parents to spank toddlers.

Given the circumstances just described, reliance on teaching alternative disciplinary techniques by itself is not sufficient as a means of ending spanking. It is also necessary to simultaneously and unambiguously advise parents to *never* spank. The necessity of advising parents to never spank was epitomized by Dr. Lewis First, quoted previously and by one mother we interviewed. Both said they were opposed to spanking. But Dr. First also said, "if a child repeatedly runs into traffic, for example, you may want to play the big card." This mother, who was also opposed to spanking when talking about other modes of discipline, said, "I use them all, but I can see with my own eyes that the alternatives often don't work. So, for her sake [the child's] and my sanity, I sometimes have to spank." Given that 80% of toddlers who have been corrected for misbehavior will repeat that same misbehavior in the same day, almost all parents will come to the same conclusion as this mother. The only way to avoid that conclusion is to remove spanking or any other hitting of children as an alternative. Unless child psychologists, parent educators, social workers, pediatricians, and others who advise parents communicate an unambiguous, *never* spank message, almost all toddlers will continue to be spanked.

Professionals Need to Be Informed

In order to effectively communicate a never-spank message, child psychologists, child psychiatrists, pediatricians, parent educators, social workers, and other professionals must themselves be informed about the research evidence and its implications. The textbooks in all these disciplines currently give very little attention to spanking. In Chapter 1 and in Douglas and Straus (2007), we reviewed 23 of the leading child development and child psychiatry textbooks. We found that the majority discussed spanking, but few wrote more than a paragraph on the topic. Moreover, none discussed the extensive research on this topic or the fact that the vast majority of this research indicates that using spanking leads to poor outcomes.

Information Professionals Need

The information that should be in child development and child psychiatry textbooks, but is not there, can be summarized as four key points on which professionals need to be informed. They are the empirical research evidence that:

•   All methods of correction and control have a high failure rate with toddlers. Therefore, nonviolent discipline strategies will erroneously be identified as not working.
•   Corporal punishment is not more effective than nonviolent modes of correction and control, even in the short run.
•   Spanking has harmful side effects.
•   Children who are not spanked tend to be the best behaved and smartest after controlling for parental education, parental warmth and support, and other variables.

Once professionals have learned about the empirical research on these four points, they will be in a better position to advise parents to never, ever, under any circumstance, hit a child as a means of correction and control. As pointed out earlier, most professionals now consider this a negative approach. The success of the never-spank approach in Sweden has shown that a never-spank approach is not only necessary in principle but that it has been very effective.

Since the passage of the no-spanking law and the steps to inform every parent, and every child, in Sweden that spanking is wrong and is contrary to national policy, the use of spanking has decreased from rates that were about the same as in the United States to a small minority of parents. So has the rate of crime, drug abuse, and suicide by youth (Durrant, 1999; Durrant & Janson, 2005). The Swedish experience shows that an absolute never-spank approach has worked to reduce use of spanking. It has also shown that the disaster foreseen by the critics of the Swedish law at the time it was passed have not occurred. Their prediction was that without the ability to spank when necessary, parents would lose control. Sweden would become a nation of kids running wild. It is not at all certain that the reduction in juvenile crime and psychological problems that occurred in Sweden since the no-spanking ban can be attributed to the reduction in spanking because so many other changes have also occurred. But it is certain that the fear that the prohibition of spanking in Sweden would result in a nation with kids running wild has not occurred.

Once child psychologists, pediatricians, social workers, and other professionals have been informed about the research and accept the implication that parents must be advised to never spank (as compared with advising parents to avoid it if you can), the implementation of a policy of informing parents about the four types of research results just listed is relatively inexpensive, although it will meet resistance and take time. Some examples include:

- Parent education programs can be revised to include the evidence that spanking does *not* work better than other disciplinary tactics, even in the short run, that it tends to make for more, rather than less, misbehavior in the long run and to specifically tell parents to never spank.
- The Public Health Service can follow the Swedish model and sponsor no-spanking public service announcements on TV, radio, milk cartons, and the Internet.
- Never-Spank posters and pamphlets can be displayed in pediatrician's offices and hospital maternity departments.
- A notice can be put on birth certificates such as:

Warning: Spanking Has Been Determined to Be Dangerous to the Health and Well-Being of Your Child—*Do Not Ever, Under Any Circumstances, Spank or Hit Your Child*

The chapters in Parts II, III, and IV of this book show that the benefits of never spanking are many, but as pointed out previously, they are virtually impossible for parents to perceive because parents cannot find out what their children will be like months or years after the spanking by observing whether the child ceased the misbehavior when they were spanked. The situation with spanking is parallel to that of smoking. Smokers could perceive the satisfaction from a cigarette but had no way to see the adverse health consequences down the road until they were informed about the research. Similarly, parents can perceive the benefit of a slap when the child stops the misbehavior. However, they have no way of seeing the adverse consequences down the road of spanking. Like smokers, they have no way of looking a year or more into the future to see if there is a harmful side effect of having hit their child to correct misbehavior. The only way parents can know this is through a major public health effort to inform all parents about the scientific evidence on the four key points listed above and by assuring parents that there is no need to put a child at risk of the harmful side effects of spanking because nonviolent methods of discipline are just as effective in the short run and more effective in the long run.

The Ethics of Advising Parents to Never Spank

Some defenders of spanking argue that it is unethical to advise parents to never spank until there is absolutely conclusive evidence on the key issues just listed (e.g., Larzelere et al., 1998). Unfortunately, this view is also prevalent, even among social scientists who are opposed to spanking. For example, one of the reviewers of a draft of this book commented, "Even though I agree with the authors [about never spanking], the primary problem as I see it is that there is not enough data to suggest that spanking—after controlling for physical abuse and other forms of harsh punishment besides spanking—is associated with criminal behavior. As

Taylor et al. (2010) points out, most studies of spanking do not control for physical abuse, including those used in Gershoff's meta-analysis. Therefore the link between harsh and punitive punishment and child delinquency may be spurious."

It is true that most studies of spanking do not control for physical abuse, but the reviewer seems to have missed the paragraph headed Confounding with Abuse a few pages earlier, which cited five studies that *did* control for physical abuse and still found that spanking was related to child behavior problems We have since added a sixth study that controlled for physical abuse and still found spanking to be a risk factor for behavior problems.

A policy statement by the National Association of Social Workers states that it "opposes the use of physical punishment in homes, schools, and all other institutions where children are cared for and educated. Effective discipline does not involve physical punishment of children" (National Association of Social Workers, 2012). But, a clear never-spank position is not held by most professionals who advise parents. As pointed out in Chapter 1, even the antispanking policy statement of the American Academy of Pediatrics includes wording that permits spanking toddlers. The surveys of psychologists and pediatricians cited in Chapter 1, and our conversations with psychologists and pediatricians, suggest that at least three quarters of American pediatricians and psychologists believe there is not sufficient evidence to advise parents to never spank. But is the evidence really not sufficient?

- First, a meta-analysis of 88 studies found 94% agreement between studies in finding harmful side effects (Gershoff, 2002).
- Second, there are now at least 18 longitudinal studies that provide evidence showing that although behavior problems cause spanking, when spanking is used to correct those problems, the long-run result is more, rather than less, misbehavior.
- Third, most of the studies controlled for other risk factors that might be the real cause of the harmful side effect.
- Fourth, there are six studies that controlled for the overlap between spanking and physical abuse. All found that spanking was nonetheless related to behavior problems.
- Fifth, thinking of spanking as a treatment for misbehavior, the U.S. Food and Drug Administration and standard clinical practice require that if there are alternative treatments without harmful side effects, the alternative should be prescribed. Absolutely conclusive evidence of harmful side effects is *not* needed to cease prescribing the treatment with harmful side effects.

The last point in this list requires some additional explanation. We discuss two aspects of this ethical requirement: transferability to other situations and availability of alternative treatment.

Transferability to other situations.   If a procedure is shown to have a negative or toxic effect under some circumstances, it becomes the obligation of those who favor the procedure under other circumstances to show that it is safe and effective under those circumstances. Defenders of spanking now recommend it only for younger children and explicitly warn against hitting older children (American Academy of Pediatrics, 1998; American Psychological Association and the American Academy of Pediatrics, 1995). Thus, having accepted the evidence that corporal punishment is harmful under one circumstance (older children), they have the obligation to provide empirical evidence that it is safe for younger children. Such evidence does not exist, and the research in Chapter 10 about corporal punishment and mental ability found the opposite (i.e., that the effects are more harmful for toddlers). The belief incorporated by many pediatricians and clinical psychologists that younger children who are hit by their parents do not experience it as traumatic is based on tradition, not empirical evidence. What evidence does exist indicates that spanking is as harmful as or more harmful to young children than to older children. This parallels research by Finkelhor and colleagues (Finkelhor, 2008; Finkelhor, Turner, & Ormrod, 2006) who investigated the similar traditional presumption that young children (age 2 to 9) who are attacked by other children, including siblings, do not run the same risk of traumatic symptoms as do older children (age 10 to 17). They found that the adverse psychological effects are as serious for the younger children in their study, just as we have found that the adverse psychological effects of spanking are as serious, or more serious, for children in the permissible-to-hit ages of 2 to 6.

Availability of alternative treatment. In medical practice, when a new drug becomes available, pediatricians are obligated to advise parents to avoid the drug currently in use if there is evidence that the old drug has harmful side effects, even *if the evidence is not conclusive,* provided an equally effective drug is available that does not have those side effects. Spanking is like the old drug with harmful side effects. Nonviolent modes of correction and control are like the new drug that is just as effective but does not have the long-term risk harmful side effects. This combination creates an ethical *requirement* to advise parents to switch to the new drug, which means use of nonviolent modes of correction and *never* spanking.

19 Implications for Crime and Violence in Society

Research has shown that physically abused children (those whose parents perpetrated severe assaults such as punching, choking, or burning the child) are more likely to engage in crime than other children (Currie, 2009; Farrington, 1978; Rebellon & Van Gundy, 2005; Widom, 1992). But does that apply to legal and morally correct spanking? This chapter addresses the following questions:

- What have studies of differences between societies in use of corporal punishment found about the relation of corporal punishment to the level of physical violence in a society?
- Do children whose parents spanked them have an increased probability of antisocial behavior as a child and criminal behavior as an adult?
- What are the processes linking spanking and crime?
- What are the implications of trends in spanking for trends in engaging in crime?

Most of the world's societies are violent in the sense that they have high rates of physical assault, homicide, and war. The United States may be one of the most violent of the advanced industrial societies. One indication of where the United States stands is the prevalence of homicides. According to the United Nations Office on Drugs and Crime, the 2008 U.S. homicide rate of 5.2 per 100,000 was more than 3 times the Canadian rate of 1.7 per 100,000, and about 5 times the rate of Western European countries. Nevertheless, using this measure, many societies are more violent. Even before the outbreak of the drug wars in Mexico in the late 1990s, the Mexican homicide rate of 11.6 was more than double that of the United States. The rate for Colombia (38.8 per 100,000) is more than 7 times higher.

Spanking and Violence

Most of the world's societies also bring up children violently by spanking them to correct misbehavior. Perhaps the correspondence between the preponderance of physical violence and that of spanking is just a coincidence. Obviously, spanking and assaults and murders differ in severity and also in the cultural definition that makes one legitimate and the other criminal. However, there is also a correspondence between the behavior involved in spanking and the behavior involved in criminal assaults and homicides that is seldom perceived.

Spanking and Homicide

Everyone understands that spanking is carried out for the morally valid purpose of correcting or controlling misbehavior. What is not understood is that almost all assaults by adults are also carried out to correct what the offender perceives as misbehavior of the victim. Marvin Wolfgang's (1958) pioneer study of all homicides in Philadelphia from 1948 to 1952 found that 37% of the murders were in response to an insult, curse, or some other affront; 13% part of a domestic quarrel; 11% a reaction to sexual infidelity; and 10% disagreements over money. Thus a total of 71% of the homicides were to correct what the offender perceived as misbehavior by the victim. The FBI Uniform Crime Reports' figures on homicides show the same thing. In 2002 and for many previous years, about three quarters of U.S. homicides were classified as parts of arguments, fights, juvenile gang killings, etc.—not part of some other crime such as robbery or rape. Typical examples include a confrontation between two men over a loan of $50 that was to be paid back in a week. Now it is three months later. They get into a fight, and one ends up dead. Physical fights between adults almost always occur over what the aggressor thinks are moral transgressions, such as not making good on a promise to pay back a loan, an insult, a member of one gang walking through the territory of another gang, or flirting with the offender's spouse or girlfriend. Thus, both spanking and most criminal violence occur in response to what the parent who spanks, or the person who assaults, believes is an outrageous or persistent misbehavior. See Wikström and Treiber (2009) for an analysis of crime as moral actions.

Moreover, like most assaults and homicides, spanking is usually impulsive, done in anger, and often regretted (see Chapter 7). Among the sample of mothers interviewed for the study on impulsive spanking in Chapter 7, 54% said that spanking was the wrong thing to have done. Durant's (1994) study of a Canadian sample revealed similar parental misgivings about spanking.

Spanking may share key elements with criminal assaults, yet that is hardly evidence that spanking is one of the factors making U.S. society so homicidal. This chapter examines that issue by reviewing empirical research on the link between spanking and societal violence, spanking and physical assaults, and other crime by individuals within a society.

Theoretical Approach

The theoretical approach of this chapter has two main elements. The first is that spanking teaches the morality of hitting to correct misbehavior. This approach is consistent with social learning theory (Akers & Sellers, 2008) and with a

key element of the *situational action theory* of crime, namely that "acts of violence are essentially moral actions and therefore can, and should be analyzed
and explained as such" (Wikström & Treiber, 2009, p. 76). It is important to
keep Wikström's specification in mind: "Morality is often discussed in terms
of whether particular actions are good or bad (virtuous or reprehensible), or
whether or not they are justified in relation to some superior moral principle. It
is important to stress that we do not use and discuss morality in these terms but
rather focus on understanding how people's actions are guided by rules about
what actions are right or wrong under particular circumstances; we classify
these rules as *moral rules*" (p. 76, note 1).

The second main aspect of our theoretical approach is the idea of cultural
spillover (Baron & Straus, 1987, 1989; Baron et al., 1988). Cultural spillover
is an aspect of the principle that human societies are social systems in the sense
that each part of society tends to influence and be influenced by the other parts,
and that includes violence (i.e., that violence in one sphere of life increases
the probability of violence in other spheres). The cultural spillover theory of
violence is explained further later in this chapter.

Societal-Level Evidence

Anthropological Studies

Societal case studies. Seventy years ago, the anthropologist Ashley Montague
argued that, "Spanking the baby may be the psychological seed of war" (Montague, 1941). He later invited eight anthropologists who had studied one of
the relatively few nonviolent societies to contribute chapters to a book called
Learning Non-Aggression: The Experience of Non-Literate Societies (Montague, 1978). Although those eight societies differed tremendously, one thing
they had in common was nonviolent child rearing (i.e., spanking or smacking
children was not part of their culturally prescribed method of child rearing).

Montague did not argue that non-spanking alone will produce a nonviolent
society. On the contrary, the eight societies described in his book show that
a great deal more is required, especially a high level of attention to a child's
needs and safety, and positive rather than punitive modes of dealing with misbehavior. If spanking is a risk factor for societal violence, it is only one of many
risk and protective factors. As a consequence, rather than a one-to-one relationship between spanking and *societal* violence, the cross-cultural evidence only
indicates that spanking is associated with an increased *probability* of societal
violence. This sort of probabilistic relationship is similar to the relationship
between characteristics or events that cause disease and the actual occurrence
of the disease. As explained in the section at the end of Chapter 1 in "Risk
Factors: The Real Meaning of Social Science Results," there is almost never a
one-to-one relation between a risk factor and the disease. Heavy smoking, for
example, does not guarantee lung cancer. Rather, it increases the risk of death
from smoking-related diseases to about one out of three (Matteson et al., 1987).

This is a large risk, but it also means that two thirds of heavy smokers do not die of smoking-related diseases. Just as most heavy smokers will not die of a smoking-related disease, most people who have been spanked a lot will not be violent adults.

Human relations area files data. In-depth analyses of child rearing in nonviolent societies are highly informative and important, but statistical evidence is also needed. One approach to statistically test the idea that corporal punishment is associated with societal violence is through analyses of the Human Relations Area Files (HRAF). The HRAF is an archive of anthropological data on over 300 societies. Levinson (1989) found that corporal punishment is used in about three quarters of the world's societies, and that the frequency of use varies greatly. Levinson also analyzed data on violence between adults and found the societies that used corporal punishment were more likely to also be societies in which wife beating was prevalent. Although the relationship that Levinson found was relatively strong (a correlation of .32) and persisted when a number of other variables had been statistically controlled, it is the *only* aspect of societal violence that Levinson found to be strongly associated with corporal punishment. Thus, analyses of the HRAF data provide only limited evidence for a link between corporal punishment and societal violence.

The International Dating Violence Study

The study in Chapter 13 on violence in the dating relationships of university students in 32 nations found that the higher the percent in each nation who were spanked or hit a lot:

- The higher the percent who approved of hitting a partner under some circumstances
- The higher the percent who actually did assault a dating partner
- The higher the percent who assaulted severely enough to injure their partner

We took this analysis one step further using a statistical method called *multilevel modeling* to see if a national context in which spanking was prevalent tended to also be national contexts in which adult violence is more common. We found that students in nations with a high rate of spanking have a higher probability of physically assaulting a dating partner than students in low spanking nations, regardless of whether they themselves were hit as children (Vanderminden & Straus, 2010).

Analysis of the same 32-nation sample found that the higher the percentage of university students who were spanked or hit a lot before age 12, the higher the percentage of students who agreed that a "A man should not walk away from a physical fight with another man." When the analysis used corporal punishment as a teenager, rather than before age 12, the link between corporal punishment and approving physical fights was much stronger. Similarly, the more corporal punishment was used in a national context, the greater the proportion of students who agreed that, "If a wife refuses to have sex, there are times when it may be okay to make her do it." This was also found for both corporal punishment as a child and as a teenager, but the link was stronger for the rate of corporal punishment as a teenager.

Why is the link between corporal punishment and adult violence stronger for corporal punishment experienced as a teen, as shown in Chapters 3 and 13? The explanation that both the public and professionals concerned with children tend to favor is that hitting young children to correct misbehavior is harmless if done in moderation or as U.S. law puts it, with reasonable force. This was the belief underlying the consensus statement issued by the American Academy of Pediatrics conference on corporal punishment. It recommends that parents avoid spanking, but it forbids it only for children under age 2 and over 6 (Friedman & Schonberg, 1996b). As pointed out in Chapter 10 on the relation of spanking to mental ability, which found more harmful effects for young children, the belief that young children are not adversely affected or affected less than adults by being a victim of crime is based on folk beliefs for which there is no scientific evidence. We suggest that the seeming more adverse effect on teenagers reflects their having been assaulted in the name of discipline for 13 or 14 years rather than 3 or 4 years.

Homicide

Perhaps the most dramatic example of the link between spanking and societal rates of violence comes from an analysis of the relation of spanking to homicide rates. Charts 19.1 and 19.2 give the results of testing the hypothesis that the more spanking is used in a society or sector of society, the more murders in that sector. Chart 19.1 uses as the cases the 32 nations where we obtained data on the percent of students who were spanked or hit a lot by their parents. It shows that the higher the percent spanked or hit a lot, the higher the national homicide rate. Chart 19.2 tested the same hypothesis but by using data on the 50 states of the United States as the societal units and using approval of spanking as the "independent variable" (i.e., the hypothesized risk factor). The chart shows that the higher the percent of the population of a state who approved of spanking children, the higher the homicide rate of the state.

Cause and effect.   In the previous paragraph, we put the term independent variable in quotation marks to highlight that both charts give the results of cross-sectional correlations. As a consequence, it is not possible to determine with this data whether it is the experience of spanking that leads to homicide or whether a society where there are norms approving violence leads parents to use violence in bringing up children. Probably both processes are at work. But whatever the causal direction, these results show that societies in which spanking is prevalent tend to be societies where there is more approval of violence

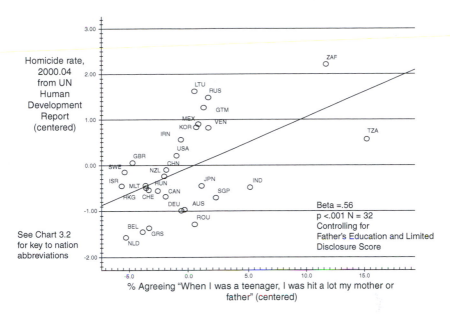

Chart 19.1 The More Spanking of Students in a Nation, the Higher the National Homicide Rate

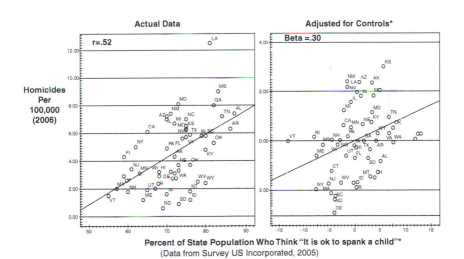

Chart 19.2 The Larger the Percent of the Population Who Approve of Spanking, the Higher the Homicide Rate (Data for the 50 U.S. States)

*Controlled for Percent: Below poverty, Black, College-educated, Metro resident

and more violence. Our interpretation is that both spanking and homicide are two reflections of a violent society. Some would label these results as *spurious* correlations. We argue that they are evidence supporting the principle that in a violent society, cultural norms approving of *pro-social* violence tend to increase the probability of violence in all spheres of life and increase the probability of violent crime (Baron & Straus, 1988; Galiani, Rossi, & Schargrodsky, 2011; Hogben, Byrne, Hamburger, & Osland, 2001). This phenomenon is discussed below as the cultural spillover theory of violence.

Attitudes Favoring Spanking and Infant Homicide Rates

Burns and Straus (in Straus, 2001b, p. 115) used data from Edfeldt (1979) on the degree to which teachers in 10 European nations approved of corporal punishment to examine the relationship between corporal punishment and societal-level violence. They found that the greater the degree of approval of corporal punishment in a nation, the higher the overall homicide rate and also the homicide rate for infants. When variables such as the gross national product and educational and military expenditures were controlled, the relationship between approval of corporal punishment by teachers and the infant homicide rate remained, but not the overall homicide rate. This seemingly strange result does not mean that teachers who favor hitting children when necessary favor murdering infants. A probable explanation is that the more a society favors spanking and other forms of morally legitimate violence, the more frequent spanking will be used, and the earlier in life it is likely to be used. In the United States, for example, Chapter 2 shows that about one third of parents hit infants. The combination of starting early, hitting a lot, and the vulnerability of infants, means that more infants are at risk of being killed in a society that favors spanking, even though no one favors killing infants. These results are also consistent with research in the United States and Canada that found that two thirds to three quarters of cases of physical abuse began as spanking and escalated into more severe and sometimes lethal assaults (Straus, 2000; 2008a).

David Gil's (1970) pioneering study of 1,380 children found that 63% of the abuse incidents were an "immediate or delayed response to specific (misbehavior) of the child." Gil concluded:

"Because culturally determined permissive attitudes toward the use of physical force in child rearing seem to constitute the common core of all physical abuse of children in American society, systematic educational efforts aimed at gradually changing this particular aspect of the prevailing child-rearing philosophy, and developing clear-cut cultural prohibitions and legal sanctions against the use of physical force as a means for rearing children, are likely to produce over time the strongest possible reduction of the incidence and prevalence of physical abuse of children." (p.141).

An in-depth study of 66 cases of physical abuse by Kadushin and Martin (1981) also found that two thirds were instances of spanking that had escalated out of control. A study of substantiated physical abuse cases in Ontario found that 85% started as attempts to correct misbehavior by the child (Trocmé,

McPhee, Tam, & Hay, 1994). The meta-analysis by Gershoff (2002) included 10 studies that investigated the relationship between spanking and physical abuse. All 10 studies found a relationship.

Other studies investigated the relation of having experienced spanking as a child and physically abusing a child later in life. For example, Straus and Yodanis (2001) studied a nationally representative sample of American parents and found that the more spanking these parents had experienced as children, the greater the probability that, in bringing up their own children, they went beyond legally permissible spanking and engaged in severe physical attacks on their children. As mentioned previously, Gershoff's meta-analysis covered 10 studies of the link between spanking and crime.

Studies like those just cited, plus clinical observation, led Zigler and Hall (1989) to conclude that "ultimate control of the abuse problem lies in changing our societal attitudes towards and acceptance of aggression as an appropriate mechanism for problem solving." A number of other leading scholars and clinicians have also concluded that reducing spanking is essential to reducing physical abuse (Feshbach, 1980; Gelles & Straus, 1988; Haeuser, 1991; Maurer, 1976; Williams, 1983), and some, such as Chaffin et al. (2004) have shown that reducing spanking actually does reduce risk for physical abuse of children.

State-to-State Difference in Corporal Punishment in U.S. Schools

Hyman and Wise (1979) published a tabulation of the extent to which corporal punishment was permitted in schools in the 1970s. At that time, only four states prohibited corporal punishment by school personnel. Some states permitted only the principal to hit children; others permitted both the principal and teachers. Thus there were considerable differences between the U.S. states in the extent to which corporal punishment was permitted in schools. We used this information to create a corporal punishment Permission Index score for each state (Straus, 2001a). At the extreme were states that permitted any school employee to hit a child. Florida even prevented individual school districts from forbidding corporal punishment. This study found that the more corporal punishment was authorized in a state, the higher the rate of violence by students and the higher the homicide rate in the state. A plausible explanation for this is that corporal punishment in schools and murders reflect state-to-state differences in an underlying tendency to use violence to correct problems. Corporal punishment in schools is an example of violence to correct a problem, and as noted earlier in this chapter, so are almost three quarters of murders in the United States. Both corporal punishment in schools and murders reflect an underlying culture of violence. There is a bidirectional relationship: As suggested in Chapters 3, 5, and 20, these cultural beliefs and norms increase the probability of corporal punishment, and corporal punishment increases the proportion of the population who subscribe to those beliefs and norms.

A generation later, another study of the relationship between school corporal punishment and homicides was published (Arcus, 2002). Arcus found that, in states that allowed corporal punishment, the probability of a homicide occurring in a school was twice that of schools in states that do not allow corporal punishment. Further, the more corporal punishment was actually used, the higher the rate of homicides in the schools of the state. These relationships remained after controlling for the poverty rate and the percent of conservative Christians in each state.

The Cultural Spillover Theory of Violence

The studies on the relationship between spanking and other forms of violence, and those described earlier in this chapter, are consistent with the idea that all types of violence tend to be related to each other. The studies we described show linkages between legitimate violence (such as spanking and executing criminals) and criminal violence such as homicide and rape. They illustrate what has been called the cultural spillover theory (Baron & Straus, 1987, 1989; Baron et al., 1988; Galiani et al., 2011; Hogben et al., 2001).

According to the cultural spillover theory, a society that uses violence for socially approved purposes such as spanking children, executing criminals, or going to war, will tend to be a society in which more citizens use violence for what the rest of the society defines as a criminal purpose. Thus, executing criminals results in a higher rather than a lower rate of homicide because, when society legitimizes killing people who do horrible things, it is associated with an increased percent of the population who take it in their own hands to kill someone who has done to them something they think is horrible (Baron & Straus, 1988; Stack, 1993; Thomson, 1999). When a society legitimizes killing by going to war, more people will perceive enemies in their daily life who warrant killing (Archer & Gartner, 1984). Even violence in the form of heavyweight boxing prize-fights has been found to be related to an increase in the rate of criminal violence (Phillips, 1983). Baron and Straus (1988) used these and other indicators of legitimate violence to create a scale to measure the extent to which the 50 states of the United States differed from each other in legitimate violence. They found that the higher the score of a state on the Legitimate Violence Index, the higher the state's homicide rate, even after controlling for other state characteristics associated with homicide such as the poverty rate and the percent of the state population in the age group with the highest homicide (age 18 to 24).

Lansford and Dodge (2008) analyzed the Standard Cross-Cultural Sample of anthropological records. This data set includes 186 cultural groups to represent the world's 200 cultural provinces. They found that frequent use of corporal punishment was related to more aggression in children, warfare, and adult interpersonal violence. These relations remained after controlling for demographic, socioeconomic, and other aspects of parenting. Lansford and Dodge concluded that frequent spanking is related to more cultural approval of violence and more actual acts of violence, and that reducing spanking by parents can lead to reductions in societal violence manifested in other ways.

The cultural spillover theory applies to cultural norms approving violence, at least in part because the use of violence for socially approved purposes is likely to be a result of and also to reinforce norms approving of violence. Thus, norms approving violence in one sphere of life will be associated with norms approving violence in other spheres of life. This is consistent with findings in Chapter 5 on approval of violence and spanking, with results in Chapters 12 and 13 on the link between being spanking and violence approval, and with the study by Lansford and Dodge described in the previous paragraph. In other words, the more children in a society who have been spanked, the greater the tendency for the society to have cultural norms that approve of, or accept other forms of, violence and the more approval of, violence in other spheres of life, the more approval of spanking. Regardless of the direction of the effect, more spanking is associated with an increased probability of violence in other spheres of life.

Individual-Level Evidence

There have been many studies of the relation of spanking to antisocial behavior and crime. Based on a review by Haapasalo and Pokela (1999) and on their own research, Farrington and Welsh (2006) concluded that "It is clear that harsh or punitive discipline (involving physical punishment) predicts a child's delinquency." This conclusion is even more clear from the results of the meta-analysis by Gershoff (2002). She analyzed 49 studies that tested the relation of corporal punishment to antisocial and criminal behavior. This included:

- Twenty-seven studies of the relationship of corporal punishment to aggression by children. All 27 found that corporal punishment was associated with an increased probability of aggression.
- Thirteen studies of the relation of corporal punishment to delinquent and antisocial behavior. Twelve of the 13 found that corporal punishment predicted an increased probability of delinquency and antisocial behavior.
- Four studies of the relation of corporal punishment to aggression as an adult. All four found that corporal punishment predicted an increased probability of aggression, as did the nine studies on this issue in Parts II and IV of this book.
- Five studies of the relation of corporal punishment to criminal and antisocial behavior as an adult. Four of the five found that corporal punishment was associated with an increased probability of crime and antisocial behavior.

Although the results of Gershoff's meta-analysis are impressive because they reveal a degree of consistency between studies that is rarely found, the evidence is weaker than it seems because most of the studies are cross-sectional, almost all are U.S. studies, and some lacked needed controls. Therefore, the following sections of this chapter provide examples of studies that used longitudinal designs or were conducted in different national contexts, or which controlled for important confounding variables such as whether there was also physical abuse.

Prevalence of Spanking

The processes that can link spanking and crime begin in infancy because, in many societies, parents start spanking children before their first birthdays. As shown in Chapter 2 and by Duggan et al. (2004), at least one third of parents in the United States hit infants. Similar results have been found for the United Kingdom (Newson & Newson, 1963). A typical example is slapping the hand of a child who pushes food from a highchair tray to the floor after being told not to do it again. This can be considered a child's first experience with violence by an adult. It is one of the reasons for entitling this book *The Primordial Violence*. It is important that the first experience of violence by adults is in the form of behavior that is morally correct, socially approved, and legal in all but a few nations because, in addition to teaching what the child is being punished for, spanking also implicitly teaches that hitting to correct misbehavior is morally correct. Our theory is that learning this behavioral script has a lifelong effect, and this script is part of the reason most violence, from simple assaults to homicides, is carried out to correct the perceived misbehavior of the person attacked. Moreover, as we pointed out earlier, the anthropologist Ashley Montague (1941) argued that spanking is one of the underlying causes of war.

As was shown in Chapter 2 on the prevalence of corporal punishment in the United States, over 90% of parents use spanking, at least occasionally, with children ages 2 to 4. Moreover, toddlers are spanked an average of 2 to 3 times a week (Giles-Sims et al., 1995; Holden et al., 1995; Stattin et al., 1995). The percentage of parents who spank decreases after children turn 5 (see Chapter 2, Chart 2.1). Even with children age 13, 40% still used corporal punishment, and at age 17, 13% still used corporal punishment. The most recent U.S. national survey of children in 2006 found that 44% of children age 8 to 10 and 15% of children age 16 to 18 had experienced corporal punishment in the previous 12 months (Martin, 2006). Moreover, among parents who continue corporal punishment into the teenage years, it is not a rare outburst. Within the subgroup of parents who use corporal punishment with teenage children, it tends to occur 4 to 5 times a year (Straus & Donnelly, 2001b).

Rates of spanking that can be compared cross-nationally were presented in Chapters 3 and 13. They are the reports of the 17,404 students in the 32 nations surveyed for International Dating Violence Study. In each of the nations, the students were asked whether they had been "spanked or hit a lot before age 12." In most of the 32 nations, over one half of the students recalled being spanked or a hit a lot. This is a lower-bound estimate because it refers to being hit a lot and because many people do not remember much of what happened when they were 2 to 5 years old, which are the peak ages for spanking. The rates ranged from less than one fifth of the students in the low spanking nations such as Sweden and the Netherlands to almost three quarters of the students in the nations where spanking was most prevalent (Taiwan and Tanzania).

Spanking and Juvenile Antisocial Behavior

The studies cited above indicate that spanking is frequent and continues for at least four or five years and, in a third or more cases, into the teenage years. We believe that being hit by parents, often for four or more years, sets in motion a number of criminogenic processes. One process is weakening the bond between parent and child, as shown in Chapters 8 and 9 and by Afifi et al. (2006). A weak bond between child and parents is a key element in the social control theory of crime (Hirschi, 1969). Social learning identifies another linking mechanism because spanking provides a behavioral model of violence. Many studies have found that the more spanking experienced as a child, the greater the support for and actual spanking of their own children (Bailey, Hill, Oesterle, & Hawkins, 2009; Muller, Hunter, & Stollak, 1995). This is illustrated by a study of 102 children age 3 to 7. The mothers were interviewed to find out about spanking. The more spanking these children experienced, the more likely they were to approve of parents spanking. However, this study made an additional unique contribution. It examined the children's strategies for dealing with a conflict with a sibling and with a peer. Two vignettes portraying typical child disagreements with

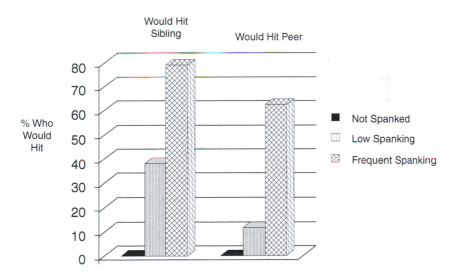

Study of 102 children age 2 to 7 who responded to vignettes depicting conflict with another child. The children were asked what they would do.

Chart 19.3   The More Children Were Spanked, the More Likely They Were to Hit Another Child with Whom They Were Having a Conflict

a peer (who grabs the child's toy) and a sibling (who changes the TV station) were used. The children were asked to pretend that they were the child in each situation and to indicate which of four responses they would choose if they were in this conflict: (a) do nothing, (b) try to find a grown-up to help, (c) suggest sharing or compromising, or (d) hit the other child. These responses were presented to the children pictorially, and they pointed to the one they would choose for each situation. The results in Chart 19.3 show that the more spanking, the more likely the child was to say they would hit the other child. Moreover, spanking was the strongest predictor of children's acceptance of aggressive problem solving, above and beyond parental acceptance, parental experience of corporal punishment, and familial demographics. A limitation of this study is that it does not rule out the possibility that the parents who spanked a lot did so to correct a child who hit other children a lot. However, the longitudinal studies described below did control for the child's misbehavior.

Longitudinal Studies

Although misbehavior does provoke spanking, 11 of 12 longitudinal studies that controlled for the level of misbehavior at the start of the study found that when parents spank, it is associated with a *subsequent* increase rather than decrease in the probability of antisocial and aggressive behavior. These studies also controlled for many possible confounding factors, such as socioeconomic status and parental warmth and support.

*   Berlin et al. (2009) studied a sample of 2,573 low-income 2-year-olds in Early Head Start programs and found that spanking at age 1 was associated with an increase in child aggression a year later. However, spanking at age 2 was not associated with more aggressive behavior at age 3.
*   Ellison, Musick, and Holden (2011) studied a U.S. national sample of 456 children and found that early spanking alone was not associated with subsequent antisocial behavior, but spanking that persisted into or began in middle childhood was. Children of mothers who belonged to conservative Protestant groups did *not* have higher antisocial behavior subsequent to spanking.
*   Grogan-Kaylor (2004) studied a sample of 4- to 14-year-old children and found that more spanking was associated with an increase in antisocial behavior two years later for Blacks, Whites, and Hispanics.
*   Lau, Litrownik, Newton, Black, and Everson (2006) studied a sample of 4-, 6-, and 8-year-olds with previous behavior problems and found that spanking was associated with a subsequent increase in externalizing problems.
*   MacKenzie et al. (2011) measured the relation of spanking at age 3 of a nationally representative sample of 779 three-year-old children to externalizing behavior at age 5. The study controlled externalizing behavior at

age 3 and 30 other variables. Despite that, they found that frequent spanking at age 3 was associated with more externalizing behavior at age 5.

- Pardini, Fite, and Burke (2008) studied a sample of 1st-, 4th-, and 7th-grade children and found that spanking was associated with a subsequent increase in both teacher- and parent-reported conduct problems. The increase was larger as age increased and if the child was Black.
- Gunnoe and Mariner (1997) studied a sample of children 4 to 11 years old and found that, for White but not for Black children, spanking was associated with more fights at school 4 or 6 years later. Over the same time span, corporal punishment was also associated with an increase in antisocial behavior for all ages for Blacks as well as Whites.
- McLoyd and Smith (2002) studied a sample of 4-year-old White, Black, and Hispanic children and found that more spanking was associated with more behavior problems six years later for all three racial or ethnic groups. However, spanking was not associated with behavior problems for children with high levels of emotional support.
- Millar (2009) studied a representative sample of 9,789 Canadian children age 4 to 11 and found that spanking was associated with a subsequent increase in hyperactivity, emotional disorders, aggression, indirect aggression, and property offenses.
- Mulvaney and Mebert (2007) studied a sample of White and Black children and found that spanking at age 3 was associated with an increase in externalizing problems in 1st grade. The increase was found for both Black and White children and was greater for children with difficult temperaments.
- Straus, Sugarman, and Giles-Sims (Chapter 6) studied a nationally representative sample of children aged 6 to 9 and found that spanking was associated with an increase in antisocial behavior two years later.
- Taylor, Manganello et al. (2010) studied a sample of 3-year-old children and found that spanking was associated with an increase in child aggression two years later.

Among these many excellent studies, the one by Millar (2009) is particularly important because it allowed comparison of the effects of spanking with the effects of other adverse childhood experiences. The study followed up a very large nationally representative sample of Canadian children who participated in the Canadian National Longitudinal Study of children. Millar's sample was large enough to include in one statistical analysis five other well-established risk factors for child behavior problems: whether a parent is depressed, inadequate supervision, lack of love and support, low income, and broken family. Each of these is associated with more spanking and therefore could be the real underlying cause of the link between spanking and child antisocial behavior. Millar found that the effect of spanking was *in addition to* and had a stronger unique effect on aggression and delinquency than these other five adverse childhood experiences.

Spanking and Adolescent and Adult Crime

Longitudinal Studies of Adolescent Crime

Four longitudinal studies found that corporal punishment was associated with crime as an adolescent or adult, controlling for the level of misbehavior that presumably elicited the corporal punishment.

- Brezina (1999) studied a nationally representative sample of 10th-grade boys and found that corporal punishment was associated with an increase in child-to-parent assault a year later.
- Foshee et al. (2005) studied a sample of 8th- and 9th-grade students and found that spanking was not associated with assaulting a dating partner for the total sample (which included many single-parent families). In the two-parent sample, maternal spanking was associated with more assaults on dating partners.
- Simons et al. (1998) studied a sample of 7th-grade boys and found that more spanking was associated with more dating violence and antisocial behavior two years later.
- Straus, Colby, and Medeiros (Chapter 15) studied a sample of children age 8 to 13 and controlled for the level of antisocial behavior that presumably led to the spanking, as well as 10 other risk factors for later crime such as low parental monitoring and support. Years later, when they were young adults, the boys who experienced spanking had higher scores on scales to measure violent crime, property crime, and overall crime.

Spanking and Physical and Sexual Assault of Partners

There are several cross-sectional studies that, even though they cannot establish which is cause and which is effect, have the merits of controlling for important variables that could be the real underlying cause of the relationship between spanking and crime, such as low socioeconomic status or a low level of parental warmth and support, and some are studies in nations other than the United States.

Research on the relationship of spanking to physically assaulting a marital or dating partner has consistently found that spanking is associated with an increased probability of assault on a marital or dating partner.

- Chapters 12 and 13 show that spanking is associated with physically assaulting a dating partner in the United States and many other nations.
- Chapter 16 shows that spanking is associated with sexual coercion and physically forced sex.
- Cast, Schweingruber, and Berns (2006) studied a sample of young married couples and found that more spanking was associated with more physical assaults against a partner.

- Foshee (Foshee, Bauman, & Linder, 1999; Foshee, Ennett, Bauman, & Suchindran, 2005) studied a sample of 8th and 9th graders and found that more spanking by mothers was associated with more assaults by females against dating partners, but not by males.

Spanking and Other Adult Antisocial Behavior and Crime

Afifi et al. (2006) studied a nationally representative sample of 5,877 U.S. adults and found that the percent with conduct disorder/antisocial behavior as adults was 32% higher for participants who had experienced corporal punishment.

A study by McCord (1997) is particularly important because the boys in the study were followed up over a 35-year period and because, like the children in Chapter 15, they were a high-risk group who many believe need strong discipline (one of the euphemisms for spanking) to keep them from a life of crime. However, Chart 19.4 shows the boys who experienced spanking were more likely to have been convicted for a serious crime, regardless of whether the father had a criminal record. Moreover, McCord (1997) found that although parental warmth and support reduced the percent of boys who were later convicted of a violent crime, the relation of spanking to crime remained.

Similar results were found using the data on 17,404 university students in the International Dating Violence Study (described in Chapter 3). Chart 19.5 clearly shows that positive parenting is associated with less crime as measured by a scale

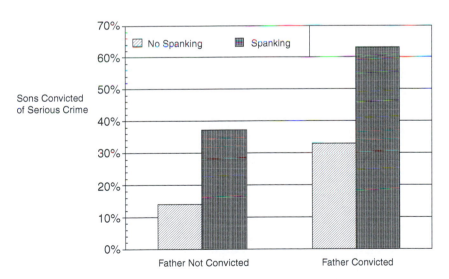

Chart 19.4   Rates of Conviction for Serious Crimes Are Higher among Sons Who Experienced Spanking and Highest among Sons of Convicted Fathers Who Experienced Spanking

*Data from McCord (1997), Table 1

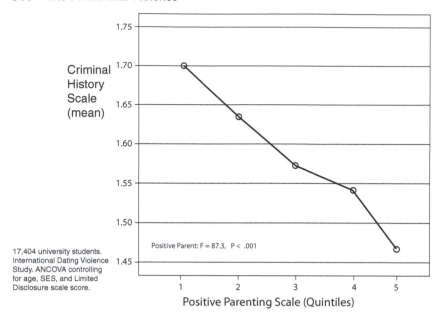

Chart 19.5   The More Positive Parenting, the Lower the Probability of Criminal Behavior

17,404 university students. International Dating Violence Study. ANCOVA controlling for age, socioeconomic status, and limited disclosure scale score.

that asked about eight criminal acts (described in Dawson and Straus, 2011). Moreover, Chart 19.6 shows that regardless of the level of positive parenting, the more spanking, the higher the score on the criminal behavior scale. (Positive parenting was measured by a six-item scale that asked about the extent to which the student's parents supervised, helped, and comforted the child).

Studies in two other nations compared the extent of criminal behavior as an adult by those whose parents depended on spanking with those whose parents did not. In Finland, Pulkkinen (1983) and in Great Britain, Farrington (1978) found that children whose parents used spanking had a greater probability for subsequently committing serious crimes.

Trends in Spanking and Implications for Crime

The longitudinal studies in Chapters 6, 10, and 15, and those summarized in this chapter provide strong evidence that spanking causes cognitive and behavioral problems. However, there are still reasons why the causal connection can be questioned, such as whether there is a genetic predisposition to violence that manifests itself in both spanking by the parents and aggression and other antisocial behavior by the child. These questions are addressed in the section, Does Spanking Really *Cause* Antisocial Behavior, in Chapter 20. Assume for

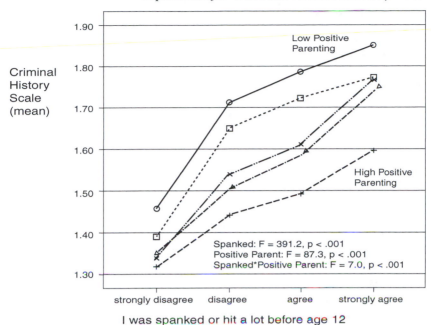

Chart 19.6 graph showing:

Criminal History Scale (mean), y-axis from 1.30 to 1.90

x-axis: strongly disagree, disagree, agree, strongly agree — labeled "I was spanked or hit a lot before age 12"

Low Positive Parenting
High Positive Parenting

Spanked: F = 391.2, p < .001
Positive Parent: F = 87.3, p < .001
Spanked*Positive Parent: F = 7.0, p < .001

Chart 19.6 Positive Parenting Reduces the Crime Rate but Does Not Reduce the Relation of Spanking to Crime

17,404 university students. International Dating Violence Study. ANCOVA controlling for age, socioeconomic status, and limited disclosure scale score.

the moment, however, that the link between spanking and an increased probability of antisocial behavior and crime is causal, what are the implications for crime rates?

There is evidence that spanking is decreasing worldwide, even in the United States, where the trend is less clear. Twenty-nine nations have prohibited spanking by parents, starting with Sweden in 1979, followed by other Scandinavian nations a few years later, Germany in 2000, and other nations since then (listed in the next chapter). Large reductions in spanking can be accomplished by such changes in national policy, as illustrated by the experience of Sweden and Germany discussed in Chapter 21. In the 1950s, 97% of Swedish parents spanked and one third did it at least daily. By 2006 it had decreased to 10% (Modig, 2009). In Germany, surveys of nationally representative samples of children age 12 to 18 found large decreases from 1992 to 2002, especially in the most severe forms of corporal punishment (Bussmann, 2004; Bussmann et al., 2011). The shift away from corporal punishment is likely to continue and probably accelerate. If spanking is one of the causes of crime, worldwide reductions in spanking should contribute to a worldwide reduction in crime, especially violent crime.

Processes Linking Spanking and Crime

In Chapter 18, we discussed the widespread belief that, as the saying goes, spanking "will teach him a lesson he won't forget." That is often true. However, this chapter shows that the lessons learned may also be conducive to violence and other crime. The most frequently mentioned of these criminogenic processes is that it is appropriate to hit people—including people we love—who misbehave, and that "might makes right." Learning the morality of hitting is an important part of the explanation of the link between spanking and crime. Many other processes are likely to also be part of the explanation. Some of them were shown by the studies in this book. They include:

- Lower self-control (Chapter 7)
- Undermining the bond between children and parents (Chapter 8)
- Lower IQ (Chapter 10)
- Lower probability of higher education (Chapter 11)
- Less conflict management skills such as explaining and negotiating (Chapter 12)

Needed Research on Mechanisms Linking Spanking and Crime

Research on the relation of spanking to child antisocial behavior and adult crime needs to examine many other processes. The examples include: anger, rage, resentment, and hostility over being repeatedly hit by parents; feeling powerless and a resulting need to demonstrate power; belief that the world is unfair; rebellion resulting from overly strict discipline enforced by spanking; low self-esteem; less well-developed conscience; alienation; hostile attribution of the intent of other people's behavior; neurological and endocrine damage (Bugental et al., 2003; Bugental et al., 2010; Tomoda et al., 2009); depression (Straus, 1994; Straus, 2001d); post-traumatic stress symptoms (Straus, 2009c); and dulled affect and empathy.

Although spanking usually secures compliance in the immediate situation, the long-term effects of spanking are more often the opposite of what, for most Americans and British people is a self-evident truth—that spanking is sometimes necessary to bring up a well-behaved child. Contrary to this belief, the studies in this book found that spanking is associated with an increased probability of 15 harmful side effects, ranging from antisocial behavior of children to reduced mental ability, depression, and crime as an adult. In the concluding chapter, we restated these in the form of a list of 15 benefits of never spanking.

Summary and Conclusions

The introduction to this chapter asked whether spanking has the same relation to crime as physical abuse. The evidence summarized suggests that it does, but with the important qualification that the "effect size" is less. For example,

Strassberg et al. (1994) found that spanking was associated with twice the number of acts of physical aggression observed among a group of kindergarten children compared with the children who were not spanked six months earlier. But physical abuse was associated with 4 times as many physically aggressive acts. Other studies that have also found that spanking has the same effect as physical abuse, but with a lower probability of the adverse outcomes for children include Afifi et al. (2006), Fergusson et al. (2008), Straus (2001a, Chapter 7), and Ulman and Straus (2003). Moreover, all the adverse effects of spanking shown in this book, and in our previous book on spanking (Straus, 2001a) and in Gershoff's meta-analysis, are also the effects of physical abuse found by numerous studies.

20 Obstacles to Accepting the Evidence

Both the amount of research and the over 90% consistency between studies of the adverse effects of spanking is remarkable. Yet all but a few parents, social scientists, and professionals who advise parents continue to believe that spanking is sometimes necessary. As pointed out in Chapter 1, this research is practically ignored in textbooks on children. If there were as much consistency in the results of research on any other aspect of parenting, it would be a major section of child psychology textbooks, rather than the current situation, which is typically a one-half page description with no recommendation to never spank. The purpose of this chapter is to suggest explanations for this discrepancy between the evidence and what the experts recommend and what parents do. Seven overlapping explanations are presented:

- The evidence, while voluminous, does not really prove that spanking *causes* child behavior problems and crime.
- Ending spanking will mean a nation with kids out of control.
- The harmful effects don't apply when spanking is the cultural norm.
- Even if the evidence on the adverse effects of spanking is strong, it is not truly conclusive, and it is therefore not ethical to advise parents to never spank.
- Parents who spank, and children who have been spanked, have no way of perceiving for themselves that spanking has harmful side effects.
- Cultural norms block accepting the evidence.

In addition to these six obstacles, the next chapter discusses the belief that, compared with other harms to which children are exposed, the adverse effects of spanking are so small that it is not worth spending limited resources on attempts to end spanking.

Does the Research Really Prove that Spanking Causes Antisocial Behavior?

Causal Sequence

Most studies that investigated the relationship of spanking to antisocial behavior or crime are cross-sectional, and therefore the results could indicate either that:

- Child antisocial behavior causes spanking
- Spanking causes antisocial behavior
- There are bidirectional effects

We believe the relationship is bidirectional. That is, the child's antisocial behavior is one of the many things that lead parents to spank, but ironically, when they spank to correct antisocial behavior, it increases rather than decreases the probability of future antisocial behavior.

Two types of research have provided evidence that spanking increases the probability of crime. First, are the longitudinal studies in Chapters 6, 10, and 15, and the many others cited in Chapter 19 that controlled for the Time 1 level of antisocial behavior that presumably led to the use of spanking and found that spanking was associated with a *subsequent* increase in antisocial and criminal behavior. Second are the results of parent-training interventions for children with problem behaviors (Crozier & Katz, 1979; Patterson, 1982; Webster-Stratton, 1990; Webster-Stratton, Kolpacoff, & Hollinsworth, 1988). These three studies evaluated programs that included steps to get parents to stop or reduce spanking. In all three, the behavior of the children improved after spanking ended. A study by Beauchaine et al. (2005) of over 500 families randomly assigned parents to either a group that had parenting interventions to reduce spanking or to a control group. The study found that one year later the children in the no-spanking intervention group had significantly less externalizing behavior problems than the control group. Similar results were found by Knox, Burkhart, and Hunter (2011).

Is the Real Cause Genetic Inheritance?

Parents who use corporal punishment may be more aggressive as a matter of genetic heritage. The association between spanking and subsequent antisocial behavior may reflect a genetic propensity to violence that is shared by parents and their children. Our view is consistent with research showing *epigenetic* effects for the interaction of genetic characteristics with many parent practices. That is, the way parents bring up children influences how the genes express themselves as the child develops. What does the research show? The studies examining the interaction of genetic heritage and parenting practices have found evidence for both genetic effects and parenting effects, and an epigenetic effect (i.e., the interaction of genetics and parenting; Burt, McGue, Krueger, & Iacono, 2005, 2007; Stams, Juffer, & Van Ijzendoorn, 2002). However, none of these three studies empirically tested the interaction of spanking with genetic characteristics.

Fortunately, a study by Boutwell et al. (2011) did test the interaction of spanking with genetic propensity to antisocial behavior. They studied a sample of 1,600 twins that enable them to compare fraternal and identical twins. They found a clear genetic effect: The higher the score on their scale of *genetic risk* that measures genetic propensity for antisocial behavior, the more antisocial behavior by the child. The crucial point for understanding the effects of spanking

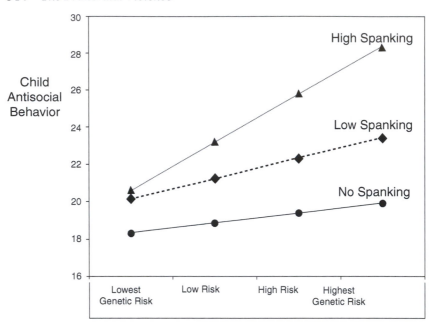

Chart 20.1   The Combination of Genetic Propensity and Spanking Results in the Most Antisocial Behavior

*After Boutwell, B. B., Franklin, C. A., Barnes, J. C., & Beaver, K. M. (2011)

is that they also found that spanking affected the relationship of genetic propensity to actual antisocial behavior. The bottom line in Chart 20.1 shows that the relation of genetic propensity for antisocial behavior to actual antisocial behavior was smallest for the children who were not spanked. The middle line shows a slightly larger relationship for the children in the low spanking group, and the top line shows that the relationship between genetic propensity and antisocial behavior was strongest for children who were spanked the most. However, as in our study of the relation of spanking to crime as an adult (Chapter 15), these relationships were found only for boys.

The Boutwell et al. study found that spanking made the biggest difference among children who were genetically more likely to be antisocial. In other words, children who are genetically more likely be antisocial are not only more likely to be spanked, they are also much more likely to be adversely affected by spanking. The chances that they will develop antisocial behaviors *increased* by being spanked. These results are consistent with the irony intended by the title of our previous book on spanking *Beating the Devil Out of Them* (Straus, 2001a). This is because the research shows that spanking, rather than beating the devil *out* of them, *brings out* the devil in them. As a consequence, one practical implication of the Boutwell et al. study is that, when there is a genetic propensity to antisocial behavior, it is even more important to avoid spanking.

Confounding with Physical Abuse

The relation of spanking to antisocial behavior and crime could occur because, among the parents who spank are some who also physically abuse the child. Although most studies of spanking do not take this into account, at least eight high quality studies have done so. All eight found that spanking is related to antisocial behavior and crime even after removing physically abused children from the sample or after controlling statistically for physical abuse (Afifi et al., 2006; Gámez-Guadix, Straus, Carrobles, Muñoz Rivas, & Almendros Rodríguez, 2010; MacMillan et al., 1999; Strassberg et al., 1994; Straus, 1990e, Chapter 23; 2001a, Chapter 8; Taylor, Manganello et al., 2010).

Cultural Context

Societies differ in respect to the cultural or statistical normativeness of spanking. It has been argued that when spanking is the norm, children will understand that it is for their own good and will not suffer adverse side effects (Deater-Deckard & Dodge, 1997). Chapter 14 presents the results of 17 studies that provided 60 comparisons of the effects of spanking in different cultural contexts. A tabulation of those studies showed that for 77% of the studies, there was a harmful side effect of spanking regardless of the normativeness of spanking in the cultural contexts. Another review of cultural context effects found similar results and concluded, "Although corporal punishment is generally related to more behavior problems regardless of cultural group, this association is weaker in countries in which corporal punishment is the norm. Yet cultures in which corporal punishment is the norm also have higher levels of societal violence" (Lansford, 2010, p. 105).

Will Ending Spanking Mean Kids Out of Control?

Many people are worried that if parents cannot spank, it will result in kids running wild. If no spanking meant no discipline (i.e., no efforts to teach and no correction of misbehavior), that would be a likely outcome. However, no spanking does not mean no discipline, or as some put it, *permissiveness* (Larzelere & Baumrind, 2010). In fact, practically all parents, including those who spank, use many other methods of teaching and correcting, starting with saying no, repositioning the child, explaining, providing an alternative activity, and time-out. Of course, as shown in Chapter 18 on why everyone resorts to spanking, these methods often do not work. In fact, for 2-year-old children, if repetition of the misbehavior in the same day is the criterion of *not working,* the failure rate for *all methods,* including spanking, is about 80% in the same day (Larzelere & Merenda, 1994). When a child has been told to stop it and an hour later repeats the misbehavior, does that mean it is time to spank? No, because as the first chart in Chapter 18 shows, a 2-year-old is just as likely to do it again two hours after being spanked. It is possible to conclude from these statistics that, with a 2-year-old, nothing works. That is correct if never repeating the misbehavior is the criterion. But that criterion is inconsistent with what is known about the limited ability of toddlers to control their own behavior. It is more consistent with the evidence on child behavior to view replacing undesirable behavior by more appropriate behavior as a gradual process. It requires repeating the correction many times, often hundreds of times, regardless of whether it is by saying no or by spanking. With consistency and perseverance, both spanking and nonviolent correction can achieve that end. But, there are two big differences.

First, parents who spank are not deterred by the fact that the child repeats the misbehavior. They spank as often as necessary until the child does learn. On the other hand, when parents start with nonviolent methods of discipline and the almost inevitable repetition of the misbehavior occurs, the cultural myth that spanking works when other methods do not, leads them to turn to spanking. That is one of the main reasons why, as documented in Chapter 2, over 90% of parents spank toddlers.

Second, at the time parents use non-violent modes of correcting misbehavior, there is no way they can observe the benefits such as closer child to parent bond and higher IQ. Those benefits, when they occur, take months or years to show up. But the repetition of misbehavior later in the same day, which occurs in about the same percentage of cases as when the child is spanked, is visible that day.

As we said, every method of teaching and controlling children, including spanking, needs to be repeated, often many, many times. If parents replace spanking with an equal level of consistency and perseverance in using the nonviolent modes of discipline they already use, the result would not be a world of kids out of control. The more likely result would be a world of better-behaved children. Consider the following:

The results of research in this book and the studies summarized by Gershoff (2002) tell us that spanking is associated with behavior problems of children. Flipping that around, those same results tell us that children of parents who do not spank have the least probability of behavior problems. They are, on average, the best behaved children. In fact, the failure to cover spanking in child development textbooks shown in Chapter 1 and in Douglas and Straus (2007) reveals that the better behavior from children who are not spanked may be the best kept secret of U.S. child psychology.

Sweden banned spanking by parents in 1979. Swedes who opposed the ban feared it would lead to a wave of delinquency. Instead, juvenile crime rates have dropped, along with juvenile drug use and suicide (Janson, Langberg, & Svensson, 2011). The specific changes are given in the next chapter. Those who favor the ban are likely to claim that it shows the benefits of avoiding spanking. That is not necessarily correct because a great many other things have changed in Sweden since 1979, and crime rates elsewhere in Europe have also decreased. Therefore, there is no way of knowing if the decrease in spanking had anything to do with the decrease in juvenile behavior problems and crime.

However, it can at least be said with certainty that fears widely expressed in 1979 of Sweden becoming a nation with kids of control has not happened.

Although no state in the United States prohibits spanking by parents, with the exception of toddlers, spanking has been decreasing. The decrease has been especially rapid in the last two decades. If spanking is necessary for effective discipline, we should be seeing an increase in juvenile behavior problems and crime. Most people in the United States think that this is what has happened. In fact, 91% of the public believes that the percentage of teenagers who commit violent crime has increased or stayed the same over the past 10 years (Guzman, Lippman, Anderson Moore, & O'HareHow, 2003). Contrary to this belief, the rate of juveniles charged with a criminal offense has decreased since the early 1990s, as has the rate of violent victimizations perpetrated by juveniles as reported in the National Crime Victimization Survey (Snyder & Sickmund, 2006). For crime in schools, tragedies such as what happened in Columbine, Colorado have captured public attention and aroused fear about the safety of children and concern for what life will be like if this continues. Again, the reality is the opposite. Both violent crime and property crime in U.S. schools have declined since the data were first gathered in 1992 (Dinkes, Kemp, Baum, & Snyder, 2009). In other nations, bullying in schools has declined since the ending of corporal punishment in schools (Molcho et al., 2009). Bullying has decreased (Finkelhor, Turner, Ormrod, & Hamby, 2010). Other youth problems have also decreased, and youth are becoming more rather than less responsible. For example, sex without a condom has decreased (Centers for Disease Control and Prevention, 2010b), and along with it births to teenage mothers (The Alan Guttmacher Institute, 2004).

Cross-Cultural Applicability of the Harmful Effects of Spanking

Most of the research on spanking is based on parents and children in Western societies. But there is enough evidence from non-Western societies to indicate that the harmful effects of spanking may be cross-culturally universal (see Chapters 3, 5, 13, 14, 16; Gardner, Powell, & Grantham-McGregor, 2007; Gershoff et al., 2010; Lansford & Deater-Deckard, 2010). Our research in Chapter 14 on spanking in cultural contexts where corporal punishment is the norm, found that the cultural context does not eliminate the harmful side effects of spanking. The review by Lansford (2010) also found that corporal punishment is related to more behavior problems regardless of cultural group. Moreover, as pointed out earlier, Lansford's review of this issue concluded that "cultures in which corporal punishment is the norm . . . have higher levels of societal violence" (Lansford, 2010, p. 105).

The fact that anthropological and cross-national studies show that parents in almost all societies spank has been used to argue that spanking may not be "something to confront with policies or laws" (Nock, 2000) and imply that such an effort is not needed or not possible. On the contrary, laws and policies to deal with behaviors that are likely to cause problems are even more important when the behavior is linked to cross-cultural or biological universals such as sex, parenthood, aging, and violence. We do not use the fact that aging, male dominance, and murder occur in every, or nearly every, society to say that nothing should be done about them. Chapter 3 on the use of corporal punishment worldwide shows that spanking was indeed found in all 32 nations studied. However, there were also very large differences between the nations in the percent of students who were spanked, and most important, Chapter 13 shows that nations with the lower rates of spanking also had lower rates of assaulting and injuring dating partners. Thus, although spanking may be just about universal, it is far from a constant. It varies from society to society and that variation is related to the level of violence in a society. The same principle applies to group differences in spanking within a society such as Blacks compared with Whites.

The difference between the treatment of spanking and aging or homicide is not that spanking is universal, whereas aging and homicide are not. Rather, spanking is treated differently because the presumed benefit of spanking "when necessary" is a deeply embedded aspect of U.S. culture, as well as many other cultures. As a consequence, almost all Americans doubt the wisdom or even the possibility of *never* spanking a child.

The Ethics of Advising Parents to Never Spank

The Ethical Obligation to Inform Parents about the Research

The research evidence on whether spanking causes violence and other crime and psychological problems is very strong but not conclusive because there have been no randomized control studies. However, as pointed out in Chapter 18 on why almost all parents spank, there are nonviolent methods of correcting and controlling behavior that are just as effective in the short run but do not have the harmful side effects of spanking. Therefore, even evidence that is not fully conclusive creates an ethical *requirement* to advise parents to avoid the medicine that has the potential of harmful side effects and to advise them to use treatments for misbehavior that are just as effective but do not have these side effects. As a consequence, professionals working with parents and those who write books and articles for parents have an *obligation* to (1) inform parents that there are nonviolent modes of discipline that are just as effective, but without the risk of the side effects of spanking and (2) advise parents to never spank and use only nonviolent modes of discipline.

Do Parents Need to Learn Alternatives for It to Be Ethical to Advise to Never Spank?

If no spanking meant no correction, it would be a disaster because children need correction and guidance to help them become responsible persons. However, as we pointed out earlier, even parents who spank the most, use many other methods of correcting misbehavior and use them much more often than they spank. For example, they tell the child to stop something or do something and explain why; they move the children; and they use nonviolent punishment such as disapproval or depriving the child of a privilege. As a consequence, the advice to never spank does not mean no correction. It mostly means leaving out the spanking part of what they do and using only the nonviolent methods of correction that almost all parents already use. If parents did this (i.e., continued correcting misbehavior but leave out the spanking part), it would increase the probability of their being effective parents, of having a closer bond with their child, and of having better behaved and more successful children. Nevertheless, it is reasonable to assume that almost all parents and children will benefit when parents also acquire new behavior management skills or improve their method of using the techniques they already use. Therefore, although it is not a prerequisite for never spanking, we believe that as many parents as possible should participate in parent education classes such as Effective Black Parenting (Alvy & Marigna, 1987); Nurturing Parenting (Bavolek, 1992–2006), Parent Effectiveness Training (Gordon, 2000), and Tripple-P (Graaf, Speetjens, Smit, Wolff, & Tavecchio, 2008).

The Moral Principle of Nonviolence

A second ethical consideration is the moral value of nonviolence. Violence has been used throughout human history to achieve socially desirable goals, but it has gradually been replaced by nonviolent alternatives (Elias, 1978; Pinker, 2011). Corporal punishment of soldiers, sailors, apprentices, and wives has been abolished. The ancient principle of an eye-for-eye has been replaced by giving kings and now governments' responsibility for dealing with criminals. In turn, governments have increasingly replaced flogging and execution of criminals or heretics with incarceration. Incarceration in turn is being replaced by various forms of therapeutic treatments, such as *restorative justice* (Johnstone & Van Ness, 2007; Menkel-Meadow, 2007).

Ironically, the family is one of the last places where violence by individual members of society to achieve socially desirable ends has persisted. Corporal punishment in schools and corporal punishment and capital punishment of criminals has been abolished in all nations of the European Union and in many other nations. Foster parents and day care teachers are not allowed to hit children in most states of the United States. However, the situation is quite different for biological parents. In all but 32 of the more than 190 nations in the world, parents are allowed to hit children for purposes of correction and control. To say that there are 32 nations where spanking is illegal overstates the extent of the movement away from spanking because in most of those nations little has been done to inform parents and children that the legal standard is *never* spank. Nevertheless, even a generation ago, the idea of legally prohibiting spanking would have been seen as utopian by some citizens and laughable or outrageous by most. Moreover, as shown in Chapter 17 on the decline of spanking, parents themselves are moving away from spanking regardless of the legal change. The evolving cultural change to end all spanking because it is inhumane and a violation of human rights (Global Initiative to End All Corporal Punishment, 2007; Newell, 2011; Pinheiro, 2006) is likely to proceed to the point where legal prohibition will be used by all nations to clarify and extend the new pattern, thus crystallizing a new stage in the social evolution of a more humane and less violent world.

Why We Don't Perceive the Connection

The evidence presented in this book, together with the many other studies cited, shows that spanking is associated with behavior problems of both children and adults. This evidence has been not presented to university students or in clinical training as indicated by its absence from child development and child psychiatry textbooks. The content analysis of textbooks on child development presented in Chapters 1 and 18 shows that almost one half of these books include nothing at all on spanking, and those that do include very little, despite the fact that it is a part of the early experience of over 90% of American toddlers and despite a degree of consistency in research results that may be greater than any other aspect of parent behavior.

As we pointed out in Chapter 1, Ross Park's argument that "attempts to treat punishment as a separate variable are bound to fail. Instead, the inherent packaged nature of parental discipline renders the attempt to answer the question about the effects of corporal punishment on children a misguided one" is like saying that it is futile to try to separate out the effects of Vitamin C because the effects depend on the whole nutritional context or futile to study the effect of reading to children because of the inherent package nature of parenting. Of course the whole nutritional package or the whole parenting package must be studied, but so must each of its parts. Parke's comments are another example of dismissing the overwhelming evidence of the harmful effects of spanking.

In some cases, the evidence is not merely ignored but denied, as we documented in Chapter 19. Still another example of ignoring the evidence about the impact of spanking is the violence of prevention programs that are implemented in a large proportion of U.S. schools. None that we know of address the most frequent type of violence encountered by teenagers—being hit by a parent. Remember that at least one third of 13- and 14-year-olds are hit by their parents each year, and that among teenagers who are hit by parents, it happens an average of about 8 times per year. It may be beyond the power of a school-based program to get parents to stop hitting their children, but if the cultural norms permitted it, they could explain that it is also wrong for parents to correct misbehavior by hitting. Until parents stop hitting children to correct their misbehavior, it is unrealistic to expect teenagers to accept the idea that hitting is not an appropriate way to deal with the misbehavior of a peer who, for example, insults him or her, jumps ahead in a line, or makes a pass at his or her girlfriend or boyfriend.

Social and Psychological Obstacles to Accepting the Evidence

In our opinion, the fundamental reason for disregarding the evidence on the links between spanking and violence is not inadequacies of the scientific evidence on the adverse effects of spanking. The more fundamental explanation lies in the contradictions between what the research says and what personal experience and cultural norms say.

Personal Experience

A major obstacle to accepting the evidence that spanking is linked to behavior problems and violence occurs because personal experience seems to contradict the research results. One aspect is rejecting the research results because the harmful outcome has not happened to them. It is difficult for most people to understand that when research shows that smoking kills, it really means it kills only a minority of heavy smokers As was pointed out in detail in Chapter 1, spanking is a risk factor, not a one-to-one causal relation. It increases the probability of crime and other social and psychological problems, but most people who were spanked, like two thirds of heavy smokers, will *not* suffer a harmful side effect. They can say, and almost everyone does say, "I was spanked and I don't beat my wife or rob banks." Additionally, it is impossible to see for yourself how things would have been different with the same amount of discipline, love, attention, etc. but *without* the spanking. Only longitudinal research on the effects of spanking, such as the studies in Chapters 6, 10, and 15, and the other longitudinal studies reviewed in Chapter 19, can show this.

Another personal experience reason for not accepting the findings from research on the harmful effects of spanking is that it requires admitting that one's parents did something seriously wrong. Similarly, there is the even greater difficulty in acknowledging that having spanked one's own children unnecessarily exposed them to risk of serious harm.

Perhaps the most important reason the evidence linking spanking to crime and violence has been ignored is that, like their children, parents cannot see for themselves the evidence of harm. As we noted earlier, the harmful side effects do not occur right away, often not for years. When they do occur, almost no one even considers the possibility that the child's violent or antisocial behavior or an adult's depression might be the result of spanking by loving parents, especially since the spanking is culturally defined as something that is sometimes necessary for the child's well-being. The harmful effects of smoking were not perceived for centuries for the same reasons. Smokers could experience the pleasure of the behavior, but they had no way of looking 10 years down the road to see the harm it might cause. Only research can show that, and even then, only if professionals and parents are informed about the results of the research. However, as we pointed out in Chapter 1 professionals and parents are not informed about the results of research on the side effects of spanking.

Cultural Norms and Myths

Much of the opposition to steps to end spanking is based on one or the other of the 10 cultural myths about spanking described in Chapter 10 of *Beating the Devil Out of Them: Corporal Punishment in American Families* (Straus, 2001a). An example is the myth that spanking works better than other methods of correction and control. As explained in Chapter 18, that myth is why, despite the fact that most people in the United States probably believe it is best to avoid spanking, almost all parents continue to spank. It is exemplified by one father who said to us "I avoid it at all costs, but there are occasions when a good swat on the behind is needed." This view is shared by many pediatricians and child psychologists. For example, Dr. Lewis First of Children's Hospital in Boston told a reporter that he was against spanking, but later in the same interview said "if a child repeatedly runs into traffic, for example, you may want to play the big card" (Lehman, 1989). The same article reports that Dr. Robert M. Reece, Director of Child Protection at Children's Hospital and also at Boston City Hospital, told the reporter that he "opposes *all* corporal punishment as ineffective, potentially dangerous, and unfair" (emphasis added). Later in the same interview he said, "Spanks anywhere but a few light blows on the buttocks or using anything other than an open hand are out of bounds and signal abuse." In short, "a few light blows on the buttocks" are not out of bounds to a pediatrician who "opposes all corporal punishment." Those same contradictory views are probably manifest in surveys of professionals by Burgess et al. (2010) and Schenck et al. (2000).

Even more deeply embedded cultural obstacles to never spanking are described in Chapter 10 of *Beating the Devil Out of Them* (Straus, 2001a) on 10 myths that perpetuate corporal punishment. Among them are the cultural norms supporting use of violence for socially desirable ends, as was illustrated in Chapter 5 on the links between approval of violence and spanking, extreme individualism, fear of government intervention in the family, and religious fundamentalists who believe that God expects parents to spank. These deep-seated aspects of American beliefs and culture are major obstacles that are slowing the eventual end of spanking as a culturally approved and prevalent method of violent child rearing. However, slowing does not mean stopping the change to a world without spanking.

Summary and Conclusions

This chapter documented numerous obstacles that have blocked a shift away from spanking that is part of the long-term social evolution toward a more humane society (Pinker, 2011; Straus, 2001d). Eventually this cultural transition will probably lead to recognition of the evidence. There are signs that illustrate both the underlying movement away from spanking and the obstacles. In 1995, the American Psychological Association and the American Academy of Pediatrics jointly published a pamphlet *Raising Children to Resist Violence: What*

You Can Do (American Psychological Association and the American Academy of Pediatrics, 1995). It says that "Hitting, slapping, or spanking children as punishment shows them that it's okay to hit others to solve problems and can train them to punish others in the same way they were punished." Despite this, the American Psychological Association has turned down resolutions advising parents not to spank, even though many years ago it passed a resolution against corporal punishment *by teachers.* Why has the American Psychological Association not done the same for corporal punishment by parents? It is not because there is scientific evidence showing that corporal punishment by teachers is harmful and a lack of such evidence for corporal punishment by parents. The evidence available at the time of harm from *teachers* using corporal punishment was minimal. There were no experiments, no longitudinal studies, and only a few—and mostly inadequate—cross-sectional studies. On the other hand, the evidence on harm from *parental spanking* is plentiful. It includes experiments, longitudinal studies, and many well-designed cross-sectional studies with numerous controls and parent-education intervention studies, and it is highly consistent. The most plausible explanation for condemning corporal punishment by teachers and not by parents is a cultural change in one but not the other. In the United States, except for states in the Deep South, there is now a moral consensus against teachers hitting, whereas as shown in Chapter 17, no such *moral passage* (Gusfield, 1981) has taken place concerning parents hitting children. Scientific evidence had little to do with the fact that as long ago as 1975, the governing Council of the American Psychological Association passed a resolution against corporal punishment by teachers, but a resolution against parents spanking has not even been put before the council.

In Chapter 1, we quoted the guidelines published in 1998 (and reaffirmed in 2004) by the American Academy of Pediatrics after years of sometimes heated debate (American Academy of Pediatrics, 1998). Although it is a strong statement against spanking, it does not include spanking in the behaviors that should *never* be used.

In 2008, a member of the California legislature introduced a bill to ban spanking of children under age 3. It received national attention, and there were editorials in many newspapers. Almost all the editorials and reader comments opposed the legislation. Like the similar legislation proposed in Massachusetts in 2005, it did get beyond the committee hearing stage. Nevertheless, the fact that this legislation was even proposed in two states is a sign that the process of change is underway. As indicated in the next chapter, that process is much further along in Europe.

21   A World Without Spanking

The idea of a world where parents *never* spank evokes a variety of images, some of them diametrically opposite.

We suggest that the majority image in the United States, and probably all but a few other nations, is that it would be a world with out-of-control children and social chaos. This is the implication of surveys such as those in Chapters 5 and 17 that found that almost three quarters of Americans think that spanking is sometimes necessary. That belief is also prevalent among professionals in the United States concerned with children (Burgess et al., 2010; Schenck et al., 2000). The opposite view of a world without spanking is that it would be a world with less violence and other crime, in part because, as shown in this book, children who grow up free of violence by their parents are more likely to be, as the saying goes, healthier, happier, and wiser than children who were spanked. It would be a world with fewer psychological problems. This is what we believe the research evidence indicates. But as indicated in Chapter 1, this evidence has not yet made its way into child development textbooks and the training of professionals who work with parents. That is probably one of the reasons the kids out of control image predominates.

Perhaps the most positive view of a world without spanking is held by a third group—those for whom ending spanking represents a major and essential gain in human rights (Durrant & Smith, 2011; Newell, 2011; Pinheiro, 2006). From a human rights perspective, ending spanking is a key step to creating a world not only in which children are better off, but which is more humane and peaceful, and, therefore, everyone is better off.

A fourth view, which we examine in this chapter, is that ending spanking by parents would not make much difference. This group focuses on the research results that show that, although spanking may have an adverse effect on children under some circumstances, the effect is small and contingent on what else the parents do. This view helps explain the seeming contradiction between the increasing proportion of the general population and professionals who are against spanking but do not see spanking as a major influence on the well-being of children unless it is done too much or is done by parents who use harsh discipline as opposed to just spanking. As a consequence, one section of this chapter examines whether ending spanking is worth the effort. After that, we examine:

- Changes in society that are indicative of a change toward a more humane and civilized society and which underlie the decrease in approval of spanking and actual spanking.
- Legislation throughout the world to end the use of spanking and all other forms of corporal punishment.
- The prospects for such legislation in the United States.
- Identification of 15 ways in which the results of our research suggest that children and society would benefit from a world without spanking.

Societal Change and Change in Spanking

Consistent with the section on economic development and the decline in spanking in Chapter 17, *Cultural Norms on The Necessity of Spanking* and in this Chapter the decrease in spanking and the decrease in juvenile violence and violent crime are probably part of a civilizing process that has been going on for centuries (Elias, 1978; Pinker, 2011). One indication is that homicide rates have been declining since the late Middle Ages (Eisner, 2003, 2008). There are many reasons for the decrease (Elias, 1978; Pinker, 2011). One is that governments have assumed the responsibility for maintaining law and order. Vendettas and duels and other forms of *self-help justice* (Black, 1983) are no longer necessary. We now have police to deter offenders. Citizens can bring their grievances to courts for settlement. Although the existence of institutionalized means of maintaining order and adjudicating conflicts has been critical for the decrease in violence, many other factors have and are contributing to the decrease in interpersonal violence. We suggest that one of them is the way children are brought up. Treating children in ways that would now be considered child abuse was once common (DeMause, 1984). Over the centuries, children have been treated more and more humanely, including less use of spanking. Such children, in turn, are more likely to grow up to treat others more humanely and less violently.

The civilizing process is continuing because, as nations become more economically developed, they also tend to become more civilized in the sense used by Elias (1978), including less violence of many types including less violent child rearing (Pinker, 2011). We analyzed the International Dating Violence Study data on 32 nations (used for Chapters 3, 12, and 16). The nations ranged from low in economic development (such as Tanzania and South Africa) to high in economic development such as Sweden and the United States. They also differed in scores on a scale to measure the national average level of violent socialization. This scale consists of eight indicators of violent socialization, such as the percent in each nation who were told to hit back if someone hit or insulted them, the percent of students who were hit a lot by their mother or father when they were teenagers, and the percent who grew up in a family in which there was violence between the parents. The results shown in Chart 21.1 strongly support the idea that the more economically developed a nation, the less violently children are brought up. For example, Switzerland (CHE), the Netherlands (NDL), Sweden (SWE), and Belgium (BEL) in the lower right corner of the chart are all high in economic development and low in

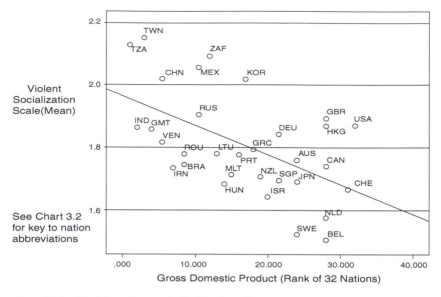

Chart 21.1   The More Economically Developed a Nation, the Less Violently Children Are Socialized

violent socialization. On the other hand, Great Britain (GBR), the United States (USA), and Hong Kong (HKG) are also high in economic development but are *above* average in violent socialization. Those cases illustrate why the correlation between economic development and violent socialization, although very high (.54) explains only 29% of the difference between nations in violent socialization. This is because economic development is only one of many things that influences violent socialization. Cases like the United Kingdom, United States, and Hong Kong that do not fit right on the trend line reflect the fact that many other national characteristics, not just the level of economic development, affect the degree to which children are brought up violently.

The results on the relation of economic development to less violent socialization are consistent with the *civilizing process* discussed previously (Eisner, 2003; Elias, 1978; Pinker, 2011). Human societies are gradually evolving to be more humane, including less violence. Violence is more and more being regarded as a problem rather than a virtue. Another example of this trend is a comparison of U.S. survey data that asked nationally representative samples of adult Americans if they agreed or disagreed that "When a boy is growing up, it's important for him to have a few fist fights." In 1968, 75% agreed (Owens & Straus, 1975). By 1995, the Gallup survey of U.S. parents described in Chapters 2 and 17 found that only 21% agreed. Because the 1968 survey included everyone age 18 or older and the 1995 survey was restricted to parents, the real decrease is probably not as great, but it is almost certain to be very large.

Seventy years ago, Montague (1941), and 40 years ago, Steinmetz and Straus (1973) argued that the family is the cradle of violence because it is where children first experience violence in the form of being hit by their parents and first observe violence between others in the form of parents and siblings hitting each other. That is also why we chose *The Primordial Violence* as the title for this book. It is a cruel irony that the institution that provides a child's first experience with love and support is also the institution that provides the child's first experience with violence. And, irony within irony, as we suggested previously, the fact that good parents do this for the morally correct purpose of producing a well-behaved child means that a child's first experience with violence is also an experience with the principle that violence is morally acceptable and is sometimes necessary in interpersonal relationships. We believe that learning the morality of violence through spanking by loving parents is an important part of the explanation for the high rates of violence in families and other spheres of life.

Of course, consistent with our repeated emphasis on multiple causation of almost all important individual and national characteristics, spanking is only one of many causes of violence and other crime. As a consequence, even if all parents stopped hitting their children, it would not mean the end of violence and other crime. Moreover, if there is a decrease, it is probably only one part of this century's long civilizing process described by Elias (1978, 1997) and Pinker (2011) that has reduced homicide rates in Europe to a 20th of what they were in the late Middle Ages (Eisner, 2003, 2008). Although less violent child rearing is only one aspect of the civilizing process, we suggest it is a crucial aspect.

The Prospects for Ending Spanking Worldwide

Despite the important reductions in violence resulting from the civilizing process, that process is far from complete. One seemingly small, but we think extremely important, part of the process that remains to be completed is ending violent socialization in the form of spanking. Spanking continues to be used by almost all parents in all but a fraction of the world's nations. Nevertheless, the movement away from spanking is accelerating. As was shown in Chapter 17, spanking is declining. Even in the United States, spanking has declined dramatically in the past 30 years for children of all ages except toddlers. The largest change has probably been in Sweden, which in 1979 was the first nation to legally ban spanking. A study of a Stockholm birth cohort born in the 1950s found that 94% of the parents spanked when these children were 3 years old. A third of them did it at least once a day. Moreover, there was not a single child in the cohort who was never spanked (Stattin et al., 1995). That is probably the situation in most of the world today. But Chart 21.2 shows the dramatic decrease in Sweden since spanking was banned in 1979 to only about 10%. Of course, the fact that 30 years after passage of the no-spanking law, at least 10% of Swedish parents were still hitting their children can be taken as support for the argument that spanking is inevitable (Nock, 2000). However, the same can be said for the fact that a certain percent of people do not always stop at stop signs. To imply, as Nock does, that there is therefore no point to prohibiting spanking is analogous to arguing that there is no point in laws requiring stopping at stop signs because, despite those laws, some people do not always stop.

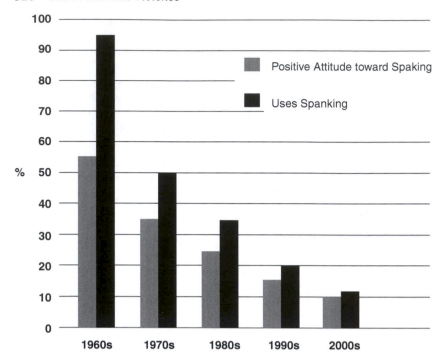

Source: Våld mot barn 2006-2007, The Swedish Child Welfare Foundation and Karlstad University

Chart 21.2   In Sweden Spanking Decreased from 90% to 10%

Modig, C. (2009). Never Violence—Thirty Years on from Sweden's Abolition of Spanking

There is unlikely to ever be a society without crime, and it is also unlikely that there will ever be a society without at least some parents hitting children, even when spanking is illegal and contrary to the beliefs and cultural norms of the population. Only time will tell if the rate of spanking in Sweden will decrease even more. However, even if spanking does not decline further, the decrease from 94% to 10% is an amazingly rapid social change in the course of only 30 years.

An important question is how much of the decrease in spanking in Sweden was the result of the no-spanking legislation. It is likely that this legislation, rather than being the prime cause of the decrease, crystallized and amplified a trend that reflected more general changes in Swedish society that have transformed the country from its extremely violent past in early modern Europe. Previous evidence of this long-term process was the 1928 law that prohibited corporal punishment in schools. That was a step in the evolutionary path toward the 1979 law prohibiting corporal punishment by parents (Bussmann et al., 2011; Durrant & Olsen, 1997; Giles-Sims & Lockhart 2005a, 2005b).

Legislation banning corporal punishment by teachers and by parents is both a reflection and a cause of the historical change toward less violent child rearing. Before such laws can be enacted, at least an influential portion of a society must believe that spanking is not appropriate in any circumstance. It seems that ending corporal punishment in schools is typically an early part of the evolutionary path leading to ending corporal punishment by parents. If so, the fact that many nations and just over one half of the states in the United States have prohibited corporal punishment in schools is a sign that the social evolution toward a less violent society is proceeding.

An almost opposite evolutionary perspective is exemplified by Nock (2000). Nock views spanking as part of human biological evolution, and therefore as something that cannot be changed. The past 100 years, and especially the past 30 years in Sweden, shows that even if there is a biological basis for spanking, social evolution can override an inherited predisposition to spank. The social evolution of Sweden in respect to humane treatment of children is an example of what is now occurring worldwide. Even Great Britain, like the United States, a bastion of support for spanking, has now prohibited corporal punishment in schools. Many other nations have ended corporal punishment in schools. This includes all 27 nations in the European Union. Moreover, among the almost one half of U.S. states that still permit corporal punishment in schools, many local school districts have banned it. These are usually urban school districts. Therefore, because the population is now primarily urban, a U.S. state can permit teachers to hit children, only a small percent of the children in the state attend schools in a *community* where this is permitted.

As for spanking by parents, by 2011, 32 other nations had followed the Swedish example and prohibited parents hitting children to correct misbehavior (Center for Effective Discipline, 2010): Austria, Bulgaria, Costa Rica, Croatia, Cyprus, Denmark, Finland, Germany, Greece, Hungary, Iceland, Israel, Kenya, Latvia, Liechtenstein, Luxembourg, Moldova, the Netherlands, New Zealand, Norway, Poland, Portugal, Romania, Spain, Tunisia, Ukraine, Uruguay, and Venezuela. This list, however, overstates the extent of change because there are large differences between nations in what is being done to implement the ban. Some have only recently changed the law, and some that changed it previously have done little to inform the public. The study by Bussmann et al. (2011) of four nations in Europe shows that st eps to inform the public about the law makes a large difference in the extent to which corporal punishment actually decreases. Sweden was not only the first nation to ban spanking, it was and is the nation with the most extensive public information effort, including television and radio announcements, and information directed at children in schools and in notices on all milk cartons informing children that parents are not allowed to hit them (Janson et al., 2011). The extensive effort to inform children and parents and to help parents who spank is probably an important part of the explanation for the decline in spanking from almost all parents to 10%.

The European Union and the United Nations committee responsible for administering the Convention of the Rights of the Child has interpreted that Convention as precluding use of spanking (Newell, 2011). Bit by bit, the committee is encouraging the member nations to end all use of spanking, and bit by bit, this is happening, usually starting with ending corporal punishment in schools.

The Prospects for Ending Spanking in the United States

The United States is among the most resistant of advanced industrialized nations to the idea of taking active steps to eliminate spanking by parents. This is indicated by a high percent of the public and professionals who continue to think that spanking is sometimes necessary (see Chapters 1 and 17). Nevertheless, change is underway as is also shown in Chapter 17. Corporal punishment is now prohibited in most American schools, and as mentioned previously, we think that prohibiting corporal punishment in schools is part of the process that is likely to eventually lead to prohibiting spanking by parents.

A few scholars are turning their attention to the legal aspects of *ending* spanking by parents (e.g., Bitensky, 1998; Pollard, 2003). However, consistent with the national consensus that spanking is sometimes necessary, the focus is on clarifying the conditions under which spanking is a "reasonable use of force" (Cope, 2010; Lambelet Coleman, Dodge, & Campbell, 2010). This seems to us to be a means of strengthening the legal basis for spanking.

Although there has been no decrease in the percent of U.S. parents who spank and slap toddlers, as shown in Chapter 17, far fewer older children are hit now than a generation ago. A U.S. branch of the organization *End Physical Punishment of Children* was established in 1989, under the name of the *Center for Effective Discipline.* It has sponsored activities such as Spank-Out Day in a number of communities. It maintains a website that informs the public about spanking and progress in ending spanking (www.stophitting.com). Three other initiatives and their websites are:

- Children Are Unbeatable (www.childrenareunbeatable.org.uk)
- End All Corporal Punishment of Children (www.endcorporalpunishment. org/index.html)
- Positive Parenting (www.positiveparenting.com/index.html)

Even among Blacks, which is a segment of the population that is highly committed to the necessity of spanking (Chung et al., 2009; Taylor, Hamvas, Rice et al., 2011), the situation is changing. The Baby College program of the Harlem Children's Zone, for example, emphasizes the importance of using verbal discipline instead of corporal punishment (www.hcz.org/programs/early-childhood).

As shown in Chapter 1, child development textbooks present little or none of the research on spanking and its harmful effects. An example of one that does discuss the adverse effects of spanking is *Infants and Children* (Berk, 2004). It provides two pages on spanking, which is more than most child development textbooks. Moreover, it is the only child development textbook we have found that cites Gershoff's meta-analysis showing that spanking is associated with many problem behaviors. But it does not discuss the pros and cons of spanking, much less recommend or even discuss the idea that children should *never* be spanked, nor do any of the other books we examined.

Nevertheless, current child development textbooks and most books of advice to parents no longer recommend spanking as they did in the early 20th century. Most of parental advice books now follow the lead of Spock and advise parents to use other modes of correction, and in respect to spanking, to "avoid it if you can." Unfortunately, as explained in Chapter 18 on why so many parents continue to spank, because of the low ability of 2-year-olds to control their own behavior, "avoid it if you can" turns out to be the equivalent of advising parents to spank, resulting in the 94% rate shown in Chapter 2. The message needs to be never spank. A small, but growing number of those who advise parents now say that.

In 2005, the annual town meeting of Brookline, Massachusetts (a politically liberal suburb of Boston) passed the following resolution by a narrow margin after a heated debate that lasted until after midnight. The article states:

- WHEREAS the nation's pediatric professionals and children's advocates advise against the use of corporal punishment of children;
- WHEREAS research shows that corporal punishment teaches children that hitting is an acceptable way of dealing with problems and that violence works;
- WHEREAS there are effective alternatives to corporal punishment of children;
- WHEREAS national surveys show that corporal punishment is common, and 25% of infants are hit before they are 6 months old;
- WHEREAS adopting national policies against corporal punishment has been an effective public education measure in various nations;
- WHEREAS accumulated research supports the conclusion that corporal punishment is an ineffective discipline strategy with children of all ages and, furthermore, that it is sometimes dangerous;
- WHEREAS studies show that corporal punishment often produces in its victims anger, resentment, low self-esteem, anxiety, helplessness, and humiliation;
- WHEREAS research demonstrates that the more children hit, the greater the likelihood that they will engage in aggression and antisocial behavior as children imitate what they see adults doing;
- WHEREAS in a study of 8,000 families, children who experience frequent corporal punishment are more likely to physically attack siblings, develop less adequately developed consciences, experience adult depression, and physically attack a spouse as an adult;
- WHEREAS, according to human rights documents, children, like adults, have the right not to be physically assaulted;
- WHEREAS the U.N. Committee on the Rights of the Child has consistently stated that persisting legal and social acceptance of corporal punishment is incompatible with the U.N. Convention on the Rights of the Child;
- WHEREAS this resolution is supported by the Massachusetts Society for the Prevention of Cruelty to Children, Massachusetts Citizens for Children, and the Massachusetts Chapter of the National Association of Social Workers;

- BE IT HEREBY RESOLVED that Town Meeting encourages parents and caregivers of children to refrain from the use of corporal punishment and to use alternative nonviolent methods of child discipline and management with an ultimate goal of mutual respect between parent and child.

Although the Brookline vote was a landmark, it remains the only jurisdiction in the United States that states that parents should not spank. Another landmark change occurred in 2004. That year, the General Conference of the United Methodist Church passed a resolution declaring that "the United Methodist Church encourages its members to adopt discipline methods that do not include corporal punishment of their children" (Swan, 2004). The significance of this resolution is threefold: First, United Methodist is the second largest Protestant church in the United States. Second, they are the first denomination in the United States to formally oppose spanking. Third, Methodism is the church of John Wesley, whose mother proudly wrote that in bringing up her children "When they turned a year old . . ., they were taught to fear the rod and to cry softly" (cited in Miller & Swanson, 1958, p. 10). That was typical of the violent era into which John Wesley was born. Today's Methodists, as well as other Americans, are living in a much less violent era. Their rejection of spanking reflects the less violent and more humane society that enabled the resolution to be passed. It is part of the civilizing process we mentioned that is likely to extend that trend and help to eventually bring about a more nonviolent society.

Blacks are another group with a strong cultural commitment to the necessity of spanking. But as was shown in Chapter 17 by Chart 17.3, the percent who believe spanking is necessary is declining, even though not as much as among Whites. Both the Black cultural commitment to spanking and the social evolution of humane standards for interpersonal relations are illustrated by the experience of one Black father who decided not to spank (Toure, 2011). He said, "A few years ago, when I knew I was heading toward becoming a parent, I began to think about what sort of parent I wanted to be. And I began to weigh whether or not I should spank. I grew up in the 1970s and was spanked—quite a bit. I think the vast majority of Black children of my generation were spanked, and nearly all the Black kids in my parents' generation were. Spanking seemed like a Black cultural imperative: Black people tell one another, 'Spare the rod, spoil the child.'" His commentary concluded that he now has two children and does not spank them. He said, "I think the home should not be a place of violence. The argument [of one of his friends] won me over."

Although U.S. culture still strongly supports spanking, and most parents of toddlers still spank, the data in Chapter 17 on the decline in the use of spanking and the discussion in the previous section indicate that important change is taking place. Child development texts are beginning to discuss the negative consequences of spanking. The United Methodist Church resolution advising parents not to spank garnered enough votes to pass. A small but growing number of parenting advice books have joined the previously lone voice of Leach (1977) in advising parents not to spank at all. We believe that the United States will eventually follow the pattern in other nations, which began with the end of corporal punishment in schools and a decline in public approval of spanking, followed by laws to discourage and later laws to ban parents spanking. These laws in turn are likely to further reduce both approval and use of corporal punishment.

Will Never Spanking Result In A Nation With Kids Out Of Control?

As we pointed out, Sweden is an important example of this process because in the span of just a generation, there have been changes not just in the law, but also major changes in public opinion and parent practices regarding spanking. These changes demonstrate that contrary to those like Nock (2000) who believe that spanking has an unchangeable inherited basis, spanking can be greatly reduced, even if not completely eliminated, when a nation makes the effort to informing everyone (including children) that spanking is unacceptable and provides information and help in using nonviolent methods of correction and control.

Sweden is also an important case study, because the fear of so many defenders of spanking is that without spanking, parents will be unable to raise well-behaved children. Four Swedish studies (summarized in Durrant & Janson, 2005; Janson et al., 2011) found that no hitting did not mean no discipline. What it has meant is that parents correct misbehavior by nonviolent methods. As a consequence, instead of what many in Sweden feared in 1979, that Swedish children would be running wild, the opposite has happened. As we noted in the introduction to this chapter, behavior problems and crime by Swedish youth have *decreased.* Durrant (2000) compared rates from 1975–1979 with rates from 1992–1996 and found the following changes:

- Convicted of theft −21%
- Convicted of narcotics trafficking −51%
- Convicted of assault/aggravated assault +54%
- Convicted of rape −48%
- Consumer of alcohol −13%
- Tried drugs −28%
- Continue to use drugs −59%
- Suicide rate −20%

The only exception to lower rates since the ban on spanking is for assaults. However, the apparent increase reflects the effects of programs against bullying in schools that were introduced during this period. Durrant points out that "What was once considered common, even expected, behavior among young males is now defined as assault. School principals must now routinely report to the police any instances brought to their attention, including threats and minor assaults. The police, in turn, have no discretionary power in registering such reports; all are entered into the criminal statistics" (Durrant, 2000 p. 450).

When Sweden banned spanking in 1979, there was widespread concern that it would results in a nation with children running wild. The opposite has happened. This cannot be attributed to less spanking because it might be the result of changes in one or more of the many other causes of crime. But we can be certain that the reduction of spanking in Sweden did not lead to an increase in crime.

Is Ending Spanking Worth the Effort?

The value of trying to reduce or end spanking has been disputed by arguing that the effect size (as indicated by the correlation between spanking and harmful side effects) is so low that ending spanking would not make an important contribution to child well-being (Larzelere & Baumrind, 2010). Although the effect size is low, the history of public health efforts provides many examples of major gains based on eliminating or reducing risk factors with a low effect size.

A Low Effect Size Is Typical of Risk Factors for Child Well-Being

A low effect size (as indicated, for example, by a low correlation) is typical of the relation between any *single* aspect of what parents do and the child's development. It could almost not be otherwise because, as pointed out in Chapter 1, there are multiple influences on how a child develops. Therefore, no single aspect of what parents do can account for much of the difference between children in variables such as delinquency, depression, and IQ. For example, cognitive stimulation of a child by parents, such as reading to the child, has been shown by many rigorous studies to be related to the child's later cognitive ability. However, the table of regression coefficients in Straus and Paschall (2009) predicting the child's later cognitive ability shows that the effect size for the relation of cognitive stimulation to cognitive ability, like the correlation for the relation of spanking to cognitive ability, is low. Despite this, educators and developmental psychologists strongly urge reading to children, as they should. Similar low correlations have been found by a large body of research on the risk and protective factors that have been the focus of national prevention and treatment programs for many physical health and mental health problems. Chart 21.3 presents some of these correlations. It shows that the effect size for spanking is low, but higher than the effect size for 8 of the 10 risk factors in the chart, each of which are the basis for national prevention efforts.

Why is the low effect size for the harmful effects of corporal punishment used to argue that ending corporal punishment is not worth the effort, but the even lower effect size for the relation of childhood exposure to lead paint to lower IQ is not seen as making the effort to eliminate lead paint not worth the effort? It is not because the effect size is low; it is because belief in the necessity of spanking is so deeply ingrained in American culture. A presumed necessity of using lead paint is not part of American cultural beliefs and norms, so the public believes those research results.

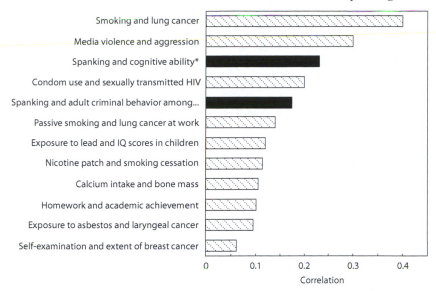

Chart 21.3 Comparison of the Effect of Spanking with Effects of Other Risk Factors
*Partial correlations from Chapter 10 and 15. Other Correlations are from Bushman & Anderson, 2001.

Cumulative Effect of a Small Risk Factor Can Be Large

A critical fact that is ignored by those who argue that ending spanking would not make an important contribution to child well-being is the wide prevalence of spanking. Because over 90% of American children are spanked as toddlers, the effect of ending corporal punishment in reducing the percent of the population who experience psychological problems or commit crimes can be much larger than the reduction that could occur from ending physical abuse, even though the effect size for abuse is 7 times greater than for spanking. This is because at least 100 times more children have experienced corporal punishment than have been physically abused. Thus, the cumulative benefit for children of ending corporal punishment is likely to be very large.

The importance of the cumulative effect is a well-established principle in public health research and intervention. A risk factor that increases the probability of a health problem by only a small amount (such as spanking) can have more impact on public health if it applies to a much larger part of the population than a risk factor that, if present, increases the probability of a harmful effect by a large amount (such as physical abuse) but which applies to only a small percent of people (Rose, 1985; Rosenthal, 1984). The following hypothetical example shows that ending spanking could do more than reducing physical abuse to reduce the probability of being arrested for a serious crime as an adult.

- Epidemiological studies such as the study in Chapter 2, suggest that over 90% of the 70 million U.S. children experienced spanking, although there is great variation in frequency and severity. This compares with perhaps 1 million who experience physical abuse (i.e., about 1%).

- The study by Afifi et al. (2006) described in Chapter 19 on spanking and crime of a U.S. nationally representative sample. They found that spanking was associated with 2.2% more cases of externalizing problems such as antisocial personality, whereas physical abuse was associated with 15.3% more cases. Thus, the adverse effect of physical abuse is 7 times greater than the adverse effect of spanking.
- Based on these data, ending all spanking could reduce antisocial behavior problems by: 0.022×70 million $= 1,540,000$ fewer cases.
- Ending all physical abuse could reduce antisocial behavior by: 0.153×1 million $= 153,000$ fewer cases
- Thus ending spanking could be associated with a 10 times greater decrease in antisocial behavior than ending physical abuse.

Because child antisocial behavior is a risk factor for crime, the example above suggests that reducing spanking could substantially reduce crime. However, that assumes that parents continue to monitor and correct misbehavior, except not by hitting the child. That is what happened in Sweden. Four Swedish studies found that no hitting did not mean no discipline (Durrant & Janson, 2005). It has meant correcting misbehavior by nonviolent methods, with many benefits for children, families, and society, as will be summarized in the next section.

Ending Spanking Is Needed to Reduce Physical Abuse

Ending spanking could not only have a positive impact on the majority of children who experience spanking, but as we pointed out earlier, it is also a crucial step in ending child physical abuse. Although the percent of spankings that escalate into physical abuse is minute, ending spanking is crucial for reducing child physical abuse because about two thirds of cases of physical abuse known to child protective services are the result of spanking that has escalated out of control (Gil, 1970; Kadushin & Martin, 1981; Trocmé, Tourigny, et al. 2003). As pointed out previously, the meta-analysis by Gershoff (2002) included 10 studies that investigated the relationship between spanking and physical abuse. All 10 studies found a relationship, as did Straus & Yodanis (2001). Thus, ending spanking and preventing physical abuse are part of the same effort. When parents no longer spank to correct misbehavior, the number of instances in which spanking escalates beyond this currently acceptable level of violence against children will decrease.

Summary and Conclusions

The potential benefits of a world without spanking are suggested by the 15 harmful side effects of spanking found by the research conducted for this book. These are summarized below. Given the millions of children who experience spanking in almost all nations, the results of this research suggest that reducing the violent child rearing that goes under the euphemism of spanking could result in a world with:

- Less antisocial behavior and delinquency as a child and as a young adult (Chapters 6, 7, 16, and 19).
- Less approval of other forms of violence such as the belief that torture is sometimes justified to obtain information critical for national defense, or that there are occasions when it is justified to slap a wife or husband (Chapters 5, 9, 12, and 13).
- Less impulsiveness and more self-control (Chapters 7 and 9).
- Better parent-child relationships (Chapters 8 and 9).
- Less risky sexual behavior as a teenager (Chapter 9).
- Less juvenile delinquency (Chapter 8).
- Less crime perpetrated as an adult (Chapters 12 through 16 and 19).
- Higher national average mental ability (Chapter 10).
- Greater probability of graduating from college (Chapter 11).
- Lower probability of depression (Chapter 12).
- Less violence against marital, cohabiting, and dating partners (Chapters 12, 13, 14).
- Less violence against nonfamily persons (Chapter 14).
- Less physical abuse of children (Chapter 14).
- Less drug abuse (Chapter 14).
- Less sexual coercion and physically forced sex (Chapter 16).

Ending spanking can reduce but not end, these personal and social problems because, as explained in the section on risk and protective factors in Chapter 1, spanking is only one of the many causes of these problems. Nevertheless, the studies in this book and the many other studies cited, makes it reasonable to think that a major reduction in spanking is likely to result in a substantial reduction in psychological problems and violence and other crime. If, for example, reducing spanking resulted in as little as a 10% reduction in these problems, that would be a profound benefit for the 10% who are spared these problems. There would also be collateral benefits. A much greater percentage would be spared the pain of being victimized by, interacting with, or caring for those with criminal behavior or psychological problems such as depression. An even larger number would be spared the trauma of having a family member victimized. The society as a whole is likely to be spared some of the economic costs of mental health treatment, crime, and prisons. Although it is impossible to know the percentages the research suggests that, in addition to many other benefits, such as a closer bond between parents and children, a society in which parents never spank is likely to be a society with fewer psychological problems and less violence and other crime.

A world without spanking is likely to have its own problems, but we believe the results from the last 50 years of research on spanking provide a basis for believing that the net effect will be a more humane world, with fewer psychological problems, better human relationships, and less violence and other crime.

Legal prohibition of spanking is an important step in reducing spanking. However, it is important to recognize that in Sweden, the nation that has made the largest change, this was accomplished by legislation setting a national standard and by informing and helping parents, not by criminal penalties. If legal changes in other nations seek to reduce spanking by punishing parents who spank rather than by informing and helping parents to correct children's misbehavior nonviolently, it would be inconsistent with the changes in society and the humanitarian goals that underlie the movement away from violent child rearing.

References

Abbey, A., & McAuslan, P. (2004). A longitudinal examination of male college students' perpetration of sexual assault. *Journal of Consulting and Clinical Psychology, 72,* 747–756.

Abma, J., Driscoll, A., & Moore, K. (1998). Young women's degree of control over first intercourse: An exploratory analysis. *Family Planning Perspectives, 30*(1), 12–18.

Acker, M. M., & O'Leary, S. G. (1988). Effects of consistent and inconsistent feedback on inappropriate child behavior. *Behavior Therapy, 19,* 619–624.

Afifi, T. O., Brownridge, D. A., Cox, B. J., & Sareen, J. (2006). Physical punishment, childhood abuse and psychiatric disorders. *Child Abuse & Neglect, 30*(10), 1093–1103.

Agnew, R. (1993). Why do they do it? An examination of the intervening mechanisms between "social control" variables and delinquency. *Journal of Research in Crime and Delinquency, 30*(3), 245–266.

Akers, R. L., & Sellers, C. S. (2008). *Criminological theories: Introduction, evaluation, and application* (5th ed.). New York, NY: Oxford University Press.

The Alan Guttmacher Institute. (2004). *U.S. teenage pregnancy statistics: Overall trends, trends by race and ethnicity, and state-by-state information.* New York, NY: Author.

Aldrich, J. H., & Nelson, F. D. (1984). *Linear probability, logit and probit models.* Newberry Park, CA: Sage.

Alvy, K. T. (1987). *Black parenting: Strategies for training.* New York, NY: Irvington Publishers.

Alvy, K. T., & Marigna, M. (1987). *Effective black parenting.* Studio City, CA: Center for the Improvement of Child Caring.

Ambati, B. K., Ambati, J., & Rao, A. M. (1998). Corporal punishment and antisocial behavior. *Archive of Pediatric and Adolescent Medicine, 152,* 303–309.

American Academy of Pediatrics. (1998). Guidance for effective discipline (RE9740). *Pediatrics, 101*(4), 723–728.

American Psychiatric Association. (1994). *Diagnostic and statistical manual of mental disorders* (4th ed.). Washington, DC: Author.

American Psychological Association and American Academy of Pediatrics. (1995). *Raising children to resist violence: What you can do.* Elk Grove Village, IL: American Academy of Pediatrics Division of Publications.

Anderson, C. A., Benjamin, A. J., Wood, P. K., & Bonacci, A. M. (2006). Development and testing of the Velicer attitudes towards violence scale: Evidence of a four-factor model. *Aggressive Behavior, 32*(2), 122–136.

Anderson, E. (1999). *Code of the street: Decency, violence, and the moral life of the inner city.* New York, NY: Norton.

Anderson, K. A., & Anderson, D. E. (1976). Psychologists and spanking. *Journal of Clinical Child Psychology, 5*(2), 46–49.

Anderson, P. B., & Struckman-Johnson, C. (Eds.). (1998). *Sexually aggressive women: Current perspectives and controversies.* New York, NY: Guilford Press.

Annerbäck, E. M., Wingren, G., Svedin, C. G., & Gustafsson, P. A. (2010). Prevalence and characteristics of child physical abuse in Sweden—Findings from a population-based youth survey. *Acta Pædiatrica, 99*(8), 1229–1236.

Annie E. Casey Foundation. (2006). *Kids count data book: State profiles of child well-being.* Baltimore, MD: Author.

Ansara, D. L., & Hindin, M. J. (2009). Perpetration of intimate partner aggression by men and women in the Philippines: Prevalence and associated factors. *Journal of Interpersonal Violence, 24*(9), 1579–1590.

Archer, D., & Gartner, R. (1984). *Violence and crime in cross-national perspective.* New Haven, CT: Yale University Press.

Archer, J. (1999). Assessment of the reliability of the conflict tactics scales: A meta-analytic review. *Journal of Interpersonal Violence, 14*(12), 1263–1289.

Archer, J. (2000). Sex differences in aggression between heterosexual partners: A meta-analytic review. *Psychological Bulletin, 126*(5), 651–680.

Archer, J. (2002). Sex differences in physically aggressive acts between heterosexual partners: A meta-analytic review. *Aggression and Violent Behavior, 7*(4), 313–351.

Arcus, D. (2002). School shooting fatalities and school corporal punishment: A look at the states. *Aggressive Behavior, 28,* 173–183.

Associated Press. (1995, September 23). Judge takes off belt, orders grandmother to give teen a whipping. *The Union Leader,* p. D10.

Aucoin, K. J., Frick, P. J., & Bodin, S. D. (2006). Corporal punishment and child adjustment. *Journal of Applied Developmental Psychology, 27*(6), 527–541.

Azrin, N. H., & Holz, W. C. (1966). Punishment. In W. K. Honig (Ed.), *Operant behavior: Areas of research and application* (pp. 380–447). New York, NY: Appelton-Century-Crofts.

Bachman, J. G. (1967). *Youth in transition.* Ann Harbor, MI: Institute for Social Research, University of Michigan.

Bailey, J. A., Hill, K. G., Oesterle, S., & Hawkins, J. D. (2009). Parenting practices and problem behavior across three generations: Monitoring, harsh discipline, and drug use in the intergenerational transmission of externalizing behavior. *Developmental Psychology, 45*(5), 1214–1226.

Bailey, W. C. (1998). Deterrence, brutalization, and the death penalty: Another examination of Oklahoma's return to capital punishment. *Criminology, 36*(4), 711–734.

Baker, P. C., Keck, C. K., Mott, F. L., & Quinlan, S. V. (1993). *NLSY child handbook: A guide to the 1986–1990 National Longitudinal Survey of Youth Child Data* (Rev. ed.). Columbus: The Ohio State University, Center for Human Resource Research.

Baker, R. K., & Ball, S. J. (1969). *Mass media and violence: A report to the National Commission on the causes and prevention of violence.* Washington, DC: Government Printing Office.

Bandura, A. (1973). *Aggression: A social learning analysis.* Englewood Cliffs, NJ: Prentice-Hall.

Bandura, A. (1977). Self-efficacy: Toward a unifying theory of behavioral change. *Psychological Review, 84,* 191–215.

Bank, L., Forgatch, M. S., Patterson, G. R., & Fetrow, R. A. (1993). Parenting practices of single mothers: Mediators of negative contextual factors. *Journal of Marriage and the Family,* 371–384.

Banks, J. B. (2002). Childhood discipline: Challenges for clinicians and parents. *American Family Physician, 66*(8), 1447–1452.

Banyard, V. L., Ward, S. K., Cohn, E. S., Plante, E. G., Moorhead, C., & Walsh, W. (2007). Unwanted sexual contact on campus: A comparison of women's and men's experiences. *Violence and Victims, 22,* 52–70.

Barkin, S., Scheindlin, B., Ip, E. H., Richardson, I., & Finch, S. (2007). Determinants of Parental Discipline Practices: A National Sample From Primary Care Practices. *Clinical Pediatrics, 46*(1), 64-69. doi: 10.1177/0009922806292644

Barnett, D., Kidwell, S. L., & Leung, K. H. (1998). Parenting and preschooler attachment among low-income urban African American families. *Child Development, 69,* 1657–1671.

Baron, L., & Straus, M. A. (1987). Four theories of rape: A macro sociological analysis. *Social Problems, 34*(5), 468–488.

Baron, L., & Straus, M. A. (1988). Cultural and economic sources of homicide in the United States. *The Sociological Quarterly, 29*(3), 371–190.

Baron, L., & Straus, M. A. (1989). *Four theories of rape in American society: A state-level analysis.* New Haven, CT: Yale University Press.

Baron, L., Straus, M. A., & Jaffee, D. (1988). Legitimate violence, violent attitudes, and rape: A test of the cultural spillover theory. In R. A. Prentky & V. L. Quinsey (Eds.), *Human sexual aggression current perspectives* (Vol. 528, pp. 79–110). New York, NY: Annals of the New York Academy of Sciences.

Basile, K. C., Chen, J., Black, M. C., & Saltzman, L. E. (2007). Prevalence and characteristics of sexual violence victimization among U.S. adults, 2001–2003. *Violence and Victims, 22,* 437–448.

Baumeister, R. F. (2001). Violent pride. *Scientific American, 284*(4), 6.

Baumeister, R. F., Heatherton, T. F., & Tice, D. M. (1993). When ego threats lead to self-regulation failure: Negative consequences of high self-esteem. *Journal of Personality and Social Psychology, 64*(1).

Baumrind, D. (1972). An exploratory study of socialization effects on black children: Some Black-White comparisons. *Child Development, 43,* 261–267.

Baumrind, D. (1991a). The influence of parenting style on adolescent competence and substance use. *Journal of Early Adolescence, 11,* 56–95.

Baumrind, D. (1991b). Parenting styles and adolescent development. In R. Lerner, A. C. Petersen, & J. Brooks-Gunn (Eds.), *The encyclopedia on adolescence* (pp. 758–772). New York, NY: Garland.

Baumrind, D. (1992a). *Family factors applied to child maltreatment.* Paper presented at the Study Panel on Child Abuse and Neglect Research, National Academy of Sciences.

Baumrind, D. (1992b). [Personal communication].

Baumrind, D. (1996). Parenting. The Discipline of controversy revisited. *Family Relations, 45,* 405–414.

Baumrind, D., Larzelere, R. E., & Cowan, P. A. (2002). Ordinary physical punishment: Is it harmful? Comment on Gershoff (2002). *Psychological Bulletin, 128*(4), 580–590.

Bavolek, S. J. (1992–2006). *The nurturing parenting programs.* Park City, UT: Family Development Resources.

Bayley, N., & Schaefer, E. S. (1964). Correlations of maternal and child behaviors with the development of mental abilities: Data from the Berkeley Growth Study. *Monographs of the Society for Research in Child Development, 29*(6), 1–80.

Beach, S. R. H., Sandeen, E. E., & O'Leary, K. D. (1990). *Depression in marriage.* New York, NY: Guilford Press.

Bean, A. W., & Roberts, M. W. (1981). The effect of time-out release contingencies on changes in child non-compliance. *Journal of Abnormal Child Psychology, 91,* 95–105.

Beauchaine, T. P., Webster-Stratton, C., & Reid, M. J. (2005). Mediators, moderators, and predictors of 1-year outcomes among children treated for early-onset conduct problems: A latent growth curve analysis. *Journal of Consulting and Clinical Psychology, 73*(3), 371–388.

Belsky, J. (1991). Psychological maltreatment: Definitional limitations and unstated assumptions. *Development and Psychopathology, 3*(1), 31–36.

Bender, H. L., Allen, J. P., McElhaney, K. B., Antonishak, J. M., Moore, C. M., Kelly, H. O., & Davis, S. M. (2007). Use of harsh physical discipline and developmental outcomes in adolescence. *Development and Psychopathology, 19*(1), 227–242.

Bennett, R. (2006). Majority of parents admit to smacking children. Retrieved from http://www.timesonline.co.uk/tol/news/uk/article644804.ece

Berger, A. M., Knutson, J. F., Mehm, J. G., & Perkins, K. A. (1988). The self-report of punitive childhood experiences of young adults and adolescents. *Child Abuse & Neglect, 12*, 251-262.

Berk, L. A. (2004). *Infants and children* (5th ed.). Boston, MA: Allyn and Bacon.

Berkowitz, L. (1983). Adversively stimulated aggression: Some parallels and differences in research with animals and humans. *American Psychologist, 388*, 1135–1144.

Berkowitz, L. (1993). *Aggression: Its causes, consequences, and control.* New York, NY: McGraw-Hill.

Berlin, L. J., Ispa, J. M., Fine, M. A., Malone, P. S., Brooks-Gunn, J., Brady-Smith, C. . . . Bai, Y. (2009). Correlates and consequences of spanking and verbal punishment for low-income White, African American, and Mexican American toddlers. *Child Development, 80*(5), 1403–1420.

Berliner, L., & Elliott, D. M. (1996). Sexual abuse of children. In J. Briere, L. Berliner, J. A. Buckley, C. Jenny, & T. Reid (Eds.), *The APSAC handbook on child maltreatment* (p. 51). Thousand Oaks, CA: Sage.

Berry, E. H., Shillington, A. M., Peak, T., & Hohman, M. M. (2000). Multi-ethnic comparison of risk and protective factors for adolescent pregnancy. *Child and Adolescent Social Work Journal, 17*(2), 79–96.

Bitensky, S. H. (1998). Spare the rod, embrace our humanity: Toward a new legal regime prohibiting corporal punishment of children. *University of Michigan Journal of Law Reform, 31*(2), 354–391.

Black, D. (1983). Crime as social control. *American Sociological Review, 48*, 34–45.

Black, R. (2010). Spanking makes kids perform better in school, helps them become more successful: Study. *New York Daily News.* Retrieved from http://www.nydailynews.com /lifestyle/2010/01/04/2010–01–04_spanking_makes_kids_perform_better_in_school_study .html

Blake, J. (2011). Differential parental investment: Its effects on child quality and status attainment. In J. B. Lancaster, J. Altmann, A. S. Rossi, & L. R. Sherrod (Eds.), *Parenting across the life span* (pp. 351–375). New Brunswick, NJ: Aldine Transaction.

Blakeslee, S. (1995, August 29). In brain's early growth, timetable may be crucial. *The New York Times,* p. C1.

Blumenthal, M. D., Kahn, R. L., Andrew, F. M., & Head, K. B. (1972). *Justifying violence: Attitudes of American men.* Ann Arbor, MI: University of Michigan.

Bodovski, K., & Youn, M. J. (2010). Love, discipline and elementary school achievement: The role of family emotional climate. *Social Science Research, 39*(4), 585–595.

Bolton, F. G., & MacEachron, A. (1987). Assessing child maltreatment risk in the recently divorced parent-child relationship. *Journal of Family Violence, 1*(3), 259–275.

Bookwala, J., Frieze, I. H., Smith, C., & Ryan, K. (1992). Predictors of dating violence: A multivariate analysis. *Violence and Victims, 7*(4), 297–311.

Bordin, I. A., Duarte, C. S., Peres, C. A., Nascimento, R., Curto, B. M., & Paula, C. S. (2009). Severe physical punishment: Risk of mental health problems for poor urban children in Brazil. *Bulletin of the World Health Organization, 87*(5), 336–344.

Boutwell, B. B., Franklin, C. A., Barnes, J. C., & Beaver, K. M. (2011). Physical punishment and childhood aggression: The role of gender and gene–environment interplay. *Aggressive Behavior, 37,* 1–10.

Boyer, J. L., & Guthrie, L. (1985). Assessment and treatment of the suicidal patient. In E. E. Beckham & W. R. Leber (Eds.), *Handbook of depression: Treatment, assessment, and research.* Homewood, IL: Dorsey Press.

Brezina, T. (1998). Adolescent maltreatment and delinquency: The question of intervening processes. *Journal of Research in Crime and Delinquency, 35*(1), 71–99.

Brezina, T. (1999). Teenage violence toward parents as an adaptation to family strain—Evidence from a national survey of male adolescents. *Youth & Society, 30*(4), 416–444.

Briere, J., & Runtz, M. (1988). Multivariate correlates of childhood psychological and physical maltreatment among university women. *Child Abuse & Neglect, 12,* 331–341.

Bronfenbrenner, U. (Ed.). (1985). *Freedom and discipline across the decades.* Weinheim, West Germany: Beltz Berlag.

Brown, C. (1965). *Manchild in the promised land.* New York, NY: Macmillan.

Bruner, J. S., Matter, J., & Papanek, M. L. (1955). Breadth of learning as a function of drive level and mechanization. *Psychological Review, 62*(1), 1–10.

Bruning, J. L., & Kintz, B. L. (1987). *Computational handbook of statistics* (3rd ed.). Glenview, IL: HarperCollins.

Bryan, J. W., & Freed, F. W. (1982). Corporal punishment: Normative data and sociological and psychological correlates in a community college population. *Journal of Youth and Adolescence, 11,* 77–87.

Bugental, D. B., Johnston, C., New, M., & Silvester, J. (1998). Measuring parental attributions: Conceptual and methodological issues. *Journal of Family Psychology, 12*(4), 459–480.

Bugental, D. B., Martorell, G. A., & Barraza, V. (2003). The hormonal costs of subtle forms of infant maltreatment. *Hormones and Behavior, 43*(1), 237–244.

Bugental, D. B., Schwartz, A., & Lynch, C. (2010). Effects of an early family intervention on children's memory: The mediating effects of cortisol levels. *Mind, Brain, and Education, 4*(4), 159–170.

Buker, H. (2011). Formation of self-control: Gottfredson and Hirschi's general theory of crime and beyond. *Aggression and Violent Behavior, 16*(3), 265–276.

Bunting, L., Webb, M. A., & Healy, J. (2010). In two minds?—Parental attitudes toward physical punishment in the UK. *Children & Society, 24*(5), 359–370.

Bureau of Justice Statistics. (2001). Bureau of Justice Statistics homicide trends in the U.S. Retrieved from http://www.ojp.usdoj.gov/bjs/homicide/gender.htm

Burgess, A., Block, S., & Runyan, D. K. (2010). *Variation in acceptable child discipline practices by child age: Perspectives of medical and legal professionals.* Unpublished paper, Chapel Hill, NC: University of North Carolina.

Bursik, R. J. (1988). Social disorganization and theories of crime and delinquency: Problems and prospects. *Criminology, 26,* 519–551.

Burt, S. A., McGue, M., Krueger, R. F., & Iacono, W. G. (2007). Environmental contributions to adolescent delinquency: A fresh look at the shared environment. *Journal of Abnormal Child Psychology, 35*(5), 787–800.

Bushman, B. J., & Anderson, C. A. (2001). Media violence and the American public: Scientific facts versus media misinformation. *American Psychologist, 56*(6/7), 477-489.

Bussmann, K. D. (2004). Evaluating the subtle impact of a ban on corporal punishment of children in Germany. *Child Abuse Review, 13,* 292–311.

Bussmann, K. D., Erthal, C., & Schroth, A. (2011). Effects of banning corporal punishment in Europe: A five-nation comparison. In J. E. Durrant & A. B. Smith (Eds.), *Global pathways to abolishing physical punishment: Realizing children's rights* (pp. 299–322). New York, NY: Routledge.

Buzawa, E. S., & Buzawa, C. G. (2003). *Domestic violence: The criminal justice response* (3rd ed.). Thousand Oaks, CA: Sage.

Byrne, B. M. (2001). *Structural equation modeling with AMOS Basic concepts, application, and programming.* Mahwah, NJ: Erlbaum.

Caldwell, B., & Bradley, R. (1984). *Home observation for measurement of the environment.* Little Rock, AR: University of Arkansas.

Caldwell, C. (2008, January 27). Old-school economics: The transition to a new economy is over. Do our candidates know it? *New York Times Magazine,* p. 11.

Calvert, R. (1974). Criminal and civil liability in husband-wife assaults. In S. K. Steinmetz & M. A. Straus (Eds.), *Violence in the family* (Chapter 9). New York, NY: Harper and Row.

Capaldi, D. M., & Eddy, J. M. (2000). Improving children's long-term well-being by preventing antisocial behavior. In A. Buchanan & B. Hudson (Eds.), *Promoting children's emotional well-being* (pp. 209–229): London, England: Oxford University Press.

Capaldi, D. M., Kim, H. K., & Shortt, J. W. (2007). Observed initiation and reciprocity of physical aggression in young, at-risk couples. *Journal of Family Violence, 22*(2), 101–111.

Capaldi, D. M., Shortt, J. W., Kim, H. K., Wilson, J., Crosby, L., & Tucci, S. (2009). Official incidents of domestic violence: Types, injury, and associations with nonofficial couple aggression. *Violence and Victims, 24*(4), 502–519.

Carrado, M., George, M. J., Loxam, E., Jones, L., & Templar, D. (1996). Aggression in British heterosexual relationships: A descriptive analysis. *Aggressive Behavior, 22,* 401–415.

Carroll, J. C. (1977). The intergenerational transmission of family violence: The long-term effects of aggressive behavior. *Aggressive Behavior, 3*(3), 289–299.

Carson, B. A. (1986). *Parents who don't spank: Deviation in the legitimization of physical force* (Unpublished doctoral dissertation). University of New Hampshire, Durham, NH.

Cascardi, M., & Vivian, D. (1995). Context for specific episodes of marital violence: Gender and severity of violence differences. *Journal of Family Violence, 10*(3), 265–293.

Cast, A. D., Schweingruber, D., & Berns, N. (2006). Childhood physical punishment and problem solving in marriage. *Journal of Interpersonal Violence, 21*(2), 244–261.

Catron, T. F., & Masters, J. C. (1993). Mothers' and children's conceptualization of corporal punishment. *Child Development, 64*(1), 1815–1828.

Center for Effective Discipline. (2010). *Discipline and the law.* Retrieved from http://www.stophitting.com/index.php

Centers for Disease Control and Prevention. (2010a). Adverse childhood experiences reported by adults—Five states, 2009. *Morbidity and Mortality Weekly Report, 59*(49), 1609–1613.

Centers for Disease Control and Prevention. (2010b). Youth risk behavior surveillance—United States, 2009. *Surveillance Summaries, MMWR 2010, 59,* (No. SS-5).

Chaffin, M., Silovsky, J. F., Funderburk, B., Valle, L. A., Brestan, E. V., Balachova, T., . . . Bonner, B. L. (2004). Parent-child interaction therapy with physically abusive parents: Efficacy for reducing future abuse reports. *Journal of Consulting and Clinical Psychology, 72*(3), 500–510.

Chan, K. L., & Straus, M. A. (2008). Prevalence and correlates of physical assault on dating partners: A comparison between Hong Kong and the US samples. *The Open Social Science Journal, 1,* 5–14.

Chan, K. L., Straus, M. A., Brownridge, D. A., Tiwari, A., & Leung, W. C. (2008). Prevalence of dating partner violence and suicidal ideation among male and female university students worldwide. *Journal of Midwifery and Women's Health, 53*(6), 529–537.

Chapple, C. L., Tyler, K. A., & Bersani, B. E. (2005). Child neglect and adolescent violence: Examining the effects of self-control and peer rejection. *Violence and Victims, 20*(1), 39–53.

Charney, E., & Weissman, M. M. (1988). Epidemiology of depressive and manic syndromes. In A. Georgotas & R. Cancro (Eds.), *Depression and Mania* (pp. 26–52). New York, NY: Elsevier Science Publishing.

Checks, J. F. (1979). Classroom discipline: Where are we now? *Education, 100,* 134–137.

Children's Institute International. (1999). Breaking the spanking habit: Survey Sponsored by Children's Institute International, conducted by Penn, Schoen & Berland, Inc., 981 adults nationwide, late April through mid-May. Los Angeles, CA.

Chung, E. K., Mathew, L., Rothkopf, A. C., Elo, I. T., Coyne, J. C., & Culhane, J. F. (2009). Parenting attitudes and infant spanking: The influence of childhood experiences. *Pediatrics, 124*(2), E278–E286.

Cicchetti, D. V. (1972). Extension of multiple-range tests to interaction tables in the analysis of variance: A rapid approximate solution. *Psychological bulletin, 77,* 405–408.

Cohen, C. P. (1984). Freedom from corporal punishment: One of the human rights of children. *New York Law School Human Rights Annual* (Vol. 2, Part 1).

Cohen, L. E., & Felson, M. (1979). Social change and crime rate trends: A routine activity approach. *American Sociological Review, 44,* 588–608.

Comer, J. P., & Poussaint, A. (1992). *Raising black children: Two leading psychiatrists confront the educational, social, and emotional problems facing black children.* New York, NY: Plume.

Conger, R. (1976). Social control and social leaning models of delinquent behavior. *Criminology, 14,* 17–39.

Connell, R. (29 December 2002). Glass-jawed guys cower as the 'weaker sex' comes out swinging. *Yomiuri Weekly.*

Connelly, C. D., & Straus, M. A. (1992). Mother's age and risk for physical abuse. *Child Abuse & Neglect, 16,* 709–718.

Coolidge, F. L., Tambone, G. M., Durham, R. L., & Segal, D. L. (2011). Retrospective assessments of childhood psychopathology by adults and their parents. *Journal of Scientific Research, 2*(3), 162–168.

Coopersmith, S. (1967). *The antecedents of self-esteem.* San Francisco, CA: W. H. Freeman.

Cope, K. C. (2010). The age of discipline: The relevance of age to the reasonableness of corporal punishment. *Law and Contemporary Problems, 73*(2), 167–188.

Council of Europe. (2005). *Eliminating corporal punishment: A human rights imperative for Europe's children.* Strasbourg, France: Council of Europe Publishing.

Covington, M. V. (1989). Self-esteem and failure in school: Analysis and policy implications. In A. M. Mecca, N. J. Smelser, & J. Vasconcellos (Eds.), *The social importance of self-esteem.* Berkeley, CA: University of California Press.

Coyl, D. D., Roggman, L. A., & Newland, L. A. (2002). Stress, maternal depression, and negative mother-infant interactions in relation to infant attachment. *Infant Mental Health Journal, 23*(1), 145–163.

Craig, S. E. (1986). *The effect of parental aggression on children's cognitive development* (Unpublished doctoral dissertation). University of New Hampshire, Durham, NH.

Crittenden, P. M. (1985). Maltreated infants: Vulnerability and resilience. *Journal of Child Psychology and Psychiatry, 26*(1), 85–96.

Crozier, J., & Katz, R. C. (1979). Social learning treatment of child abuse. *Journal of Behavioral Therapy and Psychiatry, 10,* 213–220.

Cullinan, D., & Epstein, M. H. (1982). Behavior disorders. In N. G. Haring (Ed.), *Exceptional children and youth* (3rd ed., pp. 207–239). Columbus, OH: Merrill.

Currie, J., & Tekin, E. (2009). Child maltreatment and crime: New evidence from a sample of twins (pp. 1-30). New York: Columbia Population Research Center.

Daniel, J. H. (1985). Cultural and ethnic issues: The black family. In E. Newberger & R. Bourne (Eds.), *Unhappy families: Clinical and research perspectives on family violence* (Chapter 14). Littleton, MA: PSG Publishing.

Danziger, S. K. (1995). Family life and teenage pregnancy in the inner-city: Experiences of African-American youth. *Children and Youth Services Review, 17,* 183–201.

Daro, D., & Gelles, R. J. (1992). Public attitudes and behaviors with respect to child abuse prevention. *Journal of Interpersonal Violence, 7,* 517–531.

Darts, & Laurals1. (1993, June 8). *New Hampshire Herald,* Section B.

Davidson, H. (1997). The legal aspects of corporal punishment in the home: When does physical discipline cross the line to become child abuse? *Children's Legal Rights Journal,* 18–29.

Davies, C. A., DiLillo, D., & Martinez, I. G. (2004). Isolating adult psychological correlates of witnessing parental violence: Findings from a predominantly Latina sample. *Journal of Family Violence, 19*(6), 377–385.

Davies, M. (2002). Male sexual assault victims: A selective review of the literature and implications for support services. *Aggression and Violent Behavior, 7,* 203–214.

Davis, J. A., & Smith, T. W. (1992). *The general social surveys, 1972–1991: Cumulative codebook. (No. 12).* Chicago, IL: National Opinion Research Center (NORC) IL.

Davis, T. L., & Liddell, D. L. (2002). Getting inside the house: The effectiveness of a rape prevention program for college fraternity men. *Journal of College Student Development, 43*(1), 35–50.

Dawson, G., & Fischer, K. W. (Eds.). (1994). *Human behavior and the developing brain.* New York, NY: Guilford Press.

Dawson, J., & Straus, M. A. (2011). Gender equality in society and male predominance in crime by university students in thirty-two national settings. *The Open Criminology Journal, 4,* 1–14.

Day, D. E., & Roberts, M. W. (1983). An analysis of the physical punishment component of a parent training program. *Journal of Abnormal Child Psychology, 11,* 141–152.

Day, R. D., Peterson, G. W., & McCracken, C. (1998). Predicting spanking of younger and older children by mothers and fathers. *Journal of Marriage and the Family, 60*(February), 79–94.

De Zoysa, P. T. (2005). *Parental use of physical force towards school children in the Columbo district: Prevalence, psychosocial correlates and psychological consequences* (Unpublished doctoral dissertation). University of Colombo, Sri Lanka.

Deater-Deckard, K., Bates, J. E., Dodge, K. A., & Pettit, G. S. (1996). Physical discipline among African American and European American mothers: Links to children's externalizing behaviors. *Developmental Psychology, 32*(6), 1065–1072.

Deater-Deckard, K., & Dodge, K. A. (1997). Externalizing behavior problems and discipline revisited: Nonlinear effects and variation by culture, context, and gender. *Psychological Inquiry, 8*(3), 161–175.

Deater-Deckard, K., Lansford, J. E., Dodge, K. A., Pettit, G. S., & Bates, J. E. (2003). The development of attitudes about physical punishment: An 8-year longitudinal study. *Journal of Family Psychology, 36*(4), 351–360.

DeGue, S., & DiLillo, D. (2004). Understanding perpetrators of nonphysical sexual coercion: Characteristics of those who cross the line. *Violence and Victims, 19,* 673–688.

Dekeseredy, W. S., & Schwartz, M. D. (1998). *Woman abuse on campus: Results from the Canadian National Survey.* Thousand Oaks, CA: Sage.

Dekeseredy, W. S., Schwartz, M. D., & Tait, K. (1993). Sexual assault and stranger aggression on a Canadian University Campus. *Sex Roles, 28,* 263–277.

Deley, W. W. (1988). Physical punishment of children: Sweden and the USA. *Journal of Comparative Family Studies, 19*(3), 419–431.

Demaris, A. (2005). Violent victimization and women's mental and physical health: Evidence from a national sample. *The Journal of Research in Crime and Delinquency, 42,* 384.

DeMause, L. (1984). *The history of childhood.* New York, NY: Psychohistory Press.

Demo, D. H. (1992). Parent-child relations: Assessing recent changes. *Journal of Marriage and the Family, 54.*

Dequine, K. (2011). St. Augustine High School paddling policy is "not broken," marchers say. New Orleans: *The Times-Picayune* on Nola.com. *Saturday, March 26, 2011 6:35pm updated: Monday, March 28, 2011, 7:19 AM.* Retrieved from http://www.nola.com/blogs/

DeVet, K. A. (1997). Parent-adolescent relationships, physical disciplinary history, and adjustment in adolescents. *Family Process, 36,* 311–322.

Desmarais, S. L., Reeves, K. A., Nicholls, T. L., Telford, R. P., & Fiebert, M. S. (2012). Prevalence of Physical Violence in Intimate Relationships, Part 2: Rates of Male and Female Perpetration. *Partner Abuse, 3*(2), 170–198.

Dexter, L. A. (1958). A note on selective inattention in social science. *Social Problems, 6*(Fall), 176–182.

Dinkes, R., Kemp, J., Baum, K., & Snyder, T. D. (2009). *Indicators of school crime and safety: 2009.* Washington, DC: U.S. Departments of Education and Justice.

Dinkmeyer, D., & McKay, G. D. (2008). *The parent's handbook: Systematic training for effective parenting.* Circle Pines, MN: American Guidance Services.

Dix, T., & Grusec, J. E. (1985). Parent attribution processes in the socialization of children. In I. E. Sigel (Ed.), *Parental belief systems* (pp. 201–233). Hillsdale, NJ: Erlbaum.

Dix, T., Ruble, D. N., & Zambarano, R. J. (1989). Mothers' implicit theories of discipline: Child effects, parent effects, and the attribution process. *Child Development, 60*(6), 1373–1391.

Dobson, J. C. (1988). *The strong willed child: Birth through adolescence.* Wheaton, IL: Tyndale House Publishers.

Dohrenwend, B. S., Askenasy, A. R., Krasnoff, L., & Dohrenwend, B. P. (1978). Exemplification of a method for scaling life events: The PERI life events scale. *Journal of Health and Social Behavior, 19*(2), 205–229.

Douglas, E. M., & Straus, M. A. (2007). Discipline by parents and child psychopathology. In A. R. Felthous & H. Sass (Eds.), *International handbook of psychopathology and the law.* New York, NY: Wiley.

Doyle, O., Harmon, C. P., Heckman, J. J., & Tremblay, R. E. (2009). Investing in early human development: Timing and economic efficiency. *Economics & Human Biology, 7*(1), 1–6.

Dubowitz, H., Kim, J., Black, M. M., Weisbart, C., Semiatin, J., & Magder, L. S. (2011). Identifying children at high risk for a child maltreatment report. *Child Abuse & Neglect, 35*(2), 96–104.

Duggan, A., McFarlane, E., Fuddy, L., Burrell, L., Higman, S. M., Windham, A., & Sia, C. (2004). Randomized trial of a statewide home visiting program: Impact in preventing child abuse and neglect. *Child Abuse & Neglect, 28*(6), 597–622.

DuRant, R. H., Getts, A., Cadehead, C., Emans, S. J., & Woods, E. R. (1995). Exposure to violence and victimization and depression, hopelessness, and purpose in life among adolescents living in and around public housing. *Journal of Developmental and Behavioral Pediatrics, 16,* 233–237.

Durose, M. R., Harlow, C. W., Langan, P. A., Motivans, M., Rantala, R. R., & Smith, E. L. (2005). *Family violence statistics including statistics on strangers and acquaintances* (Publication NCJ 207846). Washington, DC: National Institute of Justice, Bureau of Justice Statistics.

Durrant, J. E. (1994). *Public attitudes towards corporal punishment in Canada.* Paper presented at the International Symposium on Violence in Childhood and Adolescence, Bielefeld, Germany.

Durrant, J. E. (1999). Evaluating the success of Sweden's corporal punishment ban. *Child Abuse & Neglect, 23*(5), 435–448.

Durrant, J. E. (2000). Trends in youth crime and well-being since the abolition of corporal punishment in Sweden. *Youth & Society, 31*(4), 437–455.

Durrant, J. E., Ensom, R., & Coalition on Physical Punishment of Children and Youth. (2004). *Joint statement on physical punishment of children and youth.* Ottawa, Canada: Coalition on Physical Punishment of Children and Youth.

Durrant, J. E., & Janson, S. (2005). Law reform, corporal punishment and child abuse: The case of Sweden. *International Review of Victimology, 12*(2), 139–158.

Durrant, J. E., & Olsen, G. M. (1997). Parenting and public policy: Contextualizing the Swedish corporal punishment ban. *Journal of Social Welfare and Family Law, 19*(4), 443–461.

Durrant, J. E., Rose-Krasnor, L., & Broberg, A. G. (2003). Physical punishment and maternal beliefs in Sweden and Canada. *Journal of Comparative Family Studies, 34,* 586–604.

Durrant, J. E., & Smith, A. B. (Eds.). (2011). *Global pathways to abolishing physical punishment: Realizing children's rights.* New York, NY: Routledge.

Ealey, C. (1980). Discipline from a black perspective. *Childcare Resource Center Newsletter.* Minneapolis/St. Paul, MN.

Eamon, M. K. (2001). Antecedents and socioemotional consequences of physical punishment on children in two-parent families. *Child Abuse & Neglect, 6,* 787–802.

Eamon, M. K., & Mulder, C. (2005). Predicting antisocial behavior among Latino young adolescents: An ecological systems analysis. *American Journal of Orthopsychiatry, 75*(1), 117–127.

Easterbrook, J. A. (1959). The effect of emotion on cue utilization and the organization of behavior. *Psychological Review, 66*(3), 183–201.

Edfeldt, A. W. (1979). *Violence towards children: An international formulative study.* Stockholm, Sweden: Akademilitteratur.

Ehrensaft, M. K., Cohen, P., Brown, J., Smailes, E., Chen, H., & Johnson, J. G. (2003). Intergenerational transmission of partner violence: A 20-year prospective study. *Journal of Consulting and Clinical Psychology, 71*(4), 741–753.

Eisner, M. (2001). Modernization, self-control, and lethal violence: The long-term dynamics of European homicide rates in theoretical perspective. *British Journal of Criminology, 41,* 618–638.

Eisner, M. (2003). Long term trends in violent crime. *Crime and Justice, 30,* 83–119.

Eisner, M. (2008). Modernity strikes back? A historical perspective on the latest increase in interpersonal violence (1960–1990). *International Journal of Conflict and Violence, 2*(2), 288–316.

Elder, G. H., & Bowerman, C. E. (1963). Family structure and child-rearing patterns: The effects of family size and sex composition. *American Sociological Review, 28,* 891–905.

Elias, N. (1978). *The civilizing process* (Vol. 1 & 2). Oxford, England: Oxford University Press.

Elias, R. (1997). A culture of violent solutions. In J. Turpin & L. Kurtz (Eds.), *The web of violence* (pp. 117–147). Chicago: University of Illinois Press.

Elliott, G. C., Avery, R., Fishman, E., & Hoshiko, B. (2002). The encounter with family violence and risky sexual activity among young adolescent females. *Violence and Victims, 17*(5), 569–592.

Elliott, M. (1994, April 19). The caning debate: Should America be more like Singapore? *Newsweek, 17,* 19.

Ellison, C., Bartowski, J., & Segal, M. (1996). Conservative protestantism and the parental use of corporal punishment. *Social Forces, 74,* 1003-1028.

Ellison, C. G., & Bradshaw, M. (2009). Religious beliefs, sociopolitical ideology, and attitudes toward corporal punishment. *Journal of Family Issues, 30*(3), 320–340.

Ellison, C. G., Musick, M. A., & Holden, G. W. (2011). Does conservative Protestantism moderate the association between corporal punishment and child outcomes? *Journal of Marriage and Family, 73*(5), 946–961.

Ellison, C. G., & Sherkat, D. E. (1993). Conservative protestantism and support for corporal punishment. *American Sociological Review, 58*(1), 131–144.

Emler, N. (2002). *Self-esteem: The costs and causes of low self-worth.* York, England: York Publishing Services.

Erath, S. A., El-Sheikh, M., Hinnant, J. B., & Cummings, E. M. (2011). Skin conductance level reactivity moderates the association between harsh parenting and growth in child externalizing behavior. *Developmental Psychology, 47*(3), 693–706.

Erlanger, H. S. (1974). Social class and corporal punishment in childrearing: A reassessment. *American Sociological Review, 39,* 68–85.

Eron, L. D., Huesmann, L. R., & Zelli, A. (1991). The role of parental variables in the learning of aggression. In D. Pepler & K. Rubin (Eds.), *The development and treatment of childhood aggression* (pp. 169–188). Hillsdale, NJ: Erlbaum.

Faris, R. E. L. (1955). *Social disorganization* (2nd ed.). New York, NY: Ronald Press.

Farrington, D. P. (1978). The family backgrounds of aggressive youths. In L. A. Hersov & M. Berge (Eds.), *Aggression and anti-social behaviour in childhood and adolescence* (pp. 73–93). Oxford, England: Pergamon.

Farrington, D. P. (2011). Family influence on delinquency. In D. W. Springer & A. R. Roberts (Eds.), *Juvenile justice and delinquency* (pp. 203–222). Sudbury, MA: Jones and Bartlett Publishing.

Farrington, D. P., & Welsh, B. C. (2006). *Saving children from a life of crime: Early risk factors and effective interventions.* New York, NY: Oxford University Press.

Fauchier, A., & Straus, M. A. (2010). *Psychometric properties of the Adult-Recall form of the dimensions of discipline inventory* (Unpublished). Durham, NH: Family Research Laboratory, University of New Hampshire.

Federal Bureau of Investigation. (2007). *Crime in the United States, 2006: Uniform Crime Reports.* Washington, DC: U.S. Department of Justice.

Feldman, R., & Reznick, J. S. (1996). Maternal perception of infant intentionality at 4 and 8 months. *Infant Behavior and Development, 19*(4), 483–496.

Felson, R. B. (2000). The normative protection of women from violence. *Sociological Forum, March.*

Felson, R. B. (2002). *Violence and gender reexamined.* Washington, DC: American Psychological Press.

Felson, R. B., & Feld, S. L. (2009). When a man hits a woman: Moral evaluations and reporting violence to the police. *Aggressive Behavior, 35*(6), 477–488.

Fergusson, D. M., Boden, J. M., & Horwood, L. J. (2008). Exposure to childhood sexual and physical abuse and adjustment in early adulthood. *Child Abuse & Neglect, 32*(6), 607–619.

Fergusson, D. M., Boden, J. M., Horwood, L. J., Miller, A. L., & Kennedy, M. A. (2011). MAOA, Abuse exposure and antisocial behaviour: 30-year longitudinal study. *The British Journal of Psychiatry, 198*(6), 457–463.

Fergusson, D. M., Grant, H., Horwood, L. J., & Ridder, E. M. (2005). Randomized trial of the early start program of home visitation. *Pediatrics, 116*(6), E803–E809.

Fergusson, D. M., & Horwood, L. J. (1998). Exposure to interparental violence in childhood and psychosocial adjustment in young adulthood. *Child Abuse & Neglect, 22*(5), 339–357.

Feshbach, N. D. (1980). Tomorrow is here today in Sweden. *Journal of Clinical Child Psychology, 9*(2), 109–112.

Feshback, S. (1970). Aggression. In P. Mussen (Ed.), *Carmichael's manual of child psychology* (Vol. 2, pp. 159–260). New York, NY: Wiley.

Fiebert, M. S. (2010). References examining assaults by women on their spouses or male partners: An annotated bibliography. *Sexuality & Culture, 14,* 49–91.

Fiebert, M. S., & Gonzalez, D. M. (1997). College women who initiate assaults on their male partners and the reasons offered for such behavior. *Psychological Reports, 80,* 583–590.

Finkelhor, D. (2008). *Childhood victimization: Violence, crime, and abuse in the lives of young people.* New York, NY: Oxford University Press.

Finkelhor, D., Ormrod, R. K., & Turner, H. A. (2007). Poly-victimization: A neglected component in child victimization trauma. *Child Abuse & Neglect, 31,* 7–26.

Finkelhor, D., Turner, H., & Ormrod, R. (2006). Kid's stuff: The nature and impact of peer and sibling violence on younger and older children. *Child Abuse & Neglect, 30*(12), 1401–1421.

Finkelhor, D., Turner, H. A., Ormrod, R. K., & Hamby, S. L. (2010). Trends in childhood violence and abuse exposure: Evidence from 2 national surveys. *Archives of Pediatrics & Adolescent Medicine, 164*(3), 238–242.

Fisher, H. L., Bunn, A., Jacobs, C., Moran, P., & Bifulco, A. (2011). Concordance between mother and offspring retrospective reports of childhood adversity. *Child Abuse & Neglect, 35*(2), 117–122.

Fluke, J., Casillas, C., Capa, C., Chen, L., & Wulczyn, F. (2010, July 11–13). *The Multiple Indicator Cluster Survey (MICS) of households: Cross-national surveillance system to address disciplinary practices.* Paper presented at the International Family Violence and Child Victimization Research Conference, Portsmouth, NH.

Flynn, C. P. (1994). Regional differences in attitudes toward corporal punishment. *Journal of Marriage and the Family, 56*(2), 314–324.

Flynn, C. P. (1996a). Normative support for corporal punishment: Attitudes, correlates, and implications. *Child Abuse & Neglect, 1*(1), 47–55.

Flynn, C. P. (1996b). Regional differences in spanking experiences and attitudes: A comparison of northeastern and southern college students. *Journal of Family Violence, 11*(1), 59–80.

Flynn, J. R. (1999). Searching for justice: The discovery of IQ gains over time. *American Psychologist, 54*(1), 5–20.

Foshee, V. A., & Bauman, K. E. (1992). Parental and peer characteristics as modifiers of the bond-behavior relationship: An elaboration of control theory. *Journal of Health and Social Behavior, 33,* 66–76.

Foshee, V. A., Bauman, K. E., Ennett, S. T., Suchindran, C., Benefield, T., & Linder, G. F. (2005). Assessing the effects of the dating violence prevention program "Safe dates" using random coefficient regression modeling. *Prevention Science, 6*(3), 245–258.

Foshee, V. A., Bauman, K. E., & Linder, F. (1999). Family violence and the perpetration of adolescent dating violence: Examining social learning and social control processes. *Journal of Marriage and the Family, 61*(1), 331–342.

Foshee, V. A., Ennett, S. T., Bauman, K. E., & Suchindran, C. (2005). The association between family violence and adolescent dating violence onset: Does it vary by race, socioeconomic status, and family structure? *Journal of Early Adolescence, 25*(3), 317–344.

Foshee, V. A., Linder, F., MacDougall, J. E., & Bangdiwala, S. (2001). Gender differences in the longitudinal predictors of adolescent dating violence. *Preventive Medicine, 32*(2), 128–141.

Friedman, S. B., & Schonberg, S. K. (1996a). Consensus statements. The short- and long-term consequences of corporal punishment. *Pediatrics Supplement, 98,* 853–856.

Friedman, S. B., & Schonberg, S. K. (1996b). The short and long-term consequences of corporal punishment. *Pediatrics Supplement, 98*(4), 803–857.

Frude, N., & Goss, A. (1979). Parental anger: A general population survey. *Child Abuse & Neglect, 3,* 331–333.

Galiani, S., Rossi, M. A., & Schargrodsky, E. (2011). Conscription and crime: Evidence from the Argentine draft lottery. *American Economic Journal: Applied Economics, 3*(2), 119–136.

Gámez-Guadix, M., Straus, M. A., Carrobles, J. A., Muñoz Rivas, M. J., & Almendros Rodríguez, C. (2010). Corporal punishment and behavior problems: The moderating role of positive parenting and psychological aggression. *Psicothema, 22*(4), 529–536.

Gámez-Guadix, M., Straus, M. A., & Hershberger, S. (2011). Childhood and adolescent victimization and perpetration of sexual coercion by male and female university students. *Deviant Behavior, 32,* 712–742.

Garbarino, J., Kostelny, K., & Barry, F. (1997). Value transmission in an ecological context: The high-risk neighborhood. In J. E. Grusec & L. Kuczynski (Eds.), *Parenting and children's internalization of values: A handbook of contemporary theory* (pp. 307–332). New York, NY: Wiley.

Garber, J., Quiggle, N. K., Panak, W., & Dodge, K. A. (1991). Aggression and depression in children: Comorbidity, specificity, and social cognitive processing. In D. Cicchetti & S. Toth (Eds.), *Internalizing and externalizing expression of dysfunction* (Vol. 2). Hillsdale, NJ: Erlbaum.

Gardner, M. J., Powell, C. A., & Grantham-McGregor, S. M. (2007). Determinants of aggressive and prosocial behaviour among Jamaican schoolboys. *West Indian Medical Journal, 56*(1), 34–41.

Garner, A. S., Shonkoff, J. P., Siegel, B. S., Dobbins, M. I., Earls, M. F., Garner, A. S., . . . Wood, D. L. (2012). Early childhood adversity, toxic stress, and the role of the pediatrician: Translating developmental science into lifelong health. *Pediatrics, 129*(1), e224–e231.

Garner, J. H., & Maxwell, C. D. (2009). Prosecution and conviction rates for intimate partner violence. *Criminal Justice Review, 34*(1), 44–79.

Gelles, R. J. (1974). *The violent home: A study of physical aggression between husbands and wives.* Beverly Hills, CA: Sage.

Gelles, R. J. (1989). Child abuse and violence in single-parent families: Parent absence and economic deprivation. *American Journal of Orthopsychiatry, 59*(4), 492–501.

Gelles, R. J., & Straus, M. A. (1979). Determinants of violence in the family: Towards a theoretical integration. In W. R. Burr, F. Rueben Hill, I. Nye, & I. L. Reiss (Eds.), *Contemporary theories about the family* (Vol. 1, pp. 549–581). New York, NY: The Free Press.

Gelles, R. J., & Straus, M. A. (1988). *Intimate violence: The causes and consequences of abuse in the American family.* New York, NY: Simon & Schuster.

Gershoff, E. T. (2002). Corporal punishment by parents and associated child behaviors and experiences: A meta-analytic and theoretical review. *Psychological Bulletin, 128,* 539–579.

Gershoff, E. T. (2008). *Report on physical punishment in the United States: What research tells us about its effects on children.* Columbus, OH: Center for Effective Discipline.

Gershoff, E. T., Grogan-Kaylor, A., Lansford, J. E., Chang, L., Zelli, A., Deater-Deckard, K., & Dodge, K. A. (2010). Parent discipline practices in an international sample: Associations with child behaviors and moderation by perceived normativeness. *Child Development, 81*(2), 480–495.

Gibbs, J. (1975). *Crime, punishment, and deterrence.* New York, NY: Elsevier.

Gibson, I. (1978). *The English vice: Beating, sex and shame in Victorian England and after.* London, England: Duckworth.

Gidycz, C. A., Layman, M. J., Rich, C. I., Crothers, M., Gylys, J., Matorin, A., & Jacobs, C. D. (2001). An evaluation of an acquaintance rape prevention program: Impact on attitudes, sexual aggression, and sexual victimization. *Journal of Interpersonal Violence, 16*(11), 1120–1138.

Gil, D. G. (1970). *Violence against children: Physical child abuse in the United States.* Cambridge, MA: Harvard University Press.

Giles-Sims, J., & Finkelhor, D. (1984). Child abuse in stepfamilies. *Family Relations, 33,* 407–413.

Giles-Sims, J., & Lockhart, C. (2005a). Culturally shaped patterns of disciplining children. *Journal of Family Issues, 26*(2), 196–218.

Giles-Sims, J., & Lockhart, C. (2005b). Grid-group theory and corporal punishment. In M. Donnelly & M. A. Straus (Eds.), *Corporal punishment of children in theoretical perspective* (pp. 55–72). New Haven, CT: Yale University Press.

Giles-Sims, J., Straus, M. A., & Sugarman, D. B. (1995). Child, maternal and family characteristics associated with spanking. *Family Relations, 44*(2), 170–176.

Global Initiative to End All Corporal Punishment. (2007). Ending legalised violence against: Following up the U.N. secretary general's study on violence against children. *Global Report 2007.*

Gonzalez, M., Durrant, J. E., Chabot, M., Trocmé, N., & Brown, J. (2008). What predicts injury from physical punishment? A test of the typologies of violence hypothesis. *Child Abuse & Neglect, 32*(8), 752–765.

Goodenough, F. L. (1975 [1931]). *Anger in young children.* Westport, CT: Greenwood Press.

Gordon, T. (2000). *Parent effectiveness training: The proven program for raising responsible children.* New York, NY: New American Library.

Gottfredson, M. R., & Hirschi, T. (1990). *A general theory of crime.* Stanford, CA: Stanford University Press.

Gottfredson, M. R., & Hirschi, T. (1994). *A general theory of adolescent problem behavior: Problems and prospects.* Hillsdale, NJ: Erlbaum.

Gove, W. R., & Crutchfield, R. D. (1982). The family and juvenile delinquency. *The Sociological Quarterly, 23*(3), 301–319.

Graaf, I. D., Speetjens, P., Smit, F., Wolff, M. D., & Tavecchio, L. (2008). Effectiveness of the triple P positive parenting program on parenting: A meta-analysis. *Family Relations, 57*(5), 553–566.

Graziano, A. M., Lindquist, C. M., Kunce, L. J., & Munjal, K. (1992). Physical punishment in childhood and current attitudes: An exploratory comparison of college students in the U.S. and India. *Journal of Interpersonal Violence, 7*(2), 147–155.

Graziano, A. M., & Namaste, K. A. (1990). Parental use of physical force in child discipline: A survey of 679 college students. *Journal of Interpersonal Violence, 5*(4), 449–463.

Greenblat, C. S. (1983). A hit is a hit is a hit . . . or is it? Approval and tolerance of the use of physical force by spouses. In D. Finkelhor, R. J. Gelles, G. T. Hotaling, & M. A. Straus (Eds.), *The dark side of families* (pp. 235–260). Beverly Hills, CA: Sage.

Greven, P. (1990). *Spare the child: The religious roots of punishment and the psychological impact of physical abuse.* New York, NY: Alfred A. Knopf.

Grier, W. H., & Cobbs, P. M. (1968). *Black rage.* New York, NY: Basic Books.

Grogan-Kaylor, A. (2004). The effect of corporal punishment on antisocial behavior in children. *Social Work Research, 28*(3), 153–162.

Grogan-Kaylor, A. (2005). Corporal punishment and the growth trajectory of children's antisocial behavior. *Child Maltreatment, 10*(3), 283–292.

Grusec, J. E., Dix, T., & Mills, R. (1982). The effects of type, severity, and victim of children's transgressions on maternal discipline. *Canadian Journal of Behavioral Sciences, 14,* 276–289.

Guarendi, R., & Eich, D. P. (1990). *Back to the family: How to encourage traditional values in complicated times.* New York, NY: Villard Books.

Gulas, C. S., McKeage, K. K., & Weinberger, M. G. (2010). It's just a joke: Violence against males in humorous advertising. *Journal of Advertising, 39*(4), 109–120.

Gunnoe, M. (2009). *Never-spanked youth vs. youth spanked only during childhood: Self-evaluations on 9 outcomes.* Paper presented at the Society for Research in Child Development, Denver, CO.

Gunnoe, M. L., & Mariner, C. L. (1997). Toward a developmental-contextual model of the effects of parental spanking on children's aggression. *Archives of Pediatric and Adolescent Medicine, 151,* 768–775.

Gusfield, J. R. (1963). *Symbolic crusade: Status politics and the American temperance movement.* Urbana: University of Illinois Press.

Gusfield, J. R. (1981). *The culture of public problems: Drinking, driving and the symbolic order.* Chicago, IL: University of Chicago Press.

Guzman, L., Lippman, L., Anderson Moore, K., & O'HareHow, W. (2003). Children are doing the mismatch between public perception and statistical reality. *Child Trends, Research Brief, July.*

Haapasalo, J., & Pokela, E. (1999). Child-rearing and child abuse antecedents of criminality. *Aggression and Violent Behavior, 4*(1), 107–127.

Haeuser, A. A. (1991, September 14–17). *Reaffirming physical punishment in child-rearing as one root of physical abuse.* Paper presented at the 9th National Conference on Child Abuse and Neglect, Denver, CO.

Hakman, M., & Sullivan, M. (2009). The effect of task and maternal verbosity on compliance in toddlers. *Infant and Child Development, 18*(2), 195–205.

Hamilton, L. C. (2009). *Statistics with STATA: Updated for version 10.* Belmont, CA: Brooks/Cole Cengage Learning.

Hampton, R. L. (1987). Family violence and homicides in the Black community: Are they linked? In R. L. Hampton (Ed.), *Violence in the Black family: Correlates and consequences* (pp. 135–186). Lexington, MA: Lexington Books.

Hare, R. D., Clark, D., Grann, M., & Thornton, D. (2000). Psychopathy and the predictive validity of the PCL-R: An international perspective. *Behavioral Sciences & the Law, 18,* 623–645.

Harned, M. S. (2001). Abused women or abused men? An examination of the context and outcomes of dating violence. *Violence and Victims, 16*(3), 269–285.

Harper, F. W. K., Brown, A. M., Arias, I., & Brody, G. (2006). Corporal punishment and kids: How do parent support and gender influence child adjustment? *Journal of Family Violence, 21*(3), 197–207.

Harris, F. I. (1992, August 4). Parents shouldn't always rule out physical discipline for children. *Saint Paul Pioneer Press2.*

Harrison, M. (2011, July 20). Lawsuit filed over paddling incident. *Dekalbs Country's Oldest Newspaper: Times-Journal.*

Hawkins, J. D., & Haggerty, K. P. (2008, March 18). *Raising healthy children: A social development approach to prevention.* Paper presented at the Blueprints Conference, Denver, CO.

Heckman, J. J. (2008). Schools, skills, synapses. *Economic Inquiry, 46*(3), 289–324.

Henley, J. (2010, October 1). Middle England takes unmarried unbeliever Miliband in its stride. *The Guardian,* p. 18.

Herrera, V. M., & McClosky, L. A. (2003). Sexual abuse, family violence, and female delinquency: Findings from a longitudinal study. *Violence and Victims, 18,* 319–334.

Herzberger, S. D. (1990). The cyclical pattern of child abuse: A study of research methodology. *American Behavioral Scientist, 33,* 529–545.

Hettrich, E. L., & O'Leary, K. D. (2007). Females' reasons for their physical aggression in dating relationships. *Journal of Interpersonal Violence, 22*(9), 1131–1143.

Heuer, F., & Reisberg, D. (1992). Emotion, arousal, and memory for detail. In S. A. Christianson (Ed.), *The handbook of emotion and memory: Research and theory* (pp. 151–180). Hillsdale, NJ: Erlbaum.

Hildyard, K. L., & Wolfe, D. A. (2002). Child neglect: Developmental issues and outcomes. *Child Abuse & Neglect, 26,* 679–695.

Hindelang, M. J. (1973). Causes of delinquency: A partial replication and extension. *Social Problems, 20*(4), 471–487.

Hines, D. A. (2007). Predictors of sexual coercion against women and men: A multilevel, multinational study of university students. *Archives of Sexual Behavior, 36,* 403–422.

Hines, D. A., & Saudino, K. J. (2003). Gender differences in psychological, physical, and sexual aggression among college students using the revised Conflict Tactics Scales. *Violence and Victims, 18*(2), 197–217.

Hines, D. A., & Straus, M. A. (2007). Binge drinking and violence against dating partners: The mediating effect of antisocial traits and behaviors in a multi-national perspective. *Aggressive Behavior, 33,* 441–457.

Hirschi, T. (1969). *The causes of delinquency.* Berkeley: University of California Press.

Hirschi, T., & Gottfredson, M. R. (2005). Punishment of children from the perspective control theory. In M. Donnelly & M. A. Straus (Eds.), *Corporal punishment of children in theoretical perspective* (pp. 214–222). New Haven, CT: Yale University Press.

Hogben, M., Byrne, D., Hamburger, M. E., & Osland, J. (2001). Legitimized aggression and sexual coercion: Individual differences in cultural spillover. *Aggressive Behavior, 27*(1), 26–43.

Hoghughi, M. (1992). *Assessing child and adolescent disorders: A practice manual.* Newbury Park, CA: Sage.

Holden, G. W., Coleman, S. M., & Schmidt, K. L. (1995). Why 3-year-old children get spanked: Parent and child determinants as reported by college-educated mothers. *Merrill-Palmer Quarterly, 41*(4), 431–452.

Holden, G. W., Geffner, R., & Jouriles, E. N. (1998). *Children exposed to marital violence: Theory, research, and applied issues.* Washington, DC: American Psychological Association.

Holden, G. W., & Miller, P. C. (1997, April). *Cognitive versus emotional parenting: Alignments between child-rearing cognitions, emotions, and reported behavior.* Paper presented at the biennial meeting of the Society for Research in Child Development, Washington, DC.

Holden, G. W., & Zambarano, R. J. (1992). Passing the rod: Similarities between parents and their young children in orientations toward physical punishment. In I. E. Sigel, A. V. McGillicuddy-Delisi, & J. J. Goodnow (Eds.), *Parental belief systems: The psychological consequences for children* (2nd ed., pp. 143–172). Hillsdale, NJ: Erlaum.

Hollis, M., & Currie, D. (1994, July). Right to spank kids still sparking debate. *Gainesville Sun.*

Holmes, S. J., & Robins, L. N. (1988). The role of parental disciplinary practices in the development of depression and alcoholism. *Psychiatry, 56,* 24–36.

Horwitz, A. V., Spatz Widom, C., McLaughlin, J., & Raskin White, H. (2001). The impact of childhood abuse and neglect on adult mental health: A prospective study. *Journal of Health and Social Behavior, 4,* 184–201.

Huttenlocher, J., Waterfall, H., Vasilyeva, M., Vevea, J., & Hedges, L. V. (2010). Sources of variability in children's language growth. *Cognitive Psychology, 61*(4), 343–365.

Hyde, J. S. (1984). How large are gender differences in aggression? A developmental meta-analysis. *Developmental Psychology, 20,* 722–736.

Hyman, I. A., & Wise, J. H. (1979). *Corporal punishment in American education.* Philadelphia, PA: Temple University Press.

Institute for the Prevention of Child Abuse. (1989). Survey of Canadian parental attitudes. *Newsbrief, Special Edition #3,* 1–11.

International Association of Chiefs of Police. (1967). *Training Kely 16: Handling domestic disturbance calls.* Gaithersburg, MD: Author.

Ispa, J. M., & Halgunseth, L. C. (2004). Talking about corporal punishment: Nine low-income African American mothers' perspectives. *Early Childhood Research Quarterly, 19*(3), 463–484.

Janson, S., Langberg, B., & Svensson, B. (2011). Sweden: A 30-year ban on physical punishment of children. In J. E. Durrant & A. B. Smith (Eds.), *Global pathways to abolishing physical punishment: Realizing children's rights* (pp. 241–255). New York, NY: Routledge.

Jensen, G. F., & Brownfield, D. (1983). Parents and drugs. *Criminology, 21*(4), 543–554.

Johnston, M. E. (1984). *Correlates of early violence experience among men who are abusive toward female mates.* Paper presented at the Second National Conference for Family Violence Researchers. Durham, NH: University of New Hampshire. Research.

Johnstone, G., & Van Ness, D. W. (Eds.). (2007). *Handbook of restorative justice.* Cullompton, England: Willan Publishing.

Jordan, R. E., Cheng, K. K., Miller, M. R., & Adab, P. (2011). Passive smoking and chronic obstructive pulmonary disease: Cross-sectional analysis of data from the Health Survey for England. *BMJ Open, 1*(2), e000153–e000153.

Julian, T. W., & McKenry, P. C. (1993). Mediators of male violence toward female intimates. *Journal of Family Violence, 8*(1), 39–56.

Junger-Tas, J., Haen Marshall, I., & Ribeaud, D. (2003). *Delinquency in an international perspective: The International Self-Reported Delinquency Study.* The Hague, The Netherlands: Kugler Publications.

Kadushin, A., & Martin, J. A. (1981). *Child abuse: An interactional event.* New York, NY: Columbia University Press.

Kalmuss, D. (1984). The intergenerational transmission of marital aggression. *Journal of Marriage and the Family, 44* (February), 11–19.

Kandel, E. (1991). *Physical punishment and the development of aggressive and violent behavior: A review.* Durham, NH: University of New Hampshire, Family Research Laboratory.

Kane-Parsons and Associates. (1987). Survey conducted for Parents Magazine.

Kar, H. L., & O'Leary, K. D. (2010). Gender symmetry or asymmetry in intimate partner victimization? Not an either/or answer. *Partner Abuse, 1,* 152–168.

Katz, J., Washington Kuffel, S., & Coblentz, A. (2002). Are there gender differences in sustaining dating violence? An examination of frequency, severity, and relationship satisfaction. *Journal of Family Violence, 17*(3), 247–271.

Kaufman Kantor, G., & Straus, M. A. (1987). The drunken bum theory of wife beating. *Social Problems. 34: 213–230.*

Kendall-Tackett, K. A., Williams, L. M., & Finkelhor, D. (2001). Impact of sexual abuse on children: A review and synthesis of recent empirical studies. In R. Bull (Ed.), *Children and the law: The essential readings* (pp. 31–76).Malden, MA: Blackwell Publishers.

Kernsmith, P. D., & Kernsmith, R. M. (2009). Female pornography use and sexual coercion perpetration. *Deviant Behavior, 30*(7), 589–610.

Kidwell, J. S. (1981). Number of siblings, sibling spacing, sex, and birth order: Their effects on perceived parent-adolescent relationships. *Journal of Marriage and the Family, 43,* 315–332.

Kim, H. K., Pears, K. C., Fisher, P. A., Connelly, C. D., & Landsverk, J. A. (2010). Trajectories of maternal harsh parenting in the first 3 years of life. *Child Abuse & Neglect, 34*(12), 897–906.

Kinard, E. M. (1980). Emotional development and physically abused children. *American Journal of Orthopsychiatry, 50,* 686–689.

Kinard, E. M. (1999). Psychosocial resources and academic performance in abused children. *Children and Youth Services Review, 21*(5), 351–376.

Kirby, D. (2002). Effective approaches to reducing adolescent unprotected sex, pregnancy, and childbearing. *Journal of Sex Research, 39*(1), 51–57.

Kitzmann, K. M., Gaylord, N. K., Holt, A. R., & Kenny, E. D. (2003). Child witnesses to domestic violence: A meta-analytic review. *Journal of Consulting and Clinical Psychology, 71*(2), 339–352.

Knight, R. A. (2006). The role of psychopathy in sexual coercion against women. In C. J. Patrick (Ed.), *Handbook of psychopathy* (p. 512). New York, NY: Guilford Press.

Knight, R. A., & Sims-Knight, J. E. (2004). Testing an etiological model for male juvenile sexual offending against females. *Journal of Child Sexual Abuse, 13,* 33–55.

Knox, M., & Brouwer, J. (2008). Early childhood professionals' recommendations for spanking young children. *Journal of Child & Adolescent Trauma, 1*(4), 341–348.

Knox, M. S., Burkhart, K., & Hunter, K. E. (2011). ACT against violence parents raising safe kids program: Effects on maltreatment-related parenting behaviors and beliefs. *Journal of Family Issues, 32*(1), 55–74.

Knudsen, B., & Liszkowski, U. (2012). Eighteen- and 24-month-old infants correct others in anticipation of action mistakes. *Developmental Science, 15*(1), 113–122.

Kohn, M. L. (1969). *Class and conformity: A study in values.* Homewood, IL: Dorsey Press.

Kohn, M. L. (1977). *Class and conformity: A study in values with a reassessment* (2nd ed.). Chicago, IL: University of Chicago Press.

Kohn, M. L., & Schooler, C. (1983). *Work and personality: An inquiry into the impact of social stratification.* Norwood, NJ: Ablex Publishing.

Korsch, B. M., Christian, J. B., Gozzi, E. K., & Carlson, P. V. (1965). Infant care and punishment: A pilot study. *American Journal of Public Health, 55,* 1880–1888.

Koss, M. P., Gidycz, C. A., & Wisniewski, N. (1987). The scope of rape: Incidence, and prevalence of sexual aggression and victimization in a national sample of higher education students. *Journal of Consulting and Clinical Psychology, 55,* 162–170.

Kowaleski-Jones, L., & Mott, F. L. (1998). Sex, contraception and childbearing among high-risk youth: Do different factors influence males and females? *Family Planning Perspectives, 30*(4), 163–169.

Krafft-Ebing, R. V. (1895). *Psychopathia sexualis.* London, England: F. A. Davis.

Krahé, B., Waizenhofer, E., & Moller, I. (2003). Women's sexual aggression against men: Prevalence and predictors. *Sex Roles, 49,* 219–232.

Kramer, M. D., Krueger, R. F., & Hicks, B. M. (2008). The role of internalizing and externalizing liability factors in accounting for gender differences in the prevalence of common psychopathological syndromes. *Psychological Medicine, 38*(1), 51–61.

Lambelet Coleman, D., Dodge, K. A., & Campbell, S. K. (2010). Where and how to draw the line between reasonable corporal punishment and abuse. *Law and Contemporary Problems, 73*(2), 107–165.

Lansford, J. E. (2010). The special problem of cultural differences in effects of corporal punishment. *Law and Contemporary Problems, 73*(2), 89–106.

Lansford, J. E., Chang, L., Dodge, K. A., Malone, P. S., Oburu, P., Palmérus, K., . . . Quinn, N. (2005). Physical discipline and children's adjustment: Cultural normativeness as a moderator. *Child Development, 76,* 1234–1246.

Lansford, J. E., Deater-Deckard, K., Dodge, K. A., Bates, J. E., & Pettit, G. S. (2004). Ethnic differences in the link between physical discipline and later adolescent externalizing behaviors. *Journal of Child Psychology and Psychiatry, 45*(4), 801–812.

Lansford, J. E., & Dodge, K. A. (2008). Cultural norms for adult corporal punishment of children and societal rates of endorsement and use of violence. *Parenting: Science and Practice, 8*(3), 257–270.

Larzelere, R. E. (1986). Moderate spanking: Model or deterrent of children's aggression in the family? *Journal of Family Violence, 1*(1), 27–36.

Larzelere, R. E. (1994). Should the use of corporal punishment by parents be considered child abuse? No. In M. A. Mason & E. Gambrill (Eds.), *Debating children's lives: Current controversies on children and adolescents* (pp. 202–209). Thousand Oaks, CA: Sage.

Larzelere, R. E. (1996). A review of the outcomes of parental use of nonabusive or customary physical punishment. *Pediatrics, 98*(4), 824–831.

Larzelere, R. E., & Baumrind, D. (2010). Are spanking injunctions scientifically supported? *Law and Contemporary Problems, 73*(2), 57–87.

Larzelere, R. E., Baumrind, D., & Polite, K. (1998). The pediatric forum: Two emerging perspectives of parental spanking from two 1996 conferences. *Archives of Pediatrics and Adolescent Medicine, 152,* 303.

Larzelere, R., Cox, R., & Smith, G. (2010). Do nonphysical punishments reduce antisocial behavior more than spanking? A comparison using the strongest previous causal evidence against spanking. *BMC Pediatrics, 10*(1), 10.

Larzelere, R. E., & Merenda, J. A. (1994). The effectiveness of parental discipline for toddler misbehaviour at different levels of child distress. *Family Relations, 43,* 480–488.

Larzelere, R. E., Schneider, W. N., Larson, D. B., & Pike, P. L. (1996). The effects of discipline responses in delaying toddler misbehavior recurrences. *Child & Family Behavior Therapy, 18,* 35–57.

Lau, A. S., Litrownik, A. J., Newton, R. R., Black, M. M., & Everson, M. D. (2006). Factors affecting the link between physical discipline and child externalizing problems in Black and White families. *Journal of Community Psychology, 34*(1), 89–103.

Leach, P. (1977). *Your baby & child: From birth to age five* (3rd ed.). New York, NY: Alfred A. Knopf.

Leary, C. E., Kelley, M. L., Morrow, J., & Mikulka, P. J. (2008). Parental use of physical punishment as related to family environment, psychological well-being, and personality in undergraduates. *Journal of Family Violence, 23*(1), 1–7.

Lee, S. J., Perron, B. E., Taylor, C. A., & Guterman, N. B. (2011). Paternal Psychosocial Characteristics and Corporal Punishment of Their 3-Year-Old Children. *Journal of Interpersonal Violence, 26*(1), 71-87. doi: 10.1177/0886260510362888

Lehman, B. A. (1989, March 13). Spanking teaches the wrong lesson. *The Boston Globe.*

Levinson, D. (1989). *Family violence in cross-cultural perspective.* Newbury Park, CA: Sage.

Little, R. J. A., & Rubin, D. B. (2002). *Statistical analysis with missing data*. Hoboken, NJ: Wiley.

Loeber, R., & Farrington, D. P. (1995). Longitudinal approaches in epidemiological research of conduct problems. In F. C. Verhulst & H. M. Koot (Eds.), *The epidemiology of child and adolescent psychopathology* (pp. 309–336). Oxford, England: Oxford University Press.

Loh, C., & Gidycz, C. A. (2006). A prospective analysis of the relationship between childhood sexual victimization and perpetration of dating violence and sexual assault in adulthood. *Journal of Interpersonal Violence, 21*(6), 732–749.

Lorr, M., & Wunderlich, R. A. (1985). A measure of impulsiveness and its relation to extroversion. *Educational Psychological Measurements, 45,* 251–257.

Lucke, J. C. (1998). Gender roles and sexual behavior among young women. *Sex Roles, 39,* 273–297.

Lyndon, A. E., White, J. W., & Kadlec, K. M. (2007). Manipulation and forces as sexual coercion tactics: Conceptual and empirical differences. *Aggressive Behavior, 33*(4), 291–303.

Lyons-Ruth, K., Connell, D. B., Zoll, D., & Stahl, J. (1987). Infants at social risk: Relations among infant maltreatment, maternal behavior, and infant attachment behavior. *Developmental Psychology, 23*(2), 223–232.

Maccoby, E. E., & Martin, J. A. (1983). Socialization in the context of the family: Parent-child interaction. In P. H. Mussen (Ed.), *Handbook of child psychology: Socialization, personality and social development* (Vol. 4, pp. 1–101). New York, NY: Wiley.

Maccoby, E. M., & Jacklin, C. N. (1980). Sex differences in aggression: A rejoinder and reprise. *Child Development, 51,* 964–980.

MacKenzie, M. J., Nicklas, E., Waldfogel, J., & Brooks-Gunn, J. (2011). Corporal punishment and child behavioural and cognitive outcomes through 5 years of age: Evidence from a contemporary urban birth cohort study. *Infant and Child Development.*

MacKinnon-Lewis, C., Volling, B. L., Lamb, M. E., Dechman, K., Rabiner, D., & Curtner, M. E. (1994). A cross-contextual analysis of boys' social competence: From family to school. *Developmental Psychology, 30*(3), 325–333.

MacMillan, H. L., Boyle, M. H., Wong, M. Y. Y., Duku, E. K., Fleming, J. E., & Walsh, C. A. (1999). Slapping and spanking in childhood and its association with lifetime prevalence of psychiatric disorders in a general population sample. *CMAJ, 161*(7), 805–809.

Maiuro, R. D., Cahn, T. S., Vitaliano, P. P., Wagner, B. C., & Zegree, J. B. (1988). Anger, deficits and hostility in domestically violent versus generally assaultive men and non-violent control subjects. *Journal of Consulting and Clinical Psychology, 56*(1), 17–23.

Malamuth, N. M., Linz, D., Heavey, C. L., Barnes, G., & Acker, M. (1995). Using the confluence model of sexual aggression to predict men's conflict with women: A 10-year follow-up study. *Journal of Personality and Social Psychology, 69*(2), 353–369.

Marcos, A. E., & Bahr, S. J. (1988). Control theory and adolescent drug use. *Youth & Society, 19*(4), 395–425.

Marcum, C. D. (2010). Routine activity theory: An Assessment of a classical theory. In H. Copes & V. Topalli (Eds.), *Criminological theory: Readings and retrospectives* (pp. 43–55). New York, NY: McGraw-Hill.

Margolin, G., Vickerman, K. A., Oliver, P. H., & Gordis, E. B. (2010). Violence exposure in multiple interpersonal domains: Cumulative and differential effects. *Journal of Adolescent Health, 47*(2), 198–205.

Markie-Dadds, C., & Sanders, M. R. (2006). Self-directed triple P (positive parenting program) for mothers with children at risk of developing conduct problems. *Behavioural and Cognitive Psychotherapy, 34*(3), 259–275.

Martin, S. (2006). October 2006 youth query methodology report. Rochester, New York: Harris Interactive, Inc.

Maschi, T., Morgen, K., Bradley, C., & Hatcher, S. (2008). Exploring gender differences on internalizing and externalizing behavior among maltreated youth: Implications for social work action. *Child & Adolescent Social Work Journal, 25*(6), 531–547.

Matsuenda, R. L., & Anderson, K. (1998). The dynamics of delinquent peers and delinquent behavior. *Criminology, 36*(2), 269–308.

Matteson, M. E., Pollack, E. S., & Cullen, J. W. (1987). What are the odds that smoking will kill you? *American Journal of Public Health, 77*(4), 425–431.

Maurer, A. (1976). Institutional assault on children. *Clinical Psychologist, 29,* 23–25.

McClure, C. (2002). *Attitudes towards spanking, religion and gun ownership.* Orlando, FL: University of Central Florida.

McCord, J. (1997). Discipline and the use of sanctions. *Aggression and Violent Behavior, 2,* 313–319.

McCord, J. (2005). Unintended consequences of punishment. In M. Donnelly & M. A. Straus (Eds.), *Corporal punishment of children in theoretical perspective* (pp. 165–169). New Haven, CT: Yale University Press.

McLeod, J. D., Kruttschnitt, C., & Dornfeld, M. (1994). Does parenting explain the effects of structural conditions on children's antisocial behavior? A comparison of Blacks and Whites. *Social Forces, 73*(2), 575–604.

McLoyd, V. C., & Smith, J. (2002). Physical discipline and behavior problems in African American, European American, and Hispanic children: Emotional support as a moderator. *Journal of Marriage and Family, 64*(1), 40–53.

Medeiros, R. A., & Straus, M. A. (2006). *A review of research on gender differences in risk factors for physical violence between partners in marital and dating relationships.* Durham, NH: Family Research Laboratory, University of New Hampshire.

Meerum Terwogt, M., & Olthof, T. (1989). Awareness and self regulation of emotion in young children. In C. Saarni & P. L. Harris (Eds.), *Children's understanding of emotion* (pp. 209–237). New York, NY: Cambridge University Press.

Menkel-Meadow, C. (2007). Restorative justice: What is it and does it work? *Annual Review of Law and Social Science, 3,* 161–187.

Messman-Moore, T. L., Walsh, K. L., & DiLillo, D. (2010). Emotion dysregulation and risky sexual behavior in revictimization. *Child Abuse & Neglect, 34*(12), 967–976.

Metzler, C. W., Noell, J., Biglan, A., Ary, D., & Smolkowski, K. (1994). The social context for risky sexual behavior among adolescents. *Journal of Behavioral Medicine, 17,* 419–438.

Millar, P. (2009). *The best interests of children: An evidence-based approach.* Toronto, Canada: University of Toronto Press.

Miller, D. R., & Swanson, G. (1958). *The changing American parent.* New York, NY: Wiley.

Modig, C. (2009). *Never violence–Thirty years on from Sweden's abolition of corporal punishment.* Stockholm: Government Offices of Sweden.

Molcho, M., Craig, W., Due, P., Pickett, W., Harel-Fisch, Y., & Overpeck, M. (2009). Cross-national time trends in bullying behaviour 1994–2006: Findings from Europe and North America. *International Journal of Public Health, 54*(0), 225–234.

Molnar, B. E., Buka, S. L., Brennan, R. T., Holton, J. K., & Earls, F. (2003). A multilevel study of neighborhoods and parent-to-child physical aggression: Results from the project on human development in Chicago neighborhoods. *Child Maltreatment, 8*(2), 84–97.

Money, J. (1986). *Lovemaps: Clinical concepts of sexual/erotic health and pathology, paraphilia, and gender transposition in childhood, adolescence, and maturity.* New York, NY: Irvington Publishers.

Money, J., & Lamacz, M. (1989). *Vandalized lovemaps: Paraphilic outcome of seven cases in pediatric sexology.* Buffalo, NY: Prometheus Books.

Monroe, R. R. (1970). *Episodic behavioral disorders.* Cambridge, MA: Harvard University Press.

Montague, A. (1941, January 5). Spanking the baby may be the psychological seed of war. *Boston Sunday Globe,* p. 2.

Montague, A. (Ed.). (1978). *Learning non-aggression: The experience of non-literate societies.* New York, NY: Oxford University Press.

Moore, D. W., & Straus, M. A. (1995). *Tolerance for slapping a spouse: Higher than we thought.* Paper presented at the annual meeting of the American Association for Public Opinion Research, Fort Lauderdale, FL.

Moore, K. A., Vandivere, S., & Redd, Z. (2006). A sociodemographic risk index. *Social Indicators Research, 75,* 45–81.

Moore, M. R. (1998). *Family and community correlates of sexual debut and pregnancy among African-American female adolescents in high-poverty neighborhoods* (Doctoral Dissertation). University of Chicago, Chicago, IL.

Morris, N. A., & Slocum, L. A. (2010). The validity of self-reported prevalence, frequency, and timing of arrest: An evaluation of data collected using a life event calendar. *Journal of Research in Crime and Delinquency, 47*(2), 210–240.

Muehlenhard, C. L., & Cook, S. W. (1988). Men's self-reports of unwanted sexual activity. *Journal of Sex Research, 24,* 546–568.

Muller, R. T., Hunter, J. E., & Stollak, G. (1995). The intergenerational transmission of corporal punishment: A comparison of social learning and temperament models. *Child Abuse & Neglect, 19*(11), 1323–1335.

Mulvaney, M. K., & Mebert, C. J. (2007). Parental corporal punishment predicts behavior problems in early childhood. *Journal of Family Psychology, 21*(3), 389–397.

Mulvaney, M. K., & Mebert, C. J. (2010). Stress appraisal and attitudes towards corporal punishment as intervening processes between corporal punishment and subsequent mental health. *Journal of Family Violence, 25,* 401–412.

Murray, H. (1938). *Explorations in personality.* New York, NY: Oxford University Press.

Murray, J., Farrington, D. P., & Eisner, M. P. (2009). Drawing conclusions about causes from systematic reviews of risk factors: The Cambridge quality checklists. *Journal of Experimental Criminology, 5*(1), 1–23.

Murray, N. J., Zabin, L. S., Toledo-Dreves, V., & Luengo-Charath, X. (1998). Gender differences in factors influencing first intercourse among urban students in Chile. *International Family Planning Perspectives, 24,* 139–144.

Nabors, E. L., Dietz, T. L., & Jasinski, J. L. (2006). Domestic violence beliefs and perceptions among college students. *Violence and Victims, 21*(6), 779–795.

National Association of Social Workers. (2012). *Physical punishment of children Social Work Speaks: NASW Policy Statements, 2012–2014.* Washington, DC: National Association of Social Workers Press. Retrieved from http://www.socialworkers.org/resources/abstracts /abstracts/physical.asp

Navaro, J. (1995). Uncovering gender differences in the use of marital violence: The effect of methodology. *Sociology, 29,* 475–494.

Neal, T. (1994, May 7). Kid's defense debated in abuse bill. *The Miami Herald,* p. 1A.

Neisser, U. (1997). Rising scores on intelligence tests: Test scores are certainly going up all over the world, but whether intelligence itself has risen remains controversial. *American Scientist, 85,* 440–447.

Neisser, U., Boodoo, G., Bouchard, T. J., Jr., Boykin, A. W., Brody, N., Ceci, S. J., . . . Urbina, S. (1996). Intelligence: Knowns and unknowns. *American Psychologist, 51*(2), 77–101.

Nettler, G. (1984). *Explaining crime* (3rd ed.). New York, NY: McGraw-Hill.

Newell, P. (1989). *Children are people too: The case against physical punishment.* London, England: Bedford Square Press.

Newell, P. (2011). The human rights imperative to eliminate physical punishment. In J. E. Durrant & A. B. Smith (Eds.), *Global pathways to abolishing physical punishment: Realizing children's rights* (pp. 7–26). New York, NY: Routledge.

Newson, J., & Newson, E. (1963). *Patterns of infant care in an urban community.* Baltimore, MD: Penguin Books.

Nisbett, R. E., & Cohen, D. (1996). *Culture of Honor: The psychology in violence in the south.* Boulder, CO: Westview Press.

Nix, R. L., Pinderhughes, E. E., Dodge, K. A., Bates, J. E., Pettit, G. S., & McFadyen-Ketchum, S. A. (1999). The relation between mothers' hostile attribution tendencies and children's externalizing behavior problems: The mediating role of mothers' harsh discipline practices. *Child Development, 70*(4), 896–909.

Nock, S. L. (2000). Is spanking universal? Comments on Murray Straus. *Virginia Journal of Social Policy and the Law, 8.*

Nurius, P. S., Furrey, J., & Berliner, L. (1992). Coping capacity among women with abusive partners. *Violence and Victims, 7*(3), 229–243.

Nye, I., Carlson, J., & Gerrett, G. (1970). Family size, interaction, affect and stress. *Journal of Marriage and the Family, 32,* 216–226.

O'Hagan, K. (1993). *Emotional and psychological abuse of children.* Toronto, Canada: University of Toronto Press.

O'Keefe, M. (1997). Predictors of dating violence among high school students. *Journal of Interpersonal Violence, 12*(4), 546–568.

Olson, R. (2008, May 31). Court gets behind spanking, to a degree. *Minneapolis Star Tribune.*

Olson, S. L., Sameroff, A., Kerr, D. C. R., Lopez, N. L., & Wellman, H. M. (2005). Developmental foundations of externalizing problems in young children: The role of effortful control. *Development and Psychopathology, 17*(1), 25–45.

Osgood, D. W., Wilson, J. K., O'Malley, P. M., Bachman, J. G., & Johnston, L. D. (1996). Routine activities and individual deviant behavior. *American Sociological Review, 61*(4), 635–655.

Otterbein, K. F. (1974). *The anthropology of war.* Paper presented at the Handbook of Social and Cultural Anthropology, Chicago, IL.

Owen, D. J., Smith Slep, A. M., & Heyman, R. E. (2009). The association of promised consequences with child compliance to maternal directives. *Journal of Clinical Child & Adolescent Psychology, 38*(5), 639–649.

Owens, D. J., & Straus, M. A. (1975). The social structure of violence in childhood and approval of violence as an adult. *Aggressive Behavior, 1,* 193–211.

Palusci, V. J., Crum, P., Bliss, R., & Bavolek, S. J. (2008). Changes in parenting attitudes and knowledge among inmates and other at-risk populations after a family nurturing program. *Children and Youth Services Review, 30,* 70–89.

Panuzio, J., & DiLillo, D. (2010). Physical, psychological, and sexual intimate partner aggression among newlywed couples: Longitudinal prediction of marital satisfaction. *Journal of Family Violence, 25*(7), 689–699.

Pardini, D. A., Fite, P. J., & Burke, J. D. (2008). Bidirectional associations between parenting practices and conduct problems in boys from childhood to adolescence: The moderating effect of age and African-American ethnicity. *Journal of Abnormal Child Psychology, 36*(5), 647–662.

Parke, R. D. (1969). Some effects of punishment on children's behavior. *Young Children, 24,* 225–240.

Parke, R. D. (2002). Punishment revisited—Science, values, and the right question: Comment on Gershoff (2002). *Psychological Bulletin, 128,* 596–601.

Patterson, G. R. (1982). *A social learning approach to family intervention: III.* Eugene, OR: Castalia.

Patterson, G. R. (1995). Coercion—A basis for early age of onset for arrest. In J. McCord (Ed.), *Coercion and punishment in long-term perspective* (pp. 81–124). New York, NY: Cambridge University Press.

Patterson, G. R., DeBaryshe, B. D., & Ramsey, E. (1989). A developmental perspective on antisocial behavior. *American Psychologist, 44*(2), 329–335.

Patterson, G. R., Reid, J. B., & Dishion, T. J. (1992). *Antisocial boys: A social interactional approach* (Vol. 4). Eugene, OR: Castalia Publishing Co.

Pearlin, L. I. (1967). *Class context and family relations: A cross-national study.* Canada: Little, Brown & Company.

Perry, B. D. (2006). Applying principles of neurodevelopment to clinical work with maltreated and traumatized children: The Neurosequential model of therapeutics. In N. Boyd Webb (Ed.), *Working with traumatized youth in child welfare* (pp. 27–52). New York, NY: Guilford Press.

Peters, M. F. (1976). *Nine black families: A study of household management and child-rearing in black families with working mothers.* Ann Arbor, MI: University Microfilms.

Peterson, E. T., & Kunz, P. R. (1975). Parental control over adolescents according to family size. *Adolescence, 10*(39), 419–427.

Peterson, G. W., & Rollins, B. C. (1987). Parent-child socialization. In M. R. Sussman & S. K. Steinmetz (Eds.), *Handbook of marriage and the family.* New York, NY: Plenum Press.

Philliber, S. G., & Graham, E. H. (1981). The impact of age of mother on mother-child interaction patterns. *Journal of Marriage and the Family, 43*(1), 109–115.

Phillips, D. P. (1983). The impact of mass media violence on U.S. homicides. *American Sociological Review, 48,* 560–568.

Pick, S., & Andrade Palos, P. (1995). Impact of the family on the sex lives of adolescents. *Adolescence, 30*(119), 667–675.

Pinheiro, P. S. (2006). *Ending legalised violence against children: Global Report 2006.* Geneva, Switzerland: Global Initiative to End All Corporal Punishment of Children.

Pinker, S. (2011). *Better angels of our nature: Why violence has declined.* New York, NY: Viking.

Pinto, A., Folkers, E., & Sines, J. O. (1991). Dimensions of behavior and home environment in school-age children: India and the United States. *Journal of Cross-Cultural Psychology, 22*(4), 491–508.

Pinto-Duschinsky, M. (2011). *Bringing rights back home making human rights compatible with parliamentary democracy in the UK.* London, England: Policy Exchange.

Poitras, M., & Lavoie, F. (1995). A study of the prevalence of sexual coercion in adolescent heterosexual dating relationships in a Quebec sample. *Violence and Victims, 10,* 299–313.

Polite, K. (1996). The medium/the message: Corporal punishment, an empirical critique. *Pediatrics. The short- and long-term consequences of corporal punishment, 98*(4, Part 2), 849–852.

Pollard, D. (2003). Banning child corporal punishment. *Tulane Law Review, 77*(3), 575–657.

Power, T. G., & Chapieski, M. L. (1986). Childrearing and impulse control in toddlers: A naturalistic investigation. *Developmental Psychology, 22*(2), 271–275.

Prinz, R. J., Sanders, M. R., Shapiro, C. J., Whitaker, D. J., & Lutzker, J. R. (2009). Population-based prevention of child maltreatment: The U.S. triple P system population trial. *Prevention Science, 10*(1), 1–12

Pulkkinen, L. (1983). Search for alternatives to aggression in Finland. In A. P. Goldstein & M. H. Segall (Eds.), *Aggression in global perspective.* New York, NY: Pergamon Press.

Raghunathan, T. E., Solenberger, P. W., & Van Hoewyk, J. (2002). *IVEware: Imputation and variance estimation software user guide.* Ann Arbor, MI: Survey Methodology Program, Survey Research Center, Institute for Social Research, University of Michigan. Retrieved from ftp://ftp.isr.umich.edu/pub/src/smp/ive/ive_user.pdf

Rankin, J. H., & Kern, R. (1994). Parental attachments and delinquency. *Criminology, 32*(4), 495–515.

Rankin, J. H., & Wells, L. E. (1990). The effect of parental attachments and direct controls on delinquency. *Journal of Research in Crime and Delinquency, 27*(2), 140–165.

Rebellon, C. J., Straus, M. A., & Medeiros, R. A. (2008). Self-control in global perspective: An empirical assessment of Gottfredson and Hirschi's general theory within and across 32 national settings. *European Journal of Criminology, 5*(3), 331–362.

Rebellon, C. J., & Van Gundy, K. (2005). Can control theory explain the link between parental physical abuse and delinquency? A longitudinal analysis. *Journal of Research in Crime and Delinquency, 42*(3), 247–274.

Regalado, M., Sareen, H., Inkelas, M., Wissow, L. S., & Halfon, N. (2004). Parents' discipline of young children: Results from the national survey of early childhood health. *Pediatrics, 113*(Supplement), 1952–1958.

Resnick, M. D., Bearman, P. S., Blum, R. W., Bauman, K. E., Harris, K. M., Jones, J., . . . Udry, J. R. (1997). Protecting adolescents from harm: Findings from the national longitudinal study on adolescent health. *Journal of American Medical Association, 278*(10), 823–832.

Richardson, R. A., Abramowitz, R. H., Asp, C. E., & Petersen, A. C. (1986). Parent-child relationships in early adolescence: Effects of family structure. *Journal of Marriage and the Family, 48*(4), 805–811.

Rizzo, T. A., Metzger, B. E., Dooley, S. L., & Cho, N. H. (1997). Early malnutrition and child neurobehavioral development: Insights from the study of children of diabetic mothers. *Child Development, 68*(1), 26–38.

Roberts, M. W. (1988). Enforcing chair timeouts with room timeouts. *Behavior Modification, 12,* 353–370.

Roberts, M. W., & Powers, S. W. (1990). Adjusting chair timeout enforcement procedures for oppositional children. *Behavior Therapy, 21,* 257–271.

Rohner, R. P., Bourque, S. L., & Elordi, C. A. (1996). Children's perspectives of corporal punishment, caretaker acceptance, and psychological adjustment in a poor, biracial southern community. *Journal of Marriage and the Family, 58*(November), 842–852.

Rohner, R. P., Kean, K., J., & Cournoyer, D. E. (1991). Effects of corporal punishment, perceived caretaker warmth, and cultural beliefs on the psychological adjustment of children in St. Kitts, West Indies. *Journal of Marriage and Family, 53,* 681–669.

Rose, G. (1985). Sick individuals and sick populations. *International Journal of Epidemiology, 14*(1), 32–38.

Rosemond, J. K. (1994a). Should the use of corporal punishment by parents be considered child abuse?—Response. In M. A. Mason & E. Gambrill (Eds.), *Debating children's lives: Current controversies on children and adolescents* (pp. 215–216). Thousand Oaks, CA: Sage.

Rosemond, J. K. (1994b). *To spank or not to spank: A parents' handbook.* Kansas City, MO: Andrews & McMeel.

Rosenberg, M., Schooler, C., & Schoenbach, C. (1989). Self-esteem and adolescent problems. *American Sociological Review, 54,* 1004–1018.

Rosenthal, R. (1984). *Meta-analytic procedures for social research.* Newbury Park, CA: Sage.

Rousseau, J.-J. (1928). *The confessions of Jean-Jacques Rousseau.* Montreal, Canada: Louis Carrier.

Runyan, D. K., Shankar, V., Hassan, F., Hunter, W. M., Jain, D., Paula, C. S., . . . Bordin, S. A. (2010). International variations in harsh child discipline. *Pediatrics, 126*(3), 701–711.

Russell, E. W. (1972). Factors of human aggression: A cross cultural factor analysis of characteristics related to warfare and crime. *Behavior Science Notes, 7,* 291.

Sampson, R. J., & Laub, J. H. (1993). *Crime in the making: Pathways and turning points through life.* Cambridge, MA: Harvard University Press.

Sampson, R. J., Raudenbush, S. W., & Earls, F. (1997). Neighborhoods and violent crime: A multilevel study of collective efficacy. *Science, 277*(August 15), 918–924.

Saunders, B., & Goddard, C. (2010). *Physical punishment in childhood: The rights of the child.* Hoboken, NJ: Wiley.

Scaramella, L. V., Conger, R. D., Simons, R. L., & Whitbeck, L. B. (1998). Predicting risk for pregnancy by late adolescence: A social contextual perspective. *Developmental Psychology, 34,* 1233–1245.

Scheck, D. C., & Emerick, R. (1976). The young male adolescent's perception of early childrearing behavior: The differential effects of socioeconomic status and family size. *Sociometry, 39,* 39–52.

Schenck, E. R., Lyman, R. D., & Bodin, S. D. (2000). Ethical beliefs, attitudes, and professional practices of psychologists regarding parental use of corporal punishment: A survey. *Children's Services: Social Policy, Research & Practice, 3*(1), 23–38.

Scholer, S. J., Hamilton, E. C., Johnson, M. C., & Scott, T. A. (2010). A brief intervention may affect parents' attitudes toward using less physical punishment. *Family and Community Health, 33*(2), 106–116.

Schweinle, W., Ickes, W., Rollings, K., & Jacquot, C. (2010). Maritally aggressive men: Angry, egocentric, impulsive, and/or biased. *Journal of Language and Social Psychology, 29*(4), 399–424.

Sears, R. R., Maccoby, E. C., & Levin, H. (1957). *Patterns of child rearing.* New York, NY: Harper & Row.

Segall, M. H., Ember, C. R., & Ember, M. (1997). Aggression, crime, and warfare. In J. W. Berry, M. H. Segall, & C. Kagitcibasi (Eds.), *The handbook of cross-cultural psychology* (pp. 213–254). Needham Heights, MA: Allyn & Bacon.

Sellers, C. S. (1999). Self-control and intimate violence: An examination of the scope and specification of the general theory of crime. *Criminology, 37*(2), 375–404.

Seydlitz, R. (1990). The effects of gender, age, and parental attachment on delinquency: A test for interactions. *Sociological Spectrum, 10,* 209–225.

Sherman, L. W., Schmidt, J. D., & Rogan, D. P. (1992). *Policing domestic violence: Experiments and dilemmas.* New York, NY: The Free Press.

Shonkoff, J. P., Garner, A. S., Siegel, B. S., Dobbins, M. I., Earls, M. F., Garner, A. S., ... Wood, D. L. (2012). The lifelong effects of early childhood adversity and toxic stress. *Pediatrics, 129*(1), e232–e246.

Silverstein, M., Augustyn, M., Young, R., & Zuckerman, B. (2009). The relationship between maternal depression, in-home violence and use of physical punishment: What is the role of child behaviour? *Archives of Disease in Childhood, 94*(2), 138–143.

Simon, T. R., Anderson, M., Thompson, M. P., Crosby, A. E., Shelley, G., & Sacks, J. J. (2001). Attitudinal acceptance of intimate partner violence among U.S. adults. *Violence and Victims, 16*(2), 115–126.

Simons, D. A., & Wurtele, S. K. (2010). Relationships between parents' use of corporal punishment and their children's endorsement of spanking and hitting other children. *Child Abuse & Neglect, 34*(9), 639–646.

Simons, L. G., Burt, C. H., & Simons, R. L. (2008). A test of explanations for the effect of harsh parenting on the perpetration of dating violence and sexual coercion among college males. *Violence and Victims, 1*(23), 66–82.

Simons, R. L., Gordon Simons, L., & Wallace, L. E. (2004). *Families, delinquency, and crime: Linking society's most basic institution to antisocial behavior.* Los Angeles, CA: Roxbury Publishing.

Simons, R. L., Johnson, C., & Conger, R. D. (1994). Harsh corporal punishment versus quality of parental involvement as an explanation of adolescent maladjustment. *Journal of Marriage and Family, 56,* 591–607.

Simons, R. L., Lin, K.-H., & Gordon, L. C. (1998). Socialization in the family of origin and male dating violence: A prospective study. *Journal of Marriage and Family, 60,* 467–478.

Smith, A. B., & Durrant, J. E. (2011 (Eds.), *Global pathways to abolishing physical punishment: Realizing children's rights.* New York: Routledge.

Smith, D. E., Springer, C. M., & Barrett, S. (2010). Physical discipline and socioemotional adjustment among Jamaican adolescents. *Journal of Family Violence, 26*(1), 51–61.

Smith, J. R., & Brooks-Gunn, J. (1997). Correlates and consequences of harsh discipline for young children. *Archives of Pediatric Adolescent Medicine, 151*(8), 777–786.

Smithey, M., & Straus, M. A. (2004). Primary prevention of intimate partner violence. In H. Kury & J. Obergfell-Fuchs (Eds.), *Crime prevention—New approaches* (pp. 239–276). Mainz/Germany: Weisser Ring Gemeinnutzige Verlags-GmbH.

Snyder, H. N., & Sickmund, M. (2006). *Juvenile offenders and victims: 2006 national report.* Washington, DC: U.S. Department of Justice, Office of Justice Programs, Office of Juvenile Justice and Delinquency Prevention.

Socolar, R. R. S., & Stein, R. E. K. (1995). Spanking infants and toddlers: Maternal belief and practice. *Pediatrics, 95*(1), 105–111.

Sorenson, S. B., & Taylor, C. A. (2005). Female aggression toward male intimate partners: An examination of social norms in a community-based sample. *Psychology of Women Quarterly, 29*(1), 78–96.

Spencer, M. J. (1999). Corporal punishment and ridicule: Residual psychological effects in early adulthood. Implications for counselors. (Doctoral dissertation, Texas Tech University, 1999). *Dissertation Abstracts International. Section A: Humanities and Social Sciences, 60*(4), 1030.

Spitz, R. A. (1959). *A genetic field theory of ego formation: Its implications for pathology.* New York, NY: International Universities Press.

Spitzberg, B. H. (1999). An analysis of empirical estimates of sexual aggression victimization and perpetration. *Violence and Victims, 14*(3), 241–260.

Spock, B., & Rothenberg, M. B. (1992). *Dr. Spock's baby and child care.* New York, NY: Pocket Books.

Stack, S. (1993). Execution publicity and homicide in Georgia. *American Journal of Criminal Justice, 18*(1), 25–39.

Stams, G.-J. J. M., Juffer, F., & Van Ijzendoorn, M. H. (2002). Maternal sensitivity, infant attachment, and temperament in early childhood predict adjustment in middle childhood: The case of adopted children and their biologically unrelated parents. *Developmental Psychology, 38*(5), 806–821.

Staples, R., & Johnson, L. B. (1993). *Black families at the crossroads.* San Francisco, CA: Jossey-Bass.

Stark, R., & McEvoy, J., III (1970). Middle-class violence. *Psychology Today, 4,* 52–65.

Stattin, H., Janson, H., Klackenberg-Larsson, I., Magnusson, D., & McCord, J. (1995). Corporal punishment in everyday life: An intergenerational perspective. In *Coercion and punishment in long-term perspectives* (pp. 315–347). New York, NY: Cambridge University Press.

Steinmetz, S. K., & Straus, M. A. (1973). The family as cradle of violence. *Society, 10,* 50–56. Stempel, G. H. (2006). *Scripps-Survey SHOH34.* Athens, OH: Scripps Research Center, Ohio University.

Stempel, G. H. (2006). *Scripps-Survey SHOH34.* Athens, Ohio: Scripps Research Center, Ohio University.

Stets, J. E., & Straus, M. A. (1989). The marriage license as a hitting license: A comparison of assaults in dating, cohabiting, and married couples. *Journal of Family Violence 4*(2), 161–180.

Stets, J. E., & Straus, M. A. (1990). Gender differences in reporting of marital violence and its medical and psychological consequences. In M. A. Straus & R. J. Gelles (Eds.), *Physical violence in American families: Risk factors and adaptations to violence in 8,145 families* (pp. 151–166). New Brunswick, NJ: Transaction Publishers.

Stouthamer-Loeber, M., Loeber, R., Huizinga, D., & Porter, P. (1997). The early onset of persistent serious offending. Washington, DC: U.S. Department of Justice, Office of Justice Programs, Office of Juvenile Justice and Delinquency Prevention.

Strassberg, Z., Dodge, K. A., Pettit, G. S., & Bates, J. E. (1994). Spanking in the home and children's subsequent aggression towards kindergarten peers. *Development and Psychopathology, 6,* 445–461.

Straus, M. A. (1971). Some social antecedents of physical punishment: A linkage theory interpretation. *Journal of Marriage and the Family, 33,* 658–663.

Straus, M. A. (1976). Sexual inequality, cultural norms, and wife-beating. In E. C. Viano (Ed.), *Victims and society* (pp. 543–559). Washington, DC: Visage Press.

Straus, M. A. (1979). Measuring intrafamily conflict and violence: The Conflict Tactics (CT) Scales. *Journal of Marriage and the Family, 41,* 75–88.

Straus, M. A. (1980). *The ZP scale: A percentages Z-Score.* Durham, NH: University of New Hampshire, Family Research Laboratory.

Straus, M. A. (1987). State and regional differences in U.S. infant homicide rates in relation to sociocultural characteristics of the states. *Behavioral Sciences & the Law, 5*(1), 61–75.

Straus, M. A. (1990a). The Conflict Tactics Scales and its critics: An evaluation and new data on validity and reliability. In M. A. Straus & R. J. Gelles (Eds.), *Physical violence in American families: Risk factors and adaptations to violence in 8,145 families* (pp. 49–73). New Brunswick, NJ: Transaction Publications.

Straus, M. A. (1990b). Corporal punishment, child abuse, and wife beating: What do they have in common? In M. A. Straus & R. J. Gelles (Eds.), *Physical violence in American families: Risk factors and adaptations to violence in 8,145 families.* New Brunswick, NJ: Transaction Publishers.

Straus, M. A. (1990c). Injury, frequency, and the representative sample fallacy in measuring wife beating and child abuse. In M. A. Straus & R. J. Gelles (Eds.), *Physical violence in American families: Risk factors and adaptations to violence in 8,145 families* (pp. 75–89). New Brunswick, NJ: Transaction Publications.

Straus, M. A. (1990d). The national family violence surveys. In M. A. Straus & R. J. Gelles (Eds.), *Physical violence in American families: Risk factors and adaptations to violence in 8,145 Families* (pp. 3–16). New Brunswick, NJ: Transaction Publishers.

Straus, M. A. (1990e). Ordinary violence, child abuse, and wife beating: What do they have in common? In M. A. Straus & R. J. Gelles (Eds.), *Physical violence in American families: Risk factors and adaptations to violence in 8,145 families* (pp. 403–421). New Brunswick, NJ: Transaction Publishers.

Straus, M. A. (1991). Discipline and deviance: Physical punishment of children and violence and other crime in adulthood. *Social Problems, 38*(2), 133–154.

Straus, M. A. (1992). Children as witnesses to marital violence: A risk factor for life long problems among a nationally representative sample of American men and women. In D. F. Schwartz (Ed.), *Children and violence: Report of the twenty third Ross roundtable on critical approaches to common pediatric problems* (pp. 98–109). Columbus, OH: Ross Laboratories.

Straus, M. A. (1994). State-to-state differences in social-inequality and social bonds in relation to assaults on wives in the United States. *Journal of Comparative Family Studies, 25*(1), 7–24.

Straus, M. A. (1995a). Corporal punishment of children and depression and suicide in adulthood. In J. McCord (Ed.), *Coercion and punishment in long term perspective.* New York, NY: Cambridge University Press.

Straus, M. A. (1995b). Trends in cultural norms and rates of partner violence: An update to 1992. In S. Stith & M. A. Straus (Eds.), *Understanding partner violence: Prevalence, causes, consequences, and solutions* (Vol. Families in focus series, II, pp. 30–33). Minneapolis, MN: National Council on Family Relations.

Straus, M. A. (1998). Spanking by parents--some ideas on measurement and analysis of a neglected risk factor for serious mental health problems. *Behavioral Measurements Letter, 5*(2), 3–8.

Straus, M. A. (1999). The controversy over domestic violence by women: A methodological, theoretical, and sociology of science analysis. In X. Arriaga & S. Oskamp (Eds.), *Violence in intimate relationships* (pp. 17–44). Thousand Oaks, CA: Sage.

Straus, M. A. (2000). Corporal punishment and primary prevention of physical abuse. *Child Abuse & Neglect, 24*(9), 1109–1114.

Straus, M. A. (2001a). *Beating the devil out of them: Corporal punishment in American families and its effects on children* (2nd ed.). New Brunswick, NJ: Transaction Publishers.

Straus, M. A. (2001b). The benefits of never spanking: New and more definitive evidence. In M. A. Straus (Ed.), *Beating the devil out of them: Corporal punishment in American families and its effects on children* (2nd ed., pp. 193–215). New Brunswick, NJ: Transaction Publications.

Straus, M. A. (2001c). New evidence for the benefits of never spanking. *Social Science and Public Policy, Sept/Oct,* 52–60.

Straus, M. A. (2001d). Social evolution and corporal punishment. In M. A. Straus (Ed.), *Beating the devil out of them: Corporal punishment in American families and its effects on children* (2nd ed., Chapter 11). New Brunswick, NJ: Transaction Publishers.

Straus, M. A. (2001e). Ten myths that perpetuate corporal punishment. In M. A. Straus (Ed.), *Beating the devil out of them: Corporal punishment in American families and its effects on children* (2nd ed., pp. 149–164). New Brunswick, NJ: Transaction Publishers.

Straus, M. A. (2003). *Guide to the multidimensional neglectful behavior scales.* Durham, NH: Family Research Laboratory.

Straus, M. A. (2004). Cross-cultural reliability and validity of the revised Conflict Tactics Scales: A study of university student dating couples in 17 nations. *Cross-Cultural Research, 38,* 407–432.

Straus, M. A. (2005). Children should never, ever, be spanked no matter what the circumstances. In D. R. Loseke, R. J. Gelles, & M. M. Cavanaugh (Eds.), *Current controversies about family violence* (2nd ed., pp. 137–157). Thousand Oak, CA: Sage.

Straus, M. A. (2006). Cross-cultural reliability and validity of the multidimensional neglectful behavior scale adult recall short form. *Child Abuse & Neglect, 30,* 1257–1279.

Straus, M. A. (2008a). Commentary: The special issue on prevention of violence ignores the primordial violence. *Journal of Interpersonal Violence, 23*(9), 1314–1320.

Straus, M. A. (2008b). Dominance and symmetry in partner violence by male and female university students in 32 nations. *Children and Youth Services Review, 30,* 252–275.

Straus, M. A. (2009a, 25 September). *Differences in corporal punishment by parents in 32 Nations and its relation to national differences in IQ.* Paper presented at the 14th International Conference on Violence, Abuse and Trauma, San Diego, CA.

Straus, M. A. (2009b). The national context effect: An empirical test of the validity of cross-national research using unrepresentative samples. *Cross-Cultural Research, 43*(3), 183–205.

Straus, M. A. (2009c). Why the overwhelming evidence on partner physical violence by women has not been perceived and is often denied. *Journal of Aggression, Maltreatment & Trauma, 18*(6), 552–571.

Straus, M. A. (2010b). Prevalence and societal causes of corporal punishment by parents in world perspective. *Law and Contemporary Problems, 73*(2 Spring), 1–30.

Straus, M. A. (2011). Gender symmetry and mutuality in perpetration of clinical-level partner violence: Empirical evidence and implications for prevention and treatment. *Aggression and Violent Behavior, 16*(4), 279–288.

Straus, M. A., & Donnelly, D. A. (1994). Corporal punishment of adolescents by American parents. *Youth & Society, 24 (4) 419–442.*

Straus, M. A., & Donnelly, D. A. (2001a). The fusion of sex and violence. In M. A. Straus (Ed.), *Beating the devil out of them: Corporal punishment in American families and its effects on children* (pp. 121–136). New Brunswick, NJ: Transaction Publishers.

Straus, M. A., & Donnelly, D. A. (2001b). Hitting adolescents. In M. A. Straus (Ed.), *Beating the devil out of them: Corporal punishment in American families and its effect on children* (2nd ed., pp. 35–48). New Brunswick, NJ: Transaction Publishers.

Straus, M. A., & Fauchier, A. (2011). Manual for the dimensions of discipline inventory (DDI). Durham, NH: Family Research Laboratory, University of New Hampshire.

Straus, M. A., & Gelles, R. J. (1986). Societal change and change in family violence from 1975 to 1985 as revealed by two national surveys. *Journal of Marriage and the Family, 48,* 465–479.

Straus, M. A., Gelles, R. J., & Steinmetz, S. K. (2006). *Behind closed doors: Violence in the American family* (2nd ed.). New Brunswick, NJ: Transaction Publications.

Straus, M. A., & Gimpel, H. S. (2001). Alienation and reduced income. In M. A. Straus (Ed.), *Beating the devil out of them: Corporal punishment in American families and its effect on children* (2nd ed., pp. 137–146). New Brunswick, NJ: Transaction Publishers.

Straus, M. A., & Gozjolko, K. L. (in press). Intimate terrorism and injury of dating partners by male and female university students. *Journal of Family Violence.*

Straus, M. A., Hamby, S. L., Boney-McCoy, S., & Sugarman, D. B. (1996). The revised Conflict Tactics Scales (CTS2): Development and preliminary psychometric data. *Journal of Family Issues, 17*(3), 283–316.

Straus, M. A., Hamby, S. L., Boney-McCoy, S., & Sugarman, D. (2010). *Manual for the personal and relationships profile (PRP).* Durham, NH: University of New Hampshire, Family Research Laboratory.

Straus, M. A., Hamby, S. L., Finkelhor, D., Moore, D. W., & Runyan, D. (1998). Identification of child maltreatment with the parent-child Conflict Tactics Scales: Development and psychometric data for a national sample of American parents. *Child Abuse & Neglect, 22,* 249–270.

Straus, M. A., & Kaufman Kantor, G. (1994). Corporal punishment of adolescents by parents: A risk factor in the epidemiology of depression, suicide, alcohol abuse, child abuse, and wife beating. *Adolescence, 29*(115), 543–562.

Straus, M. A., & Kaufman Kantor, G. (2005). Definition and measurement of neglectful behavior: Some general principles and guidelines. *Child Abuse & Neglect, 29*(12), 19–29.

Straus, M. A., Kaufman Kantor, G., & Moore, D. W. (1997). Change in cultural norms approving marital violence: From 1968 to 1994. In G. Kaufman Kantor & J. L. Jasinski (Eds.), *Out of the darkness: Contemporary perspectives on family violence.* Thousand Oaks, CA: Sage.

Straus, M. A., Kinard, E. M., & Williams, L. M. (1995). The multidimensional neglectful behavior scale, form A: Adolescent and adult-recall version. Durham, NH: University of New Hampshire: Family Research Laboratory. Retrieved from http://pubpages.unh.edu/~mas2/

Straus, M. A., & Mathur, A. K. (1996). Social change and trends in approval of corporal punishment by parents from 1968 to 1994. In D. Frehsee, W. Horn, & K.-D. Bussmann (Eds.), *Family violence against children: A challenge for society* (pp. 91–105). New York, NY: Walter de Gruyter.

Straus, M. A., & Mattingly, M. J. (2007). *A short form and severity level types for the parent-child Conflict Tactics Scales.* Durham, NH: Family Research Laboratory, University of New Hampshire. Retrieved from http://pubpages.unh.edu/~mas2.

Straus, M. A., & Mickey, E. L. (2012). Reliability, validity, and prevalence of partner violence measured by the conflict tactics scales in male-dominant nations. *Aggression and Violent Behavior, 17,* 463–474.

Straus, M. A., & Mouradian, V. E. (1998). Impulsive corporal punishment by mothers and antisocial behavior and impulsiveness of children. *Behavioral Sciences & the Law, 16,* 353–374.

Straus, M. A., & Mouradian, V. E. (1999, November 19). *Preliminary psychometric data for the personal and relationships profile (PRP): A multi-scale tool for clinical screening and research on partner violence.* Paper presented at the American Society of Criminology, Toronto, Ontario.

Straus, M. A., & Paschall, M. J. (2009). Corporal punishment by mothers and development of children's cognitive ability: A longitudinal study of two nationally representative age cohorts. *Journal of Aggression, Maltreatment, and Trauma* (Vol. 18, No 5., pp. 459–483).

Straus, M. A., & Ramirez, I. L. (2007). Gender symmetry in prevalence, severity, and chronicity of physical aggression against dating partners by university students in Mexico and USA. *Aggressive Behavior, 33,* 281–290.

Straus, M. A., & Savage, S. A. (2005). Neglectful behavior by parents in the life history of university students in 17 countries and its relation to violence against dating partners. *Child Maltreatment, 10*(2), 124–135.

Straus, M. A., & Smith, C. (1990). Family patterns and primary prevention of family violence. In M. A. Straus & R. J. Gelles (Eds.), *Physical violence in American families: Risk factors and adaptations to violence in 8,145 families*. New Brunswick, NJ: Transaction Press.

Straus, M. A., & Stewart, J. H. (1999). Corporal punishment by American parents: National data on prevalence, chronicity, severity, and duration, in relation to child, and family characteristics. *Clinical Child and Family Psychology Review, 2*(2), 55–70.

Straus, M. A., Sugarman, D. B., & Giles-Sims, J. (1997). Spanking by parents and subsequent antisocial behavior of children. *Archives of Pediatric and Adolescent Medicine, 151*(August), 761–767.

Straus, M. A., & Yodanis, C. L. (1996). Corporal punishment in adolescence and physical assaults on spouses later in life: What accounts for the link? *Journal of Marriage and the Family, 58*(4), 825–841.

Straus, M. A., & Yodanis, C. L. (2001). Physical abuse. In M. A. Straus (Ed.), *Beating the devil out of them: Corporal punishment in American families and its effects on children.* New Brunswick, NJ: Transaction Publishers.

Struckman-Johnson, C. (1988). Forced sex on dates: It happens to men, too. *Journal of Sex Research, 24,* 234–241.

Substance Abuse and Mental Health Services Administration. (2005). *The NSDUH Report: Depression among adults.* Rockville, MD: Office of Applied Studies.

Sugarman, D. B., & Hotaling, G. T. (1989). Dating violence: Prevalence, context, and risk markers. In A. A. Pirog-Good & J. E. Stets (Eds.), *Violence in dating relationships: Emerging social issues* (pp. 3–31). New York, NY: Praeger.

Suitor, J. J., Pillemer, K., & Straus, M. A. (1990). Marital violence in a life course perspective. In M. A. Straus & R. J. Gelles (Eds.), *Physical violence in American families: Risk factors and adaptations to violence in 8,145 families* (pp. 305–319). New Brunswick, NJ: Transaction Publishers.

SurveyUSA. (2005). *50 state discipline survey.* Verona, NJ: SurveyUSA.

Swan, R. (2004). *Corporal punishment by parents and caretakers.* Paper presented at the General Conference 2004, United Methodist Church, Pittsburg, PA.

Swanston, H. Y., Parkinson, P. N., O'Toole, B. I., Plunkett, A. M., Shrimpton, S., & Oates, R. K. (2003). Juvenile crime, aggression and delinquency after sexual abuse: A longitudinal study. *British Journal of Criminology, 43,* 729–749.

Sweeten, G. (2009). *Scaling offending.* Paper presented at the annual meeting of the American Society of Criminology, Philadelphia, PA.

Talwar, V., Carlson, S., & Lee, K. (2011). Effects of a punitive environment on children's executive functioning: A natural experiment. *Social Development,* 1–20.

Taylor, C. A., Hamvas, L., & Paris, R. (2011). Perceived instrumentality and normativeness of corporal punishment use among Black mothers. *Family Relations, 60*(1), 60–72.

Taylor, C. A., Hamvas, L., Rice, J., Newman, D., & DeJong, W. (2011). Perceived social norms, expectations, and attitudes toward corporal punishment among an urban community sample of parents. *Journal of Urban Health, 88*(2), 254–269.

Taylor, C. A., Lee, S. J., Guterman, N. B., & Rice, J. C. (2010). Use of spanking for 3-year-old children and associated intimate partner aggression or violence. *Pediatrics,* 415–424.

Taylor, C. A., Manganello, J. A., Lee, S. J., & Rice, J. C. (2010). Mothers' spanking of 3-year-old children and subsequent risk of children's aggressive behavior. *Pediatrics, 125*(5), 1057–1065.

Teicher, M. H., Andersen, S. L., Polcari, A., Anderson, C. M., & Navalta, C. P. (2002). Developmental neurobiology of childhood stress and trauma. *Psychiatric Clinics of North American, 25*(2), 397–426.

Temple, J. R., Weston, R., Rodriguez, B. F., & Marshall, L. L. (2007). Differing effects of partner and nonpartner sexual assault on women's mental health. *Violence against Women, 13*, 285–297.

Teske, R. H. C., & Parker, M. L. (1983). *Spouse abuse in Texas: A study of women's attitudes and experiences.* Huntsville, TX: Criminal Justice Center, Sam Houston State University.

Testa, M., Hoffman, J. H., & Leonard, K. E. (2011). Female intimate partner violence perpetration: Stability and predictors of mutual and nonmutual aggression across the first year of college. *Aggressive Behavior, 37*(4), 362–373.

Tewksbury, R. (2007). Effects of sexual assaults on men: Physical, mental and sexual consequences. *International Journal of Men's Health, 6*, 22.

Thomas, K. A., & Dettlaff, A. J. (2011). African American families and the role of physical discipline: Witnessing the past in the present. *Journal of Human Behavior in the Social Environment, 21*(8), 963–977.

Thomson, E. (1999). Effects of an execution on homicides in California. *Homicide Studies, 3*(2), 129–151.

Thornberry, T. P., & Krohn, M. D. (2000). The self-report method for measuring delinquency and crime. *Criminal Justice, 4*, 34–83.

Tjaden, P., & Thoennes, N. (2000). Prevalence and consequences of male-to-female and female-to-male intimate partner violence as measured by the national violence against women survey. *Violence against Women, 6*, 142–161.

Toch, H., & Adams, K. (2002). *Acting out: Maladaptive behavior in confinement.* Washington, DC: American Psychological Association.

Tolman, R. M., & Bennett, L. W. (1990). A review of quantitative research on men who batter. *Journal of Interpersonal Violence, 5*(1), 87–118.

Tomoda, A., Suzuki, H., Rabi, K., Sheu, Y.-S., Polcari, A., & Teicher, M. H. (2009). Reduced prefrontal cortical gray matter volume in young adults exposed to harsh corporal punishment. *Neuroimage, 47*, T66–T71.

Toothaker, L. E. (1991). *Multiple comparisons for researchers.* Newbury Park: CA: Sage.

Toure. (2011). Preconceptions: Lives—A spanking questions. Retrieved from http://www.nytimes.com

Tremblay, R. E. (2003). Why socialization fails: The case of chronic physical aggression. In B. B. Lahey, T. E. Moffitt, & A. Caspi (Eds.), *Causes of conduct disorder and juvenile delinquency* (pp. 182–224). New York, NY: Guilford Press.

Tremblay, R. E. (2006). Prevention of youth violence: Why not start at the beginning? *Journal of Abnormal Child Psychology, 34*(4), 481–487.

Trocmé, N., McPhee, D., Tam, K. K., & Hay, T. (1994). *Ontario incidence study of reported child abuse and neglect* (pp. 139). Toronto, Canada: Institute for Prevention of Child Abuse.

Trocmé, N., MacMillan, H., Fallon, B., & De Marco, R. (2003). Nature and severity of physical harm caused by child abuse and neglect: Results from the Canadian incidence study. *CMAJ, 169*(9), 911–915.

Trocmé, N. M., Tourigny, M., MacLaurin, B., & Fallon, B. (2003). Major findings from the Canadian incidence study of reported child abuse and neglect. *Child Abuse & Neglect, 27*(12), 1427–1439.

Tsang, R. (1995). *Social stress, social learning, and anger as risk factors for corporal punishment.* Durham, NH: University of New Hampshire, Family Research Laboratory.

Turner, H. A., & Finkelhor, D. (1996). Corporal punishment as a stressor among youth. *Journal of Marriage and the Family, 58*(Feb), 155–166.

Turner, H. A., & Muller, P. A. (2004). Long-term effects of child corporal punishment on depressive symptoms in young adults: Potential moderators and mediators. *Journal of Family Issues, 25*(6), 761–782.

Ulman, A., & Straus, M. A. (2003). Violence by children against mothers in relation to violence between parents and corporal punishment by parents. *Journal of Comparative Family Studies, 34*(1), 41–60.

UNICEF. (1997). *United Nations Convention on the Rights of the Child.* Retrieved from http://www.unicef.org/crc/conven.htm

UNICEF. (2010). *Child disciplinary practices at home: Evidence from a range of low- and middle- income countries.* New York, NY: UNICEF.

U.S. Bureau of the Census. (2011). *Statistical abstract of the United States: 2011.* Washington, DC: U.S. Government Printing Office.

Van Zeijl, J., Mesman, J., Van Ijzendoorn, M. H., Bakermans-Kranenburg, M. J., Juffer, F., Stolk, M. N., . . . Alink, L. R. A. (2006). Attachment-based intervention for enhancing sensitive discipline in mothers of 1- to 3-year-old children at risk for externalizing behavior problems: A randomized controlled trial. *Journal of Consulting and Clinical Psychology, 74*(6), 994–1005.

Vanderminden, J., & Straus, M. A. (2010, November). *Violent socialization and its relation to physical assaults and depression in 32 nations.* Paper presented at the American Society of Criminology, San Francisco, CA.

Vissing, Y. M., Straus, M. A., Gelles, R. J., & Harrop, J. W. (1991). Verbal aggression by parents and psychosocial problems of children. *Child Abuse & Neglect, 15*(3), 223–238.

Vittrup, B., & Holden, G. W. (2010). Children's assessments of corporal punishment and other disciplinary practices: The role of age, race, SES, and exposure to spanking. *Journal of Applied Developmental Psychology, 31*(3), 211–220.

Vittrup, B., Holden, G. W., & Buck, J. (2006). Attitudes predict the use of physical punishment: A prospective study of the emergence of disciplinary practices. *Pediatrics, 117*(6), 2055–2064.

Walsh, W. (2002). Spankers and nonspankers: Where they get information on spanking. *Family Relations, 51,* 81–88.

Warr, M. (1993). Parents, peers, and delinquency. *Social Forces, 72*(1), 247–264.

Wauchope, B., & Straus, M. A. (1990). Physical punishment and physical abuse of American children: Incidence rates by age, gender, and occupational class. In M. A. Straus & R. J. Gelles (Eds.), *Physical violence in American families: Risk factors and adaptations to violence in 8,145 families* (pp. 133–148). New Brunswick, NJ: Transaction Publishers.

Webster-Stratton, C. (1984). A randomized trial of two parent-training programs for families with conduct-disordered children. *Journal of Consulting and Clinical Psychology, 52,* 666–678.

Webster-Stratton, C. (1990). Enhancing the effectiveness of self-administered videotape parent training for families with conduct-problem children. *Journal of Abnormal Child Psychology, 18*(5), 479–492.

Webster-Stratton, C., Kolpacoff, M., & Hollinsworth, T. (1988). Self-administered videotape therapy for families with conduct-problem children: Comparison with two cost-effective treatments and a control group. *Journal of Consulting and Clinical Psychology, 56*(4), 558–566.

Weiss, C. H., & Bucuvalas, M. J. (1980). Truth tests and utility tests: Decision makers' frames of reference for social science research. *American Sociological Review, 45,* 302–313.

Welsh, R. S. (1976). Severe parental punishment and delinquency: A developmental theory. *Journal of Clinical Child Psychiatry, Spring,* 17–21.

Welsh, R. S. (1978). Delinquency, corporal punishment and the schools. *Crime and Delinquency, 24,* 336–354.

Whitaker, D. J., Haileyesus, T., Swahn, M., & Saltzman, L. S. (2007). Differences in frequency of violence and reported injury between relationships with reciprocal and nonreciprocal intimate partner violence *American Journal of Public Health, 97*(5), 941–947.

White, J. W., Koss, M. P., & Kazdin, A. E. (Eds.). (2011). *Violence Against Women and Children: Mapping the Terrain.* Washington, D.C.: American Psychological Association.

White, J. W., & Smith, P. H. (2009). Covariation in the use of physical and sexual intimate partner aggression among adolescent and college-age men: A longitudinal analysis. *Violence against Women, 15*(1), 24–43.

White, K. (1993). Where pediatricians stand on spanking. *Pediatric Management, September,* 11–15.

Wiatrowski, M., & Anderson, K. L. (1987). The dimensionality of the social bond. *Journal of Quantitative Criminology, 3*(1), 65–81.

Widom, C. P., & Ames, M. A. (1994). Criminal consequences of childhood sexual victimization. *Child Abuse & Neglect, 18,* 303–318.

Widom, C. S. (1989). Child abuse, neglect, and violent criminal behavior. *Criminology, 272,* 251–271.

Widom, C. S. (1992). *The cycle of violence.* Washington, DC: National Institute of Justice.

Wikström, P.-O. H., & Treiber, K. H. (2009). Violence as situational action. *International Journal of Conflict and Violence, 3*(1), 75–96.

Williams, G. J. (1983). Child abuse reconsidered: The urgency of authentic prevention. *Journal of Clinical Psychology, 12,* 312–319.

Williams, L. (2011). Part of our culture. In R. Ray, G. W. Holden, L. Williams, T. Sharee, & D. S. Cain (Eds.), "Is spanking a Black and White issue?" *The New York Times, Room for Debate*, Opinion Pages.

Willow, C., & Hyder, T. (1998). *It hurts you inside: Children talking about smacking.* London, England: National Children's Bureau Enterprises.

Wilson, H. W., & Widom, C. S. (2008). An examination of risky sexual behavior and HIV in victims of child abuse and neglect: A 30-year follow-up. *Health Psychology, 27*(2), 149–158.

Wilson, W. J. (1996). *When work disappears : The world of the new urban poor.* New York, NY: Knopf.

Winstok, Z., & Straus, M. A. (2011a). Gender differences in intended escalatory tendencies among marital partners. *Journal of Interpersonal Violence, 26*(18), 3599–3617.

Winstok, Z., & Straus, M. A. (2011b). Perceived neighborhood violence, child misbehavior, parental approval and use of aggressive discipline tactics. *Journal of Community Psychology, 39*(6), 678–697.

Wolfe, D. A., Katell, A., & Drabman, R. S. (1982). Parent's and preschool children's choices of disciplinary childrearing methods. *Journal of Applied Developmental Psychology, 3*(2), 167–176.

Wolfe, D. A., Scott, K., Wekerle, C., & Pittman, A.-L. (2001). Child maltreatment: Risk of adjustment problems and dating violence in adolescence. *Journal of the American Academy of Child and Adolescent Psychiatry, 40,* 282–289.

Wolfgang, M. E. (1958). *Patterns of criminal homicide.* Philadelphia, PA: University of Pennsylvania Press.

Work, A. (2011, March 4). CPS to investigate spanking: City View student, 16, missed D-Hall. *Times Record News.* Retrieved from www.timesrecordnews.com

Xu, X., Tung, Y., & Dunaway, R. (2000). Cultural, human and social capital as determinants of corporal punishment: Toward an integrated theoretical model. *Journal of Interpersonal Violence, 15*(6), 603–630.

Yodanis, C. L. (1992). *Corporal punishment and the fusion of love and violence* (master's thesis). University of New Hampshire, Durham, NH.

Young, V. (1970). Family and childhood in a southern negro community. *American Anthropologist, 72,* 269–288.

Zhang, S., & Anderson, S. G. (2010). Low-income single mothers' community violence exposure and aggressive parenting practices. *Children and Youth Services Review, 32*(6), 889–895.

Zigler, E., & Hall, N. W. (1989). Physical child abuse in America: Past, present, and future. In D. Cicchetti & V. Carlson (Eds.), *Child maltreatment: Theory and research on the causes and consequences of child abuse and neglect* (pp. 38–75). New York, NY: Cambridge University Press.

Zolotor, A. J., Theodore, A. D., Runyan, D. K., Chang, J. J., & Laskey, A. L. (2011). Corporal punishment and physical abuse: Population-based trends for three-to-11-year-old children in the United States. *Child Abuse Review, 20*(1), 57–66.

Zuravin, S. J. (1988a). Child maltreatment and teenage first births: A relationship mediated by chronic sociodemographic stress. *American Journal of Orthopsychiatry, 58,* 91–103.

Zuravin, S. J. (1988b). Fertility patterns: Their relationship to child physical abuse and child neglect. *Journal of Marriage and the Family, 50,* 983–993.

Zuravin, S. J. (1991). Unplanned childbearing and family size: Their relationship to child neglect and abuse. *Family Planning Perspectives, 23,* 155–161.

Zuravin, S. J., & Greif, G. L. (1989). Normative and child-maltreating AFDC mothers. *The Journal of Contemporary Social Work,* 76–84.

Zussman, J. U. (1978). Relationship of demographic factors to parental discipline techniques. *Developmental Psychology, 14,* 685–686.

Appendix

Data and Methods Used for Empirical Research Chapters

This appendix contains material for the chapters listed below. If there is no section in this appendix for a chapter, it means that data, methods, and statistical tests are given in the chapter itself or in references cited in the chapter.

Chapter 2:   Corporal Punishment In The United States
Chapter 4:   There Was An Old Women Who Lived In A Shoe
Chapter 5:   Approval Of Violence And Spanking Children
Chapter 7:   Impulsive Spanking, Never Spanking, And Child Well-Being
Chapter 8:   The Child-To-Mother Bond And Delinquency
Chapter 9:   Spanking And Risky Sex
Chapter 11:   College Graduation
Chapter 14:   Cultural Context And The Relation Of Spanking To Crime
Chapter 15:   Spanking High-Risk Children And Adult Crime
Chapter 16:   Sexual Coercion And Sexual Assault
Chapter 17:   The Decline In Approval Of Spanking

Appendix for Chapter 2

Corporal Punishment in the United States

Table A2.1   Number of Cases in Categories Used for ANOVAs

Characteristic	Category	n	
		Prevalence	*Chronicity*
Age of child	0–1	92	43
	2–4	190	166
	5–8	230	191
	9–12	228	131
	13–17	246	70
Gender of child	Male	503	320
	Female	483	282

(Continued)

Table A2.1   (Continued)

Characteristic	Category	n	
		Prevalence	Chronicity
Gender of respondent	Male	333	181
	Female	653	420
Age of respondent	18–29	224	171
	30–39	438	285
	40+	323	146
Socioeconomic status quintiles	1 Low	203	148
	2	139	81
	3	228	145
	4	226	126
	5 High	189	101
Ethnic group	White	817	480
	Black	125	97
	Other	44	25
Single parent	Yes	324	207
	No	662	395
Region	Northeast	190	101
	Midwest	252	159
	South	328	223
	West	215	119

Table A2.2   Percent of Parents Using Specific Acts of Corporal Punishment by Age of Child

Type of Corporal Punishment	Age of Child					F	P<
	0–1	2–4	5–8	9–12	13–17		
A. Ordinary Corporal Punishment							
Spank on bottom with hand	31.8	72.1	71.2	43.1	14.0	64.6	.01
Slap on hand, arm, or leg	36.4	63.3	47.5	26.9	16.2	28.5	.01
B. Severe Corporal Punishment							
Hit on bottom with object	2.5	18.1	28.4	28.5	15.6	11.3	.01
Slap on face, head, or ears	0.5	4.8	6.9	2.9	5.8	2.6	.02
Pinch	2.8	2.8	7.9	5.1	2.3	2.8	.03
C. Other							
Shake	4.3	12.8	10.8	11.4	5.7	3.0	.02
Threatened to spank	22.8	65.5	70.7	55.6	38.9	26.8	.01

Appendix for Chapter 4

There Was an Old Woman Who Lived in a Shoe

The data set for this chapter, the 1985 National Family Violence Survey, can be downloaded from the Inter-university Consortium for Political and Social Research or ICPSR (www.lib.vt.edu/find/icpsr).

Socioeconomic status was measured using a composite created by factor analyzing data on the following five indicators: educational attainment of the husband and the wife, occupational prestige of the husband and the wife, and the couple's combined annual income. One factor ($\alpha = .80$) accounting for 56% of the variance in those indicators emerged from that analysis. Scores on that socioeconomic status factor were used in the analyses.

Analysis of covariance was used to test the hypothesis that corporal punishment increases as the number of children goes up, provided age and birth order are controlled. The analysis also controlled for family socioeconomic status and the age and gender of the parent.

Statistical Tables

Table A4.1 Bivariate Relationships between Number of Children, Corporal Punishment, and Demographic Characteristics

	Means for Each Number of Children				
	1	*2*	*3*	*4+*	*F*
A. Corporal Punishment					
Prevalence of corporal punishment	54.27	66.69	66.06	66.24	17.10***
Chronicity of corporal punishment	8.68	9.60	9.89	8.38	2.03+
B. Family and Child Characteristics					
Child's birth order	1.00	1.47	2.00	2.63	885.34***
Child's age	8.54	8.26	8.41	9.01	1.60+
Respondent age	36.61	34.53	34.63	36.00	14.73***
Family socioeconomic status	5.52	5.68	5.20	4.98	5.49***

[a]All alphas are one-tailed. ***$p < .001$ **$p < .01$ +$p < .10$

Table A4.2 Analysis of Covariance Results for Number of Children and Corporal Punishment Prevalence and Chronicity

Predictor Variable	A. Prevalence (N = 2,870)			B. Chronicity (N = 1,762)		
	DF	*F*	*b*	*DF*	*F*	*b*
Number of children	–.–	3	18.66***	–.–	3	3.51**
Child's birth order	1	3.27*	2.26	1	0.99	–0.32
Child's age	1	80.85***	–1.92	1	72.71***	–0.54

(Continued)

Table A4.2   (Continued)

Predictor Variable	A. Prevalence (N = 2,870)			B. Chronicity (N = 1,762)		
	DF	F	b	DF	F	b
Respondent gender	−0.78	1	13.38***	6.64	1	2.58+
Respondent age	1	23.40***	−0.63	1	11.01***	−0.12
Family socio-economic status	1	1.62*	.38	1	1.96*	−0.12
Residual	2861			1753		

***p < .001, **p < .01, *p < .05, *p < .10.

Post-hoc contrast analyses comparing pairs of adjusted means in Chart 4.1 revealed marginally significant differences in corporal punishment between parents with two and three children (p < .10) and between parents with three and four or more children (p < .10). In Chart 4.2, the contrast analyses revealed a marginally significant (p < .10) difference between parents with two and three children in the chronicity of corporal punishment, but no difference between those with three and four or more children.

Appendix for Chapter 5

Approval of Violence and Spanking Children

Parts of Chapter 5 report analyses of data from the Gallup survey described in Chapter 2.

Data Analysis

Analysis of variance was computed using the "regression approach" option in SPSS; namely, all effects were assessed simultaneously, with each effect adjusted for all other effects in the model. Thus, the test for each independent variable controls for the other independent variables. The means are adjusted to control for the other independent variables.

Statistical Tables

Table A5.1   Analysis of Variance for Relation of Approval of Boys Fighting and Other Variables to "A Good Hard Spanking Is Sometimes Necessary" (N = 961)

Source of Variation	Sum of Squares	DF	Mean Square	F	P
Main Effects					
Boys Fight	92620.326	2	46310.163	20.143	.001
Age of Child	39029.658	4	9757.414	4.244	.002
Gender of Child	135.415	1	135.415	.059	.808

(Continued)

Table A5.1   (Continued)

Source of Variation	Sum of Squares	DF	Mean Square	F	P
Ethnic Group	3442.852	2	1721.426	.749	.473
Gender of Parent	2355.999	1	2355.999	1.025	.312
Age of Parent	16757.977	2	8378.988	3.645	.027
Single Parent	20725.435	1	20725.435	9.015	.003
SES	3006.905	4	751.726	.327	.860
Region	50528.484	3	16842.828	7.326	.001
Two-Way Interactions					
Boys Fight × Age Of Child	24511.852	8	3063.982	1.333	.224
Boys Fight × Gender Of Child	2595.600	2	1297.800	.564	.569
Boys Fight × Ethnic Group	6128.969	4	1532.242	.666	.615
Boys Fight × Gender Of Parent	369.316	2	184.658	.080	.923
Boys Fight × Age Of Parent	7331.855	4	1832.964	.797	.527
Boys Fight × Single Parent	7761.809	2	3880.905	1.688	.186
Boys Fight × SES	8608.746	8	1076.093	.468	.879
Boys Fight × Region	11003.488	6	1833.915	.798	.572

Table A5.2   Analysis of Variance: OK for Parents to Slap Teenagers ($N = 953$)

Source of Variation	Sum of Squares	DF	Mean Square	F	p
Main Effects					
Boys fight	21728.134	2	10864.067	7.432	.001
Age of child	7682.091	4	1920.523	1.314	.263
Gender of child	.526	1	.526	.000	.985
Ethnic group	718.348	2	359.174	.246	.782
Gender of parent	285.292	1	285.292	.195	.659
Age of parent	1443.080	2	721.540	.494	.611
Single parent	1649.974	1	1649.974	1.129	.288
Socioeconomic status	12325.121	4	3081.280	2.108	.078
Region	10138.399	3	3379.466	2.312	.075
Two-Way Interactions					
Boys fight × Age of child	9916.115	8	1239.514	.848	.561
Boys fight × Gender of child	648.051	2	324.025	.222	.801
Boys fight × Ethnic group	18128.422	4	4532.106	3.100	.015
Boys fight × Gender of parent	10085.791	2	5042.896	3.450	.032
Boys fight × Age of parent	11382.203	4	2845.551	1.947	.101
Boys fight × Single parent	03827.654	2	1913.827	1.309	.271
Boys fight × Socioeconomic status	14774.556	8	1846.820	1.263	.259
Boys fight × Region	11081.880	6	1846.980	1.263	.272

Table A5.3   Analysis of Variance: Parents Who Spare the Rod/Spoil Child ($N = 910$)

Source of Variation	Sum of Squares	DF	Mean Square	F	p
Main Effects					
Boys fight	38301.052	2	19150.526	8.151	.001
Age of child	16738.143	4	4184.536	1.781	.131
Gender of child	2338.993	1	2338.993	.996	.319
Ethnic group	9881.629	2	4940.814	2.103	.123
Gender of parent	4751.092	1	4751.092	2.022	.155
Age of parent	7.063	2	3.532	.002	.998
Single parent	6.665	1	6.665	.003	.958
Socioeconomic status	20702.640	4	5175.660	2.203	.067
Region	26407.845	3	8802.615	3.747	.011
Two-Way Interactions					
Boys fight × Age of child	16137.766	8	2017.221	.859	.551
Boys fight × Gender of child	1092.375	2	546.188	.232	.793
Boys fight × Ethnic group	4241.902	4	1060.476	.451	.771
Boys fight × Gender of parent	9029.024	2	4514.512	1.922	.147
Boys fight × Age of parent	15863.558	4	3965.889	1.688	.151
Boys fight × Single parent	7208.063	2	3604.031	1.534	.216
Boys fight × Socioeconomic status	9815.364	8	1226.921	..522	840
Boys fight × Region	12918.693	6	2153.116	.916	.482

Table A5.4   Analysis of Variance: Used Corporal Punishment ($N = 960$)

Source of Variation	Sum of Squares	DF	Mean Square	F	p
Main Effects					
Boys fight	42664.543	2	21332.272	13.548	.001
Age of child	405023.371	4	101255.843	64.308	.001
Gender of child	9541.332	1	9541.332	6.060	.014
Ethnic group	7876.819	2	3938.410	2.501	.083
Gender of parent	10877.301	1	10877.301	6.908	.009
Age of parent	5066.831	2	2533.415	1.609	.201
Single parent	7542.446	1	7542.446	4.790	.029
Socioeconomic status	13085.184	4	3271.296	2.078	.082
Region	29707.932	3	9902.644	6.289	.001

(Continued)

Table A5.4 (Continued)

Source of Variation	Sum of Squares	DF	Mean Square	F	p
Two-Way Interactions					
Boys fight × Age of child	21845.502	8	2730.688	1.734	.087
Boys fight × Gender of child	2520.100	2	1260.050	.800	.450
Boys fight × Ethnic group	9814.372	4	2453.593	1.558	.184
Boys fight × Gender of parent	2484.217	2	1242.109	.789	.455
Boys fight × Age of parent	958.418	4	239.604	.152	.962
Boys fight × Single parent	757.281	2	378.641	.240	.786
Boys fight × Socioeconomic status	9912.139	8	1239.017	.787	.614
Boys fight × Region	18337.031	6	3056.172	1.941	.072

Appendix for Chapter 7

Impulsive Spanking, Never Spanking, and Child Well-Being

Data Analysis

We computed a seven-way analysis of variance using child's antisocial behavior as the dependent variable and another using child's impulsiveness as the dependent variable. The independent variables were frequency of corporal punishment, impulsivity of corporal punishment, mother's nurturing behavior, mother's non-corporal punishment discipline, child's age, child's sex, and family socioeconomic status. We restricted the analyses to the main effects and the two-way interactions of corporal punishment and impulsivity corporal punishment with the other independent variables and with each other because those were the theoretically relevant interactions for this research and because higher order interactions would have resulted in empty cells and singular variance and covariance matrices. The ANOVAs were computed using the *regression approach* option in SPSS/ PC, namely "All effects are assessed simultaneously, with each effect adjusted for all other effects in the model" (Nurius, Furrey, & Berliner, 1992, p. 257). Thus, the test for each independent variable controls for the other six independent variables.

The 189 mothers who had never used corporal punishment could not be included in the fully crossed ANOVAs because, for these mothers, the cells for impulsivity corporal punishment would have no cases and therefore singular variance-covariance matrices would result. Instead, mean antisocial behavior and child impulsiveness scores were computed separately for the no corporal punishment group as part of the process of obtaining adjusted interaction effect means (see below). Differences between these means and other main effect means were tested using Tukey-Kramer planned paired comparison tests for unequal sample sizes (Toothaker, 1991).

To obtain the interaction of corporal punishment with impulsivity of corporal punishment adjusted for the influence of all other independent variables, separate ANOVAs of corporal punishment at each level of impulsivity corporal punishment were performed with all other independent variables included in each model. The *no impulsive spanking* level ANOVAs included the never spanked group because, by definition, these mothers could not have spanked impulsively. To test differences between interaction means, Tukey-Kramer planned paired comparison tests for unequal sample sizes were performed using Cicchetti's (1972) solution to the number-of-means problem (Toothaker, 1991).

Appendix for Chapter 8

The Child-to-Mother Bond and Delinquency

Data Analysis

The child-to-mother bond scale and the delinquency scale were transformed to ZP scores (Straus, 1980). ZP scores are a linear transformation of a Z score. They have a mean of 50 and a standard deviation 20. Therefore, a ZP score of 40 is the same as a Z score of −0.5, and a ZP score of 60 is the same as a Z score +0.5. ZP scores were used for the dependent variables because it is easier for readers to understand means that are positive integers such as 40 than negative decimals such as −0.5.

A $5 \times 6 \times 2$ analysis of covariance was used to test the two hypotheses concerning the links between corporal punishment and child-to-mother bond. The dependent variable was the child-to-mother bond. The five level independent variable is corporal punishment, the six-level independent variable is nurturance, and the two-level variable is the gender of the child. Age of child and socioeconomic status were entered as covariates. This analysis used all 915 children. Tests for interactions were limited to two-way interactions because of cells with only one or zero cases with three-way interactions.

Path analysis was used to determine if there is a significant indirect path between corporal punishment and delinquency through the child-to-mother bond. It is important to keep in mind that an adequate test of this model requires that the variables in the model be in temporal order (i.e., that the corporal punishment occurred before the measures of bonding and delinquency). These data do not meet that requirement. As a consequence, the test of the path model in this paper cannot indicate that corporal punishment causes a weakening of the bond and increased delinquency. However, the results of testing the path model can falsify the hypotheses. If the paths' coefficients are not statistically significant, it would cast serious doubt on the theory.

Statistical Tables

Table A8.1   Analysis of Covariance of Child-to-Mother Bond Scale (*N* = 915)

Source of Variance	DF	Mean square	F	p<
Main Effects				
Corporal punishment	4	1514.1	4.8	.001
Nurturance	5	8066.2	25.4	.001
Gender of child	1	3782.4	11.9	.001
Interaction Effects				
Corporal punishment by nurturance	20	427.8	1.3	.140
Corporal punishment by child gender	4	472.1	1.5	.204
Nurturance by gender of child	5	745.6	2.4	.039
Covariates				
Age of child	1	13331.94	2.0	.000
Socioeconomic status	1	371.8	1.2	.279

Table A8.2   Multiple Regression Analyses for Children Age 10+ (*N* = 453)

Variable	B	SE B	Beta	T	p<
A. Dependent Variable: Child-to-Mother Bond Scale					
Corporal punishment	−1.965	.507	−.128	−3.875	.001
Nurturance	4.997	.475	.322	10.515	.001
Sex of child	4.090	1.203	.103	3.400	.001
Socioeconomic status	.215	.414	.015	.519	.604
(Constant)	4.096	6.035		.679	.498
R Square = .172					
B. Dependent Variable: Delinquency Scale					
Corporal punishment	.811	.226	.171	3.587	.001
Bond scale	−.022	.009	−.123	−2.418	.016
Nurturance	−.490	.140	−.172	−3.504	.002
Age of child	.147	.381	.018	.385	.700
Sex of child	−1.317	.377	−.165	−3.497	.002
Socioeconomic status	.122	.125	.046	.980	.329
(Constant)	10.915	2.112		5.167	.001
R Square = .137					

Appendix for Chapter 9

Study 1. Spanking and Risky Sex

The sample for this study is briefly described in Chapter 9. Additional information is presented here. Table A9.1 shows that the sample included equal numbers of males and females, and an approximately equal number of students from each grade level. Most students were 16 or 17 years old. A little over two thirds lived with both parents. About one third of students had average grades of B+ or better, and about an additional one third of students had a grade average of B or B–. About one quarter of students received average grades of C or C+ and less than 10% of students received grades that averaged lower than a C.

Measures

We used the structural equation modeling program AMOS (Byrne, 2001) to identify latent variables. For corporal punishment, a single latent variable was found to underlie the following variables: ever spanked by parents, age first spanked by father, age first spanked by mother, age when spanked most often, times spanked by father the year spanking happened most often, and times spanked by mother the year spanking happened most often. Data that was missing because the respondent reported never having been spanked was recorded as zero. All other missing data was replaced by the mean.

Two observed variables were used to create the latent variable alienated from parent: (1) Asking whether the student had considered running away from home, with responses ranging from not having considered it at all, to actually running away from home. (2) A scale measuring the perceived quality of parental interaction, consisting of the following items: "I get along with my father/stepfather," "I get along with my mother/stepmother," "My father/stepfather is understanding toward me," "My mother/stepmother is understanding toward me," "My father/stepfather does not pay attention to me," "My mother/stepmother does not pay attention to me," "My father/stepfather treats me unfairly," and "My mother/stepmother treats me unfairly." Scores were reversed as needed to make a higher score indicate a closer parent-child relationship. Each item was Z-scored, and the items were summed. Missing values were replaced with the mean, if no more than two items were missing. The scale was then Z-scored, and outliers trimmed back to 2.5 standard deviations from the mean.

Ten items intended to measure belief in traditional gender roles were available in this data set. A factor analysis found two factors. Despite the two factors, scores for the two factors created by summing the items with unique factor loadings of .5 or over were found to have a correlation of .75. We therefore used AMOS to determine if the two scales reflect a single latent variable. That turned out to be correct, and we used this variable to measure belief in traditional gender roles. All items were coded, so that high scores indicate belief in traditional gender roles.

The first scale consisted of the following items: "More encouragement in a family should be given to sons than daughters to go to college," "It is more important for boys than girls to do well in school," "If both husband and wife have jobs, the husband should do a share of the housework, such as washing dishes and doing laundry," "Girls should be more concerned with becoming good wives and mothers than desiring a professional or business career," and "Girls should have the same freedoms as boys." The second scale was created by summing the following items: "Ultimately a woman should submit to her husband's decisions," "Some equality in marriage is good, but by and large the husband ought to have the main say-so in family matters," "In groups that have both male and female members, it is more appropriate that leadership positions be held by males," "Almost any woman is better off in her home than in a job or a profession," and "A woman's place is in the home." The structural equation-modeling program indicated that the two scales' belief in traditional gender roles formed a single latent variable.

Sexual victimization was measured by questions that did not focus on molestation or incest, but instead may have been more applicable to peer relationships. Three variables in the structural equation model were identified as representing the single latent variable, Sexual Victimization. The three items were: "kissed someone when you didn't want to", "made out with someone when the respondent did not want to," and "had sexual intercourse with someone when you did not want." Fifteen percent of students reported they had been kissed by someone when they did not want to; 21% reported making out with someone when they did not want to; and 14% experienced forced sexual intercourse.

Self-esteem was measured with the following questions: "I am a person of worth," "I have a number of good qualities," "I do things as well as others," "I take a positive attitude toward myself," and "I am satisfied with myself."

Family socioeconomic status was measured using father's education, mother's education, and family income, which formed a single latent variable.

Data Analysis

We used the structural equation modeling program AMOS (Byrne, 2001) to test the hypothesized paths between corporal punishment and risky sex. The model tested included both direct effects and mediated effects. The results found that only a fully mediated model provided an adequate fit to the data. Missing values were replaced by the mean unless otherwise indicated.

Statistical Tables

Table A9.1   Prevalence of Corporal Punishment and Risky Sex, by Gender of Students

Variable	Total		Males	Females
A. Corporal Punishment				
Ever spanked by parent (%)	68.4%		67.7%	69.1%
Age most recently spanked by father*	Mean	9.6	9.7	9.4
	SD	3.6	3.6	3.6
Age most recently spanked by mother*	Mean	9.9	9.4	10.4
	SD	3.9	4.0	3.7

(Continued)

Table A9.1 (Continued)

Variable		*Total*	*Males*	*Females*
Age when spanked most often	Mean	7.8	7.8	7.7
	SD	3.5	3.4	3.7
Times spanked by father in year	Mean	2.9	3.0	2.7
most often spanked	SD	1.4	1.4	1.4
Times spanked by mother in year	Mean	2.8	2.8	2.8
most often spanked	SD	1.3	1.4	1.3
B. Risky Sexual Behavior				
Ever had sexual intercourse		42.2%	41.4%	43%
Age first had sexual intercourse**	Mean	14.6	14.4	14.8
	SD	1.6	1.8	1.5
Number of sex partners**	Mean	3.2	3.3	3.1
	SD	3.7	3.6	3.6
Times had sex in past year**	Mean	31.5	33.5	29.5
	SD	57.1	63.7	49.8
Never used condoms** (%)		16.8%	18.4%	15.2%
Never use pill** (%)		57.5%	56.3%	58.7%
Never use other contraceptives**		83.2%	83.9%	82.6%
Times purchased condoms in past year	Mean	2.5	2.8	2.2
	SD	3.6	3.3	3.9
Pregnancy***		7.9%	5.3%	10.4%

*Of those who were spanked
**Of those who have had sexual intercourse
***Males: got someone pregnant once of more, females: have been pregnant once or more

Appendix for Chapter 11

Spanking and College Graduation

Data Analysis

Logistic regression (Aldrich & Nelson, 1984; Hamilton, 2009) was used to test the hypothesis that spanking is associated with a reduced probability of college graduation. Logit was used because it permits a dichotomous dependent variable, and our theoretical focus is on a dichotomy—where or not the respondent graduated from college. Each logit model included specializations for age and whether the respondent had witnessed violence between his or her parents and educational level of the parents (1975 sample), or whether the parents were an ethnic minority (1985 sample). The analyses of the 1985 sample were weighed to correct for the oversamples of minority groups. All the independent variables were entered simultaneously.

Women have only recently achieved parity with men in college enrollment. Women are also the recipients of less spanking and other forms of corporal punishment. As a consequence, it is important to test the hypothesis separately for men and women. We therefore estimated separate logit models for men and women in 1975 and 1985, making a total of four replications of the analysis.

Table A11.1   Descriptive Statistics for Samples in Chapter 11

		1975 Survey		1985 Survey	
Variable	*Measure*	*Men*	*Women*	*Men*	*Women*
Number of cases used	N	635	780	2,150	3,118
Corporal punishment as teenager	%	71.0	56.2	58.1	44.0
Number of times	Mean	11.2	9.0	8.9	7.3
College graduate	%	28.2	16.3	31.5	19.5
Age of respondent	Mean	40.3	37.9	41.9	40.7
Violence between parents	%	16.4	15.6	12.9	13.2
Minority (Black, His-panic, Native American)	%	*	*	16.1	18.0
Father's education	% <12 Yrs	52.9	47.1	*	*
	% College Grad	6.4	7.6		
Mother's education	% <12 Yrs	44.8	41.5	*	*
	% College Grad	5.7	4.1		

Table A11.2   Summary Statistics for Logistic Regression for Effects of Corporal Punishment on College Graduation, 1975 and 1985

Independent Variable	*B*	*SE*	*Odds Ratio*
A. 1975 Survey, Men ($N = 635$)			
Corporal punishment	−.116	.049	.89**
Age	.019	.008	1.02*
Parental violence	−.458	.294	.63
Parent's education	.818	.086	2.27***
B. 1985 Survey, Men ($N = 2,150$)			
Corporal punishment	−.082	.023	.92***
Age	.419	.053	.99
Parent violence	−.109	.150	.90
Minority status	−.774	.146	.46***
C. 1975 Survey, Women ($N = 780$)			
Corporal punishment	−.082	.058	.92
Age	−.001	.009	1.00
Parental violence	−.062	.314	.94
Parent's education	.749	.098	2.11***

(Continued)

Table A11.2   (Continued)

Independent Variable	B	SE	Odds Ratio
D. 1985 Survey, Women ($N = 3,118$)			
Corporal punishment	−.083	.028	.92**
Age	−.009	.003	.99*
Parental violence	−.245	.155	.78
Minority status	−.470	.133	.63***

$p < .05$, **$p < .01$, ***$p < .001$.

Appendix for Chapter 14

Cultural Context and the Relation of Spanking to Crime

Dependent Variables

Assault of a nonfamily member. Everyone gets angry or annoyed sometimes. How often in the last 12 months did you: get into a fight with someone who doesn't live here and hit the person? Never, once, 2 to 4 times, 5 to 9 times, or 10 or more times?

Arrest. Have you been arrested for anything in the past 12 months? Yes or No?

Child aggression index. Within the last year, did (REFERENT CHILD) have any special difficulties, such as:

Temper tantrums
Disciplinary problems in school
Misbehavior and disobedience at home
Physical fights with kids who live in your house
Physical fights with kids who don't live in your house
Physical fights with adults who live in your house
Physical fights with adults who don't live in your house

Child delinquency index. Within the last year, did (REFERENT CHILD) have any special difficulties, such as:

Deliberately damaging or destroying property
Stealing money or something else
Drinking
Using drugs
Got arrested for something

Approval of partner violence. Are there situations that you can imagine in which you would approve of a husband slapping his wife's face? Yes or No? Are there situations that you can imagine in which you would approve of a wife slapping her husband's face? Yes or No?

Husband assaulted wife and wife assaulted husband. Both measures used the overall violence scale of the Form R version of original Conflict Tactics Scales as described in the appendix to (Gelles & Straus, 1988). The scores were dichotomized as 1 = one or more violent acts during the previous 12 months, 0 = no violence in previous 12 months. See Appendix C for more information on the Conflict Tactics Scales.

Severely assaulted child. This measure is from the original Conflict Tactics Scales, Form R (Gelles & Straus, 1988, Appendix B). Severe violence scale dichotomized as 1—one or more acts of severe violence (such as kicking, punching, attacks with a weapon) during the previous 12 months, 0—no violence in previous 12 months.

Substance use. In the past year, how often would you guess you:

Got drunk
Got high on marijuana or some other drug

Family socioeconomic status. A socioeconomic status index was computed using the factor score option with the Principal Components procedure of the SPSS/PC factor analysis program. Five indicators were analyzed: education of the wife and the husband, their occupational prestige scores, and the combined income of the couple. The analysis yielded a single factor that explained 43% of the variance.

Violence between parents of the respondent. "Now, thinking about the whole time when you were a teenager, were there occasions when your (father/stepfather) hit your (mother/stepmother) or threw something at her? If yes, how often did that happen? Never, once, twice, 3 to 5 times, 6 to 10 times, or 11 to 20 times? *What* about your (mother/stepmother) hitting *your* (father/stepfather)? Were there occasions when that happened when you were a teenager? If yes, how often did that happen?

Reasoning used by the respondent when dealing with misbehavior by the child. This is the reasoning scale of the Conflict Tactics Scales Form R (Gelles & Straus, 1988, Appendix B).

Physical violence between respondent and spouse. This was measured by the husband-to-wife violence and the wife-to-husband violence scales of the original Conflict Tactics Scales, Form R (Gelles & Straus, 1988, Appendix B).

Data Analysis

Logistic regression was used to test the hypothesis that spanking is associated with an increase in the probability of crime and substance abuse. The LOGIT analyses were replicated for each racial or ethnic group, controlling for socioeconomic status.

The data available in this study permitted specification of a number of additional independent variables in order to control for possible spurious effects resulting from confounding with being spanked. The *adult recall* data analyses controlled for four variables: age of respondent, family socioeconomic status, gender of respondent, and the frequency with which the respondents' parents hit each other. The *contemporaneous* data analyses controlled for seven potential confounds: age of the child, number of children in the household, gender of the child, socioeconomic status of the household, gender of the respondent, amount of *reasoning* used by the respondent when dealing with misbehavior, and the presence or absence of physical violence between the respondent and his or her spouse. As a result of these specifications, the findings to be presented should be interpreted as showing the *net effect* of spanking after controlling for the variables just listed.

In addition to these controls, it was also possible to control for the confounding of ordinary corporal punishment with physical abuse in the analyses using contemporaneous data on the children of the study participants. This was done by excluding from the sample any children who experienced one more of the items in the severe violence scale of the CTSPC. However, this could not be done for the analyses using the adult-recall data on corporal punishment experienced by the participants in the survey because no measure of physical abuse was available for them. As a consequence, the hypothesized association of spanking with later criminal behavior might be due to the inclusion in the high corporal punishment group of those who were also physically abused.

Statistical Table and Tabulation of Cultural Context Studies

Table A14.1   Logistic Regression Analysis: Base Rates, Odds Ratios, and Significance Levels by Racial and Ethnic Group

Dependent Variable		*Black*	*Hispanic*	*White*
A. Nonfamily Violence and Other Crime				
Assault of nonfamily person 1+ times by men[1]	Odds	1.13*	1.18*	1.12**
	Rate	13%	13%	10%
Assault of nonfamily person 1+ times by women[1]	Odds	1.14*	1.20*	1.12**
	Rate	11%	8%	6%
Respondent arrested[1]	Odds	1.26	1.14	1.09
	Rate	3%	1%	2%
Child aggression index of 1+	Odds	1.05*	1.08**	1.05**
	Rate	19%	17%	17%
Child delinquency index score of 1+	Odds	0.93	1.11*	1.06**
	Rate	2%	3%	2%
B. Assaults on Spouses and Children Violence				
Husband physically assaulted wife 1+ times[1]	Odds	1.16*	1.35**	1.17**
	Rate	17%	18%	11%
Wife physically assaulted husband 1+ times[1]	Odds	1.18**	1.27**	1.15**
	Rate	21%	17%	12%

(Continued)

Table A14.1 (Continued)

Dependent Variable		Black	Hispanic	White
Respondent severely assaulted child 1+ times[1]	Odds	1.26**	1.40**	1.21**
	Rate	19%	15%	10%
Approves husband slapping wife in some situations	Odds	1.17*	1.15*	1.11**
	Rate	10%	16%	13%
Approves wife slapping husband in some situations	Odds	1.10	1.24**	1.14**
	Rate	18%	23%	21%
C. Drug Abuse				
Husband used drugs 1+ times[1]	Odds	1.12	1.23*	1.20**
	Rate	9%	6%	8%
Wife used drugs 1+ times[1]	Odds	1.19*	1.20	1.08*
	Rate	6%	2%	6%

[1]In the 12 months preceding the interview, $*p < .05$, $**p < .01$.

Appendix for Chapter 15

Spanking High-Risk Children and Adult Crime

Imputation of Missing Data

The data analysis began with inspecting the frequency distributions of all variables for skewness and outliers. Initial examinations of the data indicated missing data on a number of the variables to be used in the analysis. Rather than use only cases with complete data, multiple imputation (Little & Rubin, 2002) was used. The imputation procedure, as well as analysis of the resulting data sets, was done using IVEware (Raghunathan, Solenberger, & Van Hoewyk, 2002) as an add-on to Statistical Analysis System (SAS). Multiple imputation uses a series of regression analyses to estimate missing values at each step; random values are added to the values estimated from the regression analyses to simulate random variation in individual cases. A single data set with missing values goes through this procedure multiple times, producing multiple imputed data sets. Because of the random values added to each imputed value, each data set is slightly different. The current research used five imputed data sets. Each of these data sets is then analyzed. The results from the analyses are then combined to give estimates of parameters and variances that account for the uncertainty of the imputed values, while fully utilizing all the data collected.

The hypothesis was tested using OLS regression analysis. The model employed included antisocial behavior in 1986, six control variables (child monitoring, mother's level of education, child's race, age of mother at child's birth, father's presence in the home, and number of children in the home), corporal punishment and two other aspects of parent-child interaction (cognitive stimulation and emotional support), and interaction variables to examine whether the effect of corporal punishment is contingent on six other Time 1 variables known to be related to crime: (1) corporal punishment by antisocial behavior, (2) corporal punishment by child's race, (3) corporal punishment by mother's level of education, (4) corporal punishment by cognitive stimulation, (5) corporal punishment by emotional support, and (6) corporal punishment by child's sex. None of these interactions were statistically significant. Despite the nonsignificant interaction between child's sex and corporal punishment, when examining the regression output, we discovered that when the analyses were done by the child's sex, the coefficients for corporal punishment were different (based on observation rather than statistical tests). For example, for total crime, the coefficient for corporal punishment was negative and nonsignificant, whereas the coefficient for males was *positive* and statistically significant. Logically, if the coefficient for males is statistically different from zero, it is also significantly different from a negative coefficient. This presented something of a puzzle. Further examination showed that being Hispanic and mother's age both significantly interacted with gender.

Statistical Tables

Table A15.1   Child and Family Characteristics by Sex of Child

Characteristic		Total	Females	Males
Child's Race				
	Hispanic	21%	19%	23%
	Black	51%	53%	48%
	All other	28%	28%	29%
Corporal Punishment				
	Not in past week	71%	71%	70%
	Once	15%	14%	17%
	Twice	8%	9%	8%
	Three or more	6%	7%	5%
Father in Household				
	Yes	36%	34%	38%
	No	64%	66%	62%
Child's Sex				
	Male	48%		
	Female	52%		

Table A15.2 Mean Scores for Child and Family Characteristics by Sex of Child

Characteristic	Total		Females		Males	
	M	SD	M	SD	M	SD
Child's age in months	113.32	15.98	113.04	16.39	113.63	15.56
Mother's age	17.26	1.62	17.13	1.61	17.40	1.61
Mother's education	11.01	4.47	11.01	5.84	11.01	2.18
Number of other children	2.59	1.21	2.69	1.27	2.48	1.15
Cognitive stimulation	46.38	28.81	46.83	29.70	45.90	27.87
Emotional support	45.36	29.92	43.50	29.44	47.37	30.36
Antisocial behavior	1.93	1.64	1.59	1.41	2.30	1.78
Monitoring	11.56	2.58	11.45	2.52	11.68	2.65
Total crime	1.44	2.30	0.98	1.77	1.93	2.67
Property crime	0.73	1.43	0.49	1.09	1.00	1.68
Violent crime	0.70	1.15	0.49	0.93	0.93	1.31

Table A15.3 Spanking of 8- to 13-Year-Olds by Selected Family and Child Characteristics

Family or Child Characteristic	Number of Spanks in Past Week				
	0	1	2	3 or more	Chi Square
Total	70.7%	15.1%	8.1%	6.1%	
Mother's education					
<12	68.4%	14.7%	10.7%	6.2%	6.96
12	73.6%	13.7%	6.1%	6.6%	
13+	72.6%	19.7%	3.2%	4.4%	
Child's race					
Hispanic	70.5%	18.2%	8.1%	3.2%	6.15
Black	69.4%	13.5%	9.9%	7.3%	
Other	73.5%	15.6%	4.8%	6.1%	
Child's gender					
Male	70.5%	16.6%	7.6%	5.3%	1.21
Female	71.0%	13.7%	8.6%	6.7%	
# Children in household					
1	87.5%	12.5%	0%	0%	8.97
2	81.4%	11.9%	6.7%	0%	
3	70.5%	15.1%	8.0%	6.4%	
4 or more	67.2%	16.1%	8.9%	7.8%	
Father in household					
Yes	69.6%	17.9%	6.0%	6.5%	3.18
No	71.6%	13.4%	9.4%	5.7%	

(Continued)

Table A15.3   (Continued)

Family or Child Characteristic	Number of Spanks in Past Week				
	0	1	2	3 or more	Chi Square
Mother's age at child's birth					
13–17	74.8%	11.6%	7.7%	5.8%	6.26
18–21	65.7%	19.4%	8.5%	6.4%	
Antisocial behavior quintiles					
High	62.4%	20.7%	6.8%	10.2%	44.63**
Mid-high	67.6%	16.6%	8.4%	7.3%	
Middle	77.7%	13.9%	2.7%	5.6%	
Mid-low	78.1%	11.5%	7.8%	2.6%	
Low	58.5%	14.6%	19.2%	7.7%	
Parental monitoring quintiles					
High	51.5%	20.4%	18.4%	9.8%	17.27
Mid-high	59.2%	19.4%	11.0%	10.4%	
Middle	67.2%	18.4%	5.6%	8.9%	
Mid-low	82.5%	10.2%	4.1%	3.2%	
Low	83.5%	10.9%	4.4%	1.2%	

$**p < .01$

Table A15.4   Regression Testing Relation of Corporal Punishment and Control Variables to Total Crime

	Coefficient	SE	t	p<
Intercept	2.22	1.38	1.61	0.13
Corporal punishment	0.16	0.12	1.36	0.19
Antisocial behavior	0.13	0.07	1.75	0.10
Child female	−0.92	0.22	−4.21	0.00
Hispanic	0.41	0.31	1.34	0.20
Black	0.15	0.28	0.54	0.59
Father present	−0.14	0.28	−0.51	0.61
Cognitive stimulation	0.00	0.00	−0.17	0.87
Emotional support	−0.01	0.00	−1.83	0.08
Number of children	0.06	0.09	0.61	0.55
Mother's age	0.04	0.07	0.55	0.59
Mother's education	−0.02	0.02	−0.78	0.45
Parental monitoring	−0.10	0.04	−2.39	0.03

Table A15.5 Corporal Punishment and Control Variables Regressed on Total Crime by Sex

	Coefficient	SE	t	p<
FEMALES				
Intercept	a	1.54	−0.49	0.63
Corporal punishment	−0.08	0.13	−0.61	0.55
Antisocial behavior	0.25	0.09	2.78	0.01
Hispanic	−0.35	0.35	−0.98	0.34
Black	−0.07	0.30	−0.23	0.82
Father present	−0.25	0.29	−0.88	0.39
Cognitive stimulation	0.00	0.00	0.27	0.79
Emotional support	−0.01	0.00	−1.96	0.07
Number of children	0.07	0.10	0.75	0.46
Mother's age	0.15	0.08	1.91	0.07
Mother's education	0.00	0.02	−0.19	0.85
Parental monitoring	−0.05	0.05	−0.93	0.36
MALES				
Intercept	5.28	2.38	2.21	0.04
Corporal punishment	0.47	0.20	2.28	0.03
Antisocial behavior	−0.04	0.12	−0.31	0.76
Hispanic	1.17	0.51	2.27	0.03
Black	0.19	0.49	0.39	0.70
Father present	0.26	0.47	0.56	0.58
Cognitive stimulation	0.00	0.01	0.07	0.94
Emotional support	−0.01	0.01	−0.72	0.48
Number of children	0.04	0.16	0.26	0.80
Mother's age	−0.06	0.12	−0.49	0.63
Mother's education	−0.18	0.10	−1.81	0.08
Parental monitoring	−0.14	0.07	−1.95	0.06

Table A15.6 Corporal Punishment and Control Variables Regressed on Violent Crime

	Coefficient	SE	t	p<
Intercept	1.09	0.69	1.58	0.12
Corporal punishment	0.10	0.06	1.87	0.07
Antisocial behavior	0.07	0.04	1.90	0.07
Child female	−0.43	0.11	−3.97	0.00
Hispanic	0.16	0.15	1.03	0.31
Black	0.14	0.14	1.04	0.31
Father present	−0.08	0.13	−0.64	0.53

(Continued)

Table A15.6   (Continued)

	Coefficient	SE	t	p<
Cognitive stimulation	0.00	0.00	0.14	0.89
Emotional support	−0.01	0.00	−2.92	0.01
Number of children	0.04	0.05	0.90	0.37
Mother's age	0.02	0.03	0.51	0.62
Mother's education	−0.01	0.01	−0.80	0.43
Parental monitoring	−0.05	0.02	−2.24	0.03

Table A15.7   Corporal Punishment and Control Variables Regressed on Violent Crime by Sex

	Coefficient	SE	t	p<
FEMALES				
Intercept	−0.63	0.80	−0.79	0.44
Corporal punishment	−0.01	0.06	−0.18	0.86
Antisocial behavior	0.11	0.05	2.41	0.02
Hispanic	−0.22	0.18	−1.23	0.23
Black	0.00	0.16	0.01	0.99
Father present	−0.03	0.14	−0.22	0.83
Cognitive stimulation	0.00	0.00	0.22	0.83
Emotional support	−0.01	0.00	−3.01	0.01
Number of children	0.06	0.05	1.12	0.27
Mother's age	0.08	0.04	2.08	0.05
Mother's education	0.00	0.01	−0.16	0.88
Parental monitoring	−0.01	0.03	−0.50	0.62
MALES				
Intercept	2.78	1.15	2.41	0.02
Corporal punishment	0.24	0.10	2.40	0.02
Antisocial behavior	0.00	0.06	0.07	0.94
Hispanic	0.51	0.25	2.05	0.05
Black	0.21	0.24	0.89	0.38
Father present	−0.01	0.23	−0.05	0.96
Cognitive stimulation	0.00	0.00	0.34	0.74
Emotional support	0.00	0.00	−1.36	0.19
Number of children	0.02	0.08	0.29	0.78
Mother's age	−0.04	0.06	−0.63	0.53
Mother's education	−0.08	0.05	−1.71	0.10
Parental monitoring	−0.07	0.03	−2.05	0.05

Table A15.8 Corporal Punishment and Control Variables Regressed on Property Crime

	Coefficient	SE	t	p<
Intercept	1.130	.88	1.29	0.22
Corporal punishment	0.050	.08	0.73	0.48
Antisocial behavior	0.060	.05	1.31	0.21
Child female	−0.49	0.14	−3.56	0.00
Hispanic	0.250	.19	1.31	0.21
Black	0.010	.18	0.05	0.96
Father present	−0.06	0.18	−0.32	0.75
Cognitive stimulation	0.000	.00	−0.38	0.71
Emotional support	0.000	.00	−0.65	0.53
Number of children	0.010	.06	0.26	0.80
Mother's age	0.020	.04	0.47	0.64
Mother's education	−0.01	0.02	−0.61	0.55
Parental monitoring	−0.05	0.03	−1.94	0.07

Table A15.9 Corporal Punishment and Control Variables Regressed on Property Crime by Sex

	Coefficient	SE	t	p<
FEMALES				
Intercept	−0.12	0.96	−0.12	0.90
Corporal punishment	−0.07	0.08	−0.81	0.43
Antisocial behavior	0.14	0.06	2.45	0.03
Hispanic	−0.12	0.22	−0.56	0.59
Black	−0.07	0.19	−0.37	0.72
Father present	−0.22	0.19	−1.19	0.25
Cognitive stimulation	0.00	0.00	0.25	0.80
Emotional support	0.00	0.00	−0.68	0.51
Number of children	0.02	0.06	0.27	0.79
Mother's age	0.06	0.05	1.33	0.21
Mother's education	0.00	0.01	−0.17	0.87
Parental monitoring	−0.03	0.03	−1.02	0.33
MALES				
Intercept	2.50	1.54	1.62	0.12
Corporal punishment	0.23	0.13	1.76	0.09
Antisocial behavior	−0.04	0.07	−0.54	0.59
Hispanic	0.65	0.33	1.98	0.06
Black	−0.02	0.31	−0.07	0.95

(Continued)

Table A15.9   (Continued)

	Coefficient	SE	t	p<
Father present	0.27	0.30	0.92	0.37
Cognitive stimulation	0.00	0.01	−0.14	0.89
Emotional support	0.00	0.00	−0.12	0.91
Number of children	0.02	0.10	0.18	0.86
Mother's age	−0.02	0.08	−0.28	0.78
Mother's education	−0.10	0.06	−1.53	0.14
Parental monitoring	−0.07	0.05	1.43	0.17

Appendix for Chapter 16

Sexual Coercion and Sexual Assault

Measures

Neglect was measured using the short form of the Multidimensional Neglect Scale (Straus, 2003, 2006). For this chapter, the scale was scored by adding all of the items to which the participant reported agreeing/strongly agreeing. Thus, the scores indicate the number of different types of minor neglect experiences that each respondent experienced as a child. The neglectful behavior scale has demonstrated good cross-cultural construct validity and reliability, with an overall alpha of .72 (Straus, 2003). The alpha coefficient of internal consistency reliability for this sample was .70 for males and .71 for females.

Sexual abuse was measured using the PRP scale for sexual abuse history, which is described in the chapter and in the PRP Manual (Straus, 2003; Straus et al., 2010). For this sample, the alpha coefficient was .80 for males and .79 for females.

Antisocial traits and behavior was also assessed with the PRP. It is described in the chapter and in the PRP Manual. The internal consistency reliability (Chronbach's α) was .82 for males and .81 for females. Information on the construct and concurrent validity of the antisocial traits behavior subscale is in Hines and Straus (2007). Antisocial traits and behavior scores were recoded into three categories: 1 = low antisocial traits and behavior (scores below the 25th percentile), 2 = medium antisocial traits and behavior (scores between the 25th and 75th percentile), and 3 = high antisocial traits and behavior (the top 25% of the distribution).

Data Analysis

We used multinomial logistic regression to estimate a modified path model (Hagenarrs, 1993, p. 15), where we regressed the exogenous variables (the three victimization measures and the control variables) and the mediating variable (antisocial traits and behavior) on the sexual coercion types. Then the exogenous variables were regressed on antisocial traits and behavior.

Correlations between the independent variables were calculated to assess the possibility of multicollinearity. The strongest relationships were between corporal punishment and antisocial traits and behavior ($r = .35$). The rest of the correlations ranged from .19 to .28, which suggests little risk of multicollinearity problems (Tabachnick & Fidell, 1996).

We estimated separate models for males and females because the consequences of prior victimization might be different by gender (e.g., Horwitz et al., 2001). We did not estimate separate models for each national context because, for some of the national contexts, the sample size was not sufficient for this type of multivariate analysis. However, because U.S. students are almost one third of the sample, we included a dummy variable for United States in the model. This controls for the predominance of U.S. students because the coefficients for all the other variables are the net of the effect of U.S. students in the sample.

In total, 26.7% of the male students and 19.6% of the female students [χ^2(1) $= 91.88$; $p < .001$] verbally coerced sex. Significant gender differences were found in most of verbal sexual coercion items: insisting on sex without a condom [males $= 14.9\%$, females $= 12.9\%$; $\chi^2(1) = 9.91$; $p < .01$]; insisting on sex when the partner did not want to [males $= 15.9\%$, females $= 8.2\%$; $\chi^2(1) = 178.56$; $p < .001$]; insisting on oral or anal sex [males $= 11\%$, females $= 3.8\%$; $\chi^2(1) = 264.22$; $p < .001$]; threatening the partner to have oral or anal sex [males $= 1.2\%$, females $= 1.1\%$; $\chi^2(1) = .588$; $p = .443$]; and threatening the partner to have sex [males $= 1.4\%$, females $= 0.8\%$; $\chi^2(1) = 12.00$; $p < .001$].

Physically forcing sex was reported by 2.4% of the male students and 1.8% of the female students [$\chi^2(1) = 4.83$; $p < .05$]. Rates for the specific items were 1.3% of males and 1.0% of females reported using force on the partner to have sex [$\chi^2(1) = 1.67$; $p = .19$], and 1.6% of the males and 1.0% of the females reported using force to have oral or anal sex [$\chi^2(1) = 7.35$; $p < .01$].

Statistical Tables

Table A16.1 Characteristics of Students in the Sample

Variables	X (SD)		Range
	Men	Women	
Independent Variables			
Corporal punishment	1.84 (.88)	1.68 (.87)	1–4
Sexual abuse history	0.60 (1.18)	0.70 (1.28)	0–8
Minor neglect history	1.17 (1.34)	1.02 (1.31)	0–8
Mediating Variable			
Antisocial traits and behaviors	1.81 (0.42)	1.52 (0.35)	1–4

(Continued)

Table A16.1   (Continued)

Variables	X (SD)		Range
	Men	Women	
Control Variables			
Age	22.97 (5.5)	23.13 (6.49)	18–55
Relationship length (Months)	12.82 (9.09)	15.15 (8.92)	0.60–50
Socioeconomic status (z score)	0.12 (1.01)	0.002 (.97)	–3.1–3.6
Social desirability	2.59 (.35)	2.63 (.36)	1–4
Dependent Variables			
Verbal sexual coercion (%)	26.7	19.6	
Physically forced sex (%)	2.4	1.8	

Table A16.2   Multinomial Logistic Regression Analyses Testing Paths to Sexual Coercion

	Odds ratios†			
	Model 1. Dependent variable: Medium and high antisocial behavior		Model 2. Dependent variable: Sexual coercion	
Independent variable	Medium ATB	High ATB	Verbal sexual coercion	Physically forced sex
Men				
Corporal punishment	1.64***	3.07***	1.08 ns	1.32*
Sexual abuse	1.32***	1.66***	1.20***	1.23**
Neglect history	1.07 ns	1.29***	.98 ns	1.20**
ATB	—	—	1.33***	1.69*
Control variables				
Age	.97**	.95***	1.00 ns	1.01 ns
Length of relationship	.98*	.98*	1.03***	1.02 ns
SES	0.99 ns	1.14 *	1.02 ns	1.04 ns
Social disirability	.05***	.005***	.61***	.60 ns
USA (=1)	.75*	.96 ns	1.19*	1.08 ns
	$\chi^2 (16)=1599.192$***		$\chi^2 (16)=1599.192$***	
N	1658	1545	1042	93
Women				
Corporal punishment	1.51***	2.25***	1.10**	1.24**
Sexual abuse	1.19***	1.46***	1.17***	1.14**
Neglect history	1.13***	1.37***	.98 ns	1.01 ns

(Continued)

Table A16.2 (Continued)

Independent variable	Odds ratios†			
	Model 1. Dependent variable: Medium and high antisocial behavior		Model 2. Dependent variable: Sexual coercion	
	Medium ATB	High ATB	Verbal sexual coercion	Physically forced sex
ATB	—	—	1.44***	2.08***
Control variables				
Age	.97***	.95***	.98**	.99 ns
Length of relationship	.98***	.97***	1.03***	1.03***
SES	.99 ns	1.05 ns	0.98 ns	.94 ns
Social desirability	.06***	.01***	.77**	.80 ns
USA (=1)	.70***	.72***	1.35***	1.21 ns
	$\chi^2 (16) = 3723.968$		$\chi^2 (18) = 499.998$	
N	4907	1768	1973	180

†Reference group for ATB: "low ATB"; Reference group for Sexual Coercion: "No sexual coercion." *$p < .05$, **$p < .01$; ***$p < .001$; ns=not significant.

Appendix for Chapter 17

The Decline in Approval of Spanking

Independent Variables

The year in which the survey was conducted was the independent variable for testing the hypothesis concerning changes in approval of corporal punishment by parents. The variables to investigate group differences in approval of corporal punishment were the race of the respondent, the geographic region in which the respondent lived, and the gender of the respondent. Control variables for age, income, and education were also included in the form of Z scores. The data for these three variables were transformed to Z scores before creating the merged data set. This was necessary because the various studies used different class intervals to code the data. Z scores makes them comparable in the sense that they all express the score for each respondent as the number of standard deviations above or below the mean of all respondents in that survey.

Data Analysis

The hypotheses were tested using a $7 \times 2 \times 3 \times 4$ analysis of covariance with three covariates. The seven-category variable is year (1968, 1986, 1988, 1989, 1990, 1991, and 1994), the two-category variable is gender of the respondent, the three-category variable is race (White, Black, and Other), and the four-category variable is region (Northeast, North Central, South, West). The three covariates are age, income, and education. The six sociodemographic factors in the analysis enable us to test the hypothesis that these groups do not differ significantly in approval of corporal punishment. In addition, their inclusion addresses the question of whether trends in the approval of corporal punishment reflect a change in cultural norms per se, or a change in the demographic structure of U.S. society.

Statistical Tables

Table A17.1   Analysis of Covariance of Approval of Corporal Punishment ($N = 8,477$)

Source Variation	Regr. Coef.	Sum of squares	DF	Mean Square	F	Signif. of F
Main effects		574,435.808	12	47,869.651	32.447	.001
Year		361,073.162	6	60,178 860	40.790	.001
Gender		53,$34,017	1	53,834.017	36.489	.001
Ethnic		55,619.047	2	27,809.524	IS.850	.001
Region		66,280.103	3	22,093.368	14.975	.001
Two-way interactions		175,211.069	47	3,727.895	2.527	.001
Year gender		43,236.514	6	7,214.419	4.890	.001
Year ethnic		19.565.840	12	1,630.487	1.105	.350
Year region		67,693.330	18	3,760.741	2.549	.001
Covariates		71.i20.117	3	23,706.706	16.069	.001
Age	.783	7.426.471	1	7,426.471	5.034	.025
Income	.122	148.161	1	148.161	.100	.751
Education	−.306	48.973.442	1	48,973.442	33.195	.001
Explained		820,766.994	62	13,238.177	8.973	.00 1
Residual		9,346.222.690	5.335	1,475.331		
Total		10,166,989.684	5.397	1,589.337		

Year = Year of the study
Gender = Gender of respondent (0 = Male. 1 = Female)
Ethnic = Ethnic group of respondent (1 = White. 2 = Black. 3 = Other)
Region = Region of respondent: Four census regions
Age = Age of respondent, z score, 5 categories
Income = Income of respondent, z score. 5 categories
Education = Education of respondent, z score

Author Index

Subject Index

abuse *see* physical abuse; sexual abuse
academic achievement 135–6, 157–8; *see
also* college graduation
adult crime 218–27; control variables for
221–2; corporal punishment and crime
as young adult 223–4; cross-sectional
studies of spanking and 306–7;
implications of study findings 227;
limitations for 226–7; longitudinal
studies and 306; sample and measures
for 219–22; summary and conclusions
on 225–7
Afifi, T. O. 143–4, 303, 307, 315, 336
age: age-crime curve 186; approval of
violence and spanking and 259; of
children 25–9, 69, 86, 267–8; college
graduation and 161; as control variable
236; feasibility of external control
diminishes with 283; number of
children confounding with birth order
and 58–9; of parents 29, 70; spanking
as child 44–5, 190–3, 299; spanking
before age 12 189, 193, 196; *see also*
infants; teenagers; toddlers
aggression 109; causes of 173–4;
corporal punishment, delinquency and
210; higher levels of 94; increase in
81, 82, 143, 204; sexual 229; as stable
trait 84
Agnew, R. 111–12
Ainsworth Strange Situation test 113
Alabama 72
alcohol use 204
alternative disciplinary strategies
274–5, 318–19; *see also* nonviolent
alternatives to spanking; nonviolent
discipline
American Academy of Child and
Adolescent Psychiatry 11

American Academy of Pediatrics 9, 11;
conference 26, 39, 296; consensus
statement 26, 90, 296; "Guidelines for
Effective Discipline" 273; guidelines
of 323; policy statement of 10–11, 290;
*Raising Children to Resist Violence:
What You Can Do* 323
American Family Physician 270
American Medical Association 11
American Psychological Association 11;
*Raising Children to Resist Violence:
What You Can Do* 323
Anderson, K. L. 112
Anderson, S. G. 75
anger: resentment and 282–3; spanking
in 93, 94, 95
Annie E. Casey Foundation 100
anthropological studies 294–5, 317
anticipatory socialization 251
antisocial behavior: in boys and girls
85–6, 89, 90, 104; cause-effect
relationship with 83–4, 87; causes of
21, 82, 204–5, 222; change in 87–9,
90; correlations with 87; crime and
8, 14, 32, 307–8; ethnicity and 89;
impulsive spanking relation to 100–5;
increase in 89–92; longitudinal studies
on 83–4, 91, 99; measures 98, 221,
235–6; methodological problems for
85–6; sample and measures for 84–6;
sexual coercion and 233–4, 241–2,
244; six behaviors 85; socioeconomic
status and 104–5; spanking and 218–
19, 232, 301, 303–5, 312–15; Straus
on 236, 305; studies on 43; variables
related to 100, 104–5
antisocial personality disorder 235
approval of violence and spanking
3, 51–2, 55, 63–77; age and 259;